The Girl in the Middle

The Girl in the Middle

The love-story of a monk
An autobiography

PAUL SINGLETON

Published in 1995 by

Paul Singleton, 4 Eyot Lodge, Cross Deep, Twickenham
London TW1 4QH

Cover design by Gordon Stowell
Photograph by Kenneth Markham
Photographs of Mirfield and South Africa by the author
and reproduced by kind permission of the Community of the
Resurrection

Printed in Great Britain by Intype London Ltd.

ISBN 0-9527219-0-2

The Girl in the Middle

Contents

The Girl in the Middle

Illustrations

Acknowledgements

I am deeply grateful to many friends for their encouragement, without which this book would not have progressed beyond the first draft.   In pride of place must come Angela Cassia, historian and author, who gave me exhaustive - and for her I am sure, exhausting - constructive criticism and unwavering approval in many letters from Johannesburg while she herself was busily engaged in researching and writing her own books. Then, playing a very fundamental role, Adrian McConnaughie who helped me to learn enough of the mysteries of my computer to struggle through the initial writing. Alun and Christine Glyn-Jones gave me a patient ear and sound advice on the content of the book. They are followed by my ninety-five year old neighbour Betty Abbatt, who pleaded for my little black cat to appear on the front cover and, with David and Carol Pearce and Chris Light, read and helped to correct the first draft.

My dear friend and colleague Angus Stuart, with typical generosity, sacrificed a day-off and much of his spare time in order to organise the MS and prepare the proofs - making my computer do tricks of which I did not know it was capable!   Jenny Kelly gave unstinted time to proof-reading so that the deadline could be met. I would like to thank Donald Simpson, our Archivist, for introducing me to Mark Massingham of Messrs. Intype London Ltd. Mark electrified me by saying that if he could have my copy within a fortnight he could produce the book before Christmas. He spent several hours himself, with monumental patience, helping this novice author, often I am sure beyond the call of duty, to get the book and illustrations ready for printing.   Last but by no manner of means least, I am very grateful to Peter King for introducing me to Graham Stowell who did a fantastic job in designing the cover at, literally, only a few hours notice. Thank you all very much. Your stars shine in my firmament.

Paul Singleton
December 1995

Dedication

This book is for Bar -
naturally

1

The Girl in the Middle

There was a stiff spring breeze blowing that afternoon as, hanging on to my hat I gingerly made my way down the sixty-round ladder that had taken me to the top of the chimney stack. Being the office boy of our family firm of builders and decorators, it was my job on a Friday afternoon to go round the various sites where work was in progress and pay the men their wages, and I was thoroughly enjoying my freedom from the hated office. I was not very good on ladders and I remember edging my way down carefully and rather fearfully. At last with a sigh of relief I put one foot on *terra firma* once more - and at that moment I saw a vision! The front door of the house, a mere few yards from the foot of the ladder, was flung open and a triple vision of beauty stepped on to the garden path. Their hair shone brilliantly in the spring sunshine; they stood at pause for a fleeting moment - the three most beautiful blondes I had ever seen in my life, way beyond any dream or fantasy I had so far had in my youthful and rather desperate search for love. These three girls, in that fateful and eternal moment, held me spellbound and agape as with golden hair a-frolic in the breeze, they swept upon their elegant and shapely way towards the orchard. Smartly dressed in jodhpurs and white silk blouses they gave me but a fleeting and disinterested glance as they went.

I remained momentarily transfixed then, still hanging on to my hat, I was off, scurrying back to my bicycle, intent only upon beating a hasty retreat before those exquisite girls could reappear and confound me with embarrassment. I longed to see them again but was terrified of doing so.

I was on 'auto-pilot' as I rode back to the office, unaware of roads or traffic. I was still mesmerised by the vision of those three glorious girls. But as I rode and held their faces in my mind, I realised that attractive as they all were, the most beautiful, at anyrate for me, was the girl in the middle - to my romantic young mind she was the precious pearl set between two lesser stones. As I hugged the sight of that dear face to myself, my dreaming began - dreaming that was to continue for months and years. I dreamed of what could be, or perhaps might be, one day - but my dreams were not very hopeful ones; I could not imagine putting on my Sunday best and going to woo so fair a lady. Surely such a wonder would not spare me more than the disinterested glance she had already given me; me, a mere office boy earning, at that time, five shillings a week, and clad in shabby clothes with no prospects but a life of barely making ends meet in a business I loathed. For at that time the 1930's recession had begun to bite and business was bad. Surely some knight in shining armour would come galloping on his white charger, sweep her on to his pommel and ride off with her into the sunset and they would live happily ever after. As I dreamed, I despaired. I despaired, not only because I thought this wonderful girl was far beyond my grasp, but for another factor that was at present dominating my life.

From a very early age, certainly since I was six or seven, my father had talked to me incessantly about my responsibility, as the elder son, to prepare myself to carry on the family firm as his successor. He was so obsessed about it that he insisted that my preparation for this role must exclude everything else. He made a strict rule that I was to have no girl friends, and certainly bring no girl into the house until I was sufficiently on my way towards this destiny, "Plenty of time for girls and all that sort of thing later on, first you have to learn the business". Not surprisingly I came to hate the business with all my heart, and took every opportunity that offered to escape from my dingy office.

Ours was a family business, founded by my grandfather, in which for a time all eight of his sons worked. They appear in a parish history, which contains a touching account of Grandfather's funeral:

'Among the prominent tradesmen, was the firm of Singleton, builders. All the male members of the large family were sidesmen or choristers of St James's, and the respect in which the family was held may be gauged from a report of the sudden death of Mr James Singleton, of Florence Cottage, East Bank Road, in March 1891. It tells us that he was "one of Hampton Hill's most prominent and useful inhabitants, being popular as one who is always ready to assist in any project which could be calculated to promote the welfare of those around him and the advancement of the interests of the locality. He was a large employer of local labour and Treasurer of the Working Men's Club, "an institution which he served with great zeal." On the day of his funeral "a general gloom was cast over all classes of parishioners." All shops and public houses were closed from 1.30 to 3 o'clock and blinds were drawn in private residences. The funeral procession consisted of a large number of tradesmen from Hampton Hill, Hampton, Teddington and Twickenham with many local gentry intermingled, and a strong detachment of members of the Hampton Friendly

Society, of which Mr Singleton had been for many years one of the trustees. Next came "two employees bearing a number of wreaths and emblems tastefully arranged on a raised bier". Five mourning coaches followed the plateglass funeral car, and the whole route was lined with people and at every point signs of sympathy were more than apparent". The Revd de Ricci, curate, took the service and the church "was crowded to its utmost capacity and the ceremony was most touching." Also, the scene around the grave was one to remember, many of the spectators being in tears.

'Rather a touching sequel to the funeral is an announcement that 'Messrs W and F Singleton beg to inform the customers and friends of their late father that they will continue to carry on his business under the name of James Singleton and Sons and trust that by careful and prompt attention to any orders entrusted to them to merit the continuance of their kind support' Mr William Singleton was St James's first organist. He died in 1877 and his memorial window is in the North aisle.' (*The Birth and Growth of Hampton Hill* Edited by Margery Orton)

As this account suggests, the Singletons were prominent in the neighbourhood - at the church I should think 'dominant' would probably be a more suitable word! But they seem to have been a good hearted lot and ready to help when they could. They were all indefatigable workers and no doubt beavered away helping to raise the funds for the church building, and later for the tower and spire which were added after the main church had been built. Family legend has it that when the tower and spire of St James' had been consecrated, Grandfather climbed the ladders to the pinnacle with a bag of sticky buns, which he proceeded to throw down to the children below. One of these buns was varnished and kept for years in the curio cabinet in the parlour of Florence Cottage, the family home.

My father, Ernest Singleton. was born in 1871, one of thirteen children, eight boys and five girls. All the girls died in infancy. He received what education he had, mainly the 'Three Rs' (Reading, 'Riting and 'Rithmatic), from the local Dame School and went into the family business at fifteen where he learned the rudiments of all the various trades, specialising in carpentry and joinery. The passion of his life however apart from his Christian faith, was music. From a very young age he played the piano and practiced for two hours every morning before going to the office at 7am. He was over forty when he married and by that time was

3

Myself aged 2 with
Father and Mother and
baby brother Philip

Grandparents, George and Meta Chamberlin 1923

4

widely known as a pianist and organist. When we were young we listened to a piano recital most Sunday mornings as we washed and dressed - Father playing Beethoven, Chopin, Tchaikovsky, etc. for an hour before breakfast. In those days before the advent of radio and television people made their own entertainment and Father was in great demand as a 'playing guest' at 'musical evenings' and parties.

My mother, Meta (pronounced Meeta) Elizabeth Louise Chamberlin was the oldest child of George and Meta Chamberlin and before she was married lived in the family house at Hampton Wick with her parents and younger sister Olive Mary, and 'baby brother' William. Her father was a chorister in the choir of St John the Baptist, Hampton Wick in Middlesex, just across the river from Kingston-upon-Thames, where my father was organist and choirmaster

Grandfather Chamberlin was the son of a cabinet-maker and he began his working life as a footman in one of the great houses of the land - which one I do not think I ever knew. He had learned the basics of woodworking from his father and before long left domestic service and was apprenticed to a cabinet-maker. Over the years he became a superb craftsman and by the time he had been married for a few years had become an employee at Hampton Court Palace where he eventually became Assistant Curator, in charge of the Royal Pictures.

Grandfather was very proud of the fact that Queen Mary always consulted him about the pictures she wanted taken from Hampton Court to be hung for a time in one of the other royal residences, principally Buckingham Palace, St James's Palace and Clarence House. He was then responsible for their transport and re-hanging. Apparently at that time she did a lot of swapping of pictures around the royal houses.

George Chamberlin was a handsome man with the upright stature of a guardsman, a ramrod straight back and a strong face with a large moustache, the ends of which were waxed so that they were like fierce spikes sticking straight out across his upper lip - a fact that we had to remember when, as small boys we would give him our dutiful kiss of greeting on the cheek; they could give you a nasty jab. He was as upright of character as he was physically; in fact a man of integrity. When my brother Phil and I first became fully conscious of him he and Grandma had moved from the house in Hampton Wick to Faraday Cottage at Hampton Court, one of the cottages set aside for employees in the Palace. The ground floor was the laundry where Grandma had her copper, large wooden wash-tub and huge 'dolly' almost as tall as she was herself with which she would agitate the clothes immersed in the suds. Farther back in this room were grandfather's bench and tools. It was there at the age of five that I received my first carpentry lesson - he showed me, using a brace and bit and a chisel, how to make a little punt to float in my bath. Of course he did it all really. This was on a winter's afternoon after dark and the job was done by the light, if you can call it that, of a single gas light with a fishtail burner - not even a proper mantle. Grandfather would relight his pipe periodically from the naked flame. He did some superb work in that dark laundry - beautiful cabinets in English oak with a wonderful flower in the grain; mahogany writing desks with secret drawers; and numerous chairs and tables.

He was also a great rowing man on the river and had won many trophies. When he suggested making himself a trophy case to display them, Grandma had said, "Before you make a trophy case I want a proper sideboard"; so he compromised and made a four-cupboard-and-drawer sideboard, with a trophy case above. He had acquired three beautiful Tudor linenfold oak panels that had been discarded during alterations in the Palace, and he made an exact replica for the fourth cupboard door. When the job was finished only he knew which was the copy.

Mother was the rebel of the family and when young was always kicking over the traces. She had slightly resented her sister Olive who was a great reader and later went to college and became a teacher. "Ol' always had her head in a book and I had to do all the chores", she used to complain, but they were devoted to one another in spite of their frequent differences. As was usual in those days both girls sang and learned to play the piano, so they were 'good company'. Aunt, as we always called Olive when we grew up, never married. "Never set out to get a man," Mother used to say rather scornfully. According to Mother she had one great opportunity when a young man, who later became well known as a writer, showed interest in her, but she gave him no encouragement and his interest waned. Even when they were both getting on in years, Mother still felt exasperated at what she thought of as Aunt's lack of initiative in grasping her opportunities.

As a young woman Aunt had a lot of ill-health, and suffered the physical and psychological trauma of a double mastectomy. After this the doctors said she ought to be given a lighter job for a few years, so she was appointed Head, and only, Teacher of the small Church of England school in Hampton Court Palace, a school limited to the children or dependents of employees at the Palace. Here Aunt taught two classes simultaneously. The schoolroom, in Tennis Court Lane, was a long narrow room in the middle of which stood Aunt's desk with both classes facing the middle. So much for the 'lighter job!'

For a year or so Phil and I went to this school, travelling daily by tram from Hampton. On our first day Aunt told us that at school we must call her "Miss Chamberlin", not "Auntie". At our tender age we found this most confusing; often slipping up and continuing to call her "Miss Chamberlin" when she came to family tea at the weekends, and "Auntie" in the classroom. She was a natural teacher, and always kept both classes interested and occupied.

I have always thought we were very lucky to have had Hampton Court Palace and its grounds as our playground when we were young. Grandfather would take us through 'the rooms' - the State Apartments - and give us history lessons from the paintings on the walls, all of which he knew intimately, and he would explain the different architectural periods represented in various parts of the Palace.

He would take us walking through the gardens when huge garden parties were being held to entertain dignitaries from all parts of the Empire, and colourful events they were. I was always specially impressed by the Indian princes in their full regalia, with gem-encrusted curved daggers at their waists and diamonds sparkling in the silk turbans above their fiercely black-bearded faces, their princesses, always standing or walking a pace behind them, were an exotic picture in their gorgeous saris.

We often watched the ancient game of Real Tennis being played on the Palace court farther down from the school in Tennis Court Lane. Most of the warders and attendants knew us as George Chamberlin's grandsons, and we were allowed to wander almost anywhere we wished.

Uncle Bill was the baby of the family and was rather spoilt, mainly because of ill health as a child. He had a tubercular shoulder which eventually was cured, but left his right arm shorter than his left, a great trial to him. Yet he triumphed over it to the extent of becoming a draughtsman in the firm of Weygood Otis, the builders of lifts and escalators. He was involved in the installation of the first escalators in the famous Bentalls department store in Kingston. Tragically his first wife died soon after marriage and although he married again several years later this marriage was not a success and within a couple of years or so they separated. He was an unhappy and frustrated man until he died in his early seventies.

Uncle Bill's one satisfaction in life was his music; he had a pure alto voice and after being a chorister under my father at St

John the Baptist Hampton Wick he graduated to the choir of the Chapel Royal at Hampton Court, and later belonged simultaneously to the Westminster Abbey Special Choir and the Lothbury Male Voice Choir.

It was through Grandfather's membership of Father's choir that my father and mother first met. They were married in 1914 six months or so before the beginning of The Great War when he had left the Hampton Wick church and was standing in as organist at St Mary's Hampton, the regular organist having been 'called to the Colours'. Father had been refused by the army because he was blind in one eye, though this was in no way apparent.

I was born in 1915 and my brother Philip in 1917. When I was grown up Mother told me that I had been a twin and that my twin had died some time before the birth without the doctors knowing, and as a consequence I was poisoned in the womb and was copper-coloured when I was born. She also thought this was the cause of my constant ill health as a child, and particularly, the reason why I suffered almost from birth from eczema and asthma.

Until I was nine we lived in a semi-detached house in Broad Lane Hampton, and then we bought a plot of land farther up the road which was part of the plantation bordering the grounds of the large house, Elm Lawn, owned at the time by a Mr and Mrs Stevens, friends of my parents. They were interesting people. Mr Stevens was a big bearded man and we children were very much in awe of him. They were quite well off - he was a very successful accountant and senior partner in a large firm. Mrs Stevens was East European in origin - a Czech I believe, and very musical - she had been a professional concert pianist before marriage. Her ethnic origins plus her artistic temperament made her a very volatile, and at times, explosive person. There was frequent high drama in the big house and my father was often the only person who could calm Mrs Stevens down and would be called in from time to time to exercise this pastoral role.. But she was a very generous and kind lady, as such people often are.

The Stevens had two sons and two daughters, the elder son, Monty, had just started in the business and was beyond my ken; the younger boy, John, was about eight years older than me and was at his public school at the time we built our house. To me he also seemed a creature from another planet. He would sometimes speak to us in a rather condescending way when we were small, but when we had all grown up some more we realized that he was a very nice chap indeed. The two girls we hardly ever saw in the early years, but later on we all became quite friendly. Joan was a nice level headed girl with dark hair, kind and smiling. Her younger sister, Priscilla was a very different number indeed. She had striking golden hair, was very beautiful and had her mother's volatile and fiery temperament. She was always causing ructions wherever she went - and I found her terrifyingly attractive, increasingly so as I grew up. The age disparity began to mean less of course as the years went by, and by the time I was seventeen or so and smoked a pipe, which I did from my sixteenth birthday, I could usually take her on and try to calm her tantrums, as my father had done for her mother. "I do like a man who smokes a pipe", she used to say in a voice that made me take a deep breath. She was the first pretty girl to refer to me as 'a man' and it did a lot for my ego.

So it was next door to the Stevens on land that had been theirs, that we built our own house, designed, not very well, by Uncle Fred, the senior partner in our firm

During the holidays and every weekend while Greenwood was being built, Phil and I practically lived on the site and watched with fascination every phase of the construction. I first went into the room that was to be mine by climbing a ladder before the staircase was built. The building methods were of course those of the time - the mid 1920s - and today they seem unbelievably primitive. For instance, the mortar for the brickwork was made on the site - by forming a large ring of sand in the middle of which several sacks of pure 'quick-lime' were spread, and then drenched with buckets of water. Immediately the chunks of lime would begin to crack and crumble and steam, until soon the whole thing was a boiling white cauldron - it was hot enough for the men to cook their eggs in it for their lunch, which they often did. When the lime had been slaked and had cooled down, the surrounding sand 'wall' was shovelled into it and the whole mixed well together to produce a lovely sloppy mortar just right for laying bricks. When it came to plastering the walls, the plaster had to have a binding agent, otherwise it would flake apart and fall off the walls. In this day and age it seems incredible that this binding agent was cow hair. It came in sacks, all matted and tangled together, and it smelt disgusting. Before it could be used it had to be teased out into an even texture - and this was done by placing it on a rough table and beating it with a couple of flails made of three 3 foot laths nailed together with a spacer between them producing a three-pronged flail. With one in each hand a man would spend hours beating the cow-hair until it was sufficiently broken down to mix with the plaster for the walls.

Of course all the plumbing was of lead piping, and every joint had to be 'wiped'. Wiping a joint involved opening out one of the pipes so that the other would just fit inside it; then molten lead

Greenwood, the house we built in 1926

The Choirboy brothers, myself on left

was poured over the join and as it cooled the plumber would, literally, wipe the soft molten metal around the join with a thick wad of material, impregnated with animal fat, to prevent the lead from sticking to it, and in this way he would gradually form the bulging cover to the join which is always a feature of this type of old-fashioned lead plumbing. I used to love watching this operation by our skilled plumbers - as the hot metal hit the fatty pad it smelt like the Sunday roast cooking, delicious!

We named the house 'Greenwood', rather predictably, because it was surrounded on three sides by woodland. We all loved it from the moment we moved in. We were free to roam and play in the woods and we and our friends took full advantage of this freedom. There were 'fairy dells' and wonderful places to hide, and we ran riot in this enchanting playground. I would sometimes wander from the others and penetrate deeper into the wood, half-frightened but exhilarated and it was in this woodland plantation that I had my first experiences of mystery and the 'numinous', sensing that there was a deep reality behind what could be seen - often inspired by the dappled sunshine glancing through the trees and lending an almost supernatural brightness to the greens of grass and leaf. When I read in *The Wind in the Willows* of Rat and Mole's experience on the river as they heard the heavenly music played by the Piper at the Gates of Dawn I knew just what they were feeling. I could empathise with Mole as he 'felt a great Awe fall upon him, an awe that turned his muscles to water, bowed his head and rooted his feet to the ground. It was no panic terror - indeed he felt wonderfully at peace and happy - but it was an awe that smote and held him and, without seeing, he knew it could only mean that some august Presence was very very near.'

Mother and father were often invited to dinner and a musical evening at Elm Lawn, particularly after we became their next door neighbours. When I was small I was quite a 'Mummy's boy' and often cried myself to sleep knowing that she was a long way away in the big house next door, the other side of the vast garden. Often when I did eventually sleep I had a recurrent nightmare that tortured my sleep for many years. I dreamed that I was bowling a small metal drum down a steep hill, banging it frantically with a stick to make it go faster and faster - because Daddy was coming behind me bowling a much larger drum that towered over me and any moment was going to run me down unless I could go faster, and faster, and faster. Just before it did actually crush me I would wake up, shaking and terrified.

Father built a grass tennis court in the garden, he and Mother being keen players, and we played family tennis from the first summer after we moved in. By the time Phil and I were in our early teens we regularly changed into whites after tea whenever the weather was fine and would wait to see which of our friends would turn up on a standing invitation for an evening's tennis. This was often followed after dusk by dancing in the hall. When our friends were tired of dancing they would ask my father to play the piano, which he would always rather do than dance, and most evenings would end with a piano recital, or a sing-song or both. In the winter months our house was often as full of friends in the evenings as it was in the summer, come now for music, and it would often resound with singing and laughter as Father sat for hours on the piano stool as soloist, accompanist and entertainer. In the early days when we were still small I would often lie in my bed unable to sleep and weeping with loneliness as I listened to the sounds of laughter and jollity coming from below, and longing to be down there too.

I have many unconnected but vivid memories of when we were small. Many are sad ones - I suppose because I was so frequently ill - but there are happy ones too. I remember sitting on my father's knee as he hugged me and said proudly that I was his 'son and heir' - and I would wonder what that meant; or on my mother's lap, feeling safe and full of comfort as she enfolded me in her arms and sang lullabies. They were devoted and demonstrative parents while we were young and gave us a lot of love; lots of hugs and kisses, so important for children.

I was taken by Mother to see the local contingent of the Middlesex Regiment marching through Hampton Hill as they returned from the Great War. I would have been between three and four years old and I was standing by my brother's pram waving a little Union Jack. The men wore puttees on their legs - long strips of khaki cloth wound tightly round their legs from ankle to just below the knee, standard uniform in those days but I think they had vanished before the Second World War. For me at that age they were the most visible part of the uniform, for anything else was above my eye level. One thing I could not abide was the big bass drum - as soon as this came anywhere near I would rush to Mother, because the sound of the drum gave me a pain in the tummy and I was scared stiff of it. It was several years before I could watch without distress any parade in which the bass drum was played The Scouts and Guides often marched past our house and we would stand at the front gate to watch them - but as soon as the drum came along I would rush back into the house and fling myself upon the couch in the sittingroom and cover my ears.

Another memory is of my brother Phil being operated upon for a tight ligament under his tongue which made him lisp. This was done at home by the family doctor, and Father had a special table made for the operation, much higher than a normal one, and this was put in the diningroom near the window. So far as I understand, the procedure is simply to snip the ligament, and it seems a lot of palaver for that, but that is how I remember it. What I remember most is my own anxiety about what they were going to do to my little brother - for in my book when the doctor arrived it was usually a preliminary to being hurt. The doctor's visits were nearly always on my account. He used to push up my shirt sleeve, break the top off a small glass ampule, and bringing out a large syringe he would fit a long needle to the end of it, insert the needle into the liquid in the ampule, suck it into the syringe, squirt a little bead of it out - and then plunge the fearsome needle *the whole way* into my poor unoffending little arm. I had been crying madly from the moment he arrived, and now would increase my bellows to hysterical proportions. The purpose of the exercise was to try to combat my asthma of course.

When the doctor arrived for Phil my relief that it was not for me this time was shortlived and soon replaced by a great fear for my poor defenceless little brother. Naturally I did not know what was going to be done to him, but judging by my own experience Phil was going to be hurt, and I could not bear the thought of that. It was a sunny summer's day and I was sent into the garden to play while the dreadful deed was done. I had peeped into the dining room and seen the tall table covered in a blanket and white sheet, and knew in my bones that something terrible was going to happen to him. So it was a very fearful little boy that wandered disconsolately round the garden listening for Phil to start crying like I always did - but there was not a sound, and later when I heard the front door bang I rushed back into the house to see what had happened to him. He was sleeping peacefully in his bed! - still of course under the anaesthetic, but I knew nothing of such things and so great was my relief that Phil was all right that I did not think to question the funny lingering smell of chloroform that I had not met before.

An even earlier medical memory is of being ill when staying with Grandma at Hampton Wick and her doctor calling to see me. Dr Gunther was one of the old school of GPs, and he arrived in a brougham drawn by a smart black horse, and driven by a liveried coachman. The doctor was wearing a top hat, and a frock coat, with a heavy gold watch chain and fob. After he had taken my pulse and temperature he 'shot' his stiff starched cuffs, and with a slim gold pencil wrote the prescription for my medicine on one of them.

We used to love our visits to our beloved grandmother in

13

their nice house in Cedars Road, Hampton Wick. She had a huge white cockatoo in a cage in the front parlour which we children would watch with fascination, waiting for it to speak, but of which we were very wary, for it had a formidable beak and would often threaten us through the bars of its cage. The story goes that soon after a new vicar arrived at St John the Baptist church, his wife called on grandmama one afternoon. She was shown into the front parlour by the maid who then went off to find Gran. Meantime the visitor, who had an arthritic hip, limped across the room to look at the cockatoo - which put its head on one side, gave her a beady look, and said, "Hello Cocky, got a corn?" The lady was deeply offended, and when Grandmama arrived she had to soothe a lot of feathers, but not those of the cockatoo, as she explained that his name was 'Cocky' and this was one of his few phrases.

I think few people under the age of seventy today can imagine how *quiet* life was in my parents' time and when my brother and I were very young. The occasional car or horsedrawn cart or carriage would pass our house, but there was no 'traffic'; one hardly needed to look both ways before crossing the road. When as a small child I was put to bed in the front bedroom on a summer's day for my afternoon rest, I would only hear the buzz of a bumble bee or housefly, or the "Moo" of a cow grazing in the butter-cup meadow across the road. The meadow has long ceased to exist and is now covered by roads and houses. There was no radio filling the house with music or talk. The only sound would be the murmur of conversation or the laughter of the occupants. When we children were at home we would naturally make plenty of noise from time to time as we played, but there would be no competition from other sounds. If one or other of our parents was playing the piano, which certainly happened often, this did not provide the continuous waves of sound that the radio and television do today - when they are often switched on first thing in the morning and off only last thing at night. All communication was by word of mouth, or had to be read in newspapers or letters. People tended to be more reflective in those days, and consequently escaped some of the tensions that non-stop sound and the constant and inescapable stream of ideas cause today, as they bombard our ears and minds.

Many people today would find the silences to which we were accustomed quite threatening. In those days there was plenty of 'time to stand and stare' and our spirits were enriched by the experience. The spirit of man is impoverished by many things in modern society, not least by of the lack of the experience of silence in the course of daily life and the opportunity it can give for reflection. There are growing numbers today who are seeking physical and mental relaxation through quietness and silence - witness the enormous increase in the number of retreat houses of all denominations and none, and the fact that they are full the whole year long.

As a result of my asthma I was frequently away from school during the winter. When I was reasonably clear of asthma I was plagued with eczema, on hands and legs and face - and in the summer months was away from school with this almost as often as I was away with asthma in the winter. I did very badly at school. At the age of eight, after leaving Hampton Court Palace School, I had been sent to a little private school run and owned by a Miss Tutt, but by the time I was ten my parents were told I would never be ready to sit the entrance examination for Hampton Grammar School, the best boys' school in the area, and they had set their hearts on both of us attending this school. Willie Cooke, the headmaster of the local Council School - the state funded school where the education was free - was a friend of my father, and a regular member of All Saints Church. He was a wonderful Welshman, short and fat and smiling. He had a splendid singing voice and was never missing from the choir. He also read the lessons at Evensong most Sundays with tremendous gusto and drama. When my parents told him of their anxiety he said," Why don't you send him to me for a year? - I'll get him ready for that examination."

So I went to the council school, and became acquainted with a very different type of boy from any I had so far met; most were uncouth, and they had a vocabulary that contained words I had never heard before, many of which I thought extremely funny. There was one boy I met during my first week who lived not far from us and we were soon keeping one another company on the fairly long walk to school. We used to kick a ball as we ran, with our satchels bouncing on our backs. One day I came home very amused, and I told the family as we sat at the tea table, "Johnny is so funny - this afternoon our ball went under a gate and into someones front garden, and Johnny said, O bugger, now I'll have to go in and get the fucking thing!" And I began laughing my head off. But my laughter was short-lived, for Father's face clouded over and he told me sternly not to let him hear me using such words again.

I passed the entrance examination to the Grammar School all right, but by the time I reached form 4B I was regularly at the bottom of the class, chiefly because I missed so much school through illness. As a result, when I was fifteen the doctor advised my parents to take me away from school, saying that my health might improve if I went into the office. This was decided six months before the end of the academic year - but they thought that I might as well finish off the year before leaving. The headmaster had agreed with alacrity to my being withdrawn, for he did not like failures in the school. He said scornfully; "Yes, take him away - he will never pass matric anyway". Words that rang through my head like a knell for years afterwards. Ironically it was during that last term that I began to wake up intellectually and became for the first time in my life interested in what I was learning - and able to retain what I was taught. However, the die was cast and I left school at fifteen, much to my father's satisfaction of course - I am sure he felt his plans for me and for the business were really beginning to mature. His view was that all the education I needed was just enough for me to manage the business - "The 'Three R's' are all you need, with some building construction and draughtsmanship later on", he said, "You don't want to be stuffing your head with all this algebra nonsense."

So I left school and Father took me to Barker's store in Kensington where he bought me two new suits off the peg, one grey and one brown, and some business shirts and ties. The day I started in the office I heard a friend of Father's exclaim, "Going to work in the office? But he looks no more than a child!" So, apparently, I did. Nevertheless, the doctor had been right; my health improved and I soon grew out of my new suits and had to buy more.

Next time I went shopping by myself, and only down to the village where I had seen a tailor sitting cross-legged on a small platform in the window of his shop - sewing suits by hand! For the first time in my life I had two new suits custom made by what must have been one of the last old fashioned craftsman who sewed every stitch by hand while seated cross-legged. I still remember the delight of putting on the jackets of those suits - they just slid on effortlessly and silkily because they were such a perfect fit.

For several years after moving into Greenwood we were fairly prosperous. Mother was thrilled with her new home and was able to engage a living-in nanny for us, who also doubled as a maid, helped with the housework and waited at table. When we no longer needed such close supervision there came a series of little maids, but soon after I left school this all came to an end with the sacking of the latest acquisition, a very glamorous girl who insisted on wearing bright red lipstick and as little else as possible. Father thought her a corrupting influence on 'the boys' and Mother was forced to agree. Phil and I were sorry to see her go for reasons that confirmed their opinion. She was the last of Mother's servants, for soon afterwards the Depression hit and we moved slowly but inevitably towards austerity if not actual want.

16

Greenwood was much nearer to All Saints Church, Hampton, than to St James's Hampton Hill, so after a time we transferred our allegiance. I had been in the office for about a year when Jock Murray was appointed the new vicar of All Saints. He was young and vigorous and proceeded to take the parish by storm.

Our experience of 'vicars' so far had not been very happy. The vicars of St James's where we had mostly gone as small children, and St Mary's Hampton, where Father had been organist during the 1914-18 War, and where we had gone to church on the days when he was playing the organ as a stand-in, were worthy men but were getting on in years and did little to gather young people into the fold. At that time All Saints, Hampton, was a daughter church of St Mary's and for a number of years there had been a run of very unprepossessing priests-in-charge. The whole place was run down and sad - and dead. Jock Murray came as its first vicar as soon as it was made a separate parish, and his arrival sent shock waves throughout the area. He had served his title in Pimlico. There he and his wife Marjorie had lived in a bed-sit where he said he could lie in bed while stirring the porridge on the cooker, so he knew something of the seamy side of life and was quite unshockable. He was handsome, humorous and tough.

Jock's twinkling Scotch blue eyes won hearts everywhere - although we soon discovered that they could become like gimlets and penetrate with disapproval, but he charmed everyone, young and old alike. During his first week in the parish he amazed us all by taking a parishioner in his little Austin Seven car to see her husband who was a patient in a London hospital. "He must be everso nice" was the general verdict, and it was not long before it was known that visiting the sick, whether churchgoers or not, always took priority in his life. Jock was the first 'professional priest' anyone around us had ever experienced. The other local clergy seemed concerned merely with getting people to go to church on Sundays, (what they called 'supporting the services'), and with finance. No doubt they all did more than this but it was not very obvious. In our family at anyrate we had not heard of a clergyman who was concerned to bring people to God in worship, repentance and a developing life of prayer.

So Jock was a revelation. Like all revelations he was a considerable shock to the system. On his first Sunday he told the congregation that on going through the drawers in the vestry he had found a set of white linen eucharistic vestments. He went on to explain their significance and said that as they belonged to the church he proposed to wear them at every celebration of the Holy

17

Communion, starting next Sunday. No one remembered the very first young priest-in-charge who had bought the vestments and worn them for a time - and had then either left or been told by the Vicar of Hampton to stop wearing them. They had lain in the drawer untouched and forgotten ever since. Of course tongues were soon wagging expressing dismay that the new young vicar was 'very High Church', this not least in my own family, where both Mother and Father had been brought up in the Low Church tradition, and Father had more than a touch of Calvinism in his very real and devout faith.

Naturally, being the professional he was, Jock set about teaching the Faith. The substance of his teaching can be summed up in the words appointed to be said by the Bishop on the Licensing of a Reader:

'The Church of England is part of the one, holy, catholic and apostolic Church worshipping the one true God, Father, Son and Holy Spirit. It professes the faith uniquely revealed in the holy scriptures and set forth in the catholic creeds, which faith the Church is called upon to proclaim afresh to each generation. Led by the Holy Spirit, it has borne witness to Christian truth in its historic formularies, the Thirty-Nine Articles of Religion, the Book of Common Prayer and the Ordering of Bishops, Priests and Deacons.'

I do not remember Jock ever referring to himself as an Anglo-Catholic - or giving himself any other label. He would declare roundly that the Church of England was thoroughly catholic and that he was therefore a catholic priest. He wore a full soutane cassock, single-breasted, with thirty nine buttons down the front (joking that these signified the Thirty Nine Articles of Religion!), half sleeves, and with a short cape. Thus clad he was soon to be seen everywhere in the parish - a professional priest, the 'parson,' or 'person,' of the parish, about his duties - and never off duty, a vibrant and arresting figure as he strode the streets. In those days parish visiting was considered obligatory on most afternoons and several evenings in the week, and it was not long before he knew the great majority of his parishioners and had visited most of them in their homes. While tongues continued to wag about his 'high-churchery' the great majority of the increasing congregations received his teaching like a desert the long-delayed rains.

It was not long before everyone knew that Jock was available for all, and would do everything he possibly could to help in time of trouble. The Parish Communion filled the church every Sunday at 9.30, and most of those who were there in the morning were again filling the church for Evensong, both services having a full choir of men and boys. He was a dynamic preacher and people began to come from far and wide to hear him.

Very soon the Blessed Sacrament was reserved in the Lady Chapel with a white light burning before it, and the Eucharist was celebrated daily there. We servers were expected to take it in turn to serve on weekdays as well as on Sundays - at 7am, so there was no excuse that we did not have time before going to school, or in my case, to work. My brother Phil and I were two of Jock's devotees, members of a band of a couple of dozen young people whom he had prepared for confirmation and who had responded to his teaching with great enthusiasm, so that the church and its organisations and social events became the very centre of our lives.

A year or so after Jock's arrival it was clear that the work of the parish had grown to such an extent that he needed an assistant. In due course he found just the man he was looking for, and another bombshell was dropped upon the parish in the person of The Reverend Peter Booth. The son of a wealthy member of the tobacco industry, Peter had had a privileged upbringing - public school, Pembroke College Cambridge and straight on to Ely Theological College, and then immediately to our parish of All Saints Hampton. Another good-looker, with his blond hair brushed straight back. a full and mobile mouth that quirked up at one side when he smiled - the girls almost swooned at the sight of him and some of them would ride slowly past his lodgings in the evenings in the hope of catching a glimpse of him. He was a great hit with all of us and soon had his own devoted following. It was he who organised the servers into a guild of which I became the Secretary - my first public office! - responsible for drawing up the rota of duties, and training new servers. We used to meet in Peter's study once a month for a talk from him and a general chat.

During Peter's first autumn in the parish there was an Anglo-Catholic Congress taking place at the Royal Albert Hall. The Oxford Movement, begun by Keble and Pusey just over a hundred years before, was bearing abundant fruit at that time and the Anglo-Catholic movement was on the march. Peter Booth took a party of servers to the Congress one evening and it was a revelation to us all, Phil and I were swept up in the excitement. Jock's teaching about prayer and sacraments, and all the 'sacramentals' such as the use of the sign of the cross, the vestments and ceremonial, came into its own, was confirmed and enhanced by the lectures, informal talks, and the whole spirit of the Congress. No wagging of tongues here, no mutterings of 'High Churchery', no frowns of disapproval. Everyone seemed filled with enthusiasm -

19

almost to the point of becoming 'more Catholic than the Pope!' There was for us a great sense of liberation from the dreariness and dullness that had characterised our worship in the days before Jock Murray and Peter Booth arrived to transform our whole attitude to churchgoing and the Christian faith. Here was colour and excitement, yes, and a sense of adventure, all connected with and expressing our worship of God. We had had no idea that practicing the Christian Faith could be such fun!

One of the first things we noticed on entering the Hall was the pervading smell of incense, for there had been a devotional service earlier at which it had been used. I felt slightly wicked as I sniffed it up my nostrils like some latter-day Bisto Kid, thinking Gosh, I wonder what Dad would say if he could see us here! Dad at that moment, no doubt, was sitting at home before the fire in his favourite chair with his slippers and his newspaper, snoozing the evening away.

On our arrival at the Congress Peter had said that he hoped to see one Father Millard ("Father!" - another little tingle running down the spine!) who, he explained. was a member of the Community of the Resurrection - a monk, no less. Until that moment we had had no idea there were such creatures in the good old C of E. But how to find him in such a vast throng? I asked Peter. " O, we'll find him all right", he said; "We only have to keep our ears open and sooner rather than later we shall hear him laugh." Sure enough, within a few moments there came from far above our heads a most astonishing sound - a cross between the bray of a donkey and the hideous laugh of a hyena. "Ah-ha", said Peter, "There he is, up in the second gallery". So, up the stairs we went and out on to the second gallery, where we soon found a tall figure clad in a black cassock, with a wide leather belt from which hung the bronze crucifix worn by the brethren of the Community of the Resurrection.

Father Elwin Millard CR was a jovial man and greeted Peter effusively from the midst of a circle of other friends, and then brought us all into the conversation - which was frequently punctuated by this quite extraordinary braying laugh ending in a high-pitched scream.

Here on the second gallery were more wonders to behold: stalls selling everything required for Catholic worship and devotion. I remember we bought our first little manuals of devotion from the bookstall, and small crosses painted with luminous paint which glowed in the dark. Also, greatly daring and almost with bated breath, I bought my first crucifix.

As we walked home from the station that night Phil and I

were very thoughtful, and he put our thoughts into words when he asked, "What's Dad going to say about your crucifix, are you going to tell him?" I said I had been thinking about that and had decided not tell him, but just hang it on the wall in my bedroom and say nothing about it. This I did, and the following day mother said to me, "Daddy went into your room and saw your crucifix - he said to me, 'Young Ernie (my baptismal name and always used in the family) has got a crucifix in his bedroom!!' So I said, matter-of-factly, 'Yes I know' - and he just gave me a 'look' and said 'Humph,' and walked out of the room!" Good old mother; she was twenty years younger than father, which was probably why she was more willing to change her opinions than he was, and so was much more tolerant towards us, always defending us if she could. I told Phil about all this and we had a good old giggle.

The climax of the Congress was the Pontifical High Mass celebrated at the White City Stadium on the last Sunday, and Peter took most of us servers to take part in it - all dressed up in our new purple cassocks and white cottas. Our eyes must have been like saucers when we entered the stadium, the 'congregation' packed the sides of the arena, and the wide 'aisle' down the middle was full of the most amazing sights - bishops in copes and mitres, priests in soutanes with cottas (short square-necked surplices) dripping with lace, and with birettas on their heads; servers in black or red or purple cassocks and cottas, some with albs and girdles. There were servers swinging thuribles belching clouds of incense, others with the thurible open, blowing desperately on the charcoal to make it burn - often with an anxious little 'boat boy' blowing too.

At one end of the arena a huge altar had been erected, high on a platform approached by innumerable steps. The altar was decked in a magnificent gold frontal, and upon it stood six huge baroque candlesticks with tall candles. On either side were massed choirs. The Mass was a revelation; sung to Gregorian Chants and with wonderful ceremonial and gorgeous vestments. We joined hundreds of other servers in a vast procession up the middle of the arena to seats on either side of the altar. I felt that the glory of Heaven could hardly be more breath-taking. It was here in the Albert Hall and at the Pontifical High Mass in the White City Stadium that my appreciation of the age-old rituals and ceremonials of the 'One Holy Catholic and Apostolic Church', as affirmed in the creeds, was born.

At this time I was seventeen and Phil fifteen, and we were living a fairly normal suburban family life. Phil was still at Hampton Grammar School; he would leave later and do a vocational course for a time before joining the firm. Our social life was centred upon the church and in consequence the great majority of our friends were fellow-worshippers. Phil and I had made particular friends with two brothers, fellow members of the guild of servers, Denis and Eric Rolt, whose father was a metallurgist at the National Physical Laboratory at Teddington, and we spent a good deal of time in one another's homes

Father being a sick man hardly impinged upon our social life at all. Mother gave us all the support she could, not least in our initial steps towards Catholic faith and practice. When, at different times, Phil and I decided to make use of the Sacrament of Penance we felt that we ought to tell our parents; Mother was sympathetic and Father only offered token resistance to something that he had always regarded as anathema. It was only later that we realized that he was in fact too sick and too dispirited to fight.

When Grandfather retired from the Palace, Aunt Olive bought a tiny house in Gloucester Road, Hampton, five minutes walk from Greenwood, and made a home for the old people. Uncle Bill, Mother's brother, lived in digs a short drive away, so we were a family group in the same area. As we grew up, Grandfather mellowed and he and I became particular friends. Uncle Bill became almost an elder brother to us, for he was much younger than his sisters. Today, when families are often fragmented by living so far apart, I appreciate how lucky we were to have an uncle and aunt and grandparents whom we loved and with whom we were in almost daily contact. Our normal and healthy adolescent rebellion against parents was absorbed to a great extent - we always had a 'bolt hole' that was still 'family' when home became intolerable for a time and so no harm was done - we had no need to 'drop out' even for a short while.

The only one of my father's seven brothers we had anything to do with was Uncle Fred. He did not like Mother so did not visit us at home, and contacts were confined to the office. He was only really interested in the architectural side of the business of which there was less and less as the years went by. From long before I joined the firm he had been little more than a 'sleeping partner' and had left the running of the firm, the difficult decisions and the 'hiring and firing', to my father.

As the Great Depression of the 1930s began to bite, business became more and more difficult and disheartening, There was no money about and things went progressively downhill. No one was spending money on building works; only absolutely necessary repairs to property were carried out, and paint had to be peeling off the woodwork before people would have their houses redecorated.

The salvation, for a few years, was the funeral side of the business - another aspect that Uncle Fred found distasteful and which he accordingly left to my father. Whatever happened, people had to be buried. This was probably the side of the business that my father on the contrary found most satisfying and fulfilling. Not for any ghoulish or morbid interest in death, but because he really looked upon arranging funerals and dealing with the bereaved as a sacred Christian vocation

Father was wonderful in his dealings with those who grieved; he never preached to them, but they felt comforted by his presence in the house and knew that he empathised with their grief. I am sure they always had a prominent place in his prayers. He conducted the funeral with gravity and respect, but without the dreadful over-acted solemnity and Uriah Heep 'humility' of so many modern funeral directors. He also knew that in his informal dealings with the family there was often a place for a little humour and that sometimes a laugh can release tension and bring a few crumbs of comfort.

In those days coffins were "tailor-made' by hand in our own workshops and when Father went off to the house to arrange the funeral he took with him his two-foot folding rule made of pure ivory that he kept exclusively for taking the measurements for the coffin, for of course people almost invariably died at home.

Most funerals involved burial in churchyard or cemetery, and cremation was the exception rather than the rule. The cheaper coffin was made of elm board and was french polished. The better ones were of English oak and were wax polished with home-made polish made from a mixture of pure beeswax and turpentine. Both were lined with 'swansdown and silk', the standard lining - as I typed routinely when preparing the accounts.

The Deluxe coffin, the most expensive of all, consisted of an elm 'shell' covered in purple cloth and lined with the usual 'swansdown and silk'. The body was placed in this and the cover screwed down. This elm 'shell', complete with body, was then taken down to the plumber's shop where he proceeded to cover it completely in lead sheeting about an eighth of an inch thick, which was hermetically sealed around all the joins with molten lead, smoothed to a perfectly flat finish. This outer coating of lead was then painted over with Berlin Black, which is a black paint that dries off matte - in contrast to Japan Black which is glossy. The plumber then decorated the lead covering with a diamond shaped pattern by scratching the lines with a special scriber to allow the bright metal to show through the black. Our plumber at the time was highly skilled and every lead coffin that he made was a masterpiece of his art. This lead-covered elm coffin was then put into the outer case, another coffin made of best English oak and wax polished, with brass or silver handles and engraved nameplate.

At the funeral this triple-coffin, one of elm, one of lead and one of oak, would be carried from house to hearse, hearse to church, church to grave - which could be quite a long walk through the churchyard - on the shoulders of six men. It is difficult to imagine the weight. Some firms would place the coffin on a wheeled bier to take it to the grave, but my father did not approve of this method and thought a person should be carried to the grave on the shoulders of men. The men would have sore and aching shoulders for days afterwards. Fortunately few families opted for our 'de Deluxe' model coffins!

I used to spend more time than I should have watching the coffins being made in our workshops, being fascinated by the methods used - for instance, the way the thick boards of the sides were made to bend round smoothly at the shoulder. This was done by a technique called 'kerfing' - a row of vertical cuts to within an eight of an inch of the thickness of the board were made with a handsaw about one inch apart at the position of the shoulder, for about nine inches. The thick board would then bend easily round the shaped base-board of the coffin and could be nailed in position. This called for considerable skill, for a few strokes of the saw too many and the board would break at that cut, not enough strokes and it would not bend properly, and that also could cause a break.

When the coffin was finished it would be taken to the house one evening, preferably after dark, an operation involving four men as well as Father himself. His respect for the departed and consideration for the bereaved caused him to lay down very strict rules for the behaviour of all the men concerned with the funeral. One of his strictest was that no one involved in taking the coffin to the house spoke a word from the time it was carried out of the workshop into the black van, known as the 'handy', until they had drawn away from the house on the way home.

At the house Father would ask the family to stay in one of the downstairs rooms while the men carried the coffin silently up the stairs to the bedroom where the body lay. Still in complete silence, the body was then reverently laid in the coffin, the 'swansdown and silk' draped neatly over it, with a special veil to cover the face, and then placed upon a pair of trestles. If the bedroom was small the men would probably move the bed to another room. Having left all tidy and as nicely arranged as possible, the men would then go quietly to wait in the 'handy' until father had had a few words with the family, and if they wished, conduct them to the bedroom on the first of their visits to the departed before the coffin was closed on the day of the funeral. Some, Roman Catholics especially, would keep unbleached candles burning night and day around the coffin .

I only once heard of the silence of this operation being broken . A wealthy man living in Hampton at the time owned a large Victorian house standing in extensive grounds. We did a lot of work for him over the years. Dave Singleton, a distant relation of ours, was our head carpenter. He was a fine craftsman and our client always insisted that Dave should do all his carpentry and joinery. Dave did some wonderful work for him, including lining the walls of his library, diningroom and entrance hall with oak panelling. But no job, however good it looked to everyone else, (and Dave's work always looked good), was quite good enough for our aged client, and he grumbled and groused every time a job was finished.

The day inevitably came for him to die, and Dave, now getting on in years himself and nearing retirement, naturally made his coffin - of best English oak, lined with the usual 'swansdown and silk'. Dave said he would like to be one of the four to 'take the coffin home' as we used to say. So they duly set off in the usual silence and followed the usual procedures. They carried the coffin through the beautiful hall with Dave's oak panelling gleaming in the soft lights, past the door of the oak panelled library, up the staircase which Dave had also made, into the old man's bedroom where he lay waxily upon his bed. Reverently he was lifted into his coffin and the 'swansdown and silk' carefully draped over the body leaving the face free. Dave stood for a few moments, looking down at the old man - Father thought reverently - then almost overcome with emotion he raised his hand and shook his fist in the dead man's face and hissed, "There you are you old bugger. that's the first job I've done for you you have not grumbled about!" My father did not have the heart to tick him off for breaking the silence, he could only turn away, smothering a laugh.

Years before, this client, who was a keen fly fisherman, had wanted, of all things, a trout stream created in his garden. Uncle Fred, a passionate fisherman himself, enthusiastically encouraged this whim and proceeded to design a fast-running trout stream - for a London suburban garden at Hampton! There was a central 'tower' to the house and he calculated that a large watertank built into the top of this tower would produce a sufficient head of water to provide a fast enough flow in the artificial stream. He installed a quiet electric pump that recycled the water from the final pool back to the tank in the tower. Uncle Fred even went to Scotland to arrange for the stream to be stocked with fish. It worked like a charm, though few people saw it, for the owner was something of a recluse. What eventually happened to the trout stream after the old man's death I do not know, but many years later when my brother had joined his brother-in-law's electrical business in Hampton he had occasion to go to the house about some work, and told me that the water tank was still there and the pump still operational.

Father was a gregarious man and had the ability to 'get on' with anyone. He had a profound faith, never missed his daily prayer, and the only prayer book he ever knew was the Book of Common Prayer of 1662, which indeed was open in his hand as he died. He was a man whose word was his bond, and he was respected throughout the neighbourhood for his integrity. He was loved by his very great number of friends for his compassion and his lively sense of humour. He was also a very sick man. Not long after I had joined the firm he had his first stroke and was away from the office for many weeks. This of course threw me in at the deep end and by the time I was approaching my seventeenth birthday I was running the office and taking on most of his responsibilities while he directed me as far as he was able from home. Little help came from Uncle Fred, of course!

Father's illness, with several relapses, affected his speech and seemed to make him more and more irascible, especially with me. Poor man; I had compassion for him but could not really come close to him, so unfortunately he never became my friend as well as my father. We had a rather stiff relationship, partly because of the irascibility, but mostly because I resented his refusal to let me grow up having the freedom and the fun that my contemporaries took for granted in their own lives. Phil, on the other hand, had an easy relationship with him and Father became his greatest friend. For one thing, unlike me, Phil could turn away Father's wrath with a cheeky quip that would transform his frown into a reluctant grin and a laugh. Phil and I always had a deep and affectionate relationship, and no one could ever be blessed with a finer brother than he was to me.

Apart from the prohibition of girl friends on my account, our early teenage years were quite happy except for problems with my health. So here I was at the time when the two great influences of my life made their mark upon me - my 'vision' of The Girl in the Middle and my embracing of the Catholic faith. I lived comfortably in a nice home, with a jolly but forceful mother whom I both loved and feared, an aging and failing father, a splendid and amusing brother - and I was thoroughly unhappy and frustrated.

My Christian faith was burgeoning and involvement with the church activities brought me into contact with a lot of young people of my own age, so I was not entirely bereft of feminine society and had a few innocent flirtations in the normal way, but of course it was only our young men friends that we could invite home. Notwithstanding all the other nice girls I met I was still daydreaming about that wonderful blonde, but had given up hope of seeing her again and I was still scared at the thought of doing so. It never occurred to me to go looking for her. None of the other girls could hold a candle to my blonde wonder, the sight of her had spoilt me for any other. I so longed to have a girl of my own and was unhappy and frustrated because I despaired of ever doing so.

Then the miracle happened. One day Jock Murray said to me, "The Sunday School is growing fast and I need more teachers, so I want you on Thursday evening at 7.30 sharp in my study - Sunday School Teachers preparation class; you'll start teaching on Sunday. Bring a notebook." "O Lor, must I?" "Of course; no argument." " O, all right," I said. So on Thursday evening, dutifully but not very keen on the idea at all, I went a little wearily up the vicarage stairs and into Jock's study. " O good", he said, "here you are, find a pew." Fortunately I was standing right in front of a chair, for as my eye went round the group already there I found myself staring, with open mouth, at a girl on the other side of the room in animated conversation with her neighbour. I sat down suddenly with a thump and with a racing heart - there, a few feet away, still shining in glory was - The Girl in the Middle! I was at once elated and confused. I could only sit and stare and did not hear a word of Jock's introduction of everyone, so I missed her name. But she did look across at me, cursorily but politely, and then away again to concentrate upon someone else. I noticed that I had not shrivelled to dust, so I took heart! Also I was conscious that I was better dressed this time, with a decent pair of bags and my best Harris tweed jacket - I had also worn my new 'Sammy' scarf which every well-dressed young man sported that year! - so I was not wanting to scurry away.

As the evening proceeded and we all concentrated on the instruction we were being given in the art of Sunday School teaching, the sense of awe with which I had first seen her lessened and she became just a very pretty and animated girl with a slightly husky voice - which did peculiar things to my tummy. By the end of the evening I was sufficiently emboldened to hang back until I could speak to her and introduce myself. I said I had not caught her

27

name. She said she was Barbara Baguley and she lived in Oak Avenue. O, I know where you live I said, I caught a glimpse of you once when we were doing some work at your house. I did not add that I had thought about her ever since.

Now my vision was standing next to me and although some of the glory had subsided, I could still see that she was the prettiest girl I had ever encountered and I could not wait to get to know her. "May I walk you home?" I asked. She said thanks but she was being met - and as we went out of the vicarage front door there he was, a handsome chap I had seen around from time to time, though he was not a member of the church. So off I went home with a sinking heart and muttering to myself, "There you are, I told you so, 'Adonis' has claimed her."

Come Sunday we all gathered rather nervously in the church and, having been assigned our classes, we each bore off a dozen or so rag-tag-and-bobtail kids to various parts of the church, arranged them in a circle around us, and began our teaching careers. As it happened Barbara Baguley and her class were a little way over from me and I could see her golden head bent towards the children as she talked to them. I have to admit to occasional moments of absent-mindedness while I taught my class that afternoon.

When it was over and the children were streaming ahead of us out of the church, we all loitered by the door asking one another how it had gone and comparing notes. Naturally I homed in on Barbara and we walked to the church gates chatting animatedly. This time there was no Adonis waiting for her - though in fact he lived within sight of the church - so without asking permission I began to saunter with her in the direction of her home. Before we realised it we were at her gate, and being the polite young lady she was she asked me if I would go in.

So I met the family, who all called her 'Bar'. I proceeded to do the same from then on. Only one of the other two 'golden girls' was there, her older sister Joan who lived at home and did most of the work connected with the small-holding, tending the orchard and growing the various flowers that they marketed. The elder girl, a nurse at the Great Ormond Street Hospital for Sick Children was on duty and only came home occasionally.

Bar's mother was a dear gentle lady who still retained some of her original soft Yorkshire accent. Her father was a mining engineer who came from Midlands farming stock. At this time he was in the process of inventing and marketing a special head-piece for pit-props that made the fitting and removal of them underground much simpler. Unfortunately his invention did not take on and he lost a good deal of money as a result. Bar's family

Barbara Baguley
aged 17 – the first snap

Self aged 18 with Mother

gave me a friendly welcome and I was invited to stay to tea. I walked home on air feeling that I should pinch myself to see if I was not dreaming; I could hardly believe that all this had happened, and was in my Seventh Heaven.

At home father was resting in his armchair and mother was reading and knitting. They both wanted to know how my Sunday School teaching had gone, and they put my euphoria down to the fact that I had enjoyed it immensely. Mother, shrewd lady that she was, told me later that she guessed that my happiness could not have resulted simply from finding that I had enjoyed my Sunday School teaching more than I had thought I would. I told her about meeting Bar and she immediately became my unquestioning and enthusiastic ally in my pursuit.

So at last I had met the girl of my dreams and knew I was truly in love with her and that at least she was prepared to talk to me and be friendly.

It did not take me long to discover that Bar was not very attached to Adonis. After a few weeks he disappeared from the scene, and I happily replaced him. Always welcome at her home, I began to think for the first time that I was really living. At last, incredibly, I had a girl of my own; someone I could proudly refer to as "My girl" - and what is more, my friends started chipping me and telling me I was a lucky dog for I had pinched the prettiest girl in the town! For the first time in my life I had the heady experience of being envied! My depleted ego was getting some very satisfying boosts.

Father was hanging on desperately to life and with great courage continuing to run the business with my, by now not inconsiderable, help. Uncle Fred continued to be little more than a 'sleeping partner.' There were many days when Father could not come to the office and I held the fort alone - occasionally having a surreptitious phone call to Bar where she worked as secretary to Bertie Page, one of the prominent nurserymen of the area. By this time Father had largely given up his attempts to keep strict tabs on me; perhaps he assumed that most evenings when I was not studying, Phil and I were out with the two Rolt brothers. But for me most of these meetings were a cover for seeing Bar. Mother knew this and approved. Without disloyalty to my father she let me know that she sympathised and was sorry I was not able to bring Bar to meet the family in the normal way.

It was against this background that I began to see more and more of Bar, 'My Girl'. We would meet at church and at all the parish functions and activities. On Sunday afternoons after teaching in Sunday School we usually went for cycle rides together, finishing up at her home for tea until it was time to go to church for Evensong, after which I would walk her home and we would dally for as long as we dared before parting.

It was not long before I discovered that there was another side to Bar. She was bright and vivacious for most of the time - always when she was with other people, but when we were alone a very different and very sad girl often showed her face. As our relationship developed she was able to show this face to me more and more, and we used to cycle many miles around the country roads of the neighbourhood, as they were then, with tears streaming down her face. Nor could she ever tell me what was troubling her; she used to dry her eyes after a spell of weeping and say sadly that she just felt thoroughly miserable but could not tell why.

There were various things that made her unhappy - she hated the orchard and everything to do with the picking of fruit, the cutting of flowers and the preparation of these for the market. In the summer months she was often unable to come out with me because she had to help with this work. But these were not the sort of frustrations that could be the cause of the deep unhappiness that she showed so often. However, people are usually more resilient when they are young than they are in later life, and in the main Bar was a happy and cheerful girl with a fine sense of humour. It was not until very many years later that we discovered the root cause of her depressions.

One thing Bar did in those early days of our relationship was make me determined to change my name as soon as possible. One day as we sat in companionable silence, her golden head on my shoulder, she suddenly looked up into my eyes and murmured in her husky voice, "Ten little nigger boys digging in dead earnest - poor Ernest!" - and giggled. (In those days we had not heard of 'racism'). Of course family and friends had always called me Ernie to distinguish me from my father Ernest, or Ern as he was often called, and I had for some time been uneasy about my name, thinking I would rather be called George, my other baptismal name. Until now it had been only an occasional passing thought, but in an instant, with one little joke, Bar made me determined to change it as soon as I could, although it was to take longer than I had expected before I could pluck up the courage to take such a radical step.

As our relationship progressed so my own commitment to the Christian faith developed and for a time Bar matched my stride in this, and courting and prayer, both public and private went hand in hand.

2

Courtship versus Vocation

A radical turning point in my life occurred quite unexpectedly during a Lent course preached at All Saints by the then vicar of the church of S. Michael and St George, Fulwell, a neighbouring parish. I do not remember the subject of the course, nor what the particular address was about on that Wednesday evening. But I have never forgotten how, as I listened, I had a most profound experience of the presence of our Lord, and I felt overwhelmed by the conviction that I was being called to the priesthood. For some reason Bar was not with me that evening, and I remember that I went home almost in a daze and going straight to my room without a word to anyone spent a long time in prayer; a type of prayer that I had not experienced before, in which I felt I was receiving and not giving, being held rather than reaching out. When mother saw a light under my door on her way to bed much later she looked in to see whether I was all right. I told her I was quite all right and was about to go to bed myself. She told me later that she feared I was getting 'religious mania!' Yet I was in no emotional or fanatical state, but perfectly calm and collected.

I lay awake that night thinking about the implications of the experience I had had. Priesthood? But, good heavens, one had to have an education before one could hope to be ordained, and I was an ignoramus. And what about the business? By Jove, what a wonderful way to escape its toils! I had hero-worshipped Jock Murray for years, and had added Peter Booth to my pantheon; they were 'gods' and it was pathetic, even laughable, to think I could ever follow in their footsteps.

For days I went about thinking of this momentous sense of vocation that had come to me, and that had not diminished in the least in the cold light of dawn or with the passage of time. Poor Father, I thought, whatever would he say?

A couple of weeks later I went to see Jock and told him all - expecting him to say that with my background I must be mistaken and that I should settle down to the course my life already seemed to have taken. I should by then have known him better, for he said nothing of the sort. What he said was, that a vocation needs to be tested, and in my situation that testing would probably come through what looked like the insuperable difficulties that were stacked against me. "But take heart," he said, "If God wants you to be a priest and you want to try to do his will, then nothing can ultimately stand between you and the priesthood." He advised me to say nothing to my father for a month or two - he knew what his long-nourished plans for me were, and thought I should not distress him in case this sense of vocation was a passing phenomenon and in time faded or vanished as quickly as it had come. Good advice with caution and encouragement nicely balanced.

Of course I told Bar all about it and we talked about it often. As the weeks went by the sense of vocation increased, and settled more and more firmly in my mind and heart. The way ahead looked impossibly difficult; we had no money, I did not even have Matric, I knew nothing about anything except the little needed to keep the business ticking over, as it falteringly did in spite of the recession. I had told Mother and she was sympathetic but doubtful, "Do you think you could do the studying necessary?" she said. With a hollow feeling at the pit of my stomach I said I could only try.

The day inevitably came when I had to grasp the nettle and talk to Father about it. I do not remember much of that painful interview, but I do remember being conscious that I was dealing a terrible blow to a very sick man. He was quite dreadfully upset, as I expected, but after a while when he had had a little time to get used to the fact that I was telling him I did not want to inherit the business, he suddenly stopped - and then astonished me by saying, "I am very sorry to hear of this - and yet at the same time I am very proud that a son of mine should want to be ordained. How we are going to manage I do not know, but we must trust that God will show us the way." I am ashamed to say that I had for the time being forgotten his profound faith.

Some days later Father said he had been thinking it would have been possible for him to send me to Cambridge if we had not lost so much money as a result of the recession, but even so he would try to think of some way of making it possible. Edward Wynne, later Bishop of Ely and at the time Dean of Pembroke College, was a great friend of Jock and Peter and a frequent visitor to our parish. We all knew him well and he was encouraging me to set my sights on Cambridge and look forward to the day when I could apply for a place at Pembroke. He said he could assure me of a place once I had got my Matric. Father knew that Eric Rolt was destined for Pembroke and Ely Theological college on his way to the priesthood in the steps of Peter Booth, and he half hoped that it would be possible for me to do the same.

Of course this was all pie in the sky until I had overcome the first great hurdle - for of course I could not even start on my way to ordination until I had Matriculation under my belt. How to do this looked an insoluble problem. It was four long years since I had left school, and I had done nothing academically since then except attend a few night school classes in building construction and drawing. Jock suggested that I might be able to do the necessary work by correspondence courses, so I enrolled with Wolsey Hall. Within a few weeks it became evident that I would never be able to learn in that way.

Meanwhile Jock and Peter had put their heads together, and Peter said he thought the Community of the Resurrection had a scheme by which young men who might have a vocation but had not matriculated and could not afford to pay for their education, were sent to an old student of theirs who ran a cram school at Tatterford in Norfolk. Here they were coached through Matriculation and then went on to the Community Hostel in Leeds where they read for their degree at Leeds University before going to the College at Mirfield for their final years of theology, all at the Community's expense. It sounded ideal and I was thrilled at the thought of such a wonderful opportunity, which would solve all my problems. Jock accordingly wrote to the Community at Mirfield and recommended me as a worthy candidate. But the Community turned my application down without an interview. So I was back at square one.

Not accepting defeat Jock then by-passed Mirfield and wrote direct to Father Hand the Principal of Tatterford, asking if he would take me as a paying student, and if so how much would it cost? The reply was in the affirmative and the fees would be £90 per year. I was delighted that here at last there seemed a chance, but how to find the money? - that was the rub. Jock said, "Well, if you are meant to take this opportunity the money will come - from somewhere."

That was in April I think. In May Father had a massive heart attack in the middle of the night. The family doctor, Dr Woodroffe, took Phil and me aside and told us, "Your Daddy is very very ill, and I must warn you that he may get worse." I went to see him the following morning and he was lying in bed looking dreadful. I said I was off to the office and would see him at lunch time. So off I went. We had recently, after an uphill fight, persuaded Father to let us buy an old car - I think for under £50 - because he could no longer walk very far and of course could not ride his bicycle, so I roared off to the office in this instead of taking my bike.

By mid-morning all seemed well at the office and everyone was busy so I decided to pop home to see how he was. As soon as I got into the bedroom he was very cross with me for coming home when I was supposed to be working. The poor man was justified in a way because he knew well by now that I would steal any few minutes that I could away from the office, no matter how flimsy the excuse. So, resentful but understanding, I went straight back to my desk.

About an hour and a half later Phil was on the phone asking me to go straight home as Daddy was very bad. I leaped into the car and burnt rubber to get home. Phil, shaking and with an ashen face, was waiting for me at the front gate. "I think he has gone", he said. I rushed up to the house and into the bedroom which was on the ground floor, and I saw with a glance that he had indeed died. He was sprawled on the bed, his mouth and eyes open - the open Book of Common Prayer still clasped in his hand. Mother was weeping at the side of the bed. I think I closed his eyes, gave mother a hug and then rang the doctor and Jock Murray.

The doctor arrived first and did what was necessary, then Jock came and rallied us all and told us what to do. My poor mother and brother were in a state of shock. I was not sure what I felt; certainly great loss, for basically I loved my father, but I have to confess that there was also an element of relief; I had been smarting at the ticking-off I had received earlier, and this had aroused a sense of resentment at the way I had been treated all along, with no apparent regard being paid to my own wishes and feelings. I also felt guilty because I knew in my heart that my refusal of the business had struck Father a mortal blow, proud as he said he was of my reason for doing so. But those thoughts could not be sorted out just then, and I have to confess that for a long time I felt relief that I could no longer, as I saw it, be persecuted by him.

Uncle Fred next appeared on the scene, clearly shattered; he had had no idea how ill Father had been. We had some sort of lunch I suppose because it was after lunch that mother suddenly said to me, "You had better go and fetch Barbara, you need her." So off I went, rattling along in the old car hardly believing that at last I was able to invite her to my home. She came with me gladly and was soon helping me to organise things.

By now friends had begun to arrive, and mother sat in the sitting room surrounded by them. Phil and Bar and I made numerous pots of tea while mother engaged in that very important aspect of mourning and regaled her friends with reminiscences of her past life with Father - going right back to their wedding, a recital that included laughter as well as tears; and so began the slow process of coming out of the shock. We three were in the kitchen and the serving hatch between the two rooms was slightly open, so we could hear every word. "... and," she said, "we went to

Clacton, of all places, for our honeymoon, and we tried to behave quite normally when we reached the hotel so that no one would guess that we were newly-weds. We had gone through all our clothes and suitcases to make sure there was no confetti left to give us away. We thought we had done very well until about the third day when as we were about to go out of the door of the hotel Ern noticed that it had started raining, so he opened his umbrella over our heads - and out poured handfuls of confetti! We could have murdered the wretch who had stuffed the umbrella and then rolled it up again!" "O, and it was so funny; on the first day we were walking along the promenade and Ern suddenly said, 'Do you want to powder your nose?' And I said, 'No, I don't think so, is it shiny?' 'O no, he said, I just thought you might' - "and then I noticed that we were passing the public toilets and I realised that what he really meant was, Did I want to spend a penny? but he was too shy to ask directly! Poor old Ern, but he was a dear, one of the best."

The day of Father's funeral coincided with the celebration of King George V and Queen Mary's Silver Jubilee in 1935, and that morning there was a great procession of the Terrirorial Army with its band, all the local Scouts and Guides, Brownies and Cubs, the British Legion and numerous other organisations. The procession was routed down Broad Lane, and all the banners and flags were dipped in tribute to Father as they passed our house.

As on the occasion of his own father's funeral, all the houses in the area had their blinds down, many of the shops in Hampton Hill were closed, and many followed the custom of fixing black painted boards across their shopfronts as a sign of mourning.

Father's body was taken to All Saints church where he had in the end succumbed to Jock, for he had a great regard for him though he could not accept all of his teaching. After the funeral service at All Saints, Father was buried in the family grave in the churchyard of St James' s Hampton Hill.

Following Jock's teaching Mother and Phil and I had determined that the funeral would not be an entirely sad affair. So far as we were all capable of making it so, it would be a celebration of Father's life, and a witness to his and our faith in the Risen Lord, and our belief that death has indeed been conquered and Father was entering upon a new phase of his life where suffering and sorrow were no more.

We had also decided that we were not going to wear black - on the contrary, Phil and I bought bright yellow ties and our first pairs of suede shoes to wear at the funeral! We later heard that the local men's outfitter was quite scandalised and grumbled that, "Those Singleton boys did not buy a single piece of mourning from me!" The day of the funeral was one of those wonderful hot days we sometimes get in May, and afterwards we gave everyone tea in the garden at home, and Jock came saying that that had been a very nice and cheerful Christian funeral!

The next day I reported at the office as usual and Uncle Fred said, "Well Ernie, now that your dad has died of course you will give up this nonsense about going into the Church and stay in the firm - in a year or so's time I will make you a partner." I have to confess that I got a wonderful kick out of saying, "No, sorry Uncle, but I have to try to qualify for ordination, and I shall be leaving as soon as I can arrange to go away to study," I added, "Also, my wages have been ten shillings a week for a long time now, and I think I should have a rise, in view of the fact that I am running the office by myself." The old man seemed flabbergasted, but swallowed and said, "Well, you can pay yourself a pound a week - and when you have found that you cannot manage the studying, you can come back into the firm." I remember thinking coarsely, Not on your Nelly! When I told Phil, who was now in the firm, what I had done, he said he was not going to stay with a sinking ship, and if I left he would go too as soon as he could.

After this things began happening in rapid succession; it was as if a log-jam in the river had suddenly come free and all was turbulence and activity. My beloved Aunt Olive, now having taken early retirement on a reduced pension, said she thought she could help towards my first year's fees at Tatterford. Grandfather thought he could give a little from his modest savings. Mother could only say that she thought she could clothe me but hoped to be able to do more later. So I accepted the place that I had been offered at Tatterford School for the following September. I had just enough money promised to cover one term's fees. *O lord, you* did *say Take no thought for the morrow ... So the rest is up to you if you still want me to go ahead, if you will forgive me for saying so!*

And what of my wonderful Girl in the Middle, what was happening to Bar in all this turmoil? She was giving me her moral support, but with many misgivings, the most serious of which she did not tell me for a long time. She dreaded my departure in September for three whole months, and I was dreading parting with her for that length of time. Bar only had a me-shaped void ahead of her, while I on the other hand, in spite of my fears, had something to look forward to and, however daunting, a challenge to face, which tempered my sorrow at the thought of being parted from her for so long.

The day came when I was to leave for Tatterford, and all of

us were filled with gloom. For Mother it was a second bereavement. For Phil also: he dreaded the thought of life without his elder brother to support him - he was barely eighteen at the time and very miserable, missing Father dreadfully. The whole foundation of his life had given way.

I was sad at leaving Bar, and now it had come to the point I was dreading leaving home for the first time and facing a new and no doubt very strange world, living cheek by jowl with a lot of strange young men whom I had never met before and who I felt in my bones would be far superior to me in every way. I had been warned that Tatterford was a tough place and now I felt unequal to the challenge. I was a softie; I had been brought up with more attention being paid to me than is normal on account of my frailty and my illnesses. Mother thought I would be more likely to get ill at Tatterford than at home and feared for me.

They all came up to Kings Cross station to see me off on the first leg of my journey to Peterborough where I would change on to the old M & GN line to Tatterford.

I noticed that there were one or two other young men being seen off on that train, and a few boisterous ones who were greeting one another loudly and with a lot of laughter. I studiously ignored them all as I feasted my eyes on my lovely Bar for the last time before the months of separation that stretched ahead.

With a lot of huffing and puffing and clouds of steam, and with a shrill blast from its whistle, the train pulled jerkily from Kings Cross, Phil running alongside until it gathered speed, while with a big lump in my throat I leaned out of the window waving to him and to the disconsolate little group huddled together on the platform I was leaving home for the first time, and I felt the umbilicus stretch and tear

It was not until I came home at Christmas for my first vacation that I began to realise a little of the near chaos I left behind me that day. Apart from their bereavement Mother and Phil had heavy burdens to bear to which I had given little or no attention. While I went swanning off into the blue, certainly with some apprehension, but not completely without a sense of adventure, my heaviest burden fear of the unknown and the thought of three months separation from Bar, they went home to face daunting problems. Uncle Fred was being as difficult as he could be with Mother and was only paying her a mere subsistence allowance from the business, saying that nothing more could be afforded. Phil spent a few weeks running Uncle Fred about in the car, but soon got fed up with being no more than a chauffeur and went off to Richmond and got himself a poorly paid job in the electrical department of the municipality. He then told Uncle Fred that he would be leaving on Friday. It was a doubly traumatic time for both Mother and Phil, and I have always been ashamed of how little I realised what was happening. Nor did it occur to me just how much they both relied upon me. I was a self-centred and thoughtless young man. Neither Mother nor Phil ever reproached me and I am both grateful and ashamed to this day.

The train had hardly pulled out of Kings Cross before a cheerful cove came along the corridor, one of those I had noticed on the platform, and asked if I was for Tatterford? He said he was a second year student and invited me to join the rest of them and even humped my case along for me. I was painfully shy and my inferiority complex must have stuck out a mile, but they gave me a very friendly welcome and were not a bit condescending or superior. Before long we were bowling along and getting to know one another. The 'new boys' like me soon felt at ease and the tension began to drain out of us.

Having changed trains at Peterborough the slow little country train eventually pulled into Tatterford station where the only person on the platform, apart from the stationmaster in shirtsleeves and braces, was a tall well-built figure in a rather scruffy black cassock. The second year students rushed up to him and greeted him affectionately: Father Hand, the Principal himself, come to greet his new and returning students.

He was a cheerful man and was smoking a pipe which endeared him to me at once. Already a confirmed pipe smoker myself, I always considered you could trust a man who smoked a pipe! He greeted me warmly and said he hoped I would be happy as a member of the little Tatterford family. The local carrier was outside the station with his horse and cart upon which the luggage was piled and we all began the mile long walk along the country lane, with vast open fields on either side, down the gentle hill to the ford which we crossed by the footbridge - the horse seemed to enjoy getting his feet wet - and up the other side to the tiny rather unkempt village of Tatterford, and then the School. Up the very stony drive, past the small flint-walled Tatterford Church and the ivy-covered Rectory, around the back, and there it was, Tatterford School.

In spite of the warning that life at Tatterford would be somewhat spartan I had not expected quite such a ramshackle collection of buildings. From the back of the Rectory a wooden hut extended, and this was our Refectory. A little beyond that was a World War One army hut, which was the senior dormitory. At right-angles was the only purpose-built building, a long lecture-room-cum-Common Room with the first-year dormitory above, which was approached by an outside staircase. Next came a dilapidated cowshed which was the 'ablution block' with a broad wooden bench around the walls on which stood twenty enamel bowls with a small mirror above each. In front of the bowls on the rough brick floor, that was almost permanently wet, were duckboards to stand on. In the middle of the floor by a central drain stood a large galvanised iron bath full of cold water, the only water supply. On going to wash one dipped one's bowl into the iron bath and scooped up enough water for the purpose. Inevitably some spilt on the way back to the wooden shelf - hence the almost permanently wet floor. Along a rough earth and flint path, thirty yards beyond the ablution block, stood a rough wooden 'privy' - a 'six-seater' as *The Specialist* would have said. And it was as primitive as he would have built in the Middle West.

Adjoining the ablution block was what had been the stable; it still had a couple of mangers and tethering rings attached to the walls. This was a second lecture room. The only heat provided was by means of a medium sized Tortoise stove in one corner. Another Tortoise stove stood in a corner of the Common Room. There was no other heating in the whole place, except a Valor oil heater in the Refectory which was only used in the worst weather.

Next to the stable-lecture room was a large shed housing the 'gasometer' - a huge circular contraption used for manufacturing the acetylene gas which was the means of lighting the lecture rooms and the Rectory. The Refectory was lit by oil lamps and in the dormitories we each had a candle on the small bedside chest-of-drawers.

It is not hard to imagine my feelings, pampered as I had been, when I saw this set-up. My heart quailed when I was told that at Tatterford we wash in cold water every morning, winter and summer; and that at the mid-morning break one kettle of hot water is brought from the kitchen - shaving water for twenty young men! We were allowed one bath a week, the bath being under the table in the kitchen, and were rationed to four inches of water for the purpose - a small ruler being provided for making sure we took no more! We could hardly ever have been properly clean except once a week when we had had a four-inch bath!

The domestic side of our life was ruled over by Father Hand's wife. Mrs Hand at first appeared to be a rather intimidating lady - she could certainly express her displeasure in no uncertain terms and would tolerate no nonsense, but in time we all grew to appreciate the genuine care that she had for our welfare. She did not actually come into the kitchen when we were drawing a bath, if you could call it that, but I for one felt that she was looking over my shoulder as I dutifully measured my four inches of water - at the shallow end of the bath! If we were genuinely ill she would nurse us and look after us with devotion, but we all knew better than to try a bit of malingering if we felt like wilting under the pressure and wanted only to stay hidden in the foetal position for a day under the bedclothes.

I had never played football in my life, a nasty rough game I thought it, but it was a Law of the Medes and Persians that twice a week we all turn out for at least an hour's soccer on the football field in front of the Rectory. This was really a stretch of meadow, part of the ancient glebe, with many humps and tussocks over which we tore back and forth chasing that wretched ball that I grew to hate. We shared this field with Sprig, the rectory horse, who used to get very excited when we were playing football and would tear around the edges of the field making loud and disgusting noises. Disgracefully, our game would often come to a halt while we stood and cheered him on his explosive way.

There was one other permanent member of staff, a certain Mr Hickman, known to us all as 'Old Hick', or 'Hicky'. A man of uncertain temper and great scholarship. It was rumoured that he had been sacked from more than one school for being unkind and too strict with the children, and he was immensely grateful to Father Hand for taking him on. So far as we knew he never went away, and I do not remember ever seeing him outside the grounds. He taught anything he was asked to teach, and legend has it that on one occasion Father Hand told him he had had an enquiry from a prospective student who wanted to learn Chinese. Old Hick had said, "I don't know any Chinese, but, I suppose I could mug it up in the vac." He always completed the Times Crossword puzzle while he sipped his early morning tea in bed.

It was probably the first time most of us had met an intellectual and we all regarded him with awe, and did everything we could to avoid the rough edge of his tongue when he castigated our ignorance and failure to learn. There was one certain way to make him unbend. He had an aviary in the garden in which he kept a number of most beautiful Chinese pheasants. If we came upon him feeding these colourful birds and stopped to admire them, he would actually smile and talk about them; then the next ticking- off he gave you in class might be a little milder as a a result.

Father Hand, having been trained by the Community of the Resurrection, naturally modelled Tatterford on the CR Hostel in Leeds and the College at Mirfield, and so our routine was almost monastic. Every morning we were awakened by the Hebdomodary ringing his large brass handbell through both dormitories - sometimes clanging it a few inches above the heads of well-known heavy sleepers. This signalled that there was half an hour before we were due in church for Matins and Mass. Some of us became expert at cutting it so fine that we rushed up to the church door and then walked in decorously just as the clock was about to strike. Even so, we would sometimes receive a disapproving look over the top of the Principle's specs.

Mass was followed by breakfast which was eaten in silence and on non-feast days consisted of porridge, bread and butter and marmalade. Greater Silence was kept until lectures began at nine o'clock, which left a full half hour for personal prayer and meditation after breakfast had been finished and beds had been made.

Life at Tatterford was mentally and physically tough - and to my surprise I found myself thriving upon it, at least so far as the physical toughness was concerned. I discovered a great liking for community living, and as autumn gradually changed to winter I found myself adapting, as everyone else did, to the spartan conditions and apart from the odd cold I began to feel healthier than I had ever felt before. When everywhere was covered in thick frost or under six or eight inches of snow, as occurred each winter that I spent in Norfolk, I got quite used to my morning wash consisting only of rubbing my hand over the solid ice in my tin bowl and then over my face. When we were in the lecture rooms we would wear coats and mittens, two pairs of socks, and thick scarves wound around our necks in an effort to keep warm, for the Tortoise stoves seemed to warm only their immediate vicinity. We would discard this extra clothing when the lecture or study period ended and we were free to go out for some exercise.

Weather permitting one of our favourite forms of exercise was walking for miles along the 'green lanes', which for those who do not know about them, are the grassy ways that wind through that part of Norfolk, and are said to be the ancient lanes used by mediaeval pilgrims to Walsingham. These lanes were lined by trees on either side, with vast Norfolk fields stretching beyond. I loved wandering along these green lanes at all times of the year; they were full of bird life, and pheasants and grouse roamed unconcerned as one walked by. In spring and summer the only sound was the song of the many species of birds that nested in that area. However, the majority of my walks along the green lanes were not for the purpose of bird watching. Most of the time I would be trying in vain to get the mysteries of Greek and Latin verbs into my head - declaiming them aloud to the trees and hedgerows, which I am sure absorbed them much more readily than my wretched brain.

Apart from lectures and study the students did all the chores: the only servants were a couple of maids and a cook who cooked all the meals, and we did everything else, just as the students were required to do at Mirfield. Here there was no mains water, and every drop that we drank, that was needed for cooking and for baths, had to be drawn from the Rectory well by hand, hence the four-inch-bath rule. Pumping the water was one of the best ways to get some exercise, for the pump was operated by a large wheel with a large handle and twice daily two students would turn this wheel several hundred times to keep the water tank in the Rectory roof sufficiently supplied for all these purposes. It was hard work, and by the time I went home for my first vacation I had biceps larger and harder than they had ever been before.

There was a rota, changed every week, allotting our duties. Two men were responsible for laying the tables for the meals, and for cleaning them afterwards. Two waited at table for the 'formal' meals of lunch and dinner. Two more washed the dishes after each meal. Two were responsible for keeping the two Tortoise stoves supplied with coke, and two kept the tin bath in the washroom supplied with water from another pump in the garden. This was not pure spring water like that from the main well, and often had masses of green and black aquatic beasties swimming about in it - at Tatterford in the summer months you even got used to washing in 'live' water. Two were on pump duty. Others cleaned and dusted the Common Room and lecture rooms before work began each day. On Friday afternoons we cleaned the church and the dormitories.

It was a good life, with study, manual work, recreation, exercise, corporate worship and personal prayer nicely balanced. No wonder we were healthy. Before supper we went to the church for Evensong, sung to Gregorian Chants, my first experience of Plainsong, except for that memorable High Mass at the White City two or three years before, and I have loved it ever since. Supper followed Evensong, after which we sat at our desks studying until at 9.30 the bell went for the little night office of Compline, the last service of the day, introducing Greater Silence once again. We were free to stay in the church for as long as we wished before going quietly to bed.

I grew to love this routine and I am sure it began to prepare the way for my eventual vocation to the Religious Life, though I would have scoffed at the idea at that time.

If only what I was being taught would stay in my wretched head! But no; I almost despaired. So did Father Hand. "Singleton, my dear chap," he said one day, "I really think you ought seriously to consider whether you are not wasting the money that your relations are providing to keep you here, I know with great difficulty, because you are really not managing to learn much, are you?" I had to admit that I was not. I told him I simply could not give up so long as my family were prepared to find the money for my fees. So he said no more and continued to help me in every way he could. There was just one subject with which I had no difficulty, English Literature and Language, and I think it was this that kept a glimmer of hope alive somewhere in the depths of my mind.

So, my first vacation. I had a great welcome home and I was unpacking my bags in my ground floor bedroom when the door flew open and Bar flung herself into my arms with a squeal of delight. The moment I had dreamed of for all those long weeks. The next hour was full of excited talk and many hugs and kisses. Then the door bell rang and I opened it to find a very pretty young lady standing there who said, "Is Phil in?" He came at once and I was introduced to Dorothy Hone who, he said, and was often to repeat in the years to come, had 'changed his life'. This became abundantly clear as the days and weeks went by; they clearly complemented one another, and I was thankful and delighted for them.

Phil had had a rotten time and he was long overdue for a change of luck. He told me that they had met on a coach taking a party of people from All Saints to the Albert Hall for a symphony concert. On the way home in the coach during a 'bit of larking about' Phil had got hold of one of Dorothy's shoes and when she was dropped outside her house he refused to give it back to her, saying that if she wanted it she could come and fetch it tomorrow! So perforce she hopped up her garden path - and they had clearly 'clicked', for she turned up at our front door the following evening to collect her shoe, and from that moment they never looked back. The transformation in Phil was dramatic. He was relaxed and his old cheery self. He had also grown in stature while I had been away - he knew instinctively that he was now 'head of the family' in my place and although barely eighteen he was shouldering responsibility for Mother and the family affairs quite naturally. I think he sensed that my horizons had grown wider and that I had left home for good. Of course we talked about the future; he told me about the difficulties with the business and that Uncle Fred was thinking of selling up and retiring.

Phil and Mother had put her interests in the hands of the family solicitor and it was clear that they would have to fight their corner. He did much better at this than I would have done - where I would have given in Phil was always prepared to stand and fight. He seemed to me to have a complete grasp of the situation and was obviously willing to accept the responsibility. I was relieved and profoundly grateful for this and have been ever since though, as I have said, I was not aware at the time of the full weight of the burden he was bearing so manfully.

That first vacation seemed to go in a flash; Bar and I spent as much time together as we possibly could - I trying to study in the daytime while she was at work. So also for the Easter vacation, and during these times we grew closer and closer to one another. I know I began to realise the truth in thinking of one's partner as one's 'better half', for as the weeks and months went by I really felt that we were the two halves of a single personality. We often had no need of words to communicate with one another and frequently would know what the other was thinking. In fact our friends used to say that we behaved like an established married couple.

Yet there was a worm of doubt in each of us gnawing away in the background. When the end of my first year arrived and the long summer vacation came along I had to face two unpalatable facts. First, Bar was taking up so much of my thought that I was not putting enough singleness of mind into my work. At the end of that term Father Hand had said his piece about my wasting other people's money in trying to carry on with the course. I knew that I often spent precious minutes mooning over Bar's photograph when I should have been working. I loved her 'as my own soul', but I began to see that my sense of vocation outweighed even this. I also realised that Bar was desperately lonely during the long weeks that I was away, and that our exuberant reunions and daily meetings during the vacations were placing a great strain upon her.

Secondly, Bar had a different problem, a doubt she had had from the first time I had mentioned my sense of vocation. She felt increasingly that she was not cut out to be a priest's wife. Marjorie, Jock Murray's wife, was the only priest's wife Bar knew, so for her, *ipso facto*, priests' wives had to be 'like Marjorie Murray'. Marjorie was an excellent priest's wife; she was forceful, outspoken in her support of Jock; she organised people, and loved being at the centre of things. Bar was basically a shy person and did not like the limelight or organising people or being anywhere near the centre. She was a doughty fighter when need be and when her blood was up, but the thought of taking on in cold blood the sort of things in which Marjorie excelled filled poor Bar with fear and dread. In vain I would try to persuade her that not all priests' wives were like this, nor ought they to be. I told her that in my opinion they should not become unpaid curates, nor should they try to do things in the parish for which they were temperamentally unsuited - and anyway these were the things that suitable laity ought to do. But it was no good; she felt that if I was eventually ordained she would be the wrong sort of wife for me. She was possibly right.

So we talked it all out; I told her my problems. She told me hers. She admitted that she found term times very difficult - and vacations difficult in a quite different way. It took us many weeks of that long vacation to make our most painful decision - we finally made it all alone in the front seat on the top of a red bus on the way home from a party in the pouring rain. We decided that we would meet from time to time, write to one another occasionally, but from now on we would no longer feel committed to one another. The rain streaming down the window in front of us mirrored our mood exactly, and that evening, with lumps in our throats we kissed each other goodbye.

After at last meeting my Girl in the Middle, after getting to know her, and still loving and being loved by her, my vocation to the priesthood had put her, for the time being anyway, out of my reach.

I returned to Tatterford for my second year, now a 'senior', though I do not recall any special privileges. I no longer had Bar's photograph on the top of the chest of drawers by my bed, but it was in the top drawer and for many weeks I could not resist looking at it every night before I blew out my candle.

I began again walking the green lanes cudgelling my brain to retain what I was trying to impress upon it. To my surprise and delight a few weeks later I really did begin to remember things. I am reminded of the old Irish woman on her way back from Lourdes who, when asked by Customs what she had in that bottle said piously, "Holy Wather." Upon which the Customs official withdrew the cork, sniffed the gin and thrust it under the old woman's nose saying, "Holy Water, you say?" She took one sniff and then raised her hands and her eyes to heaven and said, "O, God be praised, another miracle!" So I felt, when almost unbelievably I realised that things were at last going into my thick head and staying there - 'another miracle!'

Came the end of my second year and we sat the examination, at Tatterford in our own lecture rooms, invigilated by Old Hicky.

I failed the examination by one mark - and that in English, my best subject! So it was back to square one again - becoming such a familiar place to me! Father Hand was very disappointed for me - there were tears in his eyes when he told me the sad news. He said of course I could take the examination again in six months time in London, so I would not have to go all the way back to

Norfolk for the purpose. Naturally I would want to do some revision, but he warned me against doing too much.

"I have a suggestion that you might like to consider," he said, "I have a friend, a Miss Garrard, who runs a very nice little co-educational prep school on Epsom Common. Her Housemaster (and only master) has had a heart attack and is on sick leave for at least the next six months. How would you like to go there and try your hand at a bit of teaching? - Miss Garrard has asked me if I have a student who is at a loose end and I should be happy to recommend you". He went on, "You now have most of the necessary subjects at your finger-tips and I am sure you could do it" . With a twinkle in his eye he said, "You would have to teach Latin as well as the other subjects! I am sure the rest of the staff will be able to cover the subjects, like Geography, that you do not have." I felt like saying in broad Cockney," Wot, *me* Guvnor, *teach?*" But I suddenly knew I could do it!

The following months at the Wells House School on Epsom Common were just about the happiest time of my life so far. I loved the children, I found I could keep order - even with the flighty little minx with blue eyes and tumbling fair hair who used to pout and make goo-goo eyes at me when she did not want to do what I told her to do! I had little time to myself, and I knew the drudgery of wading through piles of exercise books correcting prep - and the boredom of taking prep; sorry for the poor little blighters biting their pencils or their nails.

Before leaving Tatterford Father Hand had talked about my next step, assuming that I passed the examination in January. Cambridge was of course out of the question; there was simply not enough money to be found. There were no such things as Local Education Authority grants in those days. It had never been much more than a pipe-dream really. He suggested I applied to St Augustine's College, Canterbury, which he said was a missionary college that took non-graduates, was well endowed and gave bursaries to needy students.

So I took a weekend off from the school and went to Canterbury. There, the Warden, Canon Tomlin, was very kind and understanding and I came away with the promise that if I passed my Matriculation examination in January they would accept me. Furthermore they would give me a bursary of sixty pounds a term so long as I could find a further forty pounds a term to make up the fees. The other stipulation was that I would be willing to go to work overseas at least for a time after I had been ordained and had served my title in this country. I said I might have a problem about that as after ordination I would have to take over responsibility for my mother and give my long-suffering brother some relief. His reply was that there were many places in the Anglican Communion overseas where he thought my mother would be happy to be with me, however I did not get the impression that he thought this a very binding commitment.

I had so far felt no particular attraction to work overseas, but I was quite prepared to give the necessary undertaking if it would open the way for me to train for ordination. I left out the matter of working overseas when I told the family about the interview - I knew Mother would immediately say she would love to come and live abroad with me, bless her, and would start making plans and building castles in the air at once. Not exactly my idea of bliss.

So back I went to my little teaching job and thoroughly enjoyed the next few months.

Of course from time to time when I went home to see the family, we were often exercised about where that enormous sum of forty pounds a term was to be found. Mother was hardly able to make ends meet; she had had to sell Greenwood and had moved into a tiny bungalow near All Saints Church, so I could not ask her for any money. Aunt had said that she thought she could provide enough for pocket money; my beloved brother promised what he could manage - but in those days forty pounds was a lot of money. As the weeks stretched into months I seemed to be at a dead end.

The time for me to resit the examination was appearing over the horizon, and, faithless wretch, I was again beginning to despair.

One Sunday I decided to go to Evensong at Christchurch, Epsom, and after the service I found myself telling the vicar of my problem. He at once said, "Come to Evensong next Sunday and stay to supper. I have Canon Hunter coming to preach. He runs a fund for helping ordinands, especially those who hope to go overseas to work".

I hardly knew how to get through the next week which seemed interminable. However Sunday evening duly arrived and I had supper at the Vicarage and was introduced to a very old clergyman, as he seemed to me then, with snow-white hair. Having heard my difficulties he invited me to lunch on the following Thursday.

Canon Hunter lived on the outskirts of Ashtead a village next to Epsom and when I was shown into his study and he had greeted me, he went to his bookshelves, with which the room was lined from floor to ceiling. and proceeded to take down volume after volume saying, "Now, my boy, you will need this; and, O yes, you must have that, very important my dear boy, and this, and O yes, of course, *that*. ..." I followed him round the room beginning to stagger slightly under the weight of the books he was thrusting upon me. When they were up to my chin, I cleared my throat and said, "Well, um, thank you very much for all these, Father, but the thing is, I shall not be able to use them very easily until I get some money." He stopped half way towards another book, turned towards me and said, "Money? O don't worry about the money, *I'll* give you the *money*," and turning back to his bookshelves he continued - "Yes, and you will want this, and this ..." Well!! One short sentence and the immense door that had seemed locked against me for ever was suddenly open wide! I nearly dropped all my lovely books, but just managed to get them to the big leather sofa and let them slither down in safety.

I went back to the school with a singing heart, and laden with the first books of what eventually became quite a comprehensive if small theological library. That dear lovely old man had joined the ranks of those who had helped me towards my goal; in fact he had removed the last practical obstacle but one; he had solved the remaining financial problem - it was now up to me. The Big One was coming up - looming now dead ahead in January - the Examination re-sit.

At the beginning of the Christmas holidays Uncle Bill took me one evening to visit some friends of his in Hertfordshire. When we went out to the car to come home we found that it was getting very foggy, and we were still some way from home when the fog was so dense that he could not see to drive. The only thing for it was for me to wind my scarf tightly around my neck and walk in the gutter shining the torch on the kerb for him to see. Young Ernie Singleton, with his weak chest, *walking* in the *fog?* Ah, but he's been to *Tatterford*, remember? So he does not have a weak chest anymore, and tonight he is *eating* the fog, bracing his shoulders, striding out and almost loving it! It took a long time to get home that night and I walked a long long way. I was soon going to be very glad of that night's blanket of fog.

It was a cold and damp morning when I left home and caught the train for London to resit the examination and I had a whole host of butterflies flapping around in my tummy. My way from Oxford Circus underground station took me past All Saints Margaret Street, and as I had time to spare I went in to say my prayers. Before leaving I bought and lit the largest votive candle they sold - and they were quite big in those days. I left it burning there as a symbol of my life, and my prayer that I might pass the examination and that, if it was God's will I would indeed be

49

ordained one day. I left the church feeling much calmer than when I went in, and all through the examination the thought of my candle burning there so steadily and so brightly, brought me serenity and banished fear. On opening the English paper that afternoon and skimming through the essay subjects; the third one down just leaped off the page to me - FOG. I wrote that essay in about ten minutes flat! Coincidence? I don't think I believe much in coincidence.

Back to school after Christmas - and then the unforgettable day when I was called to the phone. Mother saying with a sob, *"You have passed the exam!!"* Phew! *Blessing and honour and thanksgiving ....*

So now we really could start. I wrote to Canon Hunter and to the Warden of St Augustine's to tell them the good news.. The Warden confirmed my bursary, the Canon said the extra forty pounds would be paid direct to the bursar of the college. I never saw the old man again, for he died a few months later. Twice only I had seen him; at supper at the vicarage, and at lunch at his own house. But I have never forgotten him; I can still see him inundating me with books, and solving my financial problems almost dismissively as though they were the least important considerations in the world, *books* were what mattered!

So I started my three year course at Canterbury in September 1938. Several old friends from Tatterford were there, and I made a host of new ones. Again I loved the communal life, lived this time in much grander surroundings and in much greater comfort. A room of one's own! Central heating - we had not even experienced that at home! Unlimited hot water and it did not matter if your bath overflowed! We were addressed as 'gentlemen'. There were servants to do all the chores except make our beds, our rooms were cleaned by a 'scout'. A marvellous library to work in with one of the finest collections of theological and historical books to be found in any college library.

Best of all, the great Cathedral where we could worship whenever we were free to do so, and several of us would walk across to make our morning meditation there - I used to like to use one or other of the small chantry chapels, thinking of all those who had prayed there before me, back down the centuries now lost in the dim and distant past of other ages. We lived cheek by jowl with history, for in the grounds of St Augustine's are the ruins of the great Augustinian Abbey that had grown from the tiny pagan temple that St Augustine had taken over after he landed at Ebbsfleet in AD 597 and it became the first church of Western

Christendom in England. Parts of this little temple are built of Roman bricks made by Saxon brickmakers.

The college itself is mostly Victorian but with some ancient remains that have been restored. Our dining hall with the wonderful timber ceiling was the mediaeval dormitory where pilgrims from all over the world would sleep, having walked the last eighteen miles from Dover, before completing their pilgrimage the next day at the shrine of St Thomas à Becket in the Cathedral.

Arriving at St Augustine's, with matriculation successfully behind me I at last found myself ready to take the radical step of changing my 'image' by changing my name. From now on to all but family and old acquaintances I was to be George Singleton.

A new name, new activities, many new friends and constantly broadening horizons ushered me into a new and exciting life. Unremarkable to those who have gone smoothly from school to university to theological college, but to me a metamorphosis.

Rejoicing in my new-found fitness I joined the rowing club, partly because I liked the tie better than any of the other club ties! Two or three afternoons a week therefore I would cycle with the other members to our boathouse on the Stour at Sturry. The river was just wide enough for a four so long as the cox did not take us far from the middle! We were not very serious oarsmen, but we had a lot of fun. By tradition we rowed one race a year, and that was against King's School Canterbury. Of course there had to be two finishing lines as the boats could not row abreast. We always put our opponents in front because everyone knew that we could never win, and if they had been behind they would have been bumping us a few strokes from the start - it was less ignominious for them to go steaming ahead of us as we laboured in their wake. Everyone took it in good part and both crews and spectators would repair afterwards for a pint or two in the riverside pub opposite the boathouses and sing bawdy songs.

There was a well equipped carpenters' shop in the college and I became one of the three or four college carpenters who helped with small repairs and maintenance work. This being a missionary college there was also a printing shop. One of the students, Charlie Colls, happened to be a professional printer and he was immediately put in charge. In the college library there were stacks of pamphlets and magazines. that had been printed in all corners of the globe by priests who, as students, had learned their skills on the presses in the college printers' shop. So I added printing and bookbinding to my hobbies.

Nineteen thirty-eight, the year I went to St Augustine's, was also the year Neville Chamberlain came back from Germany with his fluttering piece of paper, and from then on while talking peace we were preparing for war.

An event took place in 1938 which was of great importance to me. To the delight of all the family Mother remarried, and it is worth a short diversion to say something about this. Geoffrey Bassett was a widower who lived with his ten-year-old daughter Joan in Cranmer Road, Hampton Hill, hard by St James's church. Mother had gone to keep house for him and help out as best she could. They were married a few months later and it turned out to be a very good marriage. Our step-sister Joan and Mother gradually came to terms with one another and within a couple of years were so devoted that it was easy to imagine them really mother and daughter. This was a great joy to Phil and me, for not only was Mother made happier than she had been since Father died - or even much longer because she had had a difficult time during his frequent and long illnesses, but we had gained a stepfather who could not have been kinder to us if he had been our real father - and a step-sister who was thrilled to have two big brothers. Now I need have no hesitation in mentioning the fact that I might be going to work overseas within a few years of ordination.

Geoffrey Bassett was a remarkable man; quietly spoken and unassuming, he was in fact a brilliant and innovative horticulturalist. As a student he had been trained at Wisley, and during his time there had helped to lay out the now famous Royal Horticultural Gardens. By the time he married mother he was a director of a firm of seed merchants in Covent Garden with special responsibility not only for growing the highest grade flower seeds, but far more importantly producing new varieties of flowers. This he did by patient cultivation over many years.

My favourite story is the way he transformed the old Victorian flower *nicotiana,* or Tobacco Plant. Those of my generation will remember this sweet-smelling but unprepossessing plant with greenish-white flowers that opened only after dusk, but filled the garden with its delicious scent. Geoff, as a young man, had thought how nice it would be if he could persuade it to open in the daytime.

One day he was walking round Kew Gardens with the Curator, and spotted a small plant almost hidden under a bush. He asked the Curator if he could have it. The Curator laughed and said, "Yes of course, its only a weed!" But Geoff knew that, weed or not it was of the same genus as *nicotiana,* and the point was that *it was open in the daytime,* the first such plant that he had been able to find. He very carefully dug it out with his knife, wrapped it in his handkerchief, and as soon as he decently could, left the Curator and sped back to his seed-farm at Feltham where he began a process that was to take him more than twenty years. By careful and scientific husbandry and with his habitual monumental patience, by cross-breeding that little plant he was eventually able to say, "*Eureka!*" as he regarded a test-bed of *nicotiana* flowering in broad daylight. But alas and alack, they had lost their perfume! Quite undaunted Geoff then spent a few more years restoring the scent. Now at last he had *nicotiana* flowering in the sunshine and pervading the atmosphere with its sweetness. Did he then rush it onto the market in his next promotion and cause a sensation? Not a bit of it. Smoking his pipe he looked at the plants, fingering them gently as he so often did, and thought to himself, They would look so much prettier if they were coloured instead of this rather dull greenish-white. So more years were spent making them coloured. Eventually, after more than twenty five years of patient and unhurried work, they appeared in his next annual promotion of new varieties - and caused a small sensation. So wherever you see coloured *nicotiana* growing you are looking at some of the fruits of Geoffrey Bassett's life's work.

There are many many others. Among them the dwarf *antirrhinum*, colloquially called the Snapdragon. For some time he had thought that these delightful flowers were a bit straggly for use in formal gardens; so he spent several years producing a dwarf variety that grew in a tight little bunch, ideal for formally set-out public gardens. When Mother and he were away on holiday they always walked through the local public gardens, Geoff's eyes ranging over the beds of flowers, but he would make no observations until Mother asked, "Which of these are yours, Geoff?" And almost reluctantly he would point out those that he had produced, and often it seemed that most of the flowers in sight had been 'invented' by him.

During my second year, in 1939, my brother Phil and Dorothy Hone married in the June before war was declared in September. I was Phil's Best Man, and about the only things I remember of the wedding are how splendid Dorothy looked in the dress designed and made for her by her cousin, and the fact that during the reception I sneaked out and wired a kipper on to the exhaust of Phil's car! They went about fifteen miles before they noticed the terrible smell of cooking kipper and stopped to investigate.

As my second year progressed, students and staff were almost equally divided between those who were resigned to war as inevitable, and those who refused to believe that Hitler was not bluffing. Those who favoured appeasement and those who thought we must fight.

Also during that year I became College Sacristan in charge of both the upper and lower chapels, The lower chapel was at ground level and was large enough to accommodate both students and staff. This chapel was rather 'Victorian Hideous', but I came to love it. The walls were lined with oblong tablets of plain white marble on which were engraved the names of hundreds of old students who had died in the mission field overseas. A goodly number of names were painted in red, and these were the martyrs who had died for the Faith, often in the most grisly circumstances in those days when in many parts of the mission field cannibalism was still practiced. It is said that 'the Church is built on the blood of the martyrs' and I would often reflect upon this as I worked or worshipped in that chapel, for in all those places where our old students gave their lives for the faith, thriving Christian churches came into being which continue to thrive today. The names of past students, and especially of the martyrs, were regularly remembered at the altar. Here the Eucharist was celebrated on weekdays, attendance at which was voluntary. Matins, which was compulsory, was sung in the upper chapel, with inward facing stalls on either side.

There was a lot of work involved in looking after both chapels and although I had an assistant we both often had to work in the afternoons. One never-to-be-forgotten summer afternoon I was in the lower chapel cleaning Gog and Magog - two hideous Victorian five-foot brass standard candlesticks that were so full of twists and curlicues that they took for ever to clean. With a grubby apron over my cassock I was hard at work with Brasso and rags when the Porter came in and said, "There is a lady in the Lodge to see you, sir." A lady to see *me*? I thought; I don't know any ladies in this part of the world. However, quickly taking off my apron and wiping my hands, I went out into the gateway - and there, standing in the sunshine, was Bar, looking absolutely stunning. My vision of the Girl in the Middle all over again. This time instead of beating a hasty retreat I hurried towards her with a beaming smile saying how wonderful it was to see her. I nearly kissed her, but she suddenly seemed shy and embarrassed. She said in a small voice, "Hello" - and hurried on - "I've got someone outside I would like you to meet." A frisson of foreboding went through me and I felt ice forming in the pit of my stomach as we shook hands. Without another word she led me out of the wicket gate of the entrance to where a tall young Artillery Officer was standing beside a red MG sports car. I felt as though I had been hit over the heart, as I heard Bar say, "This is Peter, and we are going to be married." *O darling,,* I thought, *why couldn't you have written to warn me?*

I suppose I said the appropriate things like "Congratulations and I hope you will be very happy" etc. I remember little of the next few minutes while we talked together beside the little car, with half of me thinking and responding, and the other half of me, my 'better-half', dying. Thankfully they could not stop for tea as they were off to see Peter's father in Pegwell Bay. So after a few more stilted words they got into the little car and drove away, Bar turning round to give me a last long look and a wave. Not a white charger, with my Girl in the Middle swept up upon the knight's pommel - just a modern little red sports car. But precisely the same effect - off into the sunset, and, I really did hope, to 'live happy ever after'. I went back wearily to Gog and Magog, and that day they really did shine. At least I was good at cleaning brass.

So that, it seemed, was the end of my idyll. I could not blame her could I? After all, we were Just Good Friends, weren't we? Well, I suppose so. Yes, of course we were - *and yet....and yet ...*

It was on the first Sunday of the new academic year in September 1939 that with everyone else we knew the worst about the international situation. The Prime Minister was to speak to the nation on the radio and it was decided that staff and students would gather in the Junior Common Room to hear the fateful broadcast. The JCR was on the first floor of the main college building, and I shall never forget how we all sat or stood in tense silence as the PM told us that there had been no reply from Herr Hitler to the French and English ultimatum, and no withdrawal of German divisions from Poland, and that therefore we were now at war with Germany - and as the broadcast ended, the air-raid sirens began their banshee wail. We were all quite appalled to hear that awful sound for the first time 'for real.'

There had been much speculation about what aerial bombardment would be like if war came. The only experience anyone had had was during the Spanish Civil War a few years ago, and everyone knew that bigger and heavier bombs would be used by the Germans. Most of us imagined that whole cities could be wiped out in a single raid with nothing left standing and with few survivors. Thus thinking we stood in stunned silence for a second, then the Warden said in a shaking voice that we should all go to the air-raid shelter. The lower chapel had been sandbagged against blast for this purpose. So everyone began streaming out of the Common Room door - and the Warden turned to me and said, "O Singleton, I think if you would, you had better stay by the radio in case there are other important announcements." So I swallowed and said I would do that. "Come and tell us if there is anything we should know," he said.

I spent the first few minutes of World War Two all by myself in the JCR expecting to hear the drone of aircraft any minute and a million high explosive bombs raining down upon my defenceless head. Of course we had had gas masks issued to us, but we did not have to don these until we heard the Air Raid Wardens' rattles announcing a gas attack, and they were no protection against high explosives, so all I could do was stay away from the windows and hope for a near-miss at the worst! I remember being enormously depressed as well as thoroughly scared.

Mercifully I was soon reprieved for the All Clear sounded about ten minutes later. It transpired that this first false alarm of the war had sounded throughout the southern half of the country

Nothing much happened during the first year of the war; a few small incursions by enemy aircraft and a little bombing, but none of the massive raids we had been expecting on the day war was declared. Some people began saying that they thought Hitler had got cold feet and was not going to prosecute the war after all. This period became known as the Phoney War, and the nation had a respite in which it prepared for the shooting war when Hitler decided it should start. The entrances to public buildings were sandbagged, shelters were built in streets, and Anderson shelters in private gardens, to be followed later by the Morrison shelter - a large steel table for erection indoors and under which six or eight people could shelter. The 'Anderson' and 'Morrison' shelters were named after the Cabinet Ministers who authorised their production and distribution. Slit-trenches were dug in public gardens and parks, windows were crisscrossed with a new self-adhesive plastic tape against bomb blast, gas masks were distributed to the whole population. The dozen or so of us who had joined the Rover Crew offered ourselves as the firefighters of the college and became expert in the operation of the stirrup-pumps. These were pumps with a hose attached; the pump was placed in a bucket of water, and fixed to it was a metal 'stirrup' that came down the outside of the bucket and that was held firm by the operators foot - thus leaving both hands free for pumping the water. Usually two people manned a pump, but they could be used by one - pumping with one hand and directing the hose with the other. We played with these pumps with great hilarity during 'fire drill', squirting more water upon one another than on our imaginary fires.

When the first harvest of the war was ready to be gathered farmers suddenly found themselves very short of workers for so many had joined the armed forces. They therefore appealed for schools and colleges to allow students to help bring in the harvest . Most of us were keen to help especially when we heard that our parties, allocated to orchards and hop gardens, were to join forces with the girls from the fifth and sixth forms of Simon Langton's School, Canterbury. We had a riotous time picking the choice Victoria plums of which there was a glut that year - the serious work from time to time deteriorating into 'plum battles' as we and the girls pelted each other with ripe fruit. Several firm friendships were established in those orchards and later in the hop gardens, one of which eventually resulted in a splendid marriage. Both Walter and Freda Lovegrove, my good friends, went on in later years to do distinguished work in this country and in South Africa.

Soon after this I sat for the first part of the General Ordination Examination, known as GOE. My learning problems had returned - 'cramming' for an examination, as I had done at Tatterford, was no real training for the mind, and it was not possible to 'cram' theology in the same way. However, I staggered along and worked hard, and for a couple of weeks or so before the exam I worked far into the night, taking caffeine tablets to keep myself awake. I think I must have been physically and mentally exhausted and apparently it showed, for Ted Sulston, my tutor, told me I should stop revising and have a few days completely off work before the exams began.

This I did and although still feeling groggy I went into the examination room in slightly better shape. Once again I failed by one mark - and again in my best subject, this time Dogmatic Theology. I was devastated, and so apparently were others, for Dr Badcock the 'Dogs" tutor, told me he could not understand it - in his booming voice, and thumping his desk with his fist, he said, " X has passed, and you have more dogmatic theology in your little finger than he has in his thick head - they must have muddled the papers!" But of course they hadn't. I would be required to sit the whole thing again in six months time, and I was back in my old familiar square once more - Square One!

My tutor, the Reverend Arthur Edward Aubrey Sulston, known to us all as Ted, was a man in a million. When the shooting war began he joined the Army as a chaplain, and some time after the war he became Overseas Secretary of the Society for the Propagation of the Gospel, the SPG. He had a prodigious memory for names, and it was said that he knew the Christian name and surname of every priest throughout the Anglican Communion world-wide who was supported by the SPG.

Until he left the staff of St Augustine's to join the Army, Ted and I used to go for long walks through the lovely Kent countryside during that blazing summer as the Phoney War came to an abrupt end and the Germans began their blitzkrieg towards the Channel ports. I am sure I was a great puzzle to him. He once said, "George, what will you do if, as you seem to think, you don't pass the exam next time?" I ruefully said I did not know. All I knew was that I could not accept defeat until it was quite impossible to go on any more; I just *had* to go on trying to get ordained - I almost said, "By hook or by crook." I said, "Do you think it is possible that our Lord could let someone have this tremendous sense of vocation but never in the end be ordained - could it be a way of refining a soul through suffering, like gold is refined in the intense heat of the crucible?" I added, "I know God does not send suffering, but he allows it!" We kicked that idea around for quite a long time as we walked, and in the end we thought we could see that it *might* be possible. I think in a strange way I felt comforted by that; I learned that even failure can be to the glory of God and that this is probably one of the things covered by St Paul's saying that 'when I am weak, then am I strong', and, 'My strength is made perfect in weakness' I also learnt that *all* things 'work together for good' for those who try to love God.

It was Herr Hitler who solved my problems for me, believe it or not. The German armies swept relentlessly and swiftly across France, sweeping our forces westwards until they had their backs to the sea. We all turned out to hand cups of tea and cigarettes to exhausted troops as their trains stopped at Canterbury East station, after they had been 'miraculously' evacuated from Dunkirk by the navy and the 'little ships' that came from every river in England and braved shot and shell to bring the men home. Our 'scout' who called me every morning used to bring me the latest news as he shook me awake. One morning he said gloomily, "Belgium's give in, sir." Two mornings later, "Holland's give in,sir." "They're in Paris, sir." and then, "France has give in, sir." And before we knew where we were the German army had taken the Channel Ports - and Dover was being shelled by long range guns from the French coast! We suddenly realised with a sinking feeling in the pit of the stomach, that the Germans were only about forty miles from us! Things really did begin to happen then. It was decreed that all non-essential personnel should leave Canterbury and move up country. The Germans were expected to invade our shores as soon as they had mustered their forces, and judging by the speed with which they had overwhelmed the continent that would not be long. A few days later the Warden announced that the college would be closed, and that arrangements had been made for our students to be dispersed to other theological colleges. We were told that we should be ready to leave within the week for the college to which we had been assigned.

We had a meeting of the Rover crew and decided unanimously that we did not want to go up-country, we wanted to stay where we were! I think we were being more lazy than brave, and we did not want to be separated from our friends - the Rover crew was a very homogeneous group in the college. So a deputation went to the Warden and suggested that the Rover crew stay behind to keep the college open and do what we could to protect it from fire. We suggested that we offer ourselves to the National Fire Service, which had already given us some training, and was, we knew, desperately in need of more men. The Warden thought this was a brilliant idea, and we were given a great welcome by the Canterbury National Fire Service (NFS).

We had a wonderful time. The Matron, who was a good sport, said she would stay too - she was sweet on the Sub-Warden who would be staying anyway, and they were happily married a couple of years later.

The NFS gave us our own trailer-pump permanently attached to the car that towed it, and parked in the 12th Century gateway of the college ready to go at a moment's notice. A rota was drawn up and there were always five men on duty by the trailer-pump, and one manning the telephone. The Porter and his wife had elected to be evacuated. There were large basements in the college, with no windows, and these made an excellent bunker-cum-dormitory. We collected all the mattresses from the rooms of the students who had gone and shared them among ourselves, so each of us slept upon a pile of six or seven mattresses. When not on duty at night we would hear the occasional bomb whistling down to crump near or far, it made no odds to us. We felt quite secure in our basement, though of course a direct hit would have been another matter.

I have two vivid recollections of those fateful days. The first is of arriving back at the beginning of the summer term, having come by train from Hampton via London. The sirens went as I arrived at the college gate; soon we heard the drone of bombers' engines, and far up in the bright blue sky we could see little shining objects, like small silver fish, streaking in straight lines towards London. This was the first of the daylight raids on London by which Goering was confident he could knock us out of the war. My heart turned over as I imagined what was about to happen in and around London and wondered whether I had seen my home and my family for the last time. What excitement when quite a short time later

59

these same bombers were fleeing back all over the sky in a mad effort to avoid the Spitfires and Hurricanes that were literally knocking them out of the sky! I saw three planes spiralling to the ground with dense black smoke pouring from them. From one of them two tiny figures leapt and soon two parachutes opened like white mushrooms bringing the airmen down to earth and, we heard later, to a prisoner of war camp. Later, when the surviving German bombers had disappeared back across the Channel, a Spitfire came roaring over the college and we watched him do a victory roll over the Cathedral.

My other vivid memory is of being on fire-watching duty one summer night on the top of one of the twin towers of our lovely gateway. The moon was shining brightly and all was still and peaceful; not a sound was to be heard, until there came the distant notes of a piano as Matron sat in her room at the foot of the tower, with the windows, open and played - Beethoven's Moonlight Sonata! That peaceful night returns to me every time I hear that music played. A more perfect setting could not be imagined.

I did not see much action myself. We were dive-bombed one afternoon while I was manning the telephone. Bombs seemed to be raining down upon us with mad shrieks and in great numbers; the dog was rushing around me barking its head off as I knelt for protection while trying to answer the telephone fixed to the wall above my head. One bomb, the noisiest and nearest, made a crater in the middle of the quad about a hundred yards away; another knocked a bit off the corner of the library; some fell in the orchard and destroyed a few very unproductive apple trees. And then they were gone. In spite of the noise not many bombs had fallen after all.

Our most weird experience occurred one dark night when the sirens sounded just after midnight and soon we could hear the throbbing drone of the bombers getting relentlessly nearer. Before long the whole of Canterbury was brightly lit by candelabra flares drifting slowly from a great height. They were so bright you could not look directly at them, and they turned the darkness into day. The phone rang and we were ordered to man our trailer pump and go out on patrol through the city. So off we went, and I for one was scared stiff. All the signs suggested that a major 'saturation' air-raid was about to build up, for as I say, the whole city was brightly illuminated. The anti-aircraft batteries had opened up and the flares looked ethereally beautiful as they drifted lazily down to the accompaniment of the cacophony from the guns.

I wish I could now go on to describe the acts of valour done by these five budding clergymen as they valiantly fought fires and brought women and children from blazing buildings as the bombs fell all around them. But no. Nothing happened at all! The guns gradually fell silent, the bombers' drone diminished in the distance, the flares petered out, the blackout descended once more and not a chink of light was to be seen - and then the All Clear sounded. Perfect anticlimax. The raid that never was. Less than an hour after we had started the old car and set off with our pump, we were back in college drinking tea.

Spitfires and Hurricanes were a common sight over Canterbury that summer. These wonderful fighters and their brave young pilots were scrambled as soon as Nazi bombers were reported heading across the channel, and we saw many a dog-fight being waged over Canterbury, the cannon and machine guns in the wings of the planes rattling and blazing, many from both sides spiralling to the ground trailing dense black smoke, or bursting into flames when the opposing fire found the petrol tank or the ammunition. As they twisted and turned, dived and climbed, the blue skies would become a tangled web of white vapour trails. Spent cartridge cases often fell tinkling around us in the streets.

Most of the families in the Cathedral Close had gone up-country, but the Archdeacons and Canons stayed behind to continue with their work. Two of them came to live in College with us, the Archdeacon of Canterbury, Canon Bickersteth, and Canon Bradfield. The latter was to gain prominence and a place in history when, as Bishop of Bath and Wells, with Michael Ramsey then Bishop of Durham, he assisted Archbishop Geoffrey Fisher at the Coronation of Queen Elizabeth II. Canon Bradfield was very kind to me. By the time that my resit of the General Ordination Examination (GOE) Part 1, and soon the examination of Part 2, were looming up, the college authorities decided that none of us could be expected to sit examinations in these conditions, and proposed asking the Bishops to ordain us on a set of essays instead.

I was talking about this to Canon Bradfield one day and told him I had vaguely thought of applying to the Bishop of Guildford because I fancied serving my title at a 'good Catholic' parish in the diocese but had heard that there were no vacancies for curates. I was in a quandary and did not know to whom I might apply. Canon Bradfield said he knew Dr Partridge, the Bishop of Portsmouth, quite well and he would mention me to him. They met regularly at Church House near Westminster Abbey, the administrative centre of the Church of England. Some time later he said that while not very keen on the idea the Bishop of Portsmouth had agreed to consider ordaining me on a set of essays - if I had a parish that would take me. But first I must write the essays.

So I went to stay in Oxford with the Society of St John the

Evangelist, the Cowley Fathers, in Marston Street, and spent three weeks or so in their Guest House writing my essays. The Bishop later told the Principal that he had heard from the Vicar of St Mark's Portsea who was looking for a deacon as one of his staff would be leaving the parish before very long, and suggested that I apply for the appointment.

This was arranged and in due course, with flights of butterflies in my tummy, off I went to Portsmouth, the great naval port and dockyard in the South of England colloquially known as 'Pompey', to find scenes of devastation that so far I had only imagined. The train ran through areas where nothing but ruined buildings could be seen, and the streets were piled with rubble. Of course Portsmouth was more in the front line than Canterbury, and being a naval port had been heavily bombed as the Germans tried to knock out the port and dockyard.

I found St Mark's to be a huge Victorian Gothic church of what, to me, was the worst sort. It was indescribably ugly. Brass and black-painted wrought iron were everywhere; the sanctuary was cramped, the stained glass windows were execrable - it is hardly an exaggeration to say that with me it was a case of hate at first sight! Across the road in the Vicarage it was a very different matter. Here was a well-built double-fronted and comfortable Victorian house, with a semi-basement, and a nice flight of stone steps leading up to the front door. Better still, the Vicar, Norman Millard and two members of his staff, who made me very welcome. They were in the middle of a game of snooker when I arrived that Saturday afternoon, and I was soon plying a cue enthusiastically if not very productively. There was a lot of laughter and they all seemed on very good terms with one another. We all sipped Scotch before the fire in the study that evening while I was put in the picture about the parish. There were two daughter churches each with its full time priest who lived in the area, one having a Deaconess as well - I would be taken to see them and meet the staff tomorrow afternoon. Here at the parish church were the Vicar and two curates, which made a total staff of six.

There had been a heavy air-raid a few nights previously, and I had arrived in what turned out to be a fairly lengthy lull. I was glad of that and it was a great luxury to sleep in a comfortable bed in a civilised bedroom for a change.

On Sunday the ugly church came alive, and I was astonished to see the numbers that came to the various services. There were, I think, two early Eucharists, and the main service at 11.00 was Matins sung with a full choir of men and boys. The church seemed comfortably full with the exception of the side aisles, and I suppose there were between three and four hundred people there, of all ages representing a good cross-section of the population. Many were in uniform, for in the parish we had part of the naval dockyard, some other naval establishments, and the barracks of the Royal Marines.

There was a similar congregation at Evensong and afterwards one of the curates, Dick Herrick, took me to a meeting of the Anglican Young People's Association (AYPA) in the Church Hall. I liked this very lively group of youngsters in the 17 to 20 age group. A large proportion of the young men worked in the Dockyard, and were therefore in a reserved occupation, and most of the girls worked in the offices there and in the city.

I had always hoped that I would begin my ministry in an out-and-out 'catholic' parish where the worship was uncompromisingly centred on the Eucharist and the full sacramental life was practiced. I had indeed already bought my trousseau - a full soutane cassock, buckled shoes and a biretta and cloak!

Before I left on the Monday morning the Vicar said that they would be glad to have me on the staff and offered me the job. I had already expected this to happen as I had the strong impression that I was not going to be turned away. One of the chief factors in my not hesitating to accept the job, apart from beggars not being able to be choosers, was the fact that Dick Herrick, the priest who would be senior to me, had been trained at Mirfield, and whatever disappointment I had about the ambience of the parish, what was good enough for Mirfield was good enough for me! So I accepted with alacrity and great gratitude.

Good heavens above! Here was a thing! It suddenly hit me - *ordination!!* I, little old Ernie Singleton who, it now seemed years ago, had told Jock Murray of his impossible dream had actually been offered a place on the staff of a large parish! Ordination really did seem to be within my grasp; if, just if, the Bishop was satisfied with the essays I had produced - or rather if his Examining Chaplains advised him that they were good enough. Back then to Canterbury, by slow war-time train making frequent detours to avoid bomb-damaged areas, none of which I noticed. I think I spent the whole journey looking into the middle distance in the sort of haze where everything seems unreal.

One last hump: *O please Lord, let the Examining Chaplains read my essays when they are feeling charitable.* And the Bishop, O the Bishop. He'd already let me know in no uncertain terms that I did not really come up to his usual standards. He was a pretty crusty prelate, as everyone knew. So the only thing to do was to sigh and say, *O Lord, the Bishop - only you can deal with the Bishop, so please* ....

I wonder how Bar is? O, I do hope she will be happy with Peter.

Pensive student, Canterbury 1940 *"Shall I ever be ordained?"*

3

Ordination in War-torn Pompey

The Bishop of Portsmouth accepted my essays and so at last ordination was in sight. I drew a big breath, said, *"Thank you Lord"* and determined to enjoy myself until the day came for me to set off for the Ordination Retreat, when all those to be ordained in the Portsmouth diocese would go and stay for three nights at or near the Bishop's house for a time of quiet and prayer before the ordination. There would be a retreat conductor, usually a senior priest of the diocese, who would give us two addresses a day to guide our thoughts and prayers, and would be available for consultation and for hearing confessions if required. The retreat would be in a couple of month's time, so I looked forward to a period without stress of any sort before I set out on my life's vocation. There were no complications; Mother and Phil were both happily married, so all was well on the home front; no ghastly examinations hanging over my head - such a relief. What bliss!

The same could not be said about the war though; that seemed to be going from bad to worse as the Nazis continued sinking vast numbers of our merchant ships and many of our naval vessels too, as well as driving us relentlessly back in North Africa. But, with the rest of the population, we had learned to some extent to take the war in our stride and while not ceasing to care I did in fact enjoy myself in a non-dramatic and pleasantly quiet sort of way during that eight-week period from April to June in 1941.

Soon after the 'shooting war' started in 1940 our old Warden at Canterbury retired and Bishop Roberts, then Bishop of Singapore, was appointed to succeed him. He and his family had left Singapore just as the Japanese were invading the peninsular and been lucky to get away. Basil Roberts and his wife Dorothy both became instantly popular with staff and students alike. Where the previous Warden and his wife, though held in considerable affection, tended to be rather formal in their relations with us, their successors were younger and much more relaxed in their approach. Of course as a result of the war formality was going by the board almost everywhere, but even so these two seemed wonderful to us. Batches of us would be invited to tea or dinner quite often, but we were told that we were also welcome to knock on the door at any time to see if either of them was free for a chat.

Dorothy Roberts, being a doctor, co-operated with Matron in looking after our health. So the Rover crew was thoroughly spoilt and we hugely enjoyed the experience. Dorothy organised poetry and play-reading evenings for us and all sorts of other semi-cultural occasions. I had also acquired a girl friend whom I had met at Canterbury East Station while we were both waiting for trainloads of children being evacuated from London to remote villages in Kent - a mystery why this should have been thought appropriate when Canterbury had been evacuated of all non-essential personnel and everyone was expecting Hitler to invade our shores at any time. My girl friend and I did not meet many trains, and I only made one trip with a Kent and County bus, taking children out into the country, on which I played the role of conductor. My heart ached for the poor little kids, each with their label and gas mask, and their pathetic little cases of basic belongings, holding hands grimly, away from home and family and everything familiar.

It was good to have some feminine company, but I did not see Ann as a substitute for Bar. We were very good friends and she did a lot for me. Ann and her widowed mother lived just outside Canterbury and Ann would often pick me up in her car and take me home for tea or dinner or a day off in congenial company. They contributed a lot to my enjoyment of my last two months at St Augustine's.

We did not have much ceremonial at the college, and I thought how splendid it would be, now that we had a Bishop as Warden, if I could persuade him to preside at Evensong in his cope and mitre - that would please us 'catholic minded' students no end. He himself was a low churchman, but when I put the idea to him he agreed at once but said, "Well George, I've never done this before, so you will have to tell me what to do." I explained the service to him and told him exactly what a bishop does, and when. I said, "There is no need to worry, I shall be your Master of Ceremonies and at your side all the time, so I can easily signal what you have to do next."

The Bishops are the successors of the Apostles and have a position of great authority in the Church. In the book of the Acts of the Apostles we read that on the first Pentecost (Whit Sunday) the Apostles were gathered together in the Upper Room when the Holy Spirit came upon them with the sound of a rushing mighty wind, and it was as though cloven tongues of fire settled upon the heads of the apostles, and they began to speak of the wonderful works of God. The special hat that a bishop wears on solemn occasions is called a 'mitre', and is shaped like, and represents, those 'cloven tongues.' Two thick ribbons hang down the back of the mitre. With the mitre the bishop wears a cope, a richly coloured cloak, and in his hand he holds his pastoral staff, usually in the form of a shepherd's crook. The crook emphasizes that the bishop's authority is that of the Good Shepherd, who lays down his life for the sheep.

At such services the Bishop wears the mitre as he walks in procession to the sanctuary, and from then on it is placed upon the altar and only worn again when he acts in his official capacity - when he pronounces the Absolution, or gives the blessing. It is the MC's job to put the mitre on his head when required.

Bishop Roberts did everything beautifully during our Solemn Evensong, with great dignity and devotion, and all went perfectly smoothly. I was feeling very pleased and relieved as we came to the end of the service and the moment for the final blessing. The bishop was seated in his chair in the sanctuary. As he was about to stand to give the blessing I took up the mitre and placed it reverently upon his head *but horror of horrors,* I had picked it up the wrong way round so that the ribbons, instead of falling neatly down the back of his head, fell down over his eyes. I have never seen a more ludicrous sight in my life. There was this tall bishop - he was about 6'4" - standing in his gorgeous cope, with his silver pastoral staff that I had put in his hand - blinded by the ribbons of his mitre! There was a stunned silence from the assembled students and staff; I was appalled and expected an outburst of laughter, but luckily everyone managed to control his amusement as I quickly whipped off the mitre and replaced it the right way round. The Bishop, who had remained perfectly calm throughout, solemnly gave the blessing, and I led him decorously out of the chapel to the vestry. But not out of earshot. Guffaws of laughter erupted as soon as we got to the vestry - and the Bishop and I joined in!

Of course, I apologised profusely, but he said something to the effect that it did not matter and anyway we must not be so solemn that we cannot enjoy the funny side when things go a little awry. A grand man that.

So in early June 1941 I left my gas mask and tin hat at Canterbury, said goodbye to my friends and went off to Portsmouth for ordination. At that time Portsmouth was under the constant threat of air-raids both day and night and the Cathedral was in one of the most dangerous zones. It was therefore not used when any large number of people would be attending a service, so the ordination was to be at the parish church of Holy Trinity, Fareham, a few miles further inland. I was put up for the nights of the ordination retreat by Father Basil Daniell, Vicar of SS Peter and Paul's, Fareham. When I rang the bell the Vicarage door was opened by a tall priest in his cassock - and he was knitting a pair of black silk socks! I thought to myself, Whatever have we here? He greeted me in a drawling voice and showed me to my room still carrying his knitting. When he noticed me glancing at this he said, "O yes, sorry to greet you with my knitting, but I have arthritis in my hands and this is the best way to prevent them from seizing up altogether." It was only then that I saw that his poor hands were swollen and misshapen and looking terribly painful. I apologised profusely for staring. Once I got used to the drawling voice I soon came to recognise a very wise and holy priest - indeed a few weeks later he agreed to be my spiritual director.

Each morning I would go early to the Bishop's chapel to spend the day in the ordination retreat. As this progressed and the fateful day came ever nearer, I became more and more uneasy about this momentous step I was taking, and a sense of profound unworthiness grew upon me. Of course one can never be worthy, and I had always been fully aware of that. But this sense of unfitness seemed to be of a different order. I now felt that to go ahead to ordination would be quite wrong. My sense of vocation had been false - probably no more than overweening pride. By the end of the retreat I felt sure I ought to withdraw.

On the afternoon before the ordination there was a rehearsal of the service in the church with the Bishop and the Archdeacon. Four deacons were to be ordained priest, and I was the only layman to be made deacon, so according to tradition I was to read the Gospel. I went through the rehearsal mechanically. I was given the Gospel book and practiced reading the Gospel set for the Ordination of Priests, as is customary. We went through the rest of the service and all was straightforward. The Bishop went off to his car immediately after the rehearsal and as soon as he had gone the Archdeacon gathered us together and said, "Look, chaps, on these occasions the Bishop is liable to change things at the last minute, so tomorrow if you find anything different from what we have done in the rehearsal, don't let it bother you, just carry on regardless." So, duly warned, off we all went back to where we were staying.

I had said nothing about my unease to anyone during the retreat or at the church, but as soon as I got back to the Vicarage and we had had supper I asked my host if he would kindly ring the Archdeacon and tell him I had decided I must withdraw from ordination. Quite calmly he drawled, "Come into the *studdaaay*." So in we went and he asked me to tell him all about it, which I proceeded to do at some length. Needless to say, he persuaded me that I had simply got cold feet, that it was quite natural that all these doubts should assail me at the last minute, and that I must stop worrying because he was convinced that I really did have a vocation. I went to bed full of gratitude and feeling happier than I had for days.

A lovely June morning greeted Trinity Sunday as I dressed myself for the first time for real in my dog collar and beautiful soutane cassock. Taking my surplice and the special stole my beloved Aunt had made me, I sallied forth on the short walk for Holy Trinity church. I arrived just as Mother, Geoff, Aunt and Phil, and my step-sister Joan were arriving, and had a few words with them before they went to their places in the church. The service began with a procession, with the Bishop resplendent in cope and mitre and walking with his pastoral staff, blessing those who genuflected as he passed by. In due course I knelt before him and he laid his hands upon my head, and a whole circle of other clergy placed their hands upon his as he made me Deacon with the words *"Take thou authority to execute the office of a Deacon in the Church of God committed unto thee; in the name of the Father, and of the Son, and of the Holy Ghost. Amen."* While I still knelt the Archdeacon placed the stole over my left shoulder and looped it together under my right arm in the manner in which a deacon wears the stole. I then rose to my feet and was presented with a leatherbound copy of the New Testament in Greek. The Gospel book was then delivered to me. I opened it where the ribbon marker was - and it opened not at the Gospel I had rehearsed yesterday, but at the Gospel for Trinity Sunday! The Gospel for Trinity Sunday in the Book of Common Prayer is a very long one indeed. I hesitated for a moment, then remembering what the Archdeacon had said at the end of the rehearsal, concluded that the Bishop had changed his mind and wanted this Gospel read instead of that for the Ordering of Priests. So I announced it and proceeded to read it.

As soon as I started I realised I had made a terrible mistake. Out of the corner of my eye I saw the Archdeacon make a move towards me - and the Bishop imperiously wave him back. So on and on I went step by wretched step through that long and it seemed interminable gospel. At last I was finished - and as soon as I closed the book, the Bishop swept down from the altar, took the book roughly from me, opened it where the *other end* of the ribbon marker was, and said, "The *Gospel* is written in ...." and proceeded to read the correct one, the one I had rehearsed the day before. I felt terrible. I wanted the earth to open and swallow me up; I felt that the Holy Spirit had not 'taken' in my ordination a few minutes before! My poor mother was beside herself with distress; she knew something awful had happened and that I was at the centre of it, but she had not quite realised what it was. I was in a complete daze for the rest of the service, thinking I *knew* I should have withdrawn. Afterwards the Archdeacon was very nice and so kind;

without actually saying so he let me know that he was furiously angry with the Bishop and looked as though he could gladly have strangled him! The others who had been made priest gathered round me for a moment, expressing sympathy before going off to relations and friends who were waiting for them. Their sympathy restored me somewhat, and though still smarting I was able to go off and comfort my mother and family, and we ended up before long being able to laugh it off. But I have been making mistakes in services ever since!

I cannot say that I enjoyed my deacon's year very much, but then who does? One is neither fish, fowl nor good red herring. There are so many things one cannot do; specially you cannot celebrate the Holy Eucharist, nor can you give the blessing; you are allowed to baptise, but you cannot conduct weddings, and you can take communion to the sick only when the elements have been consecrated at a previous Eucharist. And you can preach and you can conduct funerals.

During the first week after my ordination the Vicar gave me a street map of the parish and suggested that I ride around on my bike to get my bearings, and the feel of the parish. He gave me a list of church people whom I could visit and be sure of a warm welcome. So, on a lovely sunny afternoon in June, I tucked my cassock up around my waist, put on my black hat and set off. I went into what was to be my main visiting area, where the streets were lined with long terraces of identical little houses, every one with the front step washed and whitened daily, the windows of the front parlour sparkling clean, with Persil white net curtains and an aspidestra on a bamboo stand visible through them, *de rigueur* for a respectable front parlour window in those days. These were the homes of Able Seamen and their families and other naval personnel of similar rank.

Having paid a call on a 'friendly' house I leapt on my bike and was weaving about the road, there being no other traffic, and as I approached the right angle turn at the bottom of the street I noticed a large gateway with six blue-jackets armed with rifles and fixed bayonets standing on guard. Looking at them curiously as I approached I heard commands being given and saw the sailors spring into action and, with a lot of slapping of rifle butts and stamping of shining boots, come to attention and the salute. I wobbled to the side of the road on my bike and looked behind me thinking some top brass or other important personage must be approaching and I had better get out of the way. But the street was deserted. I did another wobble - but straightened up as I suddenly realised that they were saluting *me,* me, the newest curate, looking a mess with his cassock up round his waist! I just had the presence of mind to ride the intervening distance in a straight line, and decorously raised my hat as I passed. As I turned to the right and left them behind me I heard the CPO in charge of the squad order the Slope Arms, and then the Stand at Ease. Out of sight, I nearly fell off my bike laughing. I soon learned in Pompey that the Navy and the Marines had a great respect for the clergy, and always saluted a dog-collar.

I was in the same area a few days later, and there was no laughter this time. HMS Hood, the great battleship had been lost with all hands, and many of the devastated families lived in my area. So I was thrown into bereavement visiting at the deep end, and it was an experience I would not want any newly ordained young deacon to have to face.. I went home for days on end with a breaking heart and full of admiration for the sheer guts and fortitude and *acceptance,* of mothers and wives and sweethearts.

It was not easy to find lodgings in Portsmouth at that time and having stayed at the Vicarage for a few weeks I was offered a room by the unmarried vicar of one of the neighbouring parishes. This was not an unmitigated success; I did not find the company very congenial, and not all the training at Tatterford had prepared me for the cold. Stringent economy was the order of the day, and we barely had any heating. It was back to icy conditions in the bedroom and little better in my study, but hard by the sea and the mudflats of Portsmouth the cold seemed to be of a different order altogether from what it had been in bracing Norfolk far from the coast.

I endured for several months, and then my vicar told me that a Mrs Stevens, the widow of a local pork butcher and a member of the congregation, was willing to take me in as a paying guest. My goodness, what a transformation! The house was less than five minutes walk from the church, and from bare necessities I came to the lap of luxury; a splendid study with plump red velvet settee and armchairs, a dining table and room for my bookcases and desk. A wonderful coal fire was always burning in my grate, and I had a telephone in my room, upstairs a warm bedroom and comfortable bed. I was in clover for the next three years.

Mrs Stevens was a delightful person, the soul of kindness. We had our meals together and sometimes if I was in we would have a hot drink and a chat at the end of the day. There was also a guestroom and I was able to have family and friends to stay. Mrs Stevens still had a controlling interest in her late husband's business, so I was hardly aware that rationing existed and fed extremely well. I occasionally felt rather guilty about my standard of living, but not very often, and it did not spoil my appetite

I was put in charge of the Sunday School at the parish church and reorganised it on the lines learnt from Jock Murray, insisting on the teachers coming to a preparation class in my study - remembering him I grinned to myself as I heard myself say for the first time, "Right - Preparation Class, my study Thursday 7.30 OK?" Then I remembered that the first time I had heard those words had been the occasion when I had met the Girl in the Middle at last. *O dear. O Bar, I wonder how you are?*

The Sunday School had been run, very devotedly, by a lady who at that time seemed to me to be rather old and I considered her methods and ideas very out of date. Inevitably there would have to be a show-down if we were to get anywhere, and so arrived my first experience of conflict within the parish. In the end I had to say that I must insist on the methods I felt were right, and the lady resigned. Probably I was brash and opinionated, but I must say that after a few months of being very upset she forgave me, which I thought was very Christian of her considering that it would hardly be an exaggeration to say that the Sunday School had been her life for many years.

I baptised a large number of babies during my diaconate - and producing babies was a growth industry in Pompey during the war. Every Sunday afternoon at 3 o'clock we would have anything from six to a dozen babies and their parents and godparents and friends gathered in a crowd around the font. When they all cried at once the racket was deafening, but usually it was only two or three at a time, and the mothers would be sent with these for a walk around the church while the godparents and I got on with the important business of the baptismal rite. Often the actual baptism was a strenuous contest between officiant and baby.

One day I went into the chemist's shop opposite the church, and the other customers were five women. One of them dropped something on the floor and looked around for help, because she was heavily pregnant and could not stoop. No one moved, but the other four ladies looked at me - I suddenly realized that I was the only person there who could pick up the package, for they were all greatly pregnant! Gallant as always I swept off my big black hat and obliged with a bow.

I went into the city one evening and while I was on the trolley-bus the sirens wailed the Alert. I was on the step of the bus as it drew in to my stop in the city centre. At the head of the queue waiting to board the trolley-bus was a little man in in a long black coat wearing a bowler hat. He had a drooping moustache and looked very glum. In one hand he held a shovel, and in the other, believe it or not, he held *a Welsh harp*. Quick as a flash, our Conductor shouted to him, "O hello, mate. I see you're making sure whichever way you goes then?" In spite of the sound of enemy aircraft approaching and people beginning to run for the shelters, all on the trolley-bus and in the queue irrupted in delighted laughter.

Amid the rubble and the often smoking ruins of war-torn Pompey, both sorrow and laughter seemed highlighted. There was always genuine sympathy for those who had lost dear ones - it can hardly be an exaggeration to say that half the families living in the area had been bereaved, so there was a lot of fellow-feeling. Yet, as in other badly hit areas of Britain where there had been terrible loss of life and much bitter bereavement, genuine laughter was never far away. Not hysterical laughter, though naturally at times there was that too, but more often than not, the laughter that comes from the ability to see the funny side of even grim situations. There was also that astonishingly phlegmatic ability 'to take it' always displayed by the British people under siege. Hundreds of people got quite used to crowding into the shelters night after night as a matter of course and took it all in their stride. I like the story of the little Lancashire lad coming out after a night in the shelter, rubbing his bottom and saying to his mother, "Eee ba'goom, Moom, me boom's noom."

I spent a lot of time conducting funerals, of which there were a great number of very harrowing ones in Portsmouth at that time. Most were burials in one or other of the vast Portsmouth cemeteries, with only a very few cremations for cremation was not very often used in those days, many people being emotionally against it - in any case it was forbidden by the Roman Catholic Church.

At one of my earliest funerals the young widow sobbed and screamed and tried to throw herself into the grave. I did what I could but I felt totally unequipped to deal with such a situation. However, I did visit her several times after that trying to bring her some comfort.

I was appalled by the generally casual behaviour of the undertakers' men, who were quite lacking in the qualities on which my father used to insist. One day it was raining hard and I was conducting a funeral in the Cemetery chapel. During the service the bearers came into the small porch to shelter from the rain, and I could hear them laughing and joking while I tried to speak words of comfort and reassurance to the mourners. As we followed the coffin from the chapel we had to walk through a cloud of tobacco smoke that filled the porch. I walked ahead of the coffin with the undertaker down the paths of the cemetery to the grave. It was quite a long way, and it gave me the opportunity to tear strips off him for his men's behaviour. He started making excuses in a patronising sort of way, thinking he had got just a young rookie parson here who was still wet behind the ears. So I may have been in many respects, but one thing I did know about was funerals and how they should be conducted. So I said to him quietly but heatedly, "You can't teach me anything about funerals and how they should be conducted: I know all about it because *I have been an undertaker*, and if any of my men had behaved as yours did today I would have sacked them on the spot!" He was completely flabbergasted and our arrival at the grave saved him from having to respond. But afterwards he had the grace to apologise and said it would not happen again, nor did it, at anyrate at any funeral I was conducting. A month or so later they wrote to me and asked if I would be willing to act as chaplain to the Undertakers' Association! My vicar wrote to them and explained that as I was still only a deacon and was fully committed to work in the parish he could not agree to my accepting this kind invitation.

Preaching I found enormously daunting. During my deacon's year I had to write a number of sermons and send them for criticism to my post-ordination tutor, who was the well known theologian Canon Charles Raven, Regius Professor of Divinity at Cambridge. He gave me quite good marks, in fact he praised one of my efforts quite highly, but I do not think I ever preached one of these and I think they must have been more essays than addresses. However, I was put down to preach at Matins at St Mark's and the very thought terrified the daylights out of me. There was always a large congregation at that service. In the front row right under the pulpit sat Doctor Dewey, our local GP. He was an ex-Churchwarden, and he knew some theology. I found him quite intimidating, for as the hymn before the sermon finished, he would sit down, hitch his trousers, cross his legs, settle comfortably into the corner of his pew, screw his monocle into his eye, fold his arms - and positively glare at the preacher, with a frown on his face. To me he always looked like the judge regarding with disfavour the prisoner in the dock whom he has already decided is guilty without benefit of jury. I later discovered that he was a very nice and kind man. I wrote a sermon, of sorts, got into the pulpit - and simply read it to the congregation. It was as flat as a pancake.

The next time, about a month later I was down to preach, I decided on the Monday morning what I wanted to preach about, chose my text, wound paper into my typewriter, typed the text in red, then waited for the words to come. I sat for an hour, but nothing came. I tried again later in the day - nothing. The next day it was the same story - nothing. I tried every day that week and still nothing would come from my mind on to the paper.

On Saturday evening I panicked. I rang my friend and mentor, Dick Herrick and said, "Dick I simply cannot produce a sermon for tomorrow - I'm desperate." "I'm coming straight round." he said, and was with me within a few minutes. "What do you want to preach about?" he asked. I told him, and read my text to him. He thought for a few moments, then said. "OK, this is an emergency, so I am going to dictate a sermon to you; type it as I speak." So he did just that; right off the cuff, a perfectly adequate address. I took this to the pulpit the next morning - and read it off. Dead as a doornail; and as I came down the pulpit steps afterwards I felt as though I had sinned against the Holy Spirit!

Dick was wonderful to me; we had several sessions that following week, and the next time I was to preach I did manage to write an address, and he advised me to make notes of it and only take those to the pulpit. Come Sunday I went to church with just my notes - and fell flat on my face again, for faced with only my bare notes in the pulpit my brain siezed up and I could hardly do more than simply read the notes. Awful? It was another disaster.

Monday morning, staff meeting. No one mentioned the sermon. As we dispersed afterwards, Dick said, "Come home and have a cup of coffee." Sitting in armchairs on either side of his fireplace, coffee mugs steaming, Dick gave me one his rather unnerving quiet stares as he sipped, a small smile at the corners of his mouth. "What are we going to do about you?" A small voice from me, "I don't know." We both fell silent again; Dick thinking; me numb.

Dick put his mug down, and as he stretched his hands above his head he gave himself a little shake and said, "As a matter of fact I think I *do* know!" He continued, "We both know - don't we? - that preaching is not just a matter of thinking our own thoughts about a subject and telling the congregation what we think; it is partly that, but it is not *primarily* that." *Primarily*, it is so placing ourselves at the disposal of God that He is able to speak through us. The primary question we put to ourselves is not, What shall I preach about on Sunday? It is, What is it that God is seeking to say to these people through me on Sunday? We are fallible human beings and so will often get it wrong; we are sinful men and so the Word we preach will be diminished in its power by that. But if we believe in the grace of our ordination we must believe that in spite of our fallibility and our sinfulness, God can and will speak to his people through our lips - Right?"

"Yes, I said, that is what I have always believed."

"OK then," he continued, "*I* think that you are probably one of those people who are called simply to pray first, and last, that God will show you what He wants to say to the people through you, trusting that as you try to open yourself to him, *you will in fact know what you are to preach about.* Then I think you must *think* about that and work it out as well as you can in your mind, trusting in the guidance of the Holy Spirit. When you have thought it through for quite a while - even several days, and done any reading indicated - *then* you *pray* it through for the rest of the time before you go to the pulpit - and then you go to the pulpit with not a word written, and *preach.*"

"Good heavens," I said, "I couldn't do that, I would be scared stiff!"

Dick gave me a rather wolfish grin, then, "Yes, I expect your knees will feel like jelly as you go up the pulpit steps, but once you start speaking, I think you will be all right."

"However, don't forget that a Christian sermon is not just a one-way affair, not just the preacher talking and the congregation listening. Preaching is a sacrament; an outward and physical form of an inward and spiritual grace - there must be *giving* by the preacher and *receiving* by the congregation, both inspired by the same Holy Spirit - the Spirit desires to speak through you, to the same Spirit living and active in them. So as you 'pray your sermon' remember the congregation and *pray that they may draw from you* what each needs of the Spirit, speaking through your lips."

Every word Dick said rang true with me, and I went home feeling that he had really sorted me out.

(Dick Herrick died some years ago and I had not been in touch with him for many years. I hope that in the loving dispositions of God, he may know that I have never ceased to be grateful to him for what he did for me that morning, and many other mornings, for he did more to train me towards professionalism in my priesthood than any other person. It would be no exaggeration to say that anything that has been good and fruitful in my ministry was either directly inspired by him, or built upon the foundations he laid for me.)

The next time I was due to preach I did precisely what he had advised. I spent all the time I could spare - quite a big chunk of every morning - thinking and reading and praying about my subject - and about that daunting prospect on Sunday. I managed to keep the Saturday evening free after supper and sat in my study praying it all through.

I was trembling as I got up early the next morning. I fumbled with my collar stud. My tummy was turning over as I walked to church and I was feeling utterly miserable. I was in a daze as I assisted at the 8am Communion. I could eat little breakfast but drank several cups of strong coffee.

Another miserable walk back to church for the big one - Matins with sermon. 'Preacher: The Revd George Singleton' *"O No, please. ..."* Panic stations - *"How was I going to begin? I simply can't remember! O yes, of course! - for goodness sake get it in your thick head and remember it.! O dear, O dear ..."*

As we processed into the church my hands were clenched in my pockets, innocent of any small comforting piece of paper with a few lifesaving lines written down of what I was going to say. *What have I done? What's going to happen? I must be mad!*

The psalms.

The first lesson.

The Canticle.

The Second Lesson. *Panic! "Stop the World, I want to get off!"*

The hymn before the sermon - *"Lord, please let me die before the end of this hymn "*

He didn't.

The hymn finished; my feet took me automatically from my stall, to the pulpit. Up the steps; shaking as with ague. Everyone sat down; Dr Dewey screwed his monocle into his eye = and glared up at me.

I vaguely heard myself saying, *May the words of my lips, and the meditations of our hearts be now and always acceptable in thy sight, O Lord our strength and our redeemer.*

Then I was saying, "As I was thinking about what I was to say to you this morning ...."

I realised I had suddenly become fully conscious, perfectly calm and totally at ease!

In my minds eye I could see quite clearly the various points of the address I had prepared unfolding before me, and I found that I was talking about them almost as I would have talked about them to someone sitting in an armchair opposite me on the other side of the fire.

I was free! For the first time since I had begun trying to preach, I found myself completely free and at ease in the pulpit, and what's more, I was hugely enjoying myself!

I knew I had something to say to all those ranks of people sitting listening to me. I felt a *rapport* with them I had not felt before. I felt that the congregation and I were exploring something *together.* I was speaking, they were responding. It was a wonderful and exhilarating feeling.

I glanced down at Dr Dewey, still with the same expression on his face, and his monocle firmly in his eye, but he had been transformed since I began speaking into a kindly elderly gentleman taking a lively interest in what this young man had to say! What I had taken to be a frown was, I saw now, an expression of benign concentration.

The address had a beginning, a middle and an end; it turned out to be all of a piece. It was not a great sermon; so far as I remember no one commented on it much. In the vestry afterwards Dick just gave me a grin, and when we were alone said, "Yes, that's the way you are going to preach."

And that is the way I always have preached ever since, except on those rare occasions when I have been asked to preach on some special occasion or at some function when time has been of the essence. Then, with great toil and tribulation I have had to write what I was going to say, and it has always felt as though I have been reading an essay. I like writing to be read, but I cannot write fluently what I am going to say.

My year as a deacon lasted from the middle of 1941 to the middle of 1942, and during that time there was a lot of bombing in Portsmouth. No more of the terrible saturation blitzes that had laid waste so many areas of the city eighteen months before, but a lot of quite heavy raids nonetheless. At night we were no strangers to sticks of bombs falling across the city and our parish - making that ghastly sound of an express train coming at you from the sky at a hundred miles an hour, stopping with a mighty earth shaking explosion that seemed only yards away, Crump after crump, each louder than the last, and you wondering whether the next one was going to wipe you out or whether it would straddle you - and the crump would be beyond, wiping someone else out.

There would also be frequent 'hit and run' attacks in daylight as a German bomber would brave our defences and unload a few bombs before dashing back across the channel.

During both day and night attacks the anti-aircraft batteries, specially strengthened to protect the vital Naval base and installations, erupted with the most terrible din imaginable. As we listened to this uproar accompanying shrieking and exploding bombs we often wondered what 'secret weapons' were being deployed in the effort to bring down the bombers or warn them off.

Quite often the sirens would sound and very soon we would hear the bombers throbbing towards us, but no bombs would be dropped so it was clear that the target was further inland. On these occasions we would carry on with what we were doing and would not take shelter - indeed as the war proceeded most people became quite *blasé* and did not take shelter until the bombs really did begin to get too near for comfort.

When the occasional heavy raid occurred people would stream to the public shelters. All clergy had tin hats with a white cross on the front, and service type gasmasks, and when these raids occurred we would don our hats and go visiting in the shelters to 'keep up civilian morale.' I had to wait a while until my teeth stopped chattering with craven fear before I could do anything about keeping up anyone else's morale! As the frequency and weight of the raids gradually decreased shelter visiting ceased to be necessary as people used the communal shelters less and less and preferred to take what shelter they could in their own homes, either a "Morrison shelter" - a large steel table with enough space under it for half a dozen or so people, or the "Anderson" shelter in the garden, like a steel bicycle shed - or simply by sitting under the staircase. Another reason was that there had been some horrifying 'direct hits' on public shelters when all the occupants had been killed. So most people preferred the risk of being entombed in their own homes, and many were quite fatalistic about the dangers of war - *O well, if the bomb's got my name on it, I shall get it - if not, I shall be OK* was a very common attitude.

When the throbbing drone of approaching planes was heard and they came within range the defences did not wait to see whether we were to be the target or not and the guns would open up and the day or night would be made hideous with deafening noise.

One evening I sat writing in my study after the air-raid warning had sounded. I decided not to take shelter until the bombs, if any, had begun to fall and things got much worse. Suddenly a battery of guns opened up with the missiles making a most extraordinary sound. After the initial detonation the whole sky seemed to be filled with a shrieking 'whipping' sound that flew repeatedly back and forth from horizon to horizon. This was the first time I had heard this terrifying noise and I sat amazed and appalled as I tried to imagine whatever could make a sound like that. For an hour or more this evil whipping scream followed every firing of that particular battery, adding a new dimension to the mad cacophony of war.

A long time later I heard, or read - I forget which - that a missile had been invented which had two parts connected with a wire or chain, and as, on firing, this spread out it became a new and effective weapon against aircraft. That may have been just another of the wild rumours and surmises that were rife during the war, for I have never been able to verify it. It just might have accounted for that extraordinary sound whipping to and fro across the sky. I do not remember hearing the strange weapon being deployed during daytime raids.

What needs no verification is the way shrapnel used to fall from the sky by day and night when the guns were in action, and walking through it was like walking through a pretty lethal hailstorm. One afternoon I wanted to get home to tea when the guns opened up against a hit-and-run Dornier bomber which I happened to see circling the city, and the shrapnel began to fall. I wanted my tea so decided to take a chance and not seek shelter. Three municipal workmen were sheltering in a shop doorway across the road, and shouted to me, "Shrapnel, Father, take shelter." I waved and said, "Its all right, I've got my big black hat on." I left them killing themselves with laughter. A piece of shrapnel fell near me and I stooped to pick it up, intending to keep it as a souvenir, but it was almost red hot and I dropped it quickly. I got home to tea all right, but it was a foolhardy and thoughtless thing to do. It was only afterwards that I thought of the consequences, not only for myself, but for others, if I had been hit.

On another night there was a particularly heavy raid and a lot of damage was done in the parish. The vicar and I were in the basement of the vicarage when we heard a stick of bombs coming our way, each explosion nearer and more deafening than the last. There were six bombs in a stick, and we counted - three - four - five, gosh that was near, six like an express train driven by all the banshees in creation shrieking their heads off, *ours, this time, Lord into Thy hands, I commend* .... Tremendous explosion; the earth moving, whole basement bucking and shuddering, things falling in the garden outside, something like a load of gravel landing from a height. Silence. Good heavens, still in one piece, basement back to normal, *Blessing and honour, and thanksgiving*.....

Soon the All Clear sounded and we went out to survey the damage. There was debris everywhere, the garden littered with brickbats and rubble. The house next door but one had had a direct hit and was just a smouldering ruin. We looked at one another appalled - poor old lady, everything gone. 'Everything' meant a houseful of beautiful antique furniture worth a fortune, which the old lady - she seemed old to me and must have been all of fifty-five - spent all her days keeping in tip top condition, dusting, cleaning, polishing so that it would remain in tip-top condition as it had always been kept in her parents' day. We were desperately sorry for her and wondered how she would ever get over such a loss. She had spent the night in the shelter and when later she emerged and saw her house we expected her to break down. She looked in stunned silence at the ruin of her home, then to our utter amazement a broad smile slowly built up in her face, and rubbing her hands together she said in relief and great delight, "O Thank God *that's* all gone, now at last I'm *free!*"

By the middle of 1942 when I was nearing the end of my statutory year in the diaconate, the Royal Air Force had fought Goering's Luftwaffe back across the Channel; Portsmouth was no longer under attack, except for the occasional random intruder. The Cathedral began to be used again, and we were told that the Ordination service would be held there. This was splendid news, for I loved our Cathedral and I did not specially want to be ordained priest in a parish church. The whole scene would be different this time, for in the course of the year Bishop Partridge had died and we now had a new bishop, Bishop William Louis Anderson, who was a very different sort of prelate, kind and fatherly and very approachable.

Uppermost in my mind as the ordination on Trinity Sunday approached was the fact that soon I would celebrate the Mass for the first time, something I had looked forward to with awe and excitement for many years. My first Mass was to be on Monday, the day after the priesting, and of course it was Dick Herrick who taught me how to celebrate.

Again in 1942 we had a traditional English Flaming June, and the sunshine lifted everyone's war-jaded spirits. There was a song in my heart as I hefted my suitcase on to the bus that would once more take me to Fareham to stay with my now good friend Father Basil Daniell while I attended the ordination retreat in the Bishop's chapel. I found Basil still knitting socks, with his poor deformed hands - and idly wondered how many pairs he had knitted since I first met him a year ago, but I forbore to ask him.

Basil had taught me a great deal about the life of prayer and the spiritual responsibilities of priesthood since he had become my spiritual director, and in fact my evening talks with him during the retreat were as valuable as the retreat itself. He encouraged me to make the Mass the centre of my ministry. "Remember, it is the Priest's supreme privilege, the source of his inspiration, the supreme intercession for his people and himself, the primary channel of God's love, the 're-presentation' by which he is brought daily into the real presence of the perfect sacrifice of our Lord, offered once for all upon the Cross, his glorious Resurrection and Ascension. Through the priest at the altar the whole Church, the Mystical Body of Christ, offers the perfect Thanksgiving for all the mighty Acts of God for the salvation of the world. Through the great

Mystery of the Mass eternal realities are made present to men and women in every age - the Now becomes the Eternal Present." He also reminded me that when as layman or priest we are at the altar, we are 'compassed about by so great a cloud of witnesses' - the whole Church of God, on earth, in paradise and in heaven; space and time cease to exist. Charles Gore, Bishop of Oxford and founder of the Community of the Resurrection, when asked about the reality of Christ's presence under the forms of bread and wine in the Eucharist said, "The 'How' has no parallel in our experience" I have always believed in the 'Real Presence' and, with Gore, believe that all attempts at explanation are futile and quite unnecessary. Sufficient for me, and surely all that is necessary, the simple faith of Queen Elizabeth the First, who was no mean theologian, who said, "He took the bread and brake it, and what His Word doth make it, That I believe and take it."

The retreat over we all went into town to the Cathedral for a rehearsal - this time, thank goodness, there was another Gospeller! This time a cheerful and friendly Bishop. This time nothing, but nothing, hanging over my head. A profound sense of unworthiness, of course, but also a peaceful conviction that it really was to this that I had been called.

So, I went back to my digs where the same family party as last year had arrived, Mother and Geoff and Aunt and Phil and Joan, put up by the good Mrs Stevens.

Trinity Sunday was again a lovely morning and there was a spring in my step as I went off to the Cathedral. No new clothes this time, and the collar stud went in easily after a year's practice! A freshly laundered linen collar though, but the same soutane cassock, now shiny at seat and elbows, lending an air of experience, and suggesting that one was not quite so wet behind the ears as this time last year.

The Cathedral was lovely in the sunshine; birds were singing in the trees; the nicely proportioned cupola on the tower gleamed white like the welcoming beacon it was. Inside it was cool and peaceful with comforting shadows and open spaces, instinct with God and prayer. The congregation was beginning to assemble and the low murmur of conversation was gradually increasing.

The family went to the places reserved for relations and friends of the ordinands, and where they would be able to see all the action. I put my surplice and stole in the vestry for later, and went back to the side aisle by the sanctuary. There was over half an hour before I needed to robe.

I sat and thought back over the years - right back to that Wednesday evening in Lent at All Saints church, Hampton when during the address I suddenly knew that I had to try to become a priest. I remembered my incredulity at the idea - *I? a priest?* - but you have tó have an *education* to be a *priest!* And Jock Murray, not pooh-poohing the idea but saying, "Well, if God wants you to be a priest, and you try to do his will, then you *will* be a priest." Then Tatterford and Father Hand, "You are not really learning very much, are you?" Then Matric missed by one mark. As a result, Epsom - and if I had not had that year's teaching at the Wells House School I would not have met Canon Hunter who solved the chronic financial problem once and for all. I smiled to myself as I recalled his saying, quite offhandedly while piling me with books, "Money?, O, *I'll* give you the *money* - and you will need this, and this...." Books, *much* more important than mere money! Pipping the first part of GOE, once more by one mark All those weary returns to square one and the resultant near-despair. Staying behind in Canterbury to fight fires and protect St Augustine's - and as a result being excused examinations and being ordained on a set of essays instead - I had always been much better at writing essays than examination papers!

As I sat there by the sanctuary, literally within minutes of the end and aim of all these endeavours, was it fanciful of me to see a clear thread of the purpose and guidance of God stretching unbroken from the eighteen-year-old in the Hampton church to the twenty-five-year old sitting here in the Cathedral? I think not, and it gave me a lift of confidence and a heart of thanksgiving as I realized that soon the service would begin in which at long last and in spite of all the setbacks, all the returns to 'square one', all the heartache and, yes, all the suffering, *I would be ordained a Priest in the Church of God.* Familiar as the idea had become by now, I was suddenly so overwhelmed at the thought, that I flopped onto my knees and gave myself up to the wonder of it all thinking *"O, but who am I? who am I?*

The service began with a long procession, led by the Cathedral cross and acolytes bearing candles, followed by a full choir of men and boys in their blue cassocks and white surplices, leading the singing of one of the great processional hymns. Following the choir was a large contingent of local clergy, including the incumbents of those who were to be ordained, dressed in surplice and stole. Next the Cathedral Canons and other dignitaries, the Archdeacons, the Chancellor of the Diocese. Then the Provost of the Cathedral leading the Bishop's section of the procession. More servers, followed by the ordinands; those to be made deacon with their stoles folded over their left arms, we deacons who were to be priested still wearing ours over our left shoulders and tied under our right arms. Last of all came the Bishop with his chaplain. The Bishop, a fine figure in cope and mitre, walked with his silver pastoral staff in his left hand while with his right he blessed the people who knelt or bowed to him as he passed.

The long procession, a fine spectacle, wended its way down the south aisle of the Cathedral to the west end and then up the centre aisle of the nave and into the choir where all went to the places allotted to them. The Bishop went to his seat before the altar. His chaplain placed the pastoral staff and the mitre upon the altar.

The rite of Ordination was, as always, set within the context of the Eucharist, and after the Gloria had been sung those to be made deacon were presented to the Bishop and then ordained.

The Gospel was read by one of the new deacons, and then we who were to be priested were presented to the Bishop by the Archdeacon, who declared that he had examined us and believed us to be fit persons to be ordained to this holy office. The Bishop then addressed the congregation, saying that *"These are they whom we purpose, God willing, to receive this day unto the holy office of Priesthood.'* He told the people that we had been examined, and that nothing had been found that should prevent our being ordained. He continued, *"But if there be any of you who knoweth of any impediment, or notable crime"* which should debar any of us from this holy office, *"he must come forward and say what that impediment is."*

The Bishop then turned his attention to us and read a long exhortation about the dignity and great importance of the holy office of Priesthood, reminding us that we were *"called to be messengers, watchmen and stewards of the Lord, to teach and premonish, to lead and provide for the Lord's family, to seek for Christ's sheep that are dispersed abroad, and for his children that are in the midst of this naughty world, that they may be saved through Christ for ever."* We were to do this great work as shepherds, who, like Him, were ready to lay down our lives for the sheep, and we were always to have printed in our remembrance, how great a treasure was being committed to our charge. We were to remember that the Church and congregation whom we are called to serve was *"His spouse and His body."* So great a responsibility, he said, could only be exercised by prayer to the Holy Spirit, and study of the Scriptures.

Every one of us standing there before the Bishop was already aware of the great responsibility about to be laid upon us, and we might well have wanted to cut and run, unable to face so daunting a prospect, but as the Bishop now continued, *"We have good hope that you have well weighed and pondered these things with yourselves long before this time; and that you have clearly determined, by God's grace, to give yourselves wholly to this office, whereunto it hath pleased God to call you."*

Searching questions were put to us and in our answers we affirmed that we believed ourselves to be truly called; that *'by God's grace we will teach only what is in accordance with the teaching of Holy Scripture, that we will minister the doctrine and sacraments and discipline of Christ'* ; that we *'will banish and drive away all strange doctrine contrary to God's Word*, and finally that *'we will try to maintain and set forward quietness, peace and love among all Christian people.'*

Having reminded us of the privileges and duties of priesthood and having heard our assent to them, the Bishop then asked the whole congregation to kneel with us while all sang the great hymn to the Holy Spirit, *Veni Creator Spiritus*, 'Come Holy Ghost our souls inspire' I was now on the very brink of priesthood and I could still hardly believe it - what had for so many years seemed an impossible dream, sometimes almost an impertinent aspiration, was now coming to pass.

The last verse of the hymn summed up the whole purpose of human life, the fulfilment of all our loving, the supreme message that as priests we must take to all people:

Teach us to know the Father, Son,
and thee of both to be but One
That through the ages all along
This may be our endless song

Praise to thy eternal merit
Father, Son, and Holy Spirit

After another long prayer recalling how our Lord, after His glorious Resurrection and Ascension, sent forth into the world his Apostles, Prophets, Evangelists, Doctors and Pastors, *'by whose labour and ministry he gathered together a great flock in all parts of the world, to set forth the eternal praise of thy holy Name,'* the Bishop finally thanked God that he had called us to that same ministry.

The Bishop then rose from his knees, and as he sat in his ceremonial chair, the great breath-taking moment had arrived.

I was now so caught up with wonder and expectancy that I was hardly aware of others going before me to kneel before the Bishop - and then I was there myself.

I knelt.

I saw the beautiful embroidery of the Bishop's cope over the pure white linen of his alb.

His arms stretched out towards me as he laid his hands firmly upon my head. There was a rustling of robes as the other clergy - the Archdeacon, the Canons, my vicar Norman Millard, Dick Herrick my beloved friend, and Basil Daniell my mentor and director - surrounded me in a great circle, each with his right arm outstretched and his hand coming to rest upon the Bishop's hands. Closing my eyes I had a powerful recollection that this 'imposition of hands' for the transmission of priestly authority stretches back down the ages and centuries to the Apostles themselves.

I was overwhelmed by awe and worship as the onerous weight of the Apostolic Succession pressed upon my head and the Bishop said the solemn words:

"Receive the Holy Ghost
for the office and work of a priest in the Church of God
now committed unto thee by the imposition of our hands.
Whose sins thou dost forgive,
they are forgiven.
Whose sins thou dost retain
they are retained.
And be thou a faithful dispenser of the Word of God
and of His holy sacraments;
In the Name of the Father, and of the Son, and of the Holy Ghost.
Amen"

The circle of clergy who had joined in the laying-on-of-hands retired

The Bishop then handed me a leather-bound copy of the Revised Version of the Bible, with the words:

"Take thou authority to preach the Word of God,
and to minister the holy Sacraments
in the Congregation, where thou shalt be
lawfully appointed thereunto"

Finally the Archdeacon came to me and, untying the 'deacon's knot' under my right arm, replaced my stole to hang down straight from the neck, the symbol of the 'Yoke of Christ' and of priestly authority.

Back in my stall. I knelt with my head in my arms. A priest at last! It was all too much, too great to comprehend. I could think of no words, but of course words were not necessary, in fact they would have got in the way - so, just 'being' - quiet and still in that timeless and eternal moment, full of inexpressible thanksgiving; full of praise and wonder and joy - and love.

The rest of the service passed almost as a dream - the Creed, the sermon (I could hardly follow it) the consecration, the communion; I was grateful for the time of quiet before the blessing and the announcement of the last hymn.

I began to come to as we sang the last hymn in procession back to the vestry. There the Bishop gave us our Letters of Orders, beautifully inscribed on parchment and with the Diocesan Seal hanging from the bottom edge on a ribbon He reminded us that these were the proof of our ordination and must be kept safely, for they could not be replaced Our very caring bishop shook our hands and congratulated us, deliberately making a little joke to make us laugh and release some of the tension.

As I emerged from the vestry to go to join the family in the nave, there was a rustle and a cassocked figure emerged from the shadow of an arch and went down on his knees before me saying, "Please Father, may I have your blessing?" My dear friend and spiritual director, Basil Daniell! Instantly there was a huge lump in my throat - that *he* should ask a blessing of *me!!* For a few moments my mind went blank and I could not remember the words. Then, with a stern recollection that it would not be *I* who would be blessing, but our Lord blessing through me, I recovered and, as I laid my hands upon the bowed head of this holy man, the beautiful words returned and I blessed in His name for the first time. And who more worthy to receive it? - for had it not been for Basil's wisdom and care a year ago, when I had almost withdrawn, I might well not have been there that day.

On Monday morning there was a large congregation in the Lady Chapel of St Mark's for my first Mass. I was very nervous, and as always, I made several minor mistakes. Dick served me and kept me on the rails though and I do not suppose there were many who noticed my mistakes. I was again filled with awe and wonder but was not able to dwell upon these feelings, for I was having to attend closely to the actual mechanics of saying the service and remembering what came next! It was only as the months and years went by that I appreciated more and more what it really was that I was doing as I stood at the altar. One can never exhaust the meaning of the Mass, for it is the great mystery at the heart of Christian faith and worship and life, and ultimately unfathomable. As was customary, after the communion my mother remained at the altar rail and I gave her a large bunch of red roses. It was a very happy occasion, and we had a celebratory breakfast in the vicarage dining room.

I celebrated the Eucharist frequently, and as the rite became more familiar, I was able to think more about its nature and implications until imagination and thought were left behind and I was again lost in awe and wonder. I became more and more convinced that this rite was at the very heart of the life of the Church, the source of strength and power for the priest; the most powerful intercession of all, the source of grace and love. Standing at the altar, the focal point of the worshipping Church, I knew that we were all in the living presence both of Christ's sacrifice made once for all upon the Cross, and of the Risen and Ascended Lord, triumphant over death and sin. And that day by day our lives were renewed and empowered by Him.

Soon I was taking my full share in conducting weddings and interviewing the couples beforehand two or three times in some cases, though I do not think we were as thorough in this pastoral work as most clergy rightly are today.

Portsmouth being a busy port and dockyard there were many more weddings during the war years than in peacetime, and we would often have five or six weddings on a Saturday - I believe ten was our highest score, and sometimes it was not easy to preserve the proper dignity that should attend so important and solemn an occasion. Frequently best man and groom had repaired to the local pub to find some Dutch courage before the service. On one occasion when a Royal Navy Stoker First Class came to be married there was a lot of hilarity among the guests and I had to give them a rather tart lecture about remaining quiet, "If," I said, "this marriage is to proceed." They quietened down a bit after that, but I took a good look at the stoker and wondered just what we had here. He was a short stocky man with a round very red and shiny face, and I could smell the whiskey on his breath. He stood beside his bride with a broad grin on his face, rocking back and forth on his heels. When I asked him, "Will you take this woman to your wedded wife, etc. etc." he breathed a huge gust of whiskey fumes and, still rocking back and forth, said in a loud voice, *"NOT 'ARF."*

Another time for some reason I was left to do all the weddings on a particular Saturday; I think there were five of them. By the time I went to collect the fifth bride from the North door and lead her up the aisle I was quite punch drunk and hardly knew what I was doing - and to my horror found myself saying the introductory sentences for a funeral - "I am the Resurrection and the Life, saith the Lord..." I doubt that anyone noticed.

So many of the weddings were rushed affairs hurriedly

arranged while the naval husband was in port. And often had tragic conclusions: married one day and three days later killed in action or sunk by a U-Boat while escorting one of our vital convoys of merchant ships across the Atlantic, or a convoy to our Russian allies across the Baltic. Heartrending visits had to be paid to some of those whom we had only recently married.

I was totally immersed in the job and filled with a great joy and what today is called 'job satisfaction.' I have always been fascinated by people - as a youngster I used to go to the Hampton Court Fair not only for the swings and roundabouts, but simply to watch the crowds. Now my whole life was concerned with trying to help people, comforting and supporting them in their homes and in the hospitals. Now I was fully-fledged, no longer half-baked and limited in my scope but with all the authority of priesthood and, as I firmly believe, the special graces and spiritual powers that come from the unique gifts of the Holy Spirit in ordination. I could bless; I could absolve the guilt-ridden conscience and bring peace, I could lay hands on the sick and help either to heal or to endure. Now I could stand at the altar, the most important priestly activity of all, where my poor efforts could be caught up and perfected in the perfect activity of the One Great High Priest Himself, from whom all priesthood flows.

As every new priest discovers who tries to exercise ministry worthily, the priestly fruits of the Holy Spirit began to be evident in my work, and it was clear that there was now a new dimension in my pastoral activities. I found the deeper insights into people's minds and lives that the exercise of the priesthood brings, a source of ceaseless wonder. And the awful burdens that so many people bear with such fortitude and lack of bitterness filled my heart with admiration and respect.

The things I was doing now were the things I had seen Jock Murray and Peter Booth doing back home in Hampton, and had thought I must be mad to think I could ever do the same - and here I was just doing them as part of my regular routine, actually practicing a priestly ministry: what more could a man want in life? Well, it would have been nice to have had Bar by my side, but there - *O love, I wonder how you are? I hope you are still happy with your Peter ...*

It was during my second year of priesthood that I had a letter from Bar, telling me that her husband Peter had been posted overseas - and that she was pregnant. She said she would love to see me sometime if it ever became possible. Having no home of her own she was staying with Minka Wells, her mother-in-law at

Elstead near Haslemere. So having digested her letter, which was a touch difficult but I managed it, I replied congratulating her that she was going to have a baby but saying how sad I was for her that Peter had been sent overseas just at this particular time. I also said that I would love to see her again too, and as Haslemere was only a short distance up the line from Portsmouth, would she like to come to see me and the parish for a day?

I met her at the station in the vicar's old Riley, and we talked non-stop for practically the whole time. Mrs Stevens gave us a *tete-à-tete* lunch. It was wonderful to see her again, and she looked so bonny and smiling, though a little more awkward in her movements having put on weight for obvious reasons. After tea at the vicarage where everyone made much of this shining girl, we had a hilarious drive back to the station in the vicar's car because I suddenly kept getting in a muddle with the pre-selector gear system and we stalled several times and then proceeded in a series of jerking leaps. I drove home in a much more sober mood and forbore to look too closely at my feelings - time for Evensong, then a quick supper then my confirmation class, so the evening was mercifully full. *Thank you for letting me see her again, but O ....*

Timothy Peter was born some months later, and I was asked to baptise him and stand as one of his Godfathers, to which I readily consented. I baptised him in All Saints, Hampton, our old church as at that time Bar was living with her own family in Hanworth, nearby.

I returned to Portsmouth, and very soon afterwards 'Gussie' Davis, the priest-in-charge of one of our two daughter churches, St Francis, Hilsea, announced his resignation in order to join the Navy as a Chaplain. I was appointed to succeed him. My first independent charge! I could do almost what I liked!

St Francis, Hilsea was a dual purpose building with a large curtain that could be pulled across the sanctuary so that it could be used as a hall. It stands on the side of Central Avenue, Hilsea, which is the north western corner of Portsea Island with Portsmouth and Southsea on the southern extremity. Central Avenue is one of the main roads into Portsmouth. The area around the church consisted of a 1930s housing estate of terraced and semi-detached houses where middle ranking workers in the dockyard and offices lived, with a fair sprinkling of shore-based naval personnel, Petty Officers etc. The other side of the main road was a slum clearance area where before the war people from the notorious slums of Portsmouth had been rehoused. Without the benefit of proper rehabilitation the resettled slum dwellers had proceeded to turn their nice new estate into another slum almost as bad as the one they had left. By the time I arrived most of the fences of the originally neat little houses had been burnt as firewood, the gardens had become unkempt and the whole place was infinitely depressing.

St. Francis church was intended to serve both communities, which of course it never managed to do. The main road was a cultural as well as a physical divide between the two communities. It is nearly always the case that when a main road runs through a parish it is difficult to get those who do not live on the same side of the road as the church to come there to worship, except for those who are already really committed Christians. There were a few of these who were regular members of the St Francis congregation but they were the exceptions who proved the rule. However, the church did serve the people on the estate as far as it was able to do so, and I followed my predecessor's example by visiting on the estate regularly. There were a few house-bound people who had been regular worshippers and I took them their communion once a month. One of these, an old lady of nearly eighty, went into hospital for the first time, for a major abdominal operation. I visited her in hospital and called to see her the day she was brought home. I found her tucked up in bed, and all her old cronies sitting around the walls. As I went in she looked up at me and said, "O hello, Father. I was just tellin' 'em, it ain't the aktuel operation, its the awful prostitution wot follers."

Another day, a very hot one in August, I went to see an old woman who lived alone in a very scruffy house. I was hot and tired - and very thirsty. She was sitting at her table, covered in rather grubby and worn American cloth. She was just finishing a cup of tea, and when I came in asked me if I would like one. Breaking my normal rule I said, yes thank you, that would be nice. To my horror she poured the tea into the cup she had just used herself and pushed it across the table to me. Trying to do so inconspicuously I was careful to take the cup in my left hand. I was half way through the horrible weak and cool 'tea' when she looked up with a toothless grin and said, "Gawd, Father, ain't that funny - we're both left-'anded!"

The bane of my life was the boys' club I ran two nights a week when about twenty to thirty boys between fifteen and eighteen years of age came to play ping-pong and darts and billiards, and various other games that had been provided over the years. Most of them were real toughs, but always there were some splendid youngsters among them. I would spend the evening supervising the activities and putting loud popular music on the radiogram - I never hear an old recording of the Inkspots without being vividly reminded of the St Francis Boys' Club at Hilsea. I am afraid running boys' clubs was not my metier and I hated every minute of it and was thankful when at ten o'clock I could shout *"TIME GENTLEMEN PLEASE."*

Diagonally opposite the church on the other side of the main road was a huge Naval Transit Camp where lower-deck ranks were assembled before being sent off secretly to overseas theatres of war. The camp had a very loud public-address system, and on one of my first Sundays at St Francis' I was in the middle of my sermon and made a dramatic pause - when a gargantuan voice suddenly bellowed *DID YOU HEAR THAT? DID YOU HEAR THAT?* from across the way. I had to extend the pause until we could all stop laughing.

It was not long after I had moved into my new digs just round the corner from St Francis' that I came home for breakfast one morning to find beside my plate a letter in an all too familiar hand.

Bar, broken hearted: Peter has been posted 'Missing Believed Killed.'

4
Bereavement and Bewilderment

I was so desperately sorry for poor Bar. She was the sort of young woman who one felt instinctively ought to be protected from this sort of bereavement - but that could be said, if it can be said at all, of hundreds of young women in wartime. A nonsensical notion I suppose, but it always seemed to me that some were more vulnerable to suffering than others. Perhaps it was entirely subjective on my part, but I have always felt that Bar needed more protection than most. It was probably due to the trauma that I used to experience when in the earliest days of our getting to know one another she used to cry so copiously and was quite unable to explain why.

When the dreaded telegram had arrived from the War Office Bar was staying with her mother-in-law at Elstead, and as soon as I had read her letter I arranged with the vicar to cancel everything for the day and caught the earliest train I could from Portsmouth to Haslemere. Bar met me at the station, white faced, unsmiling, numb. We gave each other a quick little hug, and I bore her off to a nearby coffee shop and plied her with good strong coffee, saying little.

Then, as I so well remembered from what I came to think of as our 'first incarnation,' she looked at me wide eyed, and the tears welled up and flowed silently and unchecked down her cheeks. Routinely, as of old, I shook out the clean handkerchief with which, when seeing her, I always came prepared, and handed it to her without a word. "Thank God you've come," she said, and gave me a wan little apology for a smile. I said I was glad she could still cry, for it was always a release for her. She said that so far she had not been able to cry much. Soon we left the coffee shop and wandered away from the station until we found a country lane down which we sauntered.

As we strolled, still saying little, she began to sob and before long we stopped and I wrapped my arms around her as she cried as I had never heard crying before, and rarely since. She cried from the very core of her being, great wracking sobs that I thought must be tearing her heart out. She clung to me with a fierce desperation, broken hearted, the pain at last being shared, at least to some small degree.

I lost track of time as we stood there in that deserted little lane, but eventually the sobs subsided and she quietened. She dried her eyes as best she could on my sodden handkerchief, and we began to retrace our steps towards the bus stop for Elstead. While we waited she took out her compact, looked at herself in the mirror and then glanced at me with a rueful little smile, "O I do look a mess!" I refrained from telling her what she looked like to *me,* as she got to work repairing her face with lipstick and powder.

Now she could begin to talk, hesitantly at first but with growing confidence as she slipped quite naturally into the old familiar way of first crying on me and then talking to me, even though in the past she often had not known why she was crying.

In spite of our long separation, having met only once since her marriage when she came to see me in Portsmouth a few months ago, we both felt that the intervening years had rolled away and we were back in the confident roles we had played so many times in the past.

By the time we reached Elstead Bar had regained her composure and was able to make the introductions quite calmly. Having scuppered my first name 'Ernest.' she was not very enamoured of 'George', so she said to Minka, her mother-in-law, "Minka, this is 'EG'" - and from that moment and for many years, I was EG to her and to all her relations, except her mother and father who had always known me as Ernie and were not going to change now. My second change of name, and I liked it very much.

Minka was divorced from Peter Hoare's father and was now married to Lionel Wells, known to everyone as 'LW' (probably where Bar got the idea of 'EG' Minka was an arresting woman, larger than life, and I took to her at once. She was of Russian extraction, volatile, artistic, cultured, and pretty ruthless at getting her own way. She reminded me very much of Mrs Stevens our next door neighbour in Hampton. She was always very nice to me and never seemed to mind having a young dog-collar around the place. So far as I know, and from the evidence of her conversation, I do not think she had any religious convictions. But Minka tended to collect people, and I suspect I was pigeonholed under the title 'Clergymen.' Her house was full of beautiful things; I once picked up a lovely shepherdess figurine from the mantelpiece to admire and she murmured, "Don't drop it will you dear, its insured for £5000!" I very nearly did, for to me was an unimaginably large sum of money - much more than ten years' salary.

Minka was a fine pianist and had a host of well-known musicians among her friends. She organised Lunch Time Concerts in Guildford, on the lines of those at the National Gallery inspired by Kenneth Clarke, and she would put up the artists the night before.

That first day, I met Peter's sister Audrey who, with her baby daughter Celia, was staying with Minka while her Canadian Army Officer husband was away at the war. Audrey and Bar got on very well indeed and I was so glad to see this for Bar's sake. Audrey also was a fine musician, playing the pianoforte and violin, volatile like her mother and with a splendid sense of humour. She was able to make Bar laugh, and that was good.

The introductions downstairs over I was then taken upstairs for the most important of them all - Tim. He was in his play-pen in the nursery, just beginning to haul himself up on to his feet by grabbing the bars. He started burbling away in his own language as soon as we entered the room. A beautiful baby with very fair hair, much fairer than Bar's. I can see Bar now, standing and looking lovingly at Tim as he chattered away, and she murmured, "I am so thankful that at anyrate I have got something of Peter still." I picked him up and gave him a hug, and then took him downstairs for the messy procedure of giving both babies their lunch before we had ours. Tim did not want to eat, and I gained a few points by pretending that the spoonful of revolting looking mess was an aeroplane zooming in to land in his mouth. This made him laugh - and eat!

I returned to the parish that evening with an invitation to come back any time I liked and the offer of a bed if I wished. I made full use of that standing invitation in the next few weeks and months and saw a lot of Bar. Minka and her family encouraged me and made me feel perfectly at home with them. I would be urged to stay when there were special parties, especially before the Guildford Lunch Time Concerts when a number of musicians would be guests for the night as well.

Bar did not stay with Minka the whole time, but had periods either with her sister and brother-in-law, Joan and Chris Fairfield, in Surrey and sometimes with her own parents at Hanworth, not far from my own parental home in Hampton Hill. On one occasion I was staying there for a few days while Bar was with her parents. She gave me a ring to say that Minka and Audrey had invited us to meet them for tea at the Dorchester, was I free to go up to town with her? The matter needed no thought.

It was summertime and a lovely warm day. I went into the garden and picked some lilies of the valley and one or two other blooms and made them up into a nice little button-hole. Putting on my new light grey flannel suit, I borrowed mother's bike and set off to collect my fair lady. When I suggested she might like to wear the little posy, she said would I mind very much if she put it in a vase by her bed, "I would look a bit like a bride if I wore it, wouldn't I? -

O, don't be hurt darling, you do understand, don't you?" Of course I did. Anyway we had a very jolly morning, I took her to lunch - in Wardour Street where the food and service were excellent. She was thrilled when the waiter came with a silver bowl and invited her to hold out her hands to be sprinkled with rose-water. The sight of her delight sent the old familiar feelings coursing down my spine and turning my tummy over.

We met Minka and Audrey in the lounge of the Dorchester - the first time I had been in the hotel. We drew up chairs around a small table; politely I waited for the ladies to be seated, and then sat down myself - and felt as though I had sat in a puddle! Which in fact I had, for someone had spilt tea on the seat of my chair and had not reported it. The whole seat was drenched, and now so was I. I leaped to my feet, the seat of my natty light grey gent's suiting all too obviously soaked. Consternation! Minka took immediate charge of the situation, imperiously summoning the head waiter, and in spite of my embarrassment I hugely enjoyed watching her as, looking like an angry Duchess, she devastatingly poured quiet but menacing fury upon the poor man's defenceless head. By great good fortune I had brought a raincoat so was able to make myself decent. The offending chair was replaced and at last I had my elegant tea in the lounge of the Dorchester on a warm summer day - feeling uncomfortably wet and wearing a coat.

Once when I was going to see Bar for the day I was late arriving at Portsmouth station for my train to Haslemere, and as I rushed across the concourse I saw it just beginning to move. I hurtled forward through the gate to the platform, swerving to avoid the ticket collector who put his arm out to stop me, down the platform, pounding after the train as the man shouted behind me. I leapt upon the step, grabbed the door handle which nearly wrenched my arms from their sockets, managed to open the door and tumble into the corridor of the train - having a terrific fight to close the door again against the slipstream caused by the now speeding train. Having at last got my breath back standing there in the corridor, I went to slide open the door to the nearest compartment - but it was locked.

I tried the doors to all the compartments - they were all locked! So I went to the end of the corridor to go into the next coach, only to find that the connecting door was also locked. I was isolated in an empty coach at the end of the train. Not to worry, I thought, next stop I'll get off and go farther up the train. At least I knew that the door I had got in by was not locked. Then I noticed as the train drew into the station that the platform was on the other side - the other side of all those locked doors!

The penny then dropped - of course, as always the train was on the left hand track, and I was in the right hand locked corridor, a prisoner! I imagined myself unable to get off the train at Haslemere and being whisked right up to Waterloo.   There was just one possible solution - the window in the door of the compartment. One window was open just a little at the top, and as the train jolted and rattled and swerved on its way I spent quite a long time gradually opening the gap until I could get both hands on top of the window, and managed to push it down as far as it would go - to its maximum opening of about nine or ten inches. I looked dubiously at this tiny opening for some minutes; it was fairly high off the ground - the bottom of the opening just above chest-height, and it looked woefully small. It looked wide enough to accommodate my ribs, so that was all right, but hips and tummy? Of course tummy was of more modest proportions than it is today, and after all, can be drawn in. Head would be all right - not as swollen then as it sometimes is now!

Well, I thought, come on Singleton, it's your only chance. So with a prayer for help I threw my hat through the narrow opening - no turning back after that - stuck my head through and proceeded to 'climb' the other side of the corridor with my feet. As I wriggled madly in the swaying and jolting train I gave a mighty heave with my legs - and propelled myself in one decisive move half way through the window. But only half way through, *exactly* half way through, for I was neatly balanced on the axis of the window, gently swaying up and down like a human see-saw - and I could not move! I could neither get further in, nor could I get out again! We were approaching a station, and I giggled for a moment at my predicament, thinking of the reaction of anyone standing on the platform when they saw a young clergyman half in and half out of the corridor window of this compartment! It was probably the giggle that did it, no doubt tensing or flexing muscles that in the struggle I had not thought of using before - for just as the train drew into the platform I came out on to the floor of the compartment in a gush. "Gosh", I said, *"Thank you, Lord!"* I picked myself up off the floor, dusted myself down as best I could, clapped my black hat on my head, and as the train came to a standstill went to open the door intending at last to go further up the train and rejoin civilization. But guess what? Yes, *that* door was also firmly locked! I looked out of the window to attract someone's attention but the platform was deserted, no one getting on or off the train as far back as this. In a moment we were on the move again, and I was not about to try to climb out of *that* window; I'd had enough of getting through windows for the time being, thank you! So I sat and continued trying in sterterous sobs to get my breath back .

Suddenly remembering the name of that last station I realized with a sinking feeling that Haslemere, my destination, would be the next stop. *O Lord* ... I thought, whatever shall I do? I'm not entirely sure that I heard the Lord reply, *It's all right EG, I've got it all in hand* ... but I soon knew that He had, for as we drew into Haslemere station my carriage came to a halt - opposite rows of commandos with blackened faces, standing at ease in full battle kit, with fern and greenery stuck into the net covering of their tin hats, and armed to the teeth. In front of them stood their CO similarly attired - and the Station Master with a T-shaped key in his hand. He stepped forward to the door of my compartment, and as he opened it his eyes opened wide in astonishment when faced with this young clergyman. He was speechless as I smiled at him, stepped gratefully on to the platform, raised my hat to him and the CO - and, not scampering as I dearly wanted to do, walked away purposefully, and with dignity.

Anyway, when I told Bar about this escapade it gave her a good laugh, a commodity in rather short supply for her just then - she shook her head and smiling fondly said, "I don't know what I'm going to do with you!" I could have made some suggestions, but I forbore.

Apart from seeing Bar as often as possible, I also wrote to her frequently in an effort to help her to keep going. For all her vulnerability she had a hard core of toughness and she valiantly battled away in very difficult circumstances. All she had to live on was the meagre Widow's Pension, for a First Lieutenant, from the War Office. She had no house or flat, and spent her time going the rounds of various relations. She felt most at home with her sister Joan and her husband Chris, and spent a lot of her time there. To the end of her life she never forgot how good they were to her during her widowhood. Joan and Bar had always been very close, and Joan had had her first child, Roland, within a few months of Bar having Tim. The two little boys were brought up like brothers and have continued to have a special regard for one another ever since.

Chris Fairfield was in a reserved occupation and was a splendid man. He took a genuine interest in Bar's and Tim's welfare and in the early years played the role of father for him.

Back in Portsmouth I was immersed in the usual busy round of parish life. Greatly daring I bought a motor-bike, for £25, which I had to borrow from Geoff and which I paid him back in monthly instalments. It was not a very good buy and I pushed it for almost as many miles as I rode it. But when it worked it was a boon. I still had to go to the parish church most mornings for Matins, Eucharist and meditation, and the trolley buses were even more unreliable than my motorbike. I ventured one day into the city, and went to pass a trolley bus, not noticing that it had its trafficator arm out indicating that it was turning right. Another few feet and I would have made it (the story of my life, 'just another few feet', just another mark or two ....) But no; I was suddenly aware of falling - falling - and watching in slow motion a huge tyre as it bore down upon me. It hit the bike just in front of my left leg. Suddenly I was airborne. Sailing through the air in a graceful curve I landed flat on my face - at the feet of a Police Superintendent standing on the corner. Of course he 'took my name and address'; I was winded but unhurt and passers by brushed me down. I picked up my bike, and no damage having been done to either of us, I rode away.

It happened that one of my deputy-churchwardens at St Francis' was another Superintendent of Police, and when I told him about the episode he said, "O what bad luck it was at *his* feet you landed, he's so incompetent that the only convictions he ever gets in court are for driving offences; I'm afraid you are for the chop". Quite true; 'driving without due care and attention' - licence endorsed and fined £20.

As the weeks and months passed and I saw as much as possible of Bar, her attention gradually turned from mourning the past to considering the future. I knew I felt about her as I always had, for me she was still the Girl in the Middle of my life, reigning unopposed in the centre of my heart. Slowly and tentatively I began to wonder whether we had a future together. I recognised that Peter had been the great romantic love of her life, just as she had been mine. I accepted this just as I realized that so far I had not met anyone who came anywhere near to displacing her in my affections.

In the background there was always Bertie Page, Bar's former employer whose large house and nursery were next door to Bar's parental home on the borders of Hanworth and Hampton. She told me one day that Bertie had been in love with her for many years and now wanted to marry her. She said she was not really ready yet to think of remarrying.

We were both very bewildered at this time. I knew that I loved her. I believed that priesthood must take precedence over marriage - I would argue differently today. I was very fond of Tim, but on the tiny clerical salaries of those days, I did not feel up to the struggle of taking on a 'ready made' family. It was plain that what Bar craved most was security, not only for herself, but chiefly for Tim. In a sense she did not care much what happened to her; her whole life was concentrated upon Tim and his welfare. In this, although she did not articulate it, I am sure she felt that as well as loving Tim she was also serving Peter and his love for her. I did not feel I would be able to provide that sort of security.

As I say, we were both rather bewildered at this time; she had not fully come out of mourning - and in fact never would completely, I was torn yet again between priesthood and marriage. So we just went on seeing as much of each other as we could, talking and listening and hoping - and praying. One day she sighed and said, "We've got a funny love you know - we shall probably marry when we are eighty!" We often used to laugh and refer to our 'funnylove'.

Meanwhile the tide of war had turned. After the Anzio landing, where Peter had been killed, the long hard campaign in Italy eventually ground to a successful conclusion and in all theatres of war the allies were gaining the upper hand.

Talk of a Second Front in Europe was on everyone's lips, and in and around Portsmouth we began to see evidence that it was at long last under active preparation. The first sign that I noticed as I sped around in the little car some parishioners had lent me after the demise of the motorbike, was the parking spaces marked out in white paint in all the little lanes and roads in the country environs of Portsmouth - each space was numbered and had one of a variety of hieroglyphics painted next to the number. Hundreds and hundreds of them. Several weeks before D-Day these spaces began to be filled with tanks, personnel carriers, lorries, ammunition trucks, mobile guns, jeeps,ambulances etc. etc. - all the accoutrements of war that were going to France in the greatest overseas invasion in military history: Operation Overlord.

The most potent sign of something momentous pending was when huge smoke-screen trucks with gigantic chimneys were parked in the streets of our part of Portsmouth - one was immediately outside my digs - and night after night in that early summer of 1944 these machines belched out vast clouds of yellowish-grey and very oily smoke, covering the whole of the city and harbour and all the naval installations, with a heavy smoke-screen blanket. It was misery trying to sleep on those nights, not even tightly shut windows were a complete protection from the filthy smell of that awful smoke, and soon one's nose and throat felt full of the stuff.

At that time there was going to be a parish party, and we on the staff were to put on a play. The vicar was to play the part of an archdeacon, and the regulation garb for an archdeacon in those days was gaiters and apron, really a truncated cassock that came down just to knee level. So he rang up the Archdeacon and asked if he could borrow this gear; if so he would ask me to collect it. The Archdeacon readily agreed but said that I must go to his back door because his front door was out of bounds, and I must promise when I got inside the house not to look out of the front windows. He said he had had to promise the naval and military police that he would not let any visitors look out on to the Solent which his house faced. He later told me that had I looked out of his windows I would have seen shipping so closely packed in the Solent, as far as the eye could see, that it looked as if one could walk to the Isle of Wight by stepping from boat to boat

A few weeks later my organist who was a Wren officer working at General Eisenhower's HQ in one of the forts on Portsdown Hill behind Portsmouth, and from which the Solent could be clearly seen, whispered to me, "In a few day's time I shall have something very interesting to tell you, but at present my lips are sealed!!" Gosh, I thought, the balloon's about to go up - The Invasion! By now everyone knew something was afoot, and had a fair idea of what it was. Many of the roads around Portsmouth were closed, and as one went along the ones that remained open, the turrets of tanks and snouts of heavy guns were often visible above the hedges, and all was still and silent; there was a brooding air everywhere; naval and military personnel went about with serious faces. I noticed that security at the gates of the dockyard establishments, and the transit camp across the road from the church, had been strengthened.

The sun blazed down from Flaming June skies; and on most nights the thousand-bomber raids roared inexorably over our heads and when the wind was not blowing in the direction that made the smoke screen necessary, we could see the planes crowding the moonlit skies as they flew unhindered on their fell purposes. One dared not think of what carnage they would wreak when they reached their target. *O Lord, when shall we learn to talk and not to make war?*

Sure enough, on 6 June, we knew that D-Day had indeed arrived and a great armada was crossing the Channel. The Germans, though taken by surprise were counter-attacking vigorously, but we had established our bridgehead ....

That evening my Wren officer said that she was watching the whole thing as it developed, because she was one of those in the map room with a long handled wand with which little counters were pushed across the map of the English Channel, each counter representing a landing craft, supply ship, destroyer, corvette or whatever. It was she who first told me about PLUTO, the astonishing pipe-line-under-the-ocean by which petrol was pumped directly across the Channel to the supply depots in the bridgehead. Also about that incredible invention, the Mulberry Harbour, made in concrete sections at various places around the south coast, towed out on the day after D-Day and assembled as a floating harbour on the other side for the rapid supply of the armies.

Then came the time of Hitler's 'secret weapons', first the flying bomb nicknamed the 'Doodlebug', the little pilot-less plane with a puttering engine and a nose full of high explosive. By these Hitler hoped to knock out Portsmouth, but the Germans consistently got the range wrong, and we watched dozens of them by day and night as they flew over us and fell harmlessly in the New Forest. However one which we were told the Marines hit in the tail with their gunfire which tipped its nose down, and it fell on a housing estate destroying many homes - fortunately with few casualties.

The doodlebugs and later the V2 rockets did a lot of damage further inland. The rockets were terrible things, being supersonic they arrived completely without warning and exploded with devastating and completely unnerving effect.

These weapons wrought such havoc that it was decided that Bar and Tim should go up and stay with an uncle and aunt in Sutton Coldfield out of range while the danger persisted. Joan and Roland were already there.

I arranged to take the day off so that I could take Bar and Tim to Reading station and put them on the train for the Midlands. We were both miserable as Bar carried Tim and I wheeled the heavy case on the pram - not a modern folding buggy, but what my generation still calls a 'proper pram' with large wheels. The local train to Reading had been delayed as so often in wartime, and we were late arriving. The train seemed already crowded when we got to the platform and was getting ready to pull out.

I told Bar to stay where she was with Tim and the case while I whizzed along weaving in and out of the crowds, trying to find the guards' van where the pram would have to travel. Miles away, it seemed, I found it; the guard did not want to take it aboard and I argued desperately until he at last consented. Doors were slamming; "hurry up" whistles were being blown and there was a lot of shouting. I raced back to Bar and tried to find her a seat. I was beginning to despair, for the train was crowded - and at that precise moment a porter took the case from my hand and said, "Follow me sir," and briskly took us down the train where he found Bar the last seat in a compartment. He hefted the case onto the rack, and I settled Bar and Tim as best I could and kissed them both hurriedly.

The guard blew his whistle again as I stepped back on to the platform, and the porter stood beside me as we watched the train slowly pull away. I waved disconsolately but could not move for the crush of people still on the platform and only had a last fleeting glimpse of Bar and Tim, for they were not near the window. And so they went away from me. The porter, noticing my woebegone face gripped my arm and said, "Don't worry, sir, your wife and little baby will be all right." That very nearly undid me. I gruffly thanked him, thrust a generous tip into his hand, and fled the station. A tidal wave of emotion engulfed me like the breaching of a dam and I found a deserted spot behind some buildings in the station yard where I wept, great racking sobs that seemed to scour my whole being, no doubt releasing tensions that had been building up for months, now finding some release at the sympathetic word of a complete stranger. I stayed in the protective shadows of that dark corner until I had regained some control.

Back in my lonely and not very pleasant digs that night, I phoned Sutton Coldfield to find out if they had arrived safely and how they had fared. The journey had not been at all bad; everyone in the compartment had been very kind and had made a fuss of Tim and he had allowed some of them to nurse him for a time. This, said Bar, had probably saved his life, for as he was sitting on the knee of a lady opposite the train had jolted suddenly, and Bar's heavy case had fallen from the rack over her head and had landed across her knees. Had Tim been on her lap it would have landed on his head and would almost certainly have broken his neck and crushed him. As she spoke to me she was still getting over the shock.

I longed at that moment to rush to her and take her in my arms, and I heard myself say, "O darling, can't we get married, won't you marry me soon?" There was dead silence for a few moments, and I said, "Bar, are you there?" Then a small voice, "O darling, I don't think you really mean it." She had her feet more firmly on the ground than I had at that moment - perhaps she always had - and a part of me, deeper than the present emotion, knew that she was right. Ours was indeed a 'funnylove.'

We were both bewildered by the way our lives seemed continually to converge and then part again. It appeared that we had to settle for a very real but distant relationship. I know I can say that she was always *in* my life, and from what she told me in later years, she felt the same about me, I was always *in* her life. The telephone call to Sutton Coldfield was a definitive moment, and from then on we both concentrated on getting on with life in the present and tried to leave the future in other hands; we both had enough faith to believe that we could entrust our future, together or apart, to God.

I found life inexpressibly dreary now. Bar and I wrote to one another only rarely and I became increasingly lonely. From time to time I would meet a very nice girl whom I would pursue hoping that in time she would fully replace Bar in my affections. I loved them up to a point but always in the end had to face the fact that I was still hooked on my Girl in the Middle. I think I was very selfish and caused some hurt for which I am deeply sorry.

I was also feeling restless in my job and began to think it was time for a change - I had been in Portsmouth for five years, which was a long time to stay in the parish of one's title.

By now the war in Europe was clearly in its last phase and this also made me feel ready to move on. Others were on the move too. Jock Murray who, having been vicar of St Francis' Isleworth for a short time after leaving Hampton, had gone to Glasgow as Provost of St Mary's Cathedral. I now heard that he had been appointed Vicar of St Mary's Hendon in North West London, an ancient and important church and parish.

The next time I was having a few days off with mother and Geoff I gave Jock a ring and was invited to dinner. He questioned me closely about my life in Portsmouth and then asked if I felt ready for a move yet - and when I said the idea had occurred to me he asked if I would be interested in joining him as priest-in-charge of his daughter church of St Mary Magdalene, Holders Hill. He explained that the present incumbent would be moving on within the year and he would like me to take over in due course. He said it was rather a problem place and it would not be an easy job; "Its a bit of an Aegean stable," he said. "I'd like you to come in and clean it up. Anyway, think about it and let me know sometime; there's no immediate hurry."

I had always been considerably in awe of Jock Murray and I could hardly credit that the great man, who had prepared me for confirmation and taught me much of what I knew, was actually offering me a job on his staff! However, I did not need any time to think; I said at once that I would love to join him in Hendon when the job became available; I would have to give six months notice to my present vicar. He said he could not offer me the job formally until the present man gave in his notice, but he did not think it would be very long before he did so.

I went home that night feeling very excited; to work with Jock! Phew! Life took on a different complexion now and there was much to look forward to.

Victory in Europe, VE Day, eventually arrived. On the evening the Nazis surrendered I opened the church doors, switched on all the lights, and lit the candles on the altar, which could be seen from the street.

A few weeks later came the formal letter from Jock offering me the post of Priest-in-Charge of St Mary Magdalene, Holders Hill. He would like me to arrive as soon as possible. In anycase I should come to see the church and the parish the next time there was an opportunity. Then the sting in the tail: 'There is a Parsonage house that you will have to live in - you had better marry Barbara quickly; much cheaper than a housekeeper!' I took a deep breath, got out my typewriter, and replied that I would be delighted to accept his offer, that I would be going to Hampton in about a fortnight and would give him a ring to see when it would be convenient for me to come over to Hendon and 'case the joint.' I ignored the advice to marry Bar.

I had just given in my notice to my vicar when a letter came from the Bishop of Portsmouth. The atomic bombs on Hiroshima and Nagasaki having brought the war in the Far East to a rapid end, the allies were now marshalling their forces for the occupation of Japan. The Bishop said he wanted me to go to Japan as an Army Chaplain. He was furious with me for refusing on the grounds that I had already accepted a new job in the London diocese. I said that when his letter arrived I was on the point of writing to tell him about this. I must say I had slight qualms of conscience about refusing this posting - for one thing it would have been a way of fulfilling the obligation to work for a time overseas that had been attached to my college bursary. However, this job in Hendon had been tacitly agreed between Jock and me for the best part of nine months and I did not feel it would be right to back out now. Dick Herrick and my vicar both agreed that I should go to Hendon.

They too were on the move. Norman Millard, the vicar, had been appointed a Canon Residentiary of Peterborough Cathedral, and Dick and I went there in my borrowed car for his installation. In the meantime Dick remained in charge of St Mark's. Soon afterwards he in turn was offered and accepted the parish of St Michael and All Angels, Northampton, and was inducted to the living in 1947 soon after Norman Millard's successor arrived at St Mark's. So within a few months almost half the staff of St Mark's left for other jobs - we had all been together for five years or more.

From time to time during those war years Norman would take his entire staff out to dinner, nearly always at the famous Kepple's Head Hotel on the Hard near the main gate of the

Dockyard and within sight of Nelson's flagship, HMS Victory. This was a splendid place and in spite of rationing nearly always managed to produce a decent meal. It was a favourite haunt of naval officers and clergy; the place always seemed stiff with gold braid and a fairly liberal sprinkling of dog-collars. Norman gave us all a splendid farewell meal here before half of us went our several ways.

I do wish Bar and I were going to be married, it would have been so marvellous for us to have been with Jock and Marjorie. Shall I ask her again? But I didn't.

I knew she was seeing a lot of Bertie Page.

The bewilderment remained.

5
Hendon

Jock took me to see St Mary Magdalene's church in Holders Hill. The church and Parsonage were set back from the main road between Hendon and Mill Hill. Next door, just to make me feel at home, was a stonemason's yard with a lot of marble crosses, dull looking angels, open books and doric columns strewn haphazardly all over the place - an inspiring view over the fence. Beyond the stonemason's was the local Crematorium. At least I would be able to nip quickly from my front door to conduct funerals.

We went first to the church, which I liked immediately. It was a wooden dual purpose building, with a large sanctuary which could be curtained off with beautiful dark brown velvet curtains. However, it was now used almost exclusively as the church because a hall had been built behind it. The sanctuary was quite deep and wide, and on one side had a choir vestry and on the other a sacristy. The altar had six quite nice gilt wooden candlesticks and a cross. A beautiful silver sanctuary lamp hung from the middle of the arch with a red oil lamp burning. There were choir stalls and clergy stalls and a pulpit. At the west end there was a small gallery in which was installed a hand-blown organ with two manuals. My new little church had been nicely designed; in fact I thought it quite charming. I knew I was going to be very happy with this church as the centre of my work and prayer for the Church of God in Holders Hill. There was quite definitely an atmosphere in the place - it *felt* like a church. I could see it had considerable potential, and I could not wait to start making improvements.

We retraced our steps down the drive to the Parsonage: again a nicely designed small house with a deep verandah from which the front door opened. A small study on the left immediately inside the door. A medium sized kitchen, and a large sitting-room with a small dining alcove. Upstairs there was a good bathroom and three double bedrooms. The windows of the sitting room and the master bedroom above looked out on to the drive, with two long rosebeds flanking the short front path. A lovely set-up, I thought, and Jock seeing my satisfaction said, "I think and hope you will be very happy here. There are some very nice people here; some very *good* ones in the best sense of that word. There are also some who seem to get at odds with everyone else, so I am afraid it is not a very happy little place at present, and I expect you will have some difficult times, as I told you when we first talked about your coming here. But I will back you up." I was to learn that he was a hard taskmaster, but totally loyal to his staff. A grand man but not an easy one to work for.

Back at the Vicarage for lunch, Marjorie now weighed in with her good wishes for my time there and offered any help she could give. What was I going to do about a housekeeper? I told her that dear old Aunt Olive was coming to see me in and stay a few weeks while I decided. Of course Aunt was thrilled to bits at the idea, but I knew she would not want to stay for very long; it would mean too much work for her and in anycase she was committed to looking after Gran.

During lunch Marjorie enthused about the young priest whom Jock had trained in Glasgow and who was coming to join the staff at Hendon. "O, Alastair is a wonderful priest, one of the best that Jock has ever trained. He's a brilliant scholar too, he'll go a long way; it will be wonderful having him here." She went on and on about this paragon of priesthood, so much so that I began to dislike him quite heartily, and felt my old inferiority complex raising its grisly head again.

O well, I thought, he'll be at the parish church and I shall be on my own at Holders Hill, so I don't suppose I shall see much of him. Nevertheless from what I'd heard I began to dread the thought of meeting him. Marjorie, as an afterthought said, "And Peggy his wife is sweet too."

In February 1946 I moved into The Parsonage in Holders Hill, NW4. Mother and I had been to second-hand shops and bought basic furniture; the family had turned out a few unwanted items, and bits and pieces of crockery and bedding etc., and the place was livable in. In fact my sittingroom was quite cosy; I had acquired a couple of very comfortable armchairs, I had already got a desk and I had made a writing table with drawers when I was in the old firm.

The following day Mother and Geoff and Joan brought Aunt with them when they came for the Induction that evening. Usually priests-in-charge were not inducted, but Jock had laid on a big 'do' for me, even to the extent of getting the Bishop of Willesden to come and induct me in person. I was very moved; the church was packed to the doors, Jock said some nice things, the Bishop gave me a great welcome, and the parish had provided a big spread in the hall afterwards. After that the family went home, and Aunt installed herself as my housekeeper.

Aunt greatly enjoyed herself in the succeeding weeks, and the people of the parish made a great fuss of her and inevitably came under the sway of her charm. I loved having her there, not least because I knew she was so delighted to be at close quarters with me as I exercised my ministry. I believe and hope that she felt she was getting some return on all the sacrifices she had made to help me to be ordained. Also, she had told me some years before that when she was young she had wanted to be a missionary and this desire found some sort of vicarious fulfilment in those weeks as she answered the phone and took messages, and generally involved herself in my ministry and the life of the parish.

Aunt was out one late afternoon when there was a ring at the door and I opened it to find a tall young priest in a black coat standing there. He was looking at me rather severely down a longish nose, and he said,in an unmistakably Scottish voice, "You will be Ernie Singleton; I'm Alastair Haggart." O my hat, here at last was the dreaded confrontation! However, I stuck out my hand and said, "Call me George, and come on in." So in he came, and I took his coat and sat him in one of my comfy chairs which he amply filled. I said, "Is it too early for a beer?" - it was about 5.30 and of course had been dark for some time. "Not too early for me," he said. I thought I detected a note of relief in his voice. I left him while I went to get bottles of beer and glasses - and to summon up my calm and unflappable exterior. "Cheers," we said to each other, and drank long and deep. "That's good", and then, coming straight to the point: "You know George I've been dreading meeting you!" "Dreading meeting *me?*" I hooted, "Good heavens, *I* have been absolutely terrified meeting *you!!* Why on earth have you been dreading meeting *me?*" "Well," he said, "every time I've seen Marjorie Murray since I arrived in the parish a month ago she has been saying what a marvellous young priest was coming to take over St Mary Magdalene's, etc. etc." - word for word what she had said to me about him, except for the 'brilliant scholar' bit of course. I told him she had been saying precisely the same to me about him, which was why I had been dreading meeting him too. We looked at one another in astonishment and then roared with laughter, all the ice shattering and melting away in a warm wave of fellowship that endures to this day.

Alastair and Peggy and I cemented a permanent friendship there in Hendon and the three of us spent a lot of our free time together. It has been for me one of the richest friendships with which my life has been blessed, and there is none I value more.

The winter of 1946/47 was one of the hardest for many long years; the ice did not thaw on the roads for two whole months. Fortunately Aunt returned home before the worst weather arrived. I spent a great deal of my time trying to get coal for housebound people who were in danger of dying of hypothermia. The country was bankrupt after the war, rationing had been tightened, things that had been available during the war were now in short supply. Electricity and coal were rationed. It was illegal to switch on an electric fire before noon, and there were other times as well when the use of electric fires was forbidden. It was a thoroughly miserable winter and there was much privation. Our church was heated by a coke-fired boiler, and it was my responsibility to see that the fire was stoked. We could only really afford to use the boiler at weekends and in the end the frost got the better of me and the pipes burst.

The following Sunday I encouraged people to bring blankets and hot water bottles to church with them. At the Offertory, when I poured the water into the wine it froze as it went down the side of the chalice. I decided we could not worship in these conditions and the following Sunday I moved all the furniture out of my sitting room, rigged up an altar in my dining alcove, lit a good fire in the grate, and we all stood packed together like sardines, but warm and cheerful and happy. It turned out to be a super Parish Communion - which we sang in the usual way. A decibel counter would have blown its top!

I waded in at Holders Hill, and thoroughly enjoyed the work. The congregation was much more of a mixture of people from different traditions of churchmanship than the Hilsea one had been. Here there were High, Middle and Low church people. Some called me 'Father' from the start, which I liked - my predecessor had discouraged it and preferred to be called 'Mr.'. I thought 'Father' suggested the right sort of relationship between a priest and his people. I was thirty-one in 1946, and some of the older members of the congregation thought that for me to be called 'Father' seemed ridiculous - one of the ladies said to me one day, "When I hear people calling you 'Father' I want to call you 'Sonny'!" I hope I had the grace to laugh, though I'm afraid I took myself rather seriously in those days.

Dick Herrick had introduced St Mark's Portsea to the Anglican Young People's Association, which had been brought to this country from Canada by Ernie Southcott, known to all as 'Tiny' on account of his great height, a fellow student with him at Mirfield. With the AYPA the 'in' word was *Koinonia* - a New Testament Greek word meaning the many sided fellowship, that Christians ought to have with one another and with our Lord, inspired by the Holy Spirit. This *Koinonia* was one of the characteristic experiences of the early Christians as described in the Acts of the Apostles. I had seen among our own branches in Portsmouth and in those from other parishes with whom we often joined for week-end conferences, a wonderful 'coming together into a unity of people with differing backgrounds, and the growth of Christian love and mutual service.

By the time I arrived in Hendon I was very hot on *'koinonia'* and it seemed to me that this was the aspect of Christian belief and practice that I should teach to a congregation not very strong on mutual love and service. I spent most of my time in Holders Hill trying to do just that; not only by teaching, but trying to think of different practical ways in which we could actually experience the many sided truths of *'koinonia'*.

"First of all" I said, "we have a little gem of a church here; lets polish it up a bit, for if we care for the *place* of our worship our worship of God will be enriched." So we thought about our church. First, the floor. Horrible, unvarnished wood. It had never been treated by anything more than the occasional wet mop and the infrequent broom. In the course of my house-to-house visiting I had met a very nice Frenchman who told me he made a special sort of floor stain that was very hard wearing. The result of our talk was that he sent a team of men who treated the church floor with two coats of dark brown stain that left it with a slight sheen but a non-slip surface. It transformed the place - and he only charged for the cost of the materials. He was a lapsed Roman Catholic, but of course knew how to treat the Church, being one of those buttresses which stand outside and support it, rather than a pillar that supports it from the inside.

When in Portsmouth I had often gone to St Philip's church Cosham, built by Sir Ninian Comper the great Anglican church architect. His theory was that when people go into a church they ought immediately to be reminded of heaven. He had adopted what in my opinion is the most graceful of the neo-gothic styles; his churches are full of light and colour, and always have a free standing altar under a beautiful *baldachino*, a canopy standing on burnished gold pillars, suggesting the glorious 'Throne of God' - Heaven! By the time I was thinking about St Mary Magdalene's at Holders Hill Sir Ninian had died, but I knew that his son Sebastian was following in his father's footsteps and lived in Little Venice in London. I went to see him and said I wanted a refurbished sanctuary, but had very little money. He was very nice to me and came to have a look, and stayed to lunch.

Sebastian Comper cut his fees down to a minimum and produced a plan that we liked and for which we felt sure we could raise the necessary money. He brought the altar forward leaving a passageway behind it that connected the choir vestry on one side to the sacristy on the other. He made a beautifully decorated door on either side of the altar, and behind the altar a simple panelled reredos, richly painted in red and gold. What a transformation! The place looked, as indeed it was becoming, a shrine of devotion, and people said that when they went in they felt enfolded by the quiet and their spirits were uplifted by the beauty of the sanctuary. The sanctuary lamp with its live flame burning steadily gave those most important aids to worship and prayer: a sense mystery, a hint of the numinous - *a loving presence,* a serene enfolding warmth. All so vitally necessary not only for prayer and worship in the narrow sense, but for the health of the human spirit.

Having got our centre to rights, we then organised 'parish weekends' which began in church on Saturday morning with prayer for the guidance of the Holy Spirit on our fellowship, our *koinonia.* then moved to the hall for a lecture followed by group discussion of set questions. A 'bring enough for one' lunch followed where we pooled the food and then shared it out. The afternoon was free and some went home to do weekend chores; others sat in my sitting room or in the hall and chatted. After tea came another lecture and discussion groups followed by a full reporting session where each group told of its conclusions and the questions that had been raised, which we tried to answer. Evensong was sung in church, followed by a 'bring your own and share' supper. Afterwards the tables were cleared, chairs to the walls, and a few games were played to let off steam, and then records put on the old radiogram for dancing. The day ended in church again for Compline and preparation for communion tomorrow.

As is quite common when Christians have spent a day experiencing the unifying effect of thinking, talking, playing and worshipping together, the eucharistic worship on that Sunday morning had an entirely new quality to it. There was a real sense of unity among all age groups that had participated the previous day - and all age groups from teenagers and upwards had done so. The youngest participant was five and the oldest over 90! In fact we had, quite simply, experienced the presence and the guidance of the Holy Spirit, drawing us together in our Lord, binding us into one family - in short we had experienced *Koinonia.*

The usual Sunday routine was followed, early mass, Parish Communion, Sunday School in the afternoon. After Evensong we had a short summing up of the weekend, then a full scale parish party with much dancing and lots of games and tremendous hilarity and joy. The weekend ended with Compline in church, a conducted meditation, and dedication to God's service in the week to come as we were bidden to 'go forth into the world to love and serve the Lord'. We all began to realise that prayer and thinking and talking and fun and games, the whole of life, is a unity and every bit of it another facet of the worship of God through our Lord Jesus Christ who 'took our human nature upon him'. All brought about by the power and guidance of the Holy Spirit.

We also arranged a series of concerts at which we invited young music students to play in order to gain experience. Quite a large number of them were delighted to do so. For these occasions we drew the velvet curtains across the sanctuary, rearranged the chairs in semicircles so that the church was converted into a small concert hall. The municipal Parks Superintendent, who was a member of the congregation at St Mary's Hendon, the parish church, sent two men and a van full of pots of maidenhair fern and begonias, and built a wonderful bank of colour and delicate green against the dark brown curtains. In front of that stood the gleaming concert grand piano another well-wisher always provided for us. We had the programmes nicely printed on hand-made paper. We could not charge for entry as we had no entertainments licence but we were able to sell the programmes and usually made enough to break even. Before the performances I would tell the audience that this concert represented the Christian Church claiming the world of the arts for God.

At Christmas and Easter we would invite the Langley Players, formed by the priest-actor Rector of Langley, with his actress wife, son and daughter, to come with the rest of their very able company and put on Nativity and Mystery plays. These were always a tremendous success; they were acted in the open church, and always made a profound contribution to the devotional preparation for the forthcoming festival.

After Aunt had reluctantly gone home, the recently widowed mother of a priest friend of mine came as my temporary housekeeper with her two daughters, which helped them while their affairs were being sorted out. When they moved on I found a large Welsh lady who had been housekeeper in one of the local big houses and who wanted a lighter job so that she could spend most of her time doing the catering for other people's dinner parties. Looking after me was her lighter job, and we got on very well; she became a member of the congregation, very cheerful, with a great laugh - and a lot used to amuse her! She was also very heavy, and at that time I had taken over the master bedroom as my study. This was very nice: I looked out on to the drive and my lovely rose beds backed by a line of tall poplars. It was a very peaceful room, and with my desk in the window I could see everyone who came up the drive to visit me or to go on into the church. The only disadvantage of being on the first floor was that my heavy housekeeper always ran upstairs, very frequently, and when I sat at my desk I had to stop writing because the whole house shook as she came charging up the staircase. But we got on fine, and when we had our concerts and other functions in the church she would lay on wonderful buffet suppers for the musicians and actors.

St Mary Magdalene's was humming, I could hardly believe that I had been instrumental in bringing it all about. This young priest, with a chip on his shoulder because of his inferior education who had been ordained only reluctantly by his bishop, seemed to be doing quite well at Holders Hill. I have to confess that it rather went to my head and I became very conceited. Once I said to Alastair, " O well, what St Mary Magdalene's does today, every other church in the deanery starts doing tomorrow!" Alastair, guardian of my soul, looked severely down his nose and said in his lovely Scottish voice, "George, that's so nearly true that ye should never say it!"

Of course it was not all plain sailing, far from it. The difficulties about which Jock had warned me soon materialised. There were those on the Church Committee who constantly opposed me. Worse, there were the people who seemed always to be antagonising others and making trouble in the congregation. On one occasion, not long after one of our very successful parish weekends, when a further deepening of *Koinonia* seemed to have occurred, one of the trouble makers caused an unholy row to break out. I thought, O dear, Here we are again - back to square one. As so often in small closely knit communities, it was all over a fairly trivial matter. Two organizations wanted the use of the hall on the same evening; one catered for the older members of the church, and the other some of the young people. If I remember rightly the leader of the youth section asserted roundly that the young people were of course far more important. The two protagonists had fallen out before and I think it would be true to say that they could not stand one another. Well, that is only human and happens in the best regulated societies - after all, we are nowhere enjoined to *like* one another; Christian 'love of neighbour' is something different. It had something to do with churchmanship - the older member was low-church, and the young man was very 'high'. I had sympathy with both sides, for I could see the point of view of each. but that did not excuse the insensitive remark and lack of charity. The arrogant remark spoken in the heat of the moment provoked a large explosion, with the various groups in the congregation vociferously taking sides. I was enormously saddened and very angry when I heard about it.

O Lord what am I going to do with these people? And suddenly I knew. I called the culprit into my study - and as he came he was grinning and rubbing his hands. He said, "Coo, I haven't half put the cat among the pigeons!" "Yes, I said, sit down." I

114

looked at him seriously for a few moments. Then, "I think I ought to tell you that you have put the work of the Church of God here *back at least two years.*" I talked in this vein for a long time. By the end the smile had disappeared and he looked very chastened. I continued, "You can leave it as it is, and in time it will 'blow over' as we say - the wound will heal on the surface, but it will not heal inside; it will go on festering and the damage you have done will take a long long time to be repaired - it *will* be repaired in time, because the Holy Spirit always wins in the end, but in the meantime you have really thrown a spanner in the works".

"What can I do?" in a small voice, crestfallen.

"Well, there is one thing you can do, which would not only restore the situation, but could even put the work of the church here *forward* by a number of years. You could make a public confession of sin! Forgiven sin, by the wonderful dispensation of the Holy Spirit, can be the beginning of great spiritual advance, both for the individual and for the church."

He went as white as a sheet while I explained that he would not be the first Christian to do this, it was a common practice in the early church and still used today in many parts of the church.

I went on to explain that I was certainly not an advocate of the public confession of *personal* sin, as practiced by Moral Rearmament, but only, as in this case, sin that is known to all and has affected the church community.

"The way we would do it is this: after the Gospel at the Parish Communion, I would say that you have something to say to the congregation. You would then tell them that you are sorry for the distress you have caused them and ask for their forgiveness. After this you could go out of the church, if you wish, or stay. But I would then preach about the need to confess, on you part, and the obligation to forgive on ours". I concluded, "Now go into church and think about it and I will pray that the Holy Spirit will guide you as to what you should do and give you the strength to do it - I can only make the suggestion; it is for you to decide whether this is what you should do or not. I will accept your decision whatever it is".

He went out and came back some time later. He looked at me and said, "I'll do it". My admiration for him soared, for he was a good man at heart and I appreciated his sterling qualities very much. It was all very well for me to pontificate, but what a tremendous thing it was that I had suggested he should do! And what sheer guts it took for him to agree to do it!

The Parish Communion that Sunday is unforgettable, I can see it clearly in my mind as I write. A rather listless congregation assembling, a lot of people still clearly upset - a few 'regulars' had not even had the heart to come.

The Gospel is read and concluded. I begin to speak, everyone sits up suddenly and pays acute attention as what I am saying begins to sink in. The cause of all the trouble, the target of angry glances until now, going to *confess* and *apologise?!!* He steps forward to my side, and says he accepts the blame, he unreservedly apologises, and ends, "Please forgive me".

Then, back to his place, no ducking out and away, but ready to look people in the eye again.

I then say, "I hope we all realize what a courageous thing it is that we have just witnessed, how much prayer and reliance upon the Holy Spirit it must have taken. What joy there must be in the kingdom of heaven, as our Lord said, 'over one sinner that repents', what joy there should be in us too. The sin that disrupted the harmony of the church here has been forgiven by God - and let none of *us* dare to withhold our own forgiveness".

A very different congregation left the church that morning from the one that had come in. All gloom had been dispelled; there was an outpouring of joy. Several people went shyly to the forgiven man and shook his hand and gave him a smile. He and I both felt exhausted but at peace. The work of the church went forward, and the wounds were healed.

My Girl in the Middle surfaced again briefly during my time at St Mary Magdalene's. She rang me up to say that her father was dying and asking me to pray. A few days later he died and the family asked if I would conduct the funeral, which of course I was very happy to do, for I had been fond of the old man and he had always been very kind to me - he used to refer to me as 'The Bishop!'

Bar's father was another pipe smoker and therefore in my eyes a trusty. I remembered that I had always admired - and, *mea culpa*, coveted - a beautiful Dunhill pipe of his. Some time after the funeral, after what I considered a decent interval, I rang Bar up and said that if it was still around and there were no other claimants I'd love to have that pipe as a little memento of him. I said I would send it back to Dunhills and they would recondition it and fit a new mouthpiece. She was delighted with the idea and said she would take it to Dunhills herself, she knew them well because Bertie always bought his pipes there - another trusty? - well, yes he was really; a very nice chap.

A few weeks later she was on the phone again saying she had the pipe and when could she bring it over to me? She came for coffee one morning and gave me the beautiful Dunhill which became

116

my pride and joy and which I kept and smoked for many years. As always she was looking ravishing, and I kept thinking, *O dear, if only*.... However, she told me that she was going to marry Bertie quite soon; she said she really did love him, but it was a different love from the love she had had, and still had, for Peter, and Bertie understood and accepted this. I encouraged her in that belief because I was sure it was true. There may well be only one overriding love in our lives but that does not mean that there cannot be other loves and those loves can be perfectly genuine and very deep.

I became very lonely at Holders Hill and again for a time I consciously looked around to see whether I could find someone to step into the empty place in my life left by my finally giving up hope of marrying Bar. There were many very nice girls around, especially at the parish church. But I still found no-one who could really replace Bar in my heart, so I tried after a while to accept that loneliness was my lot, and as far as I could manage I stopped thinking about it.

One morning I had been into the church to say Matins, and as I came out of the church door a little black cat came up to me with his tail in the air and said, "Meeow", so I politely said "Meeow" in return and continued striding down to the house. I was wanting my breakfast and had thoughts for little else at that moment. I swept up the steps, my cassock swishing, flung open the door and slammed it behind me. As the echoes of the slam faded away into silence I heard from the other side of the door, "MEEEOOW!!" I opened the door again and there was the little black cat, still with tail in the air, who giving me a cold and offended glance, walked in as though he owned the place - and stayed for eight years.

I had been taken over and I had been given a tiny but welcome companion to relieve my loneliness just a little. He came into the kitchen and rubbed around my ankles under my cassock. Before getting my own breakfast I gave him a saucer of bread and milk. He squatted down and as he lapped and ate he began to purr - he was home. I was eating my toast and looking at the paper and there was an air of contentment in the kitchen. When he had finished he delicately licked his lips with a little pink tongue, groomed himself for a few minutes - then in an agile leap he was on my shoulders and curling himself round my neck like a fur collar.

Of course I loved him at once, and he followed me wherever I went except when I went out into the street. He would probably come as far as the gate, then sit down and watch me go. As soon as

I returned he would be ready again to be my small shadow. We got on like a house on fire; I called him Cat for the time being until a more imaginative name occurred to me. Whenever I sat down he would jump on my lap and purr, or play his favourite game of being my fur collar. I would sit reading with him draped round my neck, warm and comforting.

The question of a suitable name for Cat was solved by one of my churchwardens - he called him Satan, "because he follows you about," he said. So Satan he became. He came to church with me every morning. While I said Matins he would curl up under the prayer-desk, and would sleep while I made my meditation, and then come home with me afterwards and we would have breakfast together. The same for Evensong and supper.

There's no doubt about it,Satan was a very devout cat; he never missed a service on Sundays, and liked the Parish Communion best. He would always keep an eye on the offertory and when the sidesmen brought the collection to be presented at the altar, Satan always followed them up the aisle, tail in air and walking sedately. The people loved him, especially the children, though he always kept his dignity and would not allow overmuch familiarity.

The following Lent I asked Jock to preach a course of sermons at Evensong. Satan was in his usual place in church on the first evening. It was a good sermon and promised to be a very good course, as I had confidently expected from Jock. Satan must have thought so too, for on the following Sunday evening, just before the service was due to begin, Satan came into church, *followed by another cat.* He had brought a friend to hear the Vicar! Satan led the other cat up the aisle and the two of them sat at the foot of the pulpit. The congregation and I nearly had hysterics. Jock, busy with his notes, looked over the top of his glasses and gave a broad grin as he saw the cats. He loved animals and always treated them like human beings.

Came the Annual Parochial Church Meeting at the parish church, and as usual I was called upon to present a report on the past year at St Mary Magdalene's. Financial details, number of baptisms and communicants, various activities. All seemed quite healthy. "We have some new names for the Electoral Roll - one looking rather strange, just the one word, Satan! No, we have not been taken over by the Devil, at least I hope not. Satan is the name of the little black cat who has adopted me and taken up residence in the Parsonage. But he is a very devout cat and there is no more regular member of the congregation. He is at every service, comes to Mass regularly and always comes with me to Matins; he sits beside me and says the alternate verses of the psalms."

Much laughter, cheering up the rather dull business of the Annual Parochial Church Meeting.

On Friday morning I open the local paper, and there on page one is a headline SATAN GOES TO CHURCH. Later that morning the telephone rings. It is a reporter from the Daily Mail. "I read in your local paper, Sir, that you have a very remarkable cat, named Satan I think?" "Yes that's right." "Does he really come to church as often as the report says?" "O yes, he certainly does." "Ah, hum, er, (rather embarrassed) Does he, er, in, er - some way make some sort of response when you are, er, saying matins?" "Er, w-e-l-l," I say. "O yes, Sir, I see, a bit of poetic license I guess, Ha Ha, and why not?" Well, thank you very much, Sir." The line goes dead and I put the phone down with a grin, Silly ass!

On Monday morning a parishioner rings to ask if I have I seen the Daily Mail, because Satan is on the front page! I nip across the road to the newsagents and get a copy, and sure enough, there he is on the front page, bottom right hand corner, big letters, SATAN GOES TO CHURCH. Back home I tell Satan, "You know, you are now a very famous cat, what do you think of that, eh?" He looks at me and gives me one of his silent grins, converts it into a yawn, becomes my fur collar - and goes to sleep. *That's* the way to treat fame, I thought, just yawn at it, and go to sleep. *O Satan, I wish I could learn that lesson from you!* But, as I am sure is quite clear by now, I never did.

Apart from the' responding at Matins bit in this Satan Saga, I lie not.

When I lost my old spiritual director Basil Daniell, I asked Guy Sanderson, a friend of many years standing and a very experienced priest, if he would take me on, which he generously agreed to do. He was rector of Woodham in Surrey and he and his family always made me welcome. I saw quite a lot of him and I had told him all about Bar and how our paths seemed to keep crossing but somehow did not fuse. He was keen that I should get married and without my realizing it made opportunities for me to meet some of his young people. But of course nothing came of that and after a time he gave up.

Some time after Bar had married Bertie and I had not found anyone to take her place, it suddenly came to me one morning during my meditation that I might, just might be being called to try a vocation to the Religious Life. Good heavens, surely not, not *I!* What nonsense, I thought, I am quite unsuitable; I am built for marriage, not celibacy. I had first heard of Mirfield during the Anglo

Catholic Congress that had had such a profound influence upon me when I was in my teens. I had learned a lot about the Community from Father Hand at Tatterford, but I had not been to Mirfield until Dick Herrick took me for a priests' retreat while I was in Portsmouth. I had loved the place from that moment. But as for living that sort of life permanently, the thought never for a moment crossed my mind. I was the marrying sort ... *O Bar, if only ....*

After breakfast that morning I was on the phone to Guy. "Guy, I hope you will disabuse me of this idea at once - its quite ridiculous, but I've suddenly had the daft idea that I might be being called to try a vocation at Mirfield!" I expected a dismissive laugh and an "O no, old man, you are the marrying sort if ever I saw one." But no, instead, there was dead silence, and then he said, "Well, old man, I've thought so for a very long time, but I haven't dared to say." *Phew! Gosh! I can't believe it. O my goodness me, 'I am undone,'* as Holy Scripture has it. That needed a lot of thinking about. Of course, I reminded myself, a vocation has to be tested. I've still got lots to do here, if I try a vocation at Mirfield I'll have to leave, and I've only been here for just over two years. O no, perhaps if the idea persists - in a couple of years time when I've shot my bolt here. I'll put it out of my mind for a couple of years, then think again.

Easier said than done: like the tongue constantly returning to a hole in a tooth, I could *not* stop thinking about it, mostly with dismay.

After a few weeks I took some leave and went to Mirfield to talk to Raymond Raynes the Superior. As I arrived and was shown to my room in the Retreat House adjoining the community house, I had to admit that it all felt familiar and homely. Raymond was encouraging and after I had told him a lot about myself he said he thought I might have a vocation, but it would have to be tested. When I felt ready he would accept me as an Aspirant, that is a person who is actively thinking about trying his vocation at some future date: someone who has declared this intention, but has not finally decided to apply for admission to the Novitiate. Then, he said, if you decide to come here to try your vocation, we shall welcome you. When you arrive you will immediately become a Postulant, which means that you are now intending to try your vocation and enter the Novitiate. Whether you do so or not depends upon whether the community decides to accept you as a novice. So that the brethren can get to know you, and you can get to know them, you will live alongside us and 'live the life' with us for about six to eight weeks. If at the end of that time you still want to try your vocation I will consult the brethren in Chapter and if they agree I will admit you to the Novitiate.

While you are a Postulant you will retain the use of your own money, wear your own clothes and cassock. You will not sit in choir, but in the nave of the church. You will be free to leave at any time if you decide to do so. But you will be expected to keep the same rule as the novices, and share their life and work.

If at the end of your Postulancy you still wish to go ahead and the community agrees, you will be admitted to the novitiate one morning at a High Mass and you will be given the habit of the community, which in our case is a simple English double-breasted cassock, with one of our regulation belts with the small cross hanging from it which is the insignia of a novice. You will surrender all your money to the Bursar which will be kept in trust for you until such time as you either leave the novitiate and return to secular life, or move on to First Profession, which lasts for five years before making your Final Profession.

As soon as you become a novice you will be given a 'float' of ten pounds; from that you may take two pounds a month as what we call *Peculium*, and with that two pounds you may buy anything you like, such as sweets or tobacco etc., and you do not have to account for it. The rest of the ten pounds you spend on necessities like toothpaste, shaving cream, a new pair of socks, bus fares for local journeys, etc. With the money you will be given a form on which you make a note of all the necessary expenditure. When the ten pounds has dwindled to a couple of pounds or so you take the form to the Bursar and he replaces what you have spent, bringing your 'float' back to ten pounds again. Large necessary items of expenditure you consult the Bursar about and if he agrees he will give you the money.

The Novitiate for a priest lasts for two years, and for a layman three. During your novitiate you are free to leave whenever you decide to do so, you are under no obligation to stay. If you do stay with us it will be seven years before you make anything like an irrevocable decision, but at First Profession you state your *intention* to remain in the community for life.

Raymond explained that at Final Profession the actual vow was also an 'intention to remain for life', but it had a more irrevocable understanding attached to it than at First Profession. The founders of the Community had been against Life Vows in the traditional monastic sense.

So I went away and thought and prayed - and before I left I saw Raymond again and said that I felt pretty sure that I would ask to come to try my vocation, and if he agreed I would like to become an Aspirant at once. He agreed, and I left feeling more at peace than I had for a very long time.

Now I had to face Jock, and that was a pretty daunting prospect, for I knew that he expected me to stay on at Holders Hill for at least another two years. I thought he would go up like a rocket, though I knew he could not deny me, for I would not let him. More than this he had the greatest admiration for the Community of the Resurrection and had known many of the Fathers for a long time. Indeed both here in Hendon and in Glasgow he had invited the Community to send one of the brethren each year to preach every night in Holy Week and to conduct the Three Hours devotion on Good Friday.

So I bearded the lion in his den and told him I had asked the Superior to accept me as an Aspirant, but I hoped that it would be a year at least before I did any more about it. I would be going to Mirfield fairly frequently, and would just have to wait and see how things developed. To begin with Jock went as red as the proverbial beetroot, and I thought he was going to explode. "But my dear boy," he expostulated, "you've only just got your feet under the table at Holders Hill, you can't think of leaving yet, surely?" "I know," I said, "but you see ..." and I told him the whole story of how I had felt for years past, and how at present it all seemed to narrow down to this, a possible vocation to the Religious Life. So in the end he sighed and said, "Yes, well, I see ... I just hope it will pass and after a few months you will come and tell me that you are remaining here after all." "Dammit, boy!" he said, "I just *can't* start looking for someone else to put at Holders Hill yet!" So I said, "Don't worry its bound to be at least a year before I am sure enough either way."

So back home to Satan and my armchair and my fur collar that purred.

I have to admit that I was not really surprised to find myself getting more and more restless in the next few weeks and months as the sense of vocation to the Religious Life continued to grow. I had put my foot on the first rung of the ladder and I found myself increasingly eager to take the next step.

I am not much of a one for school or college reunions, but that year I decided to go to Canterbury for the annual reunion at St Augustine's College. As I sauntered on to the platform at Waterloo station I spied a once-familiar figure already there waiting for the Canterbury train, Charlie Colls who had taught me printing at St Augustine's. We had not met since ordination. This was a splendid reunion, for we had been good friends, but as so often happens had simply lost touch as we became engrossed in new lives centred upon our parochial ministries.

As the train trundled through the green Kent countryside

and we brought one another up to date, I suddenly asked him, "You don't want a new job do you - a nice little church and a nice little house in the same grounds, a super Vicar who can tear you off a strip, but has a heart of gold?" "Actually," he said, "I do. I'm going to get married and I'd like a change of job as well; why do you ask?" So I told him that I was off to Mirfield to see if that was the right next thing for me, and I would like to be able to give the name of my successor to my vicar at the same time as I gave him my notice. By the time we got to Canterbury he sounded as if he was hooked, and if Jock liked him, and I felt sure he would, there could be a very smooth change-over; no long and potentially damaging interregnum, and Jock need not burst a blood vessel or even have a headache.

Charlie agreed that I give his name to Jock when I gave in my notice, which I now would do as soon as possible.

Which is just how it all turned out. As I started to tell Jock I could not wait much longer to go to Mirfield, he went red in the face and started to say, "*BUT YOU SAID ....*" "Stop right there," I said, "Yes I'm giving you my notice earlier than I expected, but I am also giving you my successor" - and I told him about Charlie Colls. "He's the same churchmanship as we are, he's worked in Africa but could not stand the climate; he's fit now, he's a very good pastor and very good with difficult people; he has a splendid sense of humour, a mind of his own - and I think you and Alastair will like him." "Humph," said Jock, and gave a melodramatic sigh. "O well, you seem to have it all fixed up, so I suppose I must accept your notice and you will be free to leave in six months time. What's this chap's phone number?" - I gave him the slip of paper with Charlie's address and phone number, and Jock swivelled round in his chair and dialled the number at once. Charlie would come over the next day.

Charlie fell in love with the whole set-up at first sight, as I thought he would. He made a big fuss of Satan who signified his approval by curling up on his lap, purring. Satan gave me a cold look which said, "You are a fickle one, and no mistake. I know you are going to forsake me, but this one's got more staying-power than you have." He was quite right; Charlie and his wife stayed for five or six years, and Satan with them until, a few years on, their first baby arrived. He then had to go, for he was very jealous of the baby and a danger to him, so there was no choice. I am not quite sure what happened to him.

The parish was quite accustomed to seeing Mirfield fathers about the place, not only during Holy Week and Easter, but at other times. In fact one of them, Fr Keith Davie, had been a predecessor of mine years before at St Mary Magdalene's. I had had him back to preach one Sunday and that had been a great success. So the members of my congregation were not altogether surprised to hear that I was to try my vocation to the Religious Life in the Community of the Resurrection.

Not long after I had announced my intention, Fr Frank Biggart CR visited Jock and Marjorie, and I was invited to tea at the Vicarage to meet him. He was stationed at the London Priory, at that time in Holland Park, so I had not seen him on my visits to the Mother House at Mirfield. He was a short, birdlike man, then in his late sixties, I suppose. There was nothing 'old' about him except his appearance: he had a razor-sharp mind and a quick wit; he was reputed to have read every novel however recently published and was a great conversationalist. When I entered the drawingroom of the Vicarage that afternoon he rose from his chair, and as Jock introduced me, bowed low over my hand and glancing at Jock with a roguish look said, "Always be very deferential to your inferiors, you never know when they may become your superiors." It was a splendid tea party and Father Biggart put me perfectly at my ease and kept us all entertained with stories of the community, the eccentricities of some of the brethren, and the satisfactions and tensions of the life. I found myself wondering how I was going to get through the next few months of waiting.

I need not have worried, for there was so much to do and to arrange over and above my work, which went on as usual of course, that there was hardly time to get it all done.

It had to be faced that I might not stay at Mirfield, in which case I would need all my goods and chattels to set up home again. Most of my furniture went into store, but I distributed quite a lot around the family - the reverse process of when I came to Holders Hill and the family gave me some of the things they could spare.

What hurt most was getting rid of most of my books; I had quite a good small theological library, but I decided that apart from the standard works I would give most of it away.

It happened that on one of my last Sundays at St Mary Magdalene's, Alastair was holding the fort by himself at the parish church in Jock's absence and he 'phoned me at lunch time and said that four young priests of the Swedish Lutheran church were with them for the Parish Communion and lunch, could I entertain them to tea and Evensong? Which I was very happy to do.

As we sat in my study over tea they were bemoaning the fact that they had spent all the currency they had been allowed to bring out of Sweden and still had not been able to buy all the theological books they wanted to take home for distribution among a large group of young clergy to which they all belonged. So, beaming largesse, I waved them to my shelves and invited them to take any books they liked because I was getting rid of most of them anyway, and told them why. They were delighted and went away with large armfuls of my precious volumes.

Of course, as nearly always happens, my family were dreadfully upset about my decision to try my vocation at Mirfield, and just could not understand it, particularly my mother. That summer Geoff had to go to Holland where he had growers who grew seed for him in conditions that were ideal for those particular seeds, and which could not be found in this country. He had similar specialist growers in the South of France and in California. He was taking Mother to Holland with him and invited me to go along too.

We stayed with friends of his in Hem hard by the Zuider Zee in the area which the Nazis had flooded with fresh water during the war, when they had breached the interior dams. The land was eventually reclaimed after the liberation of Holland, leaving every building with a straight line, at a uniform height, around its walls: the 'high water line' of the flood. Below this line the walls were grey where they had been stained by the flood water. This had left behind it an immensely rich deposit of silt, several inches thick, across the whole land. The corn and wheat grown in this silt had reached a height of six or seven feet. It was a fascinating sight; we had never seen such crops - a man could walk into a field of standing corn and disappear completely from sight.

One afternoon mother and I went for a walk together and she was very depressed and began talking about my impending departure for Mirfield. She said, "This will mean a complete break between us, won't it? Much more complete than your just leaving home to be ordained: it will be a real break, won't it?" I said I supposed it would. Did I in my heart of hearts in some way welcome that idea? I think I probably did. I had felt for a long time that mother still played too dominant a role in my life; I was still psychologically tied to her apron strings. Of course this is not unique, it is a very common phenomenon, especially with a person who has been very sickly in childhood and has needed constant care and attention in order to be reared at all. It was not all on one side either, for in some ways I had remained too close to her myself. I recalled that when I was in Portsmouth during an air raid, it was the effect that my death would have upon Mother that was my chief worry, not the effect it might have upon Bar. So yes, this would be a definitive break, for her, but also for me.

Once more, then, a train took me away from family and friends, off again into the unknown. This time they wept at home; I did not want agonised farewells on the platform, nor did they want to see me off. They knew that this time, if I stayed the course, I would be gone for at least a year and would not see them in all that time, the longest I had ever been away from home. Quite naturally, I suppose, they thought of me as going off to some grim place with high walls where I would be locked away from the world. I had not thought of disabusing their minds of these popular misconceptions about monasteries; I should have been more imaginative and understanding.

I settled down in my corner seat in a Third Class Smoking compartment of the express from Euston. I was to change at Penniston and so to Mirfield station, a grim and forbidding place where I would catch the local bus to the House of the Resurrection.

Parish priest,
Hendon 1947

6
Mirfield - To Stay or Not To Stay

Mirfield railway station was said to be the first great test of the Novitiate. Legend has it that one Aspirant arrived at Mirfield station and went no further, simply waited for the next train and went home, never to try his vocation.

In 1948 the country was nearly bankrupt as a result of the war and stringently rationed for the main staples of life. The lighting on the station was just about adequate for negotiating the stairs, of which there seemed to be an inordinate number, and no porters to show the way or carry cases. No cheerful Father Hand to welcome me as on my arrival at Tatterford, no travelling companions to reassure me. Alone on that dark and damp autumn evening I struggled down the stairs lugging my case, and out to the bus stop; not much lighting there either, just one dim lamp. The bus arrived. Steamed up windows. Humping the case inside - I received the first bit of welcome, "Coom on Faaaather, let's give thee an 'and wi that caaase," Yorkshire cheer and helpfulness that I was to know well in the future and value enormously. After a couple of stops, "Next stop t'Resurrection. This'll be weer thee wants, Faaaather? A' thowt so, Ah'll 'and thee t'caaase. Joost get theesen off t'boos first like." "Thanks very much, very kind of you, Goodnight." "G'night, Faaaather, mind 'ow thee goes then."

The bus had put me down at the back door of the community house and everywhere seemed dead quiet and deserted, not a soul to be seen anywhere, so I dumped my case in the vestibule of the Retreat House, and made my way along the connecting corridor into the Community House proper. I passed the kitchens and spied the cook working over the stove, then into the front entrance hall. I realized that I had arrived before the end of Evensong, and after a moment I could hear the faint sound of singing coming up the cloister from the church. I knew the geography well of course, so I just hung about in the hall until Evensong finished. Soon I heard the sound of quietly tramping feet, and up the cloister came a steady stream of brethren in their black cassocks with grey scapulars, gradually filing into the hall and waiting quietly in silence, some going into the Community Room that opens off the hall. The Novice Guardian also arrived and seeing me standing there he beckoned me into a side room, The Guest Parlour, where we could talk. He gave me a grave welcome and said he would show me to my room after supper, and I was to follow him into the Refectory. We went back into the hall and waited with the rest of the community in silence. As the clock struck seven, the Father Steward came from the kitchen, picked up the big brass handbell from its shelf and clanged it several times. The Community Room door opened and Father Raynes, the Superior, stalked out, crossed the hall and led the way into the Refectory, the brethren following behind. The Novice Guardian led me in and stood at the head of one of the long tables, motioning me to stand by the form next to him. When everyone was in place and there was silence, the Superior began the Latin Grace, *"Oculi omnium in te sperant Domine ...."* I knew it by heart now after my several visits so was able to join in the responses. After the grace all sat, the long form I was to share was pulled out and we all stepped over the seat and sat down. Animated conversation started at once, and there was a lot of laughter and cheerfulness. The Novice Guardian asked about my journey. I greeted those sitting near me whom I knew. I was introduced to another Postulant sitting opposite: Jack Guinness, recently arrived from New Zealand to try his vocation. His first time in England, a splendid smiling face, furrowed with the creases of suffering and laughter. He had arrived the day before, and would therefore remain my senior in the Community for the whole of our time. I took to him at once.

As I had crossed the threshold that evening I automatically ceased to be an Aspirant and immediately became a Postulant, a definite step towards eventual membership of the Community.

After supper the Novice Guardian, Fr Lawrence Wrathall, took me to my room in the Retreat House. At that time the novitiate numbered over twenty, the largest it had ever been. Consequently there were not enough rooms in the Novice Wing of the Community House to accommodate them all, so the novitiate had had to overflow into the top floor of the Retreat House. Just as there had been a 'baby bulge' after the war, so there was also a 'monkish' bulge and I was part of it. The Novice Guardian repeated what I already knew, that I would follow the same routine as the novices and attend the weekly Novice Chapter in the Chapter Room, and the lectures and devotional addresses arranged from time to time for the novitiate. He advised me about what books to read, and I told him I would like to embark upon a disciplined course of theological reading as I had missed so much during the war years in college and had only been able to read rather sporadically in my parishes. He put me on the right track about this and said I should always have four books on the go - a book of dogmatic theology, one of biblical theology, one of mystical theology, prayer etc., and a novel.

As a Postulant I learnt about community customs, one of

which was going for afternoon walks. This was an important community custom, especially on Saturday and Sunday afternoons. The brethren liked to take a novice or postulant out for a walk as a good way of becoming acquainted - but a postulant or novice did not suggest a walk to a professed brother, he always waited to be invited, so never, but never, made the first move. I was told, "It is not our way," for a novice to invite a professed brother. 'Our Way' was an important phrase in the Community vocabulary, without in the least being regimented or forced into any sort of mould, we were to find that 'our way' governed a lot of things in the communal life, there were 'unwritten laws and customs' and we gradually learnt them. It was not 'our way' for a postulant or novice to call professed brethren simply by their Christian names, as they do among themselves, but always with the prefix 'Father', or 'Brother' in the case of a professed lay brother. There were one or two brethren whom I had met several times while at Holders Hill; One in particular, a great music lover, I had invited as a special guest to one of the evening concerts at St Mary Magdalene and he had been very friendly. So when I saw him later that first evening I gave him a broad grin and expected if not a word at least a smile and a wave - but he looked right through me with a set face. No word. No wave. I was quite hurt and wondered what was biting him or what I had done. I discovered later that he did not recognise such low forms of life as Postulants; he might *occasionally* deign to have a few words with a junior novice, but you had to be fairly well on in the novitiate before he really began to give you any attention. That is, except when he might decide to take you for a walk. Then he would be his old self, cheerful and laughing, or talking seriously and listening to your opinions. But back home for a quick wash before tea, and be alongside him at the urn in the refectory getting your cup of tea, and he would look right through you again, back to square one. I learnt the hard way that one of the tests of the postulancy and novitiate was accepting being ignored by most of the brethren most of the time. Very good for the soul! As I have admitted, I was pretty pleased with myself at that time. I had acquired a reputation as a 'successful parish priest', whatever that means, and I found this treatment particularly galling. In retrospect I saw that it was very salutary for me.

When my first Christmas came I was still only a postulant, but on Christmas Day the distinction between postulants, novices and brethren was to all intents and purposes ignored. On Christmas Eve all the younger brethren who were at home at Mirfield helped in decorating the church and building the Crib in front of the altar of the Holy Nativity. The first Solemn Eucharist of

Christmas was at 11.30pm so that the consecration came at midnight. In the course of the service the *Bambino*, the figure of the Holy Child, was blessed and at the end was carried in procession to the Crib and placed in the manger. Candles were lit around the Crib symbolising the Light of Christ. Everyone then went to bed. The next morning the usual offices were said and those brethren who wished to do so said their mass. After breakfast there was a second Solemn Eucharist. After this everyone gathered in the main entrance hall where a fire was blazing in the grate and half a dozen pokers had been stuck into the fire. On the hearth stood a number of earthenware jugs of ale. Enough chairs had been collected from empty rooms in the house to accommodate all the brethren. On the hall table were boxes of biscuits, chocolates, candied fruit, nuts and raisins etc. All this transformed the hall into one large family sittingroom. As soon as most of the brethren were present the Superior swept in and wished everyone a Happy Christmas, and then, he proceeded to thrust red hot pokers into the jugs, making the Mirfield Christmas treat of mulled ale, and soon we were all sitting around the fire drinking this splendid brew with much laughter and high spirits. The Superior was in very good form and held the floor telling amusing stories. Like so many men of stature he had a schoolboy sense of humour and his laughter at his own jokes and his sense of fun were infectious.

The lunch that followed was a real feast, a traditional turkey, plum pudding, wine and all the trimmings. We even had crackers and wore paper hats. For many of the brethren lunch was followed by an equally traditional Christmas Afternoon walk. After supper most of the brethren went to their rooms, except the Superior who sat in an armchair by the fire, gathered the novices around him and any other brethren who had stayed, and regaled us all with stories and reminiscences, mostly about the community and its work in South Africa, especially Sophiatown where he had done some wonderful work, and Rhodesia. By the time we went to Compline on Christmas Day we felt that the Community of the Resurrection really was a family.

I weathered my postulancy and in the New Year Philip Smith, Jack Guinness and I were accepted for the Novitiate. Philip and I would have to take other names because there was already a Philip (Fr Speight) and a George (Fr Sidebotham) in the community, and if a postulant had the same name as a living member he had to change it on becoming a novice. The Superior interviewed postulants before he admitted them to the novitiate and it was at this interview that the change of name was discussed. Raymond Raynes said to me, "O well, you are all right, you can revert to your first name, we have not got an Ernest in the Community." I said, "O please not, Superior, its a name I have been trying to get rid of for years." He said rather sardonically, "Why? It's a perfectly good name!" I took a deep breath and decided I was not *yet* living under obedience and I would have a last fling of self-will - and proceeded to tell him why I had got rid of 'Ernest' in the first place, "You see," I said, "there was this gorgeous blonde, and one day as she lay in my arms she looked deep into my eyes and said, in her husky voice, 'Ten Little Nigger Boys digging in dead earnest, Poor Ernest!'" Raymond suddenly lost his severe 'Superior' look, grinned quickly, and said, "O I see, well, in that case .... What name do you want to take?" There had been two names suggested that Philip and I could choose between, Luke and Paul. He had had first choice because he was senior to me, and said he would like to take Luke - and I, thankfully, had been left with Paul, which is what I had wanted all along. So I told the Superior that if he had no objection I would like to take 'Paul.' He agreed. I was delighted with this third, and I hoped final, change of name. I had practiced signing Paul Singleton and had found that the 'l' of Paul flowed quite nicely into the capital 'S' of Singleton. Very satisfactory! *Thank you Lord,* I breathed, *from now on I will start being obedient and not arguing the toss and trying to get my own way.*

With admission to the novitiate, things once more took on a different hue, and I found myself loving the life - to say more every day would hardly be an exaggeration. I would pause sometimes in what I was doing and think to myself: How lucky I am to be here; what a wonderful place to be, what a wonderful life to live! *Thank you, Lord.*

I used to be very bad at getting up in the morning and it was a daily struggle to get washed and shaved and dressed in time to *walk* (Novices, like nurses, do not *run)* through the corridors of the Retreat House and the Community House and along the cloister to the church and thence to my stall before the clock struck and everyone stood for the start of Matins. But once that had been done the day unfolded smoothly in a wonderfully balanced and satisfying way. Greater Silence was observed from Compline the previous night until after *Terce* the next morning. So Matins was followed by the short office of *Prime*, after which most priest brethren and novices would say Mass every day, or at least several days a week. I was one of the majority who liked to say my daily mass. To make this possible there were seventeen altars at Mirfield, apart from the High Altar in the great sanctuary. Nine were in the main church, seven in the lower church beneath, and one in the Retreat House Oratory. Most days there were so many priests wishing to say mass that it was necessary for several masses to be said before Matins, and the majority after Prime. Very often there was a priest saying mass, with a server, at every altar in both upper and lower churches simultaneously. In the large sacristy there was a vestment chest for every altar containing a set of vestments in each of the five liturgical colours, a chalice and paten, burse and veil and all the necessary linen. I thought it all inspiring and wonderful, I suppose in a way the fulfilment of the yearnings that had been aroused by the Anglo Catholic Congress and my subsequent vocation to the priesthood. After making our thanksgiving after mass we would go to the refectory for breakfast, which was an informal meal. Within the forty or so minutes allowed for breakfast a brother would enter and leave the refectory when he wished, helping himself to porridge and bread and butter and marmalade and tea (a choice of coffee only on Sundays and Greater Feast Days). And, it being a silent meal, brethren would often take a book to read, or simply sit and think while they had their breakfast.

After breakfast there was time to make beds and tidy rooms, and then make one's meditation for half an hour or so before going into choir in the church at nine to recite the 'little hour' of Terce.

The church at Mirfield was built on a hillside and entry to the lower church is also at ground level. The first part of the church, designed by Walter Tapper and built in 1912, was the Chapel of the Resurrection. The chapels of the Ascension, Holy Cross, and the main sanctuary were built later. The Sanctuary is in Red Runcorn stone and very spacious and beautiful. The inspiration is Byzantine, the community having turned away from the Gothic and Romanesque designs that had been suggested by previous architects. The nave had been built in the thirties, and stone being by then far too expensive, the building had been completed in brick with the interior walls plastered. The interior of the nave was painted cream, as was the lower church. Purists thought it a bit of a hotchpotch, but I found it very satisfying. For me the massive red stone pillars of the sanctuary housing the High Altar dedicated to the mystery of the Holy Trinity, in a splendid open space, have a great dignity, appropriately symbolising the worship of God as the central work and activity of the community. The Choir and Nave, being more simply built of brick and plaster painted white, expressed for me the simplicity of life which was the community's interpretation of the vow of poverty. Nothing was spared when it was for the glory of God. Everything as simple and unobtrusive as possible where it concerned our own life.

Of all the holy places I already knew none could compare for

132

me, with the Chapel of the Resurrection in the Community Church at Mirfield. This great apsidal chapel behind the high altar was flanked by the Chapel of the Holy Cross on one side, and that of the Ascension on the other. The altar of the Chapel of the Resurrection stood beneath a *baldachino*, from the ceiling of which was suspended the golden hanging pyx, a casket in which the Blessed Sacrament, the consecrated bread from the Eucharist, was reserved for the communion of the sick, and therefore always available. This was an ancient English method of reserving the Blessed Sacrament, and did not suffer from the 'pin-point' focus of a tabernacle on the altar or an aumbry at the side, and allowed a more diffused attention to the mystery of our Lord's special presence associated with the Eucharist. This chapel drew me like a magnet and it became my favourite place of prayer. I was not alone in this; for it was not often that there was no one praying there and frequently a considerable number, particularly in the early morning, before any of the services, and at night before and after Complne.

It was in the choir before the High Altar that the daily offices, which punctuate the day with corporate prayer and worship, were recited and sung, and it was here that the Solemn Eucharists were sung on Sundays and the greater festivals of the church's year. The high barrel roof of the building made for a wonderful resonance ideally suited to the singing of plainsong, the quiet cadences of which gained an added beauty as they soared into the great spaces above the choir.

Being now a novice, and therefore 'of' the community, though not yet 'in' it, I found it most satisfying to begin each day singing and reciting the praises of God in choir in this wonderful building, whose very walls seemed impregnated with prayer.

Silence plays a very important part in the Religious Life, and there are two sorts. Greater Silence is in force from after Compline, the last office of the day, until after Terce, which with us was said after breakfast, at 9am. During Greater Silence there is no speaking unless it is absolutely necessary. Lesser Silence governs the rest of the day apart from times of recreation after lunch and after supper. During Lesser Silence one is encouraged to talk only when necessary for work or duties about the house or grounds.

The purpose of these silences is to help the brethren to maintain their recollection of the presence of God at all times, and to think of all their work, whether intellectual or manual, in the Bursar's office, the kitchen or the grounds, or travelling and preaching and teaching, as equally part of the worship that is summed up and expressed directly so many times a day in the church. All to the glory of God and for the welfare of the Church and

133

Community Church, Mirfield High Mass – Western Rite 1960

Chapel of the Resurrection

the world. This, of course, is or should be the aim of every Christian life - the glory of God in and through all that one does. There was a famous comedian who had a close association with the community who used to say he liked to be on the boards at 9 o'clock in the evening because he knew that at that time the brethren would be singing Compline in the church at Mirfield, worshipping God through prayer as he was worshipping God by making people laugh.

The Community of the Resurrection was founded by Bishop Charles Gore, Bishop of Oxford, and the first professions were made in the chapel of Pusey House in Oxford. Gore described their small band as 'a few Christian gentlemen living simply and trying to be good'. They started warily, not making life vows, but expressing an 'intention to remain members for life.' Gore refused to be called Superior and was called Senior. It was Walter Frere, later to become Bishop of Truro (while remaining a member of the community), who became the first true Superior and was given that title. He guided the fledgling community much more in the direction of traditional monasticism and was the main author of the Rule, and wrote the commentary upon it. By the 1940's the Rule and the Frere Commentary were bound up in the one book and, at anyrate for postulants and novices, were a second Bible - to be studied and thought about and applied to one's own life.

The Community of the Resurrection interpreted the traditional religious vow of poverty as simplicity of life, as owning nothing and having as few 'necessities' as possible. Everything necessary for life and health and work was supplied by the community and belonged not to *me* but to *us*. The brethren tried to reproduce the life of the first Christians who, according to the Acts of the Apostles 'remained faithful to the teaching of the apostles, to the brotherhood,to the breaking of bread and to the prayers ... and they owned everything in common' (Acts 2: 42 & 44). The vow of obedience certainly means that you promised to do what you were told by your superiors, but this did not mean a slavish obedience. In practice a brother was not *ordered* to do something, but *asked* if he would. If he was asked to do something that for some reason he thought inappropriate or open to some other objection, he was under an obligation to state his reasons 'patiently and opportunely.' If, having done so, his superior still asked him to do what he had been asked, then he concurred without further demur. The Rule stated, however, that in the last resort no brother might be asked to do anything that was against his conscience.

When I went to Mirfield in the late 1940s Raymond Raynes the Superior was gradually leading the community towards a more strict monasticism, egged on by most of the junior brethren who wanted a stricter rule and a full monastic habit. Mirfield Fathers did not wear a monastic habit in the strict sense of the term, but an ordinary Anglican wrap-over cassock. A monastic touch was supplied by a grey *scapular* - that is a long strip of grey material, that hangs back and front from the shoulders nearly to the hem of the cassock (from the 'scapular' bones of the shoulders). This had originated simply as an apron to keep the cassock clean and was washable. Only after I had been in the community for several years was one permitted to wear the scapular when travelling.

I joined the 'pro-monastic' band of opinion as I came very much under the influence and sway of the Superior - he had joined my pantheon of heroes and I swallowed everything he said, hook line and sinker. Many of the more senior brethren were dubious about this trend.

However, the Rule of the Community was a very liberal one and far from forcing brethren into any sort of mould, gave real freedom for the fullest possible development of every brother's character and talents. That, it has always seemed to me, is the fundamental genius of the Community of the Resurrection, a marvellous liberating freedom in the framework of benign discipline. For me it epitomised the old saying, that 'you are never so free as when you are bound.' As the months went by I found myself expanding in wonder as I learned to live the life.

The 'Daily Office' consisted of seven short 'services' that were recited every day in choir - Matins, Prime (before Mass), Terce (after breakfast), Sext (before lunch), None (after tea), Evensong (before supper) and Compline to close the day. These were seen to be the setting for the Eucharist which was always the centre of the worship - like a great diamond in a setting of lesser stones, and it was from the worship in the Daily Office and Eucharist that all the works of the community flowed, and to which they were returned in the ceaseless round of prayer and praise, all *ad maiorem gloriam Dei,* all to the greater glory of God.

It may seem from all this that life in the community was a very solemn affair, but that is far from the truth. Indeed, during my very first visit to the community with Dick Herrick, when I had only recently been ordained priest, during Lesser Silence on my first morning I heard echoing through the silent corridors that cross between bray of donkey and laugh of hyena, and my mind flew back to the Albert Hall in the 1930s - Ho Ho, I thought, Fr Elwin Millard - keeping Lesser Silence; 'in the spirit,' he would claim, if not in the letter! On another occasion, I was walking sedately past the sanctuary on my way out of the church after Terce. Some small way ahead was a junior brother recently professed. He was a tall and well-built man and was walking more than sedately, in fact as if he were a procession all to himself, and he was looking quite pleased with himself. Just beside me was a lay brother who had been professed for many years, a fine down-to-earth Yorkshireman. As we both glanced rather amusedly at the newly professed brother sailing on ahead, he turned to me and said, *sotto voce*, "Smoog Booger!" and gave me a charming but wicked grin! In the Greater Silence! In the church! A senior brother to a novice! I barked a laugh that I could only cut off in the middle as I whipped out my handkerchief! I always loved that lay brother. (I think perhaps I ought to explain for those whom he would call *Sootherners* that in Yorkshire, 'bugger' is not a rude word, as it is in the South. Indeed it can be a term of affection or at least camaraderie - I have myself been greeted jovially by a local friend at Mirfield with, "Hello, Faather, y'owd booger 'ow are y'then?" having my hand pumped at the same time).

In the same grounds, on the other side of the community church there was another large complex of buildings, the College of the Resurrection, where our theological students, having obtained their degrees at Leeds University were given their final two years of theological training. This was one of the original works of the community begun not very long after it was founded and established itself at Mirfield. As one would expect, the proximity of the college, always filled with lively young men, had also a cross-fertilizing effect upon the community, and together with our external work helped us to be open to what the next generation were thinking. Over the years several old students, having had a few years in the parochial ministry, returned to find their full vocation in the community itself.

We novices saw little of the students except at tea on Sunday afternoons when they had a standing invitation to take tea with the brethren in the front hall of the community house. After profession, however, it was as common for brethren to go for walks with students as with their own brethren or novices. There were various directions one could take from the mother house on setting off for a walk; one was down what was known as The Clough, a narrow and rocky pathway going steeply down hill to the Huddersfield road in the valley. There one crossed the road, then the river Calder, then a canal and a railway line, all within a distance of a few hundred yards, and so gain the moors stretching away in the distance.

One of the things that I valued most was that for the whole of the first year I did not go away from the Mother House; it was deliberate community policy that a novice remained at home for the first year, and in his second year went away only rarely. So I had the best part of two years to read more widely than I had done before, and with more help. Help was not confined to supervised reading; one seemed to absorb knowledge at Mirfield. In my day there were some renowned scholars in the Community not least Fr Lionel Thornton, one of the famous theologians of his day. All were generous in giving the fruits of their learning to their brethren and the novices.

Regular features of life were the learned lectures given to the community by one or other of the academic brethren. When Michael Ramsey, later Archbishop of Canterbury, was a Canon of Durham Cathedral he used to come to Mirfield from time to time for a scholarly disputation with Dr Thornton, and we novices were allowed to 'sit in' on these occasions, and we listened in awe to the debates of the two great men. Much of it was in Latin and Greek, and some in Hebrew. I don't think more than a couple of the novices were able to follow the arguments very closely, I certainly could not. But we all got something from these sessions and most of us found them thrilling. However little we understood, something rubbed off on to us, of that I am certain.

In my novitiate great stress was laid upon making a clean break with one's previous life. We were encouraged not to write to old friends; there had to be a process of withdrawal, so that we might concentrate as totally as possible on learning to live the Religious Life as interpreted by the Rule of the Community. To this end we were encouraged to open ourselves by reading and prayer to the guidance of the Holy Spirit in the deepening of our spiritual life. This may sound a very self-centred aim, but that is not so. In this first year of withdrawal novices were not only preparing for full membership of the Community but also for taking a full part eventually in the multi-faceted works of the Community for the good of the Church and for mankind. While we did not write to our friends, we were encouraged to keep them very much in our prayers. We were encouraged to keep in touch with our families, but had to learn that a religious must maintain a certain detachment even from them.

It is not uncommon for an elder son to be rather dominated by his mother, and as I have said earlier, this was particularly so in my case because owing to my frailty when young I had had to be cosseted. Mother knew that a more definite break in our relationship would occur when I went to Mirfield, as she had said on our walk in Holland the previous summer. She found this extremely difficult to accept, and during my first year in the novitiate she became increasingly unhappy, writing miserable letters to me pleading with me to leave and return to parish life. I was very troubled by these letters and told the Novice Guardian about them. He astonished me by suggesting that I invite Mother and Geoff to stay for a few days as guests of the Community. I had no idea that such a thing was possible, "But Father," I said, "what about all this business of standing back from the family with a degree of detachment?" He told me that having them to stay here was quite a different matter from going to stay with them.

Gosh, I thought, whatever will Geoff say when he is expected to stay in a monastery - I bet he will want to run a mile! So I wrote inviting them, half expecting Mother to say that she would come by herself, but not a bit of it - she replied by return of post to say that they would both love to come.

At the Novice Guardian's suggestion I had asked a lady who lived just across the road from the main gates of the Mother House if she could put them up, and she had agreed to do so. This was splendid, for poor old Geoff would hopefully not be too overwhelmed by the monastic life of the Community.

I met them at Huddersfield station and after a few awkward moments at the beginning we were talking animatedly as the bus took us to Mirfield. On the way, outside Huddersfield, I pointed out to them the Community Church, with its green barrel roof and twin squat towers clearly visible on the hillside, looking, I thought, like a lion crouching ready to pounce - the Lion of Judah!

They both took immediately to the very nice Yorkshire lady in whose house they would stay. She had given them a very comfortable bedroom and the sitting room on the front of the house, with a view of the Community Church and the Mother House across the road. I first took them round the church and the garden, introducing them to any brethren and novices we happened to meet. No keeping me in my place now; every one was welcoming and kind. I could sense Mother and Geoff beginning to thaw out a little. They came to Evensong and after supper the Novice Guardian came across to their 'digs' to welcome them and was very kind and gentle and put them at their ease.

It was summertime and we were blessed with brilliantly sunny and warm weather for the whole of their visit. They came to Compline and made their way back by themselves. The following day I went to see them at coffee time, and there paying them a call and sitting beaming in a comfortable armchair was Fr Keble Talbot. Keble had been superior of the community for several years; now getting old he was officially 'retired.' He was a most remarkable man, well known up and down the country and abroad, often in Court circles and a confidant of the King, for he came, as several of the early brethren had, from aristocratic stock. Like most real aristocrats he had no 'side' to him whatever, and could get on with anyone, completely at his ease wherever he went and in whatever company. He was one of the kindest, most holy and most friendly men I had ever met, so gloriously *human*. No keeping novices in their place with him, he was beyond all that, and like everyone else, I was devoted to him. Perhaps Fr Wrathall the Novice Guardian had tipped him the wink that my parents were here and were not very happy about my intention to try my vocation. So he had decided to come calling, and here he was, the great and kindly man, a brilliant raconteur, and he had Mother and Geoff hanging on his every word. They were laughing their heads off at one of his stories as I arrived, and Geoff had tears running down his cheeks with laughter, which was an endearing habit of his. Keble did more than anyone else to reconcile them to my being there, and without any solemn lectures about the nature and purpose of the religious life - simply by being himself, and showing them that those who follow this way are perfectly ordinary human beings who enjoy life as much as the next man, and do not spend all their time being solemn and 'holy' in the accepted sense of that word. Various other brethren came to visit in the sitting room across the road, and Mother and Geoff gradually responded like Geoff's flowers, opening to the warmth of the sun.

When the time came to say Goodbye they were both thoroughly relaxed and happy; there were no tears. As we waited for the bus to Huddersfield station, Mother turned to me and said in her forthright way, "Well, if you have the chance to stay here for the rest of your life and don't take it, you will be a bigger fool than I take you for!" I caught the bus back to Mirfield grinning with relief and amusement. No more miserable pleading letters, simply 'Please give my love to Fr Keble, and to Frs X and Y and Z.'

So, with an easier mind, back to learning to live the religious life, and of course, for all my continuing contentment, this was not an easy road. The cliche about being able to choose one's friends but not one's relations is just as true in a community. A community is a family and the Rule exhorts one to do one's whole duty to each of the brethren. Men and women who don the religious habit do not change into saints, they remain frail human beings with irritating habits, cussed and self-willed, and one cannot escape them. The tensions, likes and dislikes that one had in one's previous life are present in the cloister, sometimes even redoubled in intensity, so there are many struggles and many failures.

A lay brother and I went for a walk one Sunday afternoon; he had just been in a bit of a row and had behaved badly. He admitted this to me very glumly as we walked, and said, "O dear, I hope they will forgive me" - and then he brightened and said with a grin, "Well, they've *got* to, haven't they?" And that is the key to living in community - whatever a brother has done, however badly he has offended, you have to forgive him, just as we are forgiven by God. Christian 'brotherly love' is the hallmark of true community life, and it has always been the hallmark of the Community of the Resurrection, or 'CR' as it is popularly abbreviated. It does not mean that everyone has to *like* everyone else, preference and compatibility play the same part in relationships as they do outside. It is the constant striving for true *caritas,* true Christian love, the self-sacrificing service of others in the name of Christ, that makes all the difference in a community. My own experience suggests that when you try to do this, however half-heartedly, you often find yourself quite liking people whom you once heartily disliked. In fact a visitor once remarked, "The extraordinary thing is that they all seem so fond of one another."

A very great impression was made upon me by my experience of Holy Week and Easter at Mirfield. During the year the Community received a very large number of invitations from parishes up and down the country for one of the brethren to preach the next Holy Week and Easter - far more invitations than there were brethren available. So all able-bodied brethren were sent out in response to these invitations, and the Mother House and the priories were denuded. The only ones remaining at home therefore were the brethren who were on the staff of the College, postulants, novices and the infirm. Priest novices in their second year of the Novitiate were also sent out to preach. 'Preaching Holy Week' in those days involved preaching at the Eucharist and Evensong on Palm Sunday, every night in Holy Week, conducting the Three Hours Devotion on Good Friday, and finishing off one's course on Easter Day.

Because there were so few brethren left at home the students of our College took over the entire provision of the rites and ceremonies of Holy Week and Easter, except of course for the priestly functions. They did this with great efficiency and devotion. All through the year our students joined in the liturgical life of the community and provided cantors, readers and servers, so they were no strangers to this side of the community life and worship; indeed we believed that what they learnt through this participation in the spiritual life of the community was a very important part of their training for the priesthood.

In Holy Week the students shared the stalls in choir with those brethren and novices who had not gone out to preach, and they joined in the whole round of the Daily Office, and all the extra liturgical events that are special to this period of the Church's year.

Community and students kept the whole of Holy Week as a retreat. Greater Silence was in force all day and every day from the Monday until breakfast on Easter Day. The emphasis of course was on the last week of our Lord's life and ministry from the Entry into Jerusalem on Palm Sunday until the Crucifixion on Good Friday and the Resurrection on Easter Day.

I found it a wonderful experience as each day brought one nearer to the agony in the Garden of Gethsemane, the Arrest, the Trial, with the three-fold denial by Peter, and the Crucifixion - upon which we meditated for the three hours from noon to 3pm on Good Friday. We remembered very specially all our brethren throughout the land who were at that time helping people in the parishes to 'keep watch' at the foot of the Cross and to see the implications for their own lives of the lengths to which God has gone to bring men and women back, through repentance and forgiveness, to the knowledge and experience of His love.

For me one of the most moving experiences of that absorbing and inspiring week was the monastic service of *Tenebrae*, from the Latin word for darkness, which was held on Thursday, Friday and Saturday in Holy Week. This consisted in the recitation of psalms and readings from Holy Scripture. In the middle of the Choir there was a stand with a chevron shaped rack on which there burned thirteen candles, one candle standing at the peak of the chevron and represented our Lord; on either side were six other candles representing the twelve disciples. There was no lighting apart from these candles. As each section of the service was concluded one candle was extinguished, until at the end there was just the candle representing our Lord left burning. After the final psalms and reading, in total silence the Sacristan quietly took that one candle and 'hid it in an obscure place' in our case behind an altar. The church was then in total darkness for several minutes. Suddenly there was an almighty bang, as the senior brother in choir banged his book hard on his stall. The lone candle was then brought back, replaced on the stand, and we all left the church in its glimmering light.

The symbolism was the gradual defection of the disciples, one by one, as the Crucifixion approached, until our Lord is left alone. The hiding of the candle represented the burial of Jesus in the tomb for three days. The banging of the book was his resurrection from the dead. The return of the candle represented the Risen Life of Christ the Light of the World. Guided by this Light, we went on our way.

I do not think anything before that experience of Tenebrae had made me realize quite so deeply the terrible loneliness our Lord must have suffered as his disciples faded away and forsook him.

The most triumphal moment of all came as the great Easter ceremonies were performed from before dawn on Easter Day. We all assembled in our stalls in choir by the bare minimum of lighting; there was quite a large congregation of local people in the nave, and as we all waited in silence there was a palpable air of suppressed excitement and expectancy. As the clock struck the hour the ceremony of the New Fire was begun. Out on the balcony at the West End of the church the 'sanctuary party' in golden vestments had assembled, and the 'New Fire' had been struck - traditionally in the primitive way with a flint and kindling, (I think we decided that a cigarette lighter was a suitable modern equivalent!) This New Fire represented the Resurrection of Christ, from it one candle of the 'triple candle' was lit, with the cry, "The Light of Christ" and the procession entered the church. This 'triple candle' - three candles twisted into one - represented the Holy Trinity, and as the procession moved forward the other two were lit with the same cry, "The Light of Christ." Every member of the congregation and the brethren in the choir were holding candles which they lit from the Triple Candle as it passed slowly up the nave, through the choir to the high altar. The darkened church gradually filled with light as more and more candles were lit - a 'new dawn' of faith and light for the world. And so into the Solemn Eucharist of Easter, a very special feast for the Community of the Resurrection, called to go from the worship of the Risen Lord out into the world to proclaim his truth and try to reveal his light to all mankind, in preaching and teaching and service.

During their second year, as well as preaching Holy Week, priest novices went out a few times, usually in the locality, to start 'getting the feel' of some of the community work. My first assignment was a Quiet Day for a parish about twenty miles away. During the following Lent I was sent to a church in Bradford to preach a course of sermons on the Sunday evenings. I was rather apprehensive about this, thinking that the Yorkshire people would not take much notice of a mere southerner. I had had a Yorkshireman friend in college and he had a chip on his shoulder about us southerners - he disliked us on the whole, thinking us 'la-di-da' effete and insincere. I thought the Bradford people would similarly tend to write me off. However I was a bit of a chameleon where speech and accent were concerned, and often tended to pick up some of the intonations of local speech, quite unconsciously. On that first rather nervous Sunday in Bradford, I was saying goodbye to people after the service, when a large comfortable Yorkshire lady came and shook my hand saying, "Ee, Faather, A' can tell tha's Yorksheer!" I was delighted, and did not disabuse her!

Later still in my novitiate I was sent out with one of the professed brethren to assist him in conducting a Mission in a parish not far from London. This was the first time I had been away for more than twenty-four hours since my arrival, and I found it a little bewildering to be rushing through the countryside in the train. The whole tempo of my life had slowed down and to re-enter the hurly burly of 'the world' was quite unnerving for a while. I soon readjusted of course and by the time we got to the parish where the mission was to be held I was ready and eager for the fray. We took a couple of our theological students from the College at Mirfield as assistants. This was a fairly small parish and did not call for the large team of helpers and visitors that would have been organized for a larger parish. I enjoyed this experience very much. Fr Cledwyn Evans who was the missioner preached the basics of the Christian Faith and life every night for ten days. The days of the old fashioned 'hellfire' mission sermon were long gone, thank goodness, and a mission by now simply involved a reasoned presentation of the Faith with no reliance on stirring up the emotions. Emotions often are deeply stirred of course, but they are not whipped up deliberately. The students would be out all day visiting in the parish and suggesting that people take this rare opportunity to hear the Christian Faith explained in a series of inter-related addresses. The church was packed every night and the mission had a great impact. I did some of the visiting, but was mainly concerned with helping with the counselling of people who had been touched by the teaching and needed individual help, and with hearing the confessions of those who wished to make use of that sacrament. On revisiting the parish six months or so later we found that the faith and spiritual life of those who were already practising members of the church had been deepened, those who had been only occasional worshippers were now more regular, and many who had never worshipped in the church before were now to be seen quite often. The whole tone of the worship had developed and the spiritual life of the parish had been deepened. Concomitant with this there was a greater concern by the congregation to express their worship in service to others. I was very impressed with this method of bringing the Faith to the people.

So the months sped by and election for profession began to appear on the horizon. I desperately wanted to be professed in the Community, but two thirds of the brethren, voting in General

Chapter, had to agree that I should be professed, and I was scared that I would not command this number of votes.

The eczema that had plagued me as a youngster had never properly cleared - for much of the time in Portsmouth I had had to wear white cotton gloves because my hands were covered with it, which I found very embarrassing. It gave me a feeling of being 'unclean.' It had eased a little in Hendon and I was fairly clear of it during the first part of the novitiate, for which I was profoundly grateful. But as the time of decision came nearer the eczema reappeared on my chest and torso. I had in the end to report this to the Infirmarian because the itching was almost intolerable. He sent me to the local doctor who in turn referred me to a consultant dermatologist in Leeds. Such a kind and sensitive man he was, and he said that he felt sure this was caused by the stress of wondering whether the community would elect me to profession, or whether I had not made the grade and would be told that they did not think I had a vocation. I told him I was petrified at the thought of being a 'failure' again. He said, I think you will find that when the decision has been made and you know, the eczema will soon fade away.

The day then came when, with the other five novices, Nicolas Graham, Humphrey Whistler, Luke Smith, Cecil Cohen and Jack Guinness, who had also come to the end of their novitiate, I formally applied to the Superior in writing, for admission to First Profession and membership of the Community. A few days later, during General Chapter, which is the 'parliament' of the community consisting of all professed brethren, the Superior put our names forward for debate. At the end of the debate each of us was voted on by secret ballot.

Those of us up for election were waiting together in a room near the Chapter Room, feeling very jittery. As soon as the votes had been counted the Superior came sweeping into the room and said, "You have all been elected" - What relief! What joy! He also told us the date of the profession. So we were able to write to our families and invite them to come to Mirfield for the occasion.

Mother and Geoff and Aunt and my brother Phil said they would come, and I arranged accommodation for them in the house where Mother and Geoff had stayed on that transforming visit nearly two years ago.

The profession took place in January, during the normal Christmas Chapter when all brethren who are in the country stay for about two weeks to 'live the common life,' to debate the Community business and look to its finances. Those who were to be professed were in retreat for most of the week before the profession, and so incommunicado to the outside world. A look out of the windows made us feel completely cut off from the world, for the fog was thick all that week, and I could not help wondering on the evening before whether the family had arrived safely. I was much relieved when a note was passed to me by the Novice Guardian saying that they were all comfortably ensconced in the house opposite.

From Compline the night before the profession the brethren-elect kept an all-night vigil in the church, and the rest of the brethren got up at various times in the night to spend a hour or so with them before returning to bed. There were no set rules about how the vigil was to be kept. Some remained in their stall in choir for the greater part of the time - we were encouraged to regard our stall in choir as our 'home.' Others made a 'pilgrimage' round the church, praying at each of the Stations of the Cross, visiting the side altars, each with its special dedication - the Holy Nativity, Holy Cross, The Ascension, the tombs of Charles Gore the Founder, and of Walter Frere the first Superior and main architect of the Rule. Most of us spent the greater part of the time in the Chapel of the Resurrection in the presence of the Blessed Sacrament, often prostrate before the altar symbolising our intention to submit entirely to the will of God expressed in loving obedience to the Rule and the will of our superiors.

That night of vigil was one of the most inspiring experiences of my life. The warm silence of the church, instinct with prayer, lit just sufficiently to see one's way about; the soft tread of brethren arriving to pray with us for a while or departing having done so, all made us feel wrapped around in caring love. Love is at the very heart of the Religious Life, and as I kept vigil I faced yet again the fact of my Girl in the Middle.

I recalled how, three years ago I had rung Guy Sanderson and told him about the idea that I might have a religious vocation. How the conviction had grown that I was being called to love God direct and not through a single human channel. Direct, through a life of poverty, chastity and obedience, and by keeping myself free from any single human love, to grow in love and service for all men. I had had two years of testing this sense of vocation and now felt secure in the belief that it really was to this that I was called. I knew that Bar and Tim were well cared for by Bertie Page, and I was able during my vigil, admittedly after a little sigh, to lay them on the altar - and leave them there.

In the small hours the vigil ended and each of us went to his room and slept for a few hours before the usual rising time when we hauled ourselves from bed and began the day which was to see us received into the great Community of the Resurrection as full members.

The rite of profession was incorporated in the High Mass. At the end of Prime all the professed brethren moved into the sanctuary and stood on either side of the High Altar in a large crescent facing towards the choir. The Superior stood in the middle of the communion step with a prayer desk before him. Each brother-elect was led to the prayer desk and stood while the Novice Guardian presented him to the Superior for profession. Questions and answers followed until the Superior invited the brother-elect to make his profession, in which he stated that he felt truly called by God to this life, and pledged himself to obedience to the Rule and Constitution of the Community of the Resurrection, with a firm intention to continue in this community for the rest of his life. He made his profession kneeling at the prayer desk in front of the Superior, who then formally admitted him to the Community. The newly professed brother signed the profession document from which he had just read, and rising, took it and placed it upon the altar. He returned to the Superior who girded him with the broad leather belt from which now hung the bronze crucifix, the insignia of a professed brother and which had now replaced the small cross of a novice. The Superior then took him by the hand and led him round the crescent of the brethren, presenting him to each brother in turn, who took his right hand and kissed it in welcome and acceptance. The Superior then led him to his stall in the choir, bowed to him, and returned to repeat the process for each of the other brethren making their profession. This ceremony was watched with fascination by the families and friends seated in the nave. My old friend Alastair Haggart was with my family, having come all the way from Perth. How delighted I was to see him there! I had arranged for him to have a room in the retreat house, and it was wonderful to have him under the same roof.

The profession ceremony led straight into the High Mass, in which the theme was of great thanksgiving and praise - special soaring plainsong chants had been arranged and practised by the Precentor and the hand-picked band of cantors chosen for the occasion; rousing popular hymns for the sake of the large congregation consisting of the students from the college as well as the special guests. The organist played triumphal music and the whole service was a glorious pean of thanksgiving and praise to God. The best gold vestments gleamed, and the incense filled the great church, and our nostrils, with the very smell of worship. As the final blessing was given the organist surpassed himself and produced from the organ a transport of glorious sound.

Then everyone was more than ready for a 'talking breakfast'

in the refectory - and a *cooked* one as for a major feast day! But best of all, a moment we had all been looking forward to - the right now to call all the professed brethren simply by their Christian names without the prefix 'Father'! We had all gone in awe of the 'great ones' in the community, especially the Reverend Father Doctor Lionel Thornton, DD! We had all said at one time or another, "I can't *imagine* calling Fr Lionel simply 'Lionel'!" What a cheek! But there he was as I went into the refectory, sitting at the head of one of the side tables, beaming with *bonhomie* - as I approached him he rose and stretched out his hand and grasped mine, saying, "Welcome Paul," and I replied quite spontaneously, "Thank you *Lionel* " - and moved on to collect bacon and eggs, thinking, *I've done it!!* Other brethren were crowding round to shake our hands and say, "Welcome!"

At last I was able to join Alastair and Phil who had come to have breakfast in the refectory while Geoff and Mother and Aunt returned to their digs, for women were not allowed in the refectory. The rest of the day we could spend as we wished; the newly professed were given a 'day off,' being obliged only to attend the offices.

Alastair and I saw the family off at Huddersfield station and then back in my room we had a long talk; it was a long time since we had seen one another and we had a lot of catching up to do. Too soon it was time for his bus to Leeds and the train to Scotland.

So began my life as a fully professed priest brother of the Community of the Resurrection - and the eczema was gone within a fortnight!

The newly professed Mirfield
Father 1950

7

The London Priory

'The immediate worship and service of God' is a phrase that occurs very frequently in the Rule of the Community of the Resurrection as again and again it is emphasised that this is the *raison d'etre* of the community, and that nothing must be allowed to take priority over it. For this reason it is also stated that external work must be carefully balanced by time 'spent quietly at home'.

It was not long after profession that I began to be very busy with external work, and my time had to be carefully regulated so that I kept the proper balance. I very much enjoyed the work: travelling all over the country to towns and cities I had not visited before I found very exciting. I also enjoyed the work of preaching and teaching, conducting retreats and missions.

I was very nervous when I was given my first retreat to conduct for a community of nuns, and I went around the brethren asking for any advice they could give me. Old Bishop Rupert Mounsey CR was quite a pal of mine, now getting very old, I would walk him slowly round the garden as he hung on to my arm. One day I said to him, "Rupert, tell me about conducting retreats for Sisters." He thought for a minute and then said in his rather tart way, "It's funny about sisters you know. You will notice that they take down every word you say. I remember once sitting in the conductor's chair on the chancel step ready to begin my first address, and there they all were, with their little notebooks on their knees and pencils poised. The first words of my address were, 'Under every one of those wimples, is a woman' - and they all wrote it down!"

I also asked Fr Frank Biggart about sisters' retreats, and he gave me some very good advice, which he rounded off by saying, "And my dear, be very wary of the Reverend Mother Superior, there is no scratch like the scratch of a *consecrated claw!*" I am glad to say that being scratched by a 'consecrated claw' did not come my way, and all the Mothers Superior with whom I had contact were delightful people and I grew to love conducting sisters' retreats more than any others. I think Fr Frank Biggart was being amusingly naughty!

Soon after profession I had a wonderful holiday. One day a letter arrived out of the blue from an old parishioner in Portsmouth enclosing a cheque for one hundred pounds. She said she had appreciated the help I had tried to give her during the war when her son, an only child, had been shot down and killed in the Royal Air Force, and asked me to accept the money as a token of gratitude. I took the letter and cheque to the Superior and asked what I should do about it. He told me to write and explain that I was not able to accept money for myself, but if she cared to give it to the community we would be very grateful. The lady replied saying that she was happy to give the money to CR and added, '... but if you can have some pleasure from it as well, I shall be very pleased....' So back I went to the Superior and gave him the cheque - and told him what she had said. He said, "Well, you can have twenty-six pounds - what would you like to do with it?" I said I would like to go to Sweden, "One of those Swedish priests we had staying a few months ago asked if it would be possible for me to go to Sweden this summer. If so, he would take his holiday at the same time and take me around." Raymond said he would like me to accept this invitation because he wanted us to keep in touch with the Swedish Church - "...so you can have £26.00 for the trip."

Why twenty *six* pounds, I was never able to fathom, but that was the sum. That twenty-six pounds together with the usual annual holiday allowance from the Bursar paid my return fare to Gothenburg, and all I needed in the way of pocket money!

We toured Sweden in Ake's little car staying with friends of his, and had a splendid time. He was a wonderful and amusing companion. One day he said, "Today we are going up country to the great lakes and we are going to have tea with a priest friend of mine and his delightful family." We drove through magnificent country into huge forests that bordered some of the great lakes of Sweden. In the afternoon we arrived at Ake's friend's rectory, a beautifully designed house built of wood. While we were having tea in his study, the Rector got up from his chair, went to a bookshelf and took down a slim black book which he handed to me saying, "Have you seen this book before, Father?" I opened it - and found myself looking at my own bookplate! A lino-cut made for me by my sister-in-law Dorothy. He saw my surprise and said, "That was given to me by one of the Swedish priests who visited you just before you joined your community - you gave them a lot of books, and we shared them out when they got home."

I had been invited as an external observer to a Christian Youth Conference that was being held at Visbe on the island of Gotland in the middle of the Baltic - called the 'Island of Ruins and Roses'. The organiser of the conference was one of the young priests who had visited me in Holders Hill, hence the invitation. I was to sail on the midnight ferry from a small port in the South of Sweden. The previous night Ake and I were much further North, so we had to make a very early start the next morning, for we had a very long drive ahead of us. We had breakfast, consisting of a boiled egg in which strips of raw fish were dunked, put a few bread rolls in our pockets and set off, Ake driving like Jehu. We had no time to stop for meals, only for 'pit stops' at filling stations. From time to time we munched a rather dry bread roll. Hungry and tired we got to the jetty just before midnight. The ferry from Gotland was very late arriving and had only just docked. People were disembarking as we got there- several being carried off on stretchers. It transpired that heavy storms were raging in the Baltic, hence the late arrival, and the stretcher cases were those who had been incapacitated by sea-sickness. It would be some time before the ferry could be turned round for the return trip. Ake was to stay the night with friends and was anxious about keeping them up late, so I told him to go and I would just wait until I was allowed on board. He had told me that a cabin had been booked for me and my ticket would be on board in the Pursar's office. So off he went and I sat on my suitcase with a small crowd of other passengers and waited. I was very hungry by now, the last roll had disappeared a long time ago, I tightened my belt a notch. At long last we were allowed to board and I took my place in the queue. The Purser was a rather disgruntled looking woman who, unlike most Swedes, did not speak English very well. "No, no cabin; no ticket!" "What?!!" "Nothing - for you!"- peering at my passport. "Wait here," she commanded, pushing me aside, while she continued dealing with the long queue of other passengers.

When she had finished with them, she turned her attention to me once more. "You must pay ticket," she said. I offered her a traveller's cheque, "No, no," she said, "Swedish." I showed her that I only had the equivalent of five shillings sterling in Swedish money - there had been no time to stop at a bank, and I had relied upon being able to cash a cheque at the Purser's office on board. She looked exasperated and gave me a long considering look. I suppose what she saw was enough to put anyone off - a young monk in a black habit with a huge 'shovel' hat with the brim supported by strings to the crown. I was in the middle of my 'super-high-church' period! However, she decided that I could share a cabin with three other men but I would have to pay when we arrived in Visbe. With a sigh of relief I thanked her - and rubbing my tummy said rather desperately, "Food, please?" She frowned again and said, "No food; closed" - and went away.

At least there was water in the cabin, and I drank copiously of that - trying to remember how long it is that a man can stay alive on water only. I felt sure it would be long enough for the seven hour crossing to Gotland. But I was so *hungry!* I tried to be a good religious and accept the hunger as a piece of extra fasting. I was not very successful though. Anyway, I tightened my belt until I could just about breathe, and as the ferry began to move away from the jetty I followed the example of my three companions, and curled up in my bunk. It was not long before we were out in the open sea and pitching and rolling with tremendous abandon. I like the movement of a ship at sea and did not mind being storm-tossed, which on this night was an advantage because it kept my attention away from my hunger pains. We could only have caught the tail end of the storm, for after three hours or so the ferry stopped being tossed about and the boat was simply rolling in the swell as the seas abated. Surprisingly I must have slept because before I knew it, the light was shining through the porthole and we were motoring to the jetty in the harbour of Visbe. I began to feel hungry again, and sipped the last of the water, hoping that the priest who would be meeting me off the boat would take me to breakfast before we did anything else. I joined the long queue for passport control, and by the time I got there, wondering how I was going to get money to pay for my fare, the unfriendly Purser was there - with a smile on her face and very apologetic, saying in broken English that my ticket should have come across on last night's boat but had been forgotten. It had been waiting for us when we docked and now all was well. It was now 7.45am and we were nearly an hour late, I hurried down the gangway on to the jetty with my battered case, eagerly looking around for a dog-collar.

No dog-collar.

A lovely summer morning, so he's probably in casual clothes.

No one was around who could conceivably be a priest in casuals. By now everyone else had disembarked and I could see the last of the passengers disappearing down the jetty. I was left alone, and a touch forlorn.

I sat on my case, thinking someone is bound to turn up and if I move I might miss them. So, one monk with cropped head, sitting on a battered case, plus outlandish hat. It was very peaceful; seagulls crying, sun shining, ferry hissing quietly and, tranquil after its labours, towering over this lone figure. Nothing moved, I did not appreciate it all very much, I was so very very *hungry*.

I prayed to St Christopher, patron saint of travellers, *O Saint Chris, please do something*. Although I did not hear it, he must have said *"Willco,"* or whatever the heavenly equivalent is, for in the distance, coming towards me was a lady struggling along hauling a yelling child in each hand. Her English was not very good but she was profuse in her apologies; her husband had had to go to the other end of the island I gathered; I could not make out why. I was to follow her to a car; children on the back seat still screaming. Whizzing round the streets, stopping in a narrow street outside a stone terraced house with iron railings flanking three steps to the front door. Children still screaming, poor girl looking frantic as she knocked on the door. It was opened by a woman in an apron to whom I was delivered. "My husband come afternoon," the young mother said, sped back to her car and roared off. I was taken in and shown a room on the ground floor on the left of the front door. I dumped my case and turned and said, hopefully, "Food?" and rubbed my tummy. My hostess said, "No food - bed only," O NO, I thought; I shall pass out, I'm so *hungry*. Using mostly dumb-show I managed to elicit that there was a food shop in the square at the end of the street - which opened at 9am. It was now 8.20 *only 8.20!* So I managed to do my belt up one more notch, and lay down on my bed exhausted. At 8.45 I sallied forth, almost slavering at the thought of food, left out of the front door, to the end of the street, which opened into a busy market square dominated by a huge Romanesque cathedral. I noticed on the other side of the square a short queue of people and guessed right first time - they were waiting for the cafe to open. Like everything in Sweden it looked very clean and inviting, and I thankfully joined the queue. I was receiving many curious glances as I waited, wondering how I was going to order as much food as could be had for the five shillings or so I had in my pocket, when a girl standing next to me said, "Are you from England, Father?" *'O YES!'* I almost shouted, in relief that someone could speak English. She told me that she had lived in London for three years as an *au pair* - she certainly spoke English very well. I told her my plight, showed her how much money I had, and asked her to order for me as much to eat as it would buy when we got inside. Soon the door opened and we streamed in. My little angel did me proud, and before long I was tucking into two boiled eggs, large rolls and butter - and a pot of splendid strong coffee. I lingered a long time over my last cup, and then, feeling very tired but comfortably replete decided to go back to my 'digs' and get some sleep - exploring the cathedral could wait. I would indulge myself and say my morning office after I had rested and washed and shaved. So out I went into the cathedral square - to face another appalling dilemma - I saw there were five or six streets converging on the square. In which one was I staying? I had been so intent upon finding food that I had not given a thought to the name of my street! I tried to remember what aspect of the cathedral I had seen as I entered the square? Not the one I could see now. I crossed over to the other side and looked back - that looked vaguely better. But I

154

still could not decide. I thought I was more or less right, but there were still at least two if not three streets to choose between - so it was back to St Christopher, *Sorry to trouble you again St Chris - thank you for your previous favour. But I'm lost, please help. I'm just going to walk and trust you to take my feet in the right direction for my digs.* So I walked, hardly looking where I was going. I was in a street; terraced houses, built of stone. On and on - then, *O yes, three steps flanked by iron railings. Thank goodness (& St Chris).* I almost ran up the steps, opened the front door - and, confidently, the first door on the left - and went straight into a bedroom where a woman stood half-dressed by the side of the bed, who gaped at this apparition of a monk with cropped head and huge hat. She let out a prodigious scream as I turned and fled, slamming the front door behind me. I went rapidly up the street, getting as far from the disaster area as possible, scared of being arrested, but fortunately there were no police to be seen. I gradually recovered my composure, and soon I saw an identical set of three steps with railings. This time I tapped on the front door and opened it cautiously, the door on the left was ajar - and, yet another experience of blessed relief on this crazy journey, I could see the corner of my case beside the bed. No prizes for guessing what I did next - I loosened my belt and flopped on the bed - and slept for the best part of three hours!

My priest friend appeared soon after I had got up and washed and shaved, full of apologies. He had taken three coach loads of young people to see some ancient buildings at the other end of the island; they had made an early start and had come to the docks to meet me off the boat, intending taking me with them. They had been told the ferry would be very late and it was not known what time it would arrive, so they had not been able to wait. He had telephoned his wife and told her to meet me and take me to my digs; he was sorry she did not have much English - please come now to lunch with them and try to forgive!

The next five or six days were enchanting. This youth conference was housed in college buildings and I was collected every morning in time for breakfast in the college dining hall. I was kept busy most of the day with groups of flaxen haired young people coming to talk to me, take me for walks, tell me what their lectures and discussions had been about, and often to sit on the floor in front of me asking questions about the monastic life, about prayer, about the Church of England.

I found Gotland aptly named the 'Island of Ruins and Roses,' for mediaeval ruins were all over the place and all were covered in pink rambler roses just now in full bloom. My friends told me that they thought I must be the first religious to set foot on the island, since the Reformation! If that were so, no wonder I received so many curious glances - sometimes even frank stares. It was a great privilege to be with them all, and I could see that the Christian Church in Sweden represented by these splendid young people was very much alive and very well.

By the time I had been professed for about two years it seemed that an increasing amount of my external work was being done in the South of England. It was for this reason that while chatting with the Superior I said that if he thought of moving me from the Mother House I would be delighted to be transferred to the London Priory in Holland Park. This looks like another exercise of 'self will' on my part, but CR has always accepted that brethren have natural preferences about where they would like to live and work, and they are not discouraged from making these preferences known - people tend to do their best work in an environment that they find agreeable and that is a suitable sphere for the type of work that they do. Every brother knows and accepts that the Superior may have other ideas and may say, No. It was not very long after this that Raymond called me into his office and said he wanted me to go to the London Priory. Naturally I was very pleased - even though the Prior at the time was a brother I found rather difficult. However, this is not at all an uncommon difficulty in the religious life and I lost no sleep over it.

I am reminded of a Roman Catholic monk, I think it was the famous Dom John Chapman OSB, who when asked by his Novice Master just before his profession, "My son, what has been your greatest difficulty during your novitiate?" answered with courageous honesty, "*You* Father!"

I joined the brethren at the London Priory soon after Easter in 1952. I had always loved London and I arrived at a time when it was looking its best - and I was to live in a gracious house in one of the very gracious streets of the west end of the city. What bliss! The house backed on to Holland Park proper, and the curving tree-lined street was in the first delicate green of Spring. The Priory was a four-story building with a semi-basement. The front door, flanked by two Corinthian pillars was approached by a broad flight of stone steps. The chapel had been formed from the dining-room, and the drawing-room across the hall was the library. The refectory was in the semi-basement. I was given a very spacious and elegant room on the first floor in the front of the house and had a bow window, which seemed to me to be the peak of luxury. All the rooms had their own wash basins, which was another great luxury.

From here I was sent out all over the South of England and

I thoroughly enjoyed myself. I had loved my time at the Mother House, and still loved the place - but it *was* rather grim and dark compared with here. For one thing at Mirfield all the trees and bushes were covered in soot from the industrial areas that were so near. The London Priory, dedicated to StPaul, with its lovely trees and light rooms was a tremendous contrast and joy. I loved the chapel; if I could not pray in my beloved Chapel of the Resurrection, then this was the next best thing and it felt like the centre of our 'home'. I treated my new Prior with great respect for I found him as difficult and prickly as ever, more so in fact because in a small house there is little scope for taking avoiding action. I enjoyed all the other brethren very much. The great Dr Lionel Thornton himself was one of them. He was a tall imposing man of generous build and walked the Priory with head in air and heavy deliberate tread. Nearly always lost in thought he was rarely conscious of the more mundane areas of daily life, but occasionally at meal times would be full of *bonhomie* and his face would go bright pink with laughter. I became very fond of him and found that all my previous awe evaporated as I got to know him better. He used to amuse us by the way he would take little incidents with the greatest seriousness - he preferred his own company when taking his afternoon walk. One day he told us at tea that he had been walking through Kensington Gardens when a man had stopped him and asked whether he understood Greek? "I said, 'Yes I do' - and as that seemed to be all he wanted to know, I walked on." He was completely serious and could not understand our amusement. On another occasion the doctor put him on a strict diet - he had blood pressure and was overweight. The Steward accordingly provided him with a special diet lunch - and happened to notice later in the meal that Lionel was tucking in to what everyone else was eating. He said, "O, Lionel, I've prepared your special diet, didn't you see it?" Lionel, with a slight frown, said quite forcefully, "*Yes*, I've had my diet, and now I am having *this*!" Retreat of baffled Steward to have a word in the ear of the Infirmarian, who later, as the Rule says, 'patiently and opportunely' explained to the great Doctor that being on a diet meant that you only ate your diet, not the ordinary food as well. From then on without demur poor Lionel ate lettuce leaves and tomato and cottage cheese, or whatever, instead of the roasts and toad-in-the-hole and stews that the rest of us enjoyed.

Not long after the Community was founded, the Fraternity of the Resurrection was formed. A growing number of priests and lay men and women had expressed a desire to have some association with the community and to live under a Rule in their secular life. Most religious orders have their 'Third Order' of associated clergy and laity, and the Fraternity of the Resurrection was ours. There were three grades, Priest Companions, Lay Companions and Associates. The latter were people who felt unable to commit themselves to the rule that applied to Companions, but still wanted to 'belong'. Companions followed quite a strict rule of life that covered such matters as frequency of communion, confession, Bible reading, prayer and almsgiving. Each reported from time to time on the keeping of this rule to a Warden, who was a professed member of the Community. Soon after profession we had each been given a list of members of the Fraternity to look after as their Wardens. Often Companions would use their Warden as their spiritual director, and this could involve a lot of correspondence. I enjoyed this work and it was a privilege to try to help people with their reading and their prayers.

After I had been at the London Priory for a while, Raymond Raynes, the Superior, began taking me as his assistant to what had become known as his 'Holy Parties'. These were house parties held at South Park near Blechingley, the home of some old friends of his. Uvedale Lambert, Lord Lieutenant of Surrey and Master of Fox Hounds at the time, and his charming American wife Melanie would invite twenty or so guests for the weekend in order to listen to Fr Raynes explaining the basics of the Christian Faith. The guests were drawn from what I suppose one must call the 'educated upper classes'. Two daily lectures were held in the spacious and very comfortable library of the house, and Raymond would talk for forty minutes or so. He sat in a large armchair by the log fire that burnt brightly in winter, with the guests gathered around him, also sitting comfortably. He was a powerful speaker, though he hardly ever raised his voice and his audiences were always engrossed. He was completely uncompromising; there was nothing mealy-mouthed about him: he taught the full Catholic Faith of the Anglican Church. Raymond always had a tremendous impact, and over the years more and more people let it be known that they would like to be invited to one of his Holy Parties. He brought many to the Christian faith, and helped many more to sort out their intellectual and emotional problems. I count it a very great privilege to have been associated with these Holy Parties for a number of years and I made some very good friends there. Apart from the lectures and the time spent in pastoral counselling, the weekends were very happy house parties in a gracious house and grounds. On Saturday and Sunday afternoons there were horses in the stables to be borrowed by those who wanted to ride, and being in the heart of the country there was abundant scope for walking. In the summer there was

158

the tennis court which was often in use. Next to the house was an ancient chapel and Raymond and I took it in turns to say mass there every morning. If we both wished to celebrate on the same day there was always someone who would get up early in order to provide us with a congregation. Above the chapel was a self-contained flat, known in the family as 'The Priests' Hole' where one or other of us slept when there were not enough rooms in the house. As the Holy Parties grew in numbers over the years some of the guests had to be farmed out to friends in the neighbourhood, but everyone ate in the large dining room at South Park. Mealtimes there were often hilarious occasions. In fact the Holy Parties were mixtures of gravity and gaiety in almost equal measure.

I once said to Raymond that I wondered whether it would be a good idea to organise an Instruction Weekend, as a follow-up of the Parties, at the Community's retreat house at Hemingford Grey near Huntingdon in Cambridgeshire. It seemed to me that a number of people went away from a Holy Party wanting the chance to receive more instruction than we had had time to give them. He said he thought it was a good idea and told me to book a weekend and see what response there was. So I booked the following Whitsun weekend, from Friday evening to Tuesday morning, and it turned out to be a great success; some of the old stagers came along, people who were already practising the full Catholic faith, and about half were those who were still 'enquiring' as a result of the Holy Parties. We followed much the same pattern as at South Park, with the addition of keeping silence until morning coffee in order to give instruction on prayer, with a devotional address in the chapel after breakfast.

During the first of these weekends I suggested that on Whit Sunday morning, being the 'birthday' of the Christian Church instead of worshipping in our own chapel we might go to the local parish church for the Parish Communion at 11 o'clock. We did this, and after the service someone suggested that we all went to the local pub hard by for a celebratory drink. Everyone thought this a marvellous idea, so we crowded into the bar. Being carried away by the moment and full of euphoria, I raised my glass to our crowd that dominated the bar and said "Thank God for the Catholic Church!" - and we raised the roof with our laughter.

It was from the London Priory that I went to conduct my first mission, to St Alban's Church, Bournemouth, in 1952. This was part of the Mission to Bournemouth, in which every Anglican church had its missioner and a team of assistants. We began preparation for the mission a year before, and I had visited the parish several times, talking to the Parochial Church Council, encouraging the formation of prayer groups to start praying at once for the guidance of the Holy Spirit, and teams of visitors from the congregation to go round the parish, getting people accustomed to the idea of what was going to happen next year. This parish visiting was always very productive and by the time the mission team arrived the following year the parish priest invariably knew far more about his parish and the needs of his people than he had ever done before.

I took with me a lay brother from Mirfield, two nuns, two of our students, and a few lay people, nine or ten people altogether, and by the time we all arrived to begin the mission a lot of work had been done. The parish was full of expectancy and not a little excitement. This time I did all the preaching, and with the team out visiting most of the day the church was full every night for the mission service. This consisted of hymns and prayer and two addresses - sometimes there would be a tableau to illustrate the teaching, and we made sure that we had with us on the team someone able to act as producer of the tableaux, and a 'mistress of the wardrobe' responsible for the costumes. This mission gained a lot because everyone knew that there was a similar one being conducted in every Anglican church in the city, and the Mission to Bournemouth had a tremendous impact. All the churches were packed every night, and towards the end of the mission most of them reported that for several nights there had been 'standing room only' by the time the service began. The mission ended with a tremendous service of re-dedication - and a most exuberant parish party!

Soon after this I conducted a mission in Godstone, not far from South Park where the Holy Parties were held, and I already knew many of the local people. The South Park 'regulars' were a great help and did a lot of the visiting with the parish teams before the mission, and with the visiting team during it.

An amusing incident occurred on this mission. At this time I was still in my very *very* High Church period, and I wore the 'hat with strings' that had come my way at a 'share out' after one of the older brethren had died. One early evening as dusk was falling, I decided to pay a few visits nearby before preparing for the service, so, donning my big hat and long black cloak, I sauntered along to a row of cottages nearby. Simply 'on spec' I knocked on the door of a cottage in the middle of the row. The door was opened by a man in his shirtsleeves and braces, whose eyes flew wide open, and before I could say a word he shouted, "My God, the Pope!!" - and slammed the door in my face!

This mission saw the beginning of my career as an amateur photographer. I took on my team a young man who lived in London and was at the time rather mixed up. I had met him at a Holy Party, to which he had been brought by his current girl friend who lived in the neighbourhood.

I found myself talking to him idly one day about what I considered the unimaginative state of Mirfield Publications. Having done a little printing at St Augustine's I was very critical of what I considered the dull formats and presentation of many of our very good publications. "For one thing," I said, "we ought to be producing a book about the religious life in general, and the Community in particular, that would make people want to pick it up and read it - we need something like Picture Post, full of photographs and short but informative descriptions and explanations of the life." He agreed and became quite enthusiastic.

A few days later he came to me and said that months ago he had bought all the equipment he needed to become a press photographer. He said he knew now that he never would be a photographer, and would like to give me the equipment so that I could take the pictures needed to bring Mirfield Publications up to date! I was astonished and delighted, and could hardly believe it! Of course I had to ask the Superior's permission to accept this gift. I am glad to say that Raymond was almost as enthusiastic as I was. He told me to tell the generous donor how grateful the Community was for such a splendid gift. He said that I could have the equipment *in usum*. This meant that it did not belong to me, but while I needed it for the work of the Community I had it 'for use'. There was a lovely Rolleiflex camera with its professional standard tripod, and all the necessary flash guns, filters and light meters and other equipment. I took to photography at once and before long we produced the first of the Picture Post style books about the Community. I did the photography and dealt with the format and lay-out, and Fr Jonathan Graham wrote the text.

While I was at the London Priory Trevor Huddleston was going great guns in South Africa and was beginning to be known around the world as the prophetic voice condemning the evil of Apartheid. He was at that time Father Provincial of the Community in Southern Africa, the Superior's deputy there. Trevor was not, however, confining his work exclusively to the non-European population, he was also very active among the whites, and was doing everything he could to bring the two communities together. He was especially concerned with fostering good race relations in the Anglican churches.

The Community had built a charming retreat and conference house in Rosettenville near Johannesburg, opposite St Peter's Priory. St Benedict's House was open to people of all races, and while the Nationalist Government did all they could to enforce apartheid everywhere in South Africa, they did not trouble us much at St Benedict's, turning a blind eye to our flagrant breaches of the law - because they suddenly realized that the place was useful to them. On the not infrequent occasions when black diplomats from other countries visited South Africa the Community was asked to put them up at St Benedict's. This saved the Government the embarrassment of having to explain that no hotel in Johannesburg was permitted to have them. So they brought them to St Benedict's. The only alternative would have been a sleazy lodging house in one of the African townships.

One of the very popular ways of teaching the Faith and making it possible for people of all races to meet, was Trevor's idea of having evening lectures in the large sitting room at St Benedict's. These were by invitation, and they soon became so popular, and so many people from both sides of the racial divide crowded the room, that they became known as Shoe Parties, after the nursery rhyme lady who lived in a shoe and had *so* many children. The lectures were not on narrowly Christian topics: Trevor invited people specialising in a wide range of subjects to speak. The Shoe Parties were as popular with the speakers as they were with the invited audience.

At that time we were very conscious at the London Priory that we were not making the impact upon London that we felt we should, and we began to wonder whether we could emulate Trevor and hold Shoe Parties there too. At the bottom of our garden there was a quite attractive wooden summer-house and we began to think of turning it into a small hall and making it sufficiently comfortable to attract sophisticated Londoners to hear lectures, in our case specifically about the Christian Faith. This scheme was adopted and we were given a grant from the Bursar for extending the summer-house the full width of the garden, and even managed to form a tiny kitchen at one end. We bought nice 'pot' crockery - from Wedgwood, no less! Jack Linscott, an old friend of mine, had become a Lay Oblate of the Community. Having retired from business he was invited to come to live at the Priory and deal with all the invitations and bookings. There was a lot of work involved for which none of us could spare the time.

So the London Shoe Parties took off in a big way and a lot of very interesting people came to them. Some of the people who had been influenced by the Superior's Holy Parties at South Park used to bring their unbelieving or half-believing friends, and in the few years that they continued, the Shoe Parties had a considerable effect. I made some wonderful friends through these parties who showed me great kindness and generosity for many years.

All these activities, at South Park and in the London Priory brought me into contact with a stratum of society that so far I had only vaguely glimpsed from a distance. I began to number people with titles and riches among my friends and those who sought my help and guidance in both confessional and counselling session. I began to stay from time to time in wealthy and aristocratic homes. A far cry from the dingy office of the village builder and undertaker - and from the poverty-striken dunce walking the green lanes of Norfolk trying vainly to cram the principal parts of Greek verbs into his thick head! I regret to say that the thick head began to swell. I became more and more insufferable - years later my nieces admitted that they called me 'Old Bighead,' and I could understand why.

I learnt many things in the London Priory. I learnt, for instance, the importance of our religious habit with its broad belt and crucifix. I had cause to remember the Superior once saying, "The habit of a religious is his armour." I quickly learnt, as many young religious have to learn, that there are a few women for whom his vow of chastity is a challenge, and who will, by devious means try to seduce him. Sometimes the temptation is so strong that the only thing to do is to hold on tight to your crucifix - and run away! Of course there are also the occasions when the young religious finds the bonds of the vow of chastity creaking with the strain of being attracted by a woman in his pastoral care. If he knows that the attraction is reciprocated, and he usually does, then a dangerous situation can arise. Sometimes it can be resolved by a great act of faith and rededication on the part of both, and can develop into a disciplined and very rewarding friendship enfolded in the love of our Lord. At other times there has to be a decisive breaking of the relationship with unavoidable distress. I went through both experiences when I was a junior brother. I thank God for the enriching friendships, and I humbly ask pardon for any distress I caused in those that had to be broken.

One day the Prior came in to see me and said he had been asked if one of the brethren could be sent to Merstham in Surrey to speak to a group of City businessmen on one evening a week during Lent, and would I please do this? It was an assignment that was to begin a life-long friendship. Robin Johnston was a young Lloyds Underwriter and a regular member of the congregation of Merstham Parish Church. He had a number of cronies living in the neighbourhood who did not do much about churchgoing, so Rob had invited them to a drinks party and had said to them, "Look here chaps, Lent is coming up and *I* think we ought to learn a bit more about the Christian Faith. There's this community of Anglican monks that has a house in London, and I thought we might ask if one of them would come and talk to us once a week during Lent - nothing very churchy, just a nice evening party, here in my drawing-room. We'd have the drinks out of course, because I'm sure they are not teetotal or stuffy, and after he's talked we can shoot questions at I'm. What do you say?" They all said, "Agreed!" And the lot fell upon me!

They were wonderful evenings. Robin and his wife Dorothy and their three young children made me very welcome and gave me supper each week before the others arrived. Several of the men had been at Winchester with Robin and were now fellow Underwriters at Lloyds, two were stockbrokers, one a local doctor and one was in shipping. I managed to survive their questioning - mainly thanks to listening to Raymond Raynes at the Holy Parties - and it turned out to be one of the most enjoyable occasions of the whole of my ministry.

One evening I was talking to one of the Wykehamist stockbrokers, and started enthusing about a novel I had just read. I asked, "Have you read it?" He looked rather embarrassed and said, "I'm ashamed to say, Father, that I have not read a book since I left school." I was flabbergasted! A man with a top class education like he had had, and never reads a book! I covered my confusion and we were soon chatting about other things. Of course I have met other well educated people since then and know that there are many who never open a book, but at the time it was a revelation.

The next interesting job that came my way was the appointment as External Chaplain to Benenden School. I was to go down to Benenden two or three times a term and talk to the girls. My first visit was on a cold and wet winter's afternoon. I went down by train to Cranbrook station, which was on a tiny branch line, the train consisting of two old coaches behind a small 'puffing billy' locomotive. I was feeling very nervous. I was expecting very high powered and highly educated women on the staff and the thought of the headmistress, no doubt an authoritarian blue-stocking with a withering glance, made me tremble. They had sent a car to collect me from the station and as it dropped me at the imposing front door it was already dark. The driver motioned vaguely at the door, said, "Just ring the bell Father," and drove off.

I found the bell push but could not hear whether it rang, so I waited in the semi-darkness before this intimidating door, and the butterflies were doing aerobatics in my tummy. I seemed to have waited a long time wondering whether to ring again; my hand was hovering over the bellpush, when I heard as from a great distance the steady sound of a ponderous tread, slowly increasing in volume until at long last the deliberate stride stopped on the other side of the door, which slowly opened to reveal a large butler in full morning dress rig. He bowed slightly to me and invited me to enter. My coat and hat were taken and hung on a stand by the door, and then, taking my bag he invited me kindly to follow him. He was every inch the butler and everything was done with great solemnity. I followed him across the vast open space of the hall, trying to keep to my own stride and not match his like a raw recruit following his sergeant major, though that was pretty much how I felt.

At long last he stopped at a door, knocked and was bade enter - he opened the door announcing, Father Singleton, Miss Clarke, and showed me into a room full of light, with chintzy furniture and a blazing log fire. From behind the desk in the middle of the room rose the dreaded Headmistress of Benenden - whereupon the ogress immediately metamorphosed into a most charming and cheerful lady, who gave me a warm greeting, sat me in a comfortable armchair by the fire and rang the bell for tea. All my butterflies went to their hangars, or wherever butterflies go when they are not flying around, and in no time we were both perfectly at ease as she told me that she had succeeded the co-founders of the school, the Misses Bird, Hindle and Sheldon who had asked her to take over the headship from them. Miss Clarke was herself an old Benenden girl, and thought this invitation a great honour. I am sure they could not have found a more worthy successor, for I thought her a wonderful headmistress, with a most natural, affectionate and 'un-bossy' way with the girls.

My job was to talk to the girls about the Christian faith of course and try to answer their questions. These talk and question sessions were held, of all places, on the main staircase; the girls would arrange themselves on the whole length of the staircase, and I would sit on the top step. As I talked, their eager young faces looking up at me were like a bed of flowers. I found it highly delightful.

At dinner that first night, I met the rest of the resident staff and they were all very nice people and not in the least intimidating. I enjoyed my visits to Benenden.

To my regret the Princess Royal did not arrive at the school until a few years later when one of the other brethren had taken over from me. He was very impressed with her and used to say quite often, "As I said to HRH the other day ...." Needless to say I was quite jealous!

When, to his great delight, my friend Fr Claude Lunniss was sent back to South Africa, I succeeded him as Chaplain to Bickersteth House, a residential club for Christian girls working in London, which involved celebrating the Eucharist on Saturday mornings in the chapel and on the Friday evening giving an address to the residents and staff. There was also a good deal of counselling and hearing of confessions involved. The club is just off Campden Hill Square and was only a short walk from the Priory. Until just before I became Chaplain, the Warden had been the redoubtable Miss Goffe who ruled the roost in no uncertain way, and referred to the members as "My Gels." "Now, Father," she would say, "I think my Gels need to be reminded of their Christian obligations in Lent," or whatever.   The speaker at my first Bickersteth House jamboree was a vibrant young lady with a vintage Roedean voice. Her name was Dorothy. Very soon afterwards she married Deane Yates whom the Bishop of Johannesburg had just appointed Headmaster of St John's College, Johannesburg.

Another 'first' for me at the London Priory was my first visit to France, and this again was through the great generosity of friends. I had met Tom and Willa Jameson at the Priory Shoe Parties. They asked me if I could visit them in their home near Oxford because they had a lot of questions for which there was not time in the open meetings. Tom was a Captain RN in the Fleet Air Arm and was working at the Ministry of Defence. I stayed with them for a few days in their beautiful Elizabethan house in a small village deep in the lovely countryside of Oxfordshire. We had a number of question-and-answer sessions during those few days, and it turned out to be the beginning of a wonderful friendship.The following year they invited me to go to France with them for two weeks, all expenses paid. My Prior gave me rather grudging permission to accept this munificence

I have never forgotten that holiday - not least because they said I could help with the driving. We went to Calais from Lydd airport in Hampshire by a funny little transport plane that could carry only two cars, and drove towards Paris. The first night Willa and a woman friend who was also with us stayed in the guest house at Cluny, the famous Benedictine monastery, and Tom and I in the monastery itself. Breakfast the next morning consisted of bread-and-milk and fruit! But the coffee was excellent! No one had so far suggested that I should drive, and I assumed we were waiting until we got to the other side of Paris and on to quieter roads. Imagine my horror when on the outskirts of Paris, Tom stopped the car and said, "There you are Fr Paul you can drive now." Phew, the blighter! However I immediately put on my unflappable air and, pretending to be perfectly at ease, drove off on the 'wrong' side of the road for the very first time.

As I am sure he had intended all along, Tom had thrown me in at the deep end, for our route took us right into the heart of Paris, down the Champs Elysee and round the Arc de Triumph. People seemed to be sounding their horns all the time, drivers shouted and waved and gesticulated as they tore about in a manic fashion, shaking their fists as they cut in in front of me - and the gendarmerie constantly blew their whistles, which they held permanently in their mouths, as they pointed imperiously at me and waved their arms telling me where I must go. As we arrived at the hotel I was more than ready for an aperitif before lunch. To put it delicately, I was in a 'muck sweat'. Continental driving held no fears for me from then on, and I was grateful to Tom for this drastic introduction to the skill.

During the next few days I fell ever more deeply in love with Paris. I found the city and the people enchanting. I loved sitting in the dappled sunshine under a tree in Montmartre drinking strong coffee and watching the people - and how I wished I had tried a bit harder with my French at school! And the churches where I could hive off to make my meditation and say my office seemed to me to be places of real devotion, in spite of the hordes of tourists and sightseers. The Sacre Coeur, at which I arrived breathless and perspiring having toiled up all those steps, I thought full of the numinous, and the same applied to Notre Dame and St Sulpice where I loved the 'dim religious light'. There were always people praying in these churches.

Naturally, as this was my fist time in Paris we did all the tourist things, walked along the banks of the Seine, which in spite of my habit made me feel romantic, and sauntered in sunshine through the Tuillerie Gardens. Willa and her friend wanted to buy perfume at one of the famous houses, so I also went for the ride. We sat in opulence while glamorous assistants brought different perfumes, putting a tiny spot of each upon the backs of the women's hands for them to sample the fragrance. Impetuously I put out my hand too, and the young assistant giggled as she put an exotic spot on my wrist and said, "Ooo la la, Monsieur le Cure!" much to everyone's amusement.

One evening we met a friend of Tom and Willa's, a French businessman who took us out to dinner in a splendid restaurant. I was very impressed because he wore on his lapel the narrow red thread of the Legion d'Honeur, awarded for his bravery and services to France in the Resistance during the war. On our way south after leaving Paris we stayed a night with his family in Brittany.

We then had a week on the south coast where we stayed just outside Antibes and wallowed in glorious sunshine and sea. One day we tore ourselves away from the coast to go up into the mountains to Grasse to see Monet's famous chapel, the glorious riot of colour filling me with delight. On the homeward journey we went to Sens and after visiting the Cathedral we lunched in its shadow and I sampled my first *escargot*. Delicious!

Brethren who become very involved in the work of the Community in this country often come to fear that they might one day be sent to South Africa, and I was no exception. Africa in general had held a fascination for me from the time I had been enthralled by Rider Haggard (the exploits of Umslopogaas with his battle axe that made a neat little hole in the heads of his enemies!) and all the other intrepid explorers of the Dark Continent - but I did not want to be sent there to work. I was much too engrossed in my present activities. I had rather 'got above myself,' and had begun to think myself indispensable in the London scene of the Community. Unbeknown to me it was considered fairly widely, that I needed a change of venue. At Easter Chapter in 1956 the blow fell. Raymond Raynes called me to his office and said, "Paul I want you to go to South Africa in the autumn, to Sophiatown, is that all right?"

I swallowed hard and said, "Yes, Superior, of course. When do you want me to go?" He said he thought sometime in August; "You will have a lot of handing over to do and it would be nice for you to be at General Chapter in July, so, yes get a passage on the mailship sometime in August. Before you go you can have a bit of holiday with your family."

So that was that. Trevor Huddleston had been recalled in a whirl of publicity, and I was to go out to replace him *numerically*. No one could 'replace' Trevor, least of all me. I was simply being sent to make up the numerical strength of the community. I was being sent to Sophiatown, the African town that Trevor made famous in his book *Nought for Your Comfort*. As soon as it became known that I was going to South Africa I began to be plagued by the press, and although I said quite definitely that I was *not*, repeat *NOT*, the famous Fr Trevor Huddleston's successor, they did not believe me. My picture appeared, in the Evening News I think it was headlined 'Fr Huddleston's Successor in South Africa.' After that I got quite cunning at avoiding the press, and anyway I was rarely in London from then on until I sailed.

The family were upset about my move, knowing that South Africa is a violent place - Geoff said, "I'm sorry you are going, it's dangerous out there isn't it?" They also knew that in the normal course of events I would not be home for at least five years, when I would be due for my first furlough. The saddest of all I think, was my old grandmother; we were very fond of one another and she knew that it was very unlikely that she would still be alive when I returned in five years time. It was something I could not bear to think of very much, and nor could she.

Of course there were many farewells to be said. Tom Jameson was now in command of the Royal Naval Air Station in Londonderry and I was invited to go to stay with them for a long weekend to say goodbye. I had not been to Ireland so was eager for this opportunity.

I went to Liverpool and boarded the steamer for the night crossing. Having found my cabin, which I was to share with another man, I went on deck to smoke my pipe and survey the scene. I was standing amidships watching people coming aboard up the gangway, and the various bustling activities going on, when a little old Irish lady, dressed all in black came on board. As she got to me she stopped, curtsied, crossed herself and said, "God bless y' Faarther." She continued across the deck to the other rail, looked over the side for a moment, turned on her heel, came straight back, stopped, curtsied, made the sign of the cross and said, "God bless y' again Faarther," and went on her way.

My cabin companion was an Irishman, who fetched me a coffee just as I was about to turn in on my bunk, told me all his troubles while he took frequent and generous 'nips' from a bottle of whiskey, would not let me go to bed and got more and more loquacious and more and more emotional and drunk as the night wore on and the boat rolled and ploughed its way to his native heath. I did manage to get to bed at last, and by the time I got on deck the next morning and went in search of breakfast he had vanished.

Tom met me at Londonderry station in his official car, the first time I had ridden in a car flying a pennant. As we went sweeping through the country lanes I was very amused to see sailors, when they saw the car approaching, almost falling off their bikes so that they could stand at attention and salute as it swept by. I kept still of course, realizing that, unlike Portsmouth in wartime, it was Tom's uniform, not mine that they were saluting. Tom sat there beside me covered in gold braid, looking like the Duke of Edinburgh as he returned the salutes. There had recently been an upsurge of IRA violence, and there was tight security at the Naval airbase. As we arrived we passed through mountains of barbed wire, and there were armed Naval personnel everywhere.

169

Dinner that night had all the atmosphere of a Wardroom: Tom and his officers in dress uniform, the ladies in long dresses - and I wore my cassock with a clean scapular! That is one of the advantages of wearing a cassock all the time, it is not only your 'armour' but also your universal dress and can be worn anywhere - tuck it up in your belt while you dash out to feed the pigs, for instance, pull it down again and throw on a clean scapular, and go straight out to a dinner party: wonderfully versatile gear with minimum complications.

That was a splendid weekend and we even managed a trip over the border into the Republic to meet some of Tom's *Jameson* relations of Irish whiskey fame.

On the morning I was to leave, Tom said he had to go to the base to take the salute of a squadron of helicopters that was taking off, to be replaced by another from the mainland later that day. He asked whether I would like to join him. So we went out to the airfield and Tom made me stand with him on the saluting dais. In front of us were lined up, in three rows, the departing squadron of helicopters with their rotors ticking over. As Tom stood to attention the throttles were opened and the planes all rose as one and hovered stationary about fifty feet from the ground - and then, astonishingly, still in perfect unison and formation, they dipped their noses as Tom came to the salute, straightened up with a roar of revving engines and wheeled away to the right, or I suppose I should say to starboard, gaining height all the time. We watched them until they became faint dots in the sky. I would not have missed that display of precision flying for anything; it was thrilling.

Back then to London to continue with my final preparations for departure, white cassocks to be fitted, mailboat tickets to be collected, arrangements to be made to be chaplain of the ship on the voyage. The Society for the Propagation of Christian Knowledge, the Church publishing company that had bookshops all over the world, appointed a chaplain for the mailships, and if a member of CR was travelling he was nearly always the first to be invited. While in London I had served on the board of SPCK, and the Managing Director offered me the job as soon as I gave him my resignation and told him the reason for it. The job carried a concessionary fare, which pleased the Community's Bursar.

As the Superior had suggested, I had a short holiday with the family, and while there I took the opportunity of getting in touch with Bar. She invited me to lunch, and we sat in the garden in deckchairs before the meal and chatted very amicably and without embarrassment. She was looking as lovely as ever and maturing into a very handsome young woman. I think she was more relaxed than I had ever seen her. Tim was at school at Cranleigh, and at lunch it was clear that she was very fond of Bertie, and he was devoted to her. From what she had told me I knew he was very fond of Tim and was being a very good stepfather. I was happy for them both.

I spent the night before I sailed, at home with mother and Geoff. In the morning Gran and Aunt came from their flat nearby, and I left them all there - Gran standing on the front step with tears streaming down her poor old face, and waving her white hanky as I disappeared from view and from her life, and she from mine.

I was thankful that I had let it be known that I would rather get the boat train from Waterloo by myself and once again not have an emotional farewell on the platform.

I was very glum as the train sped through the Hampshire countryside. I realized how much I loved this land with its woods and green fields and rich hedgerows, and I wondered when I would see it again - *if* I would ever see it again.

So one very downhearted young religious arrived on the dockside at Southampton and looked with scant enthusiasm at the pale mauve side of the RMS Stirling Castle towering above him. Lugging my case up the gangway I reported at the Purser's desk and was told how to find my cabin. The cabin door was shut, but I could hear voices! Check the cabin number and deck. Yes, correct. So I tapped on the door and a voice I knew said, Come in! Noel Davey, Managing Director of SPCK with his secretary, come to see me off with a bottle of wine and a huge bunch of flowers! What a wonderful surprise, and what a wonderful gesture! They must have taken the day off from the office in Northumberland Avenue just to see me off. I felt overwhelmed by their kindness, and my spirits began to lift. Noel introduced me to the First Officer, who welcomed me aboard as their chaplain, and we made a date for me to be shown the facilities for services, after we had sailed. When all visitors were asked to leave the ship as the time for sailing approached, Noel and his secretary went ashore. As we cast off, with a long booming blast from the siren, I stood by the rail and waved to my friends as they stood diminishing on the dockside. *O dear, I wish I had married Bar and we were comfortably ensconced in a nice parish in England. Nonsense, this is your vocation. Yes, Lord, sorry.*

The First Officer introduced me to the Captain on the bridge, then took me to see the main lounge where he said I could hold a Communion service at 8 o'clock on the two Sunday mornings, and another general service for all comers at 9.30am. He showed me the library where I could celebrate every morning at 8 o'clock if I wished, and the cupboard where all the vestments and the chalice and paten were kept. The front of the cupboard folded down to make a small temporary altar. There was also a notice board by the Purser's desk where I could post any notices I wanted displayed. He said that he would announce on the tannoy that there would be a celebration of Holy Communion in the library at 8o'clock the next morning, and I was not to hesitate to ask him about anything I wanted or was uncertain about. Then he introduced me to the voyage doctor who said he would let me know of any sick people who might appreciate a visit. I'm sure there will be some, he said, there always are!

So for twelve days the Stirling Castle became my parish. Wearing a cassock I had a pretty high profile and I did not need to go looking for like-minded friends, they came to me and introduced themselves. Several who were regular travellers in the Union Castle Line ships knew other members of the Community, for it was only the Superior and other big shots in CR who flew to S Africa. The rest of us invariably went by sea.

On my first morning three people turned up for the 8 o'clock Communion service in the library, and there was always at least one other person every morning of the voyage, so I was able to celebrate daily. On each of the Sundays we had several people at the early service in the lounge, and about fifty, to a hymns and prayers and address service at 9.30. These services introduced me to quite a large number of people, and again and again I had to deny that I was Fr Huddleston's successor. There were many who came to me to say how much they admired the work he had done; some very cross that he had been recalled. Also a significant number came to tell me how wicked he was and that he was undermining the state and they were glad he had been recalled. I suppose of the people I met the majority were in favour of apartheid, and it was only the committed Christians, as distinct from 'churchgoers', and a few deeply thinking people of no particular faith, who saw how evil it was. A number of families on board were emigrating to South Africa, and it saddened me to hear them trying to justify apartheid before they had even set foot in the country - they were eagerly looking forward to a lifestyle, with cheap servants to do all the work in house and garden, that they could never have afforded in Britain. I made friends with people of all denominations, and met with almost universal kindness.

I had recently delivered a lecture on 'The Resurrection - True or False?' at one of the Priory Shoe Parties and I had put it in my bag, 'just in case.' After dinner one night, I mooted the idea of repeating it to a delightful young Methodist couple who had become special friends, and they were enthusiastic and said they would certainly like to hear it. So I put up a notice saying I would deliver the lecture in the library one evening after dinner and would answer questions afterwards. I thought we might get a dozen or so, but at least thirty people crammed into the small library, and we had to open the windows on to the deck so that those who could not squeeze in could lean through the windows to listen.

There was much that I enjoyed on that voyage, but I was thankful that it was not longer than twelve days. I got very bored with all the deck games and competitions which did not appeal to me, and the dancing in the evenings from which I was naturally precluded. I did so admire the young officers, led by the First Officer, who hosted all this frenetic gambolling night after night as part of their job.

When the day came for Crossing the Line, to which all the children and young people had looked forward with mounting excitement, I discreetly went visiting in the First Class area of the ship and from a safe distance watched King Neptune come aboard, capture his victims who had not crossed the Line before, cover them in lather and proceed to shave them with a huge wooden razor, and then dunk them in the pool afterwards. I had not crossed the line before either, and was determined not to become a victim. So I wore one of my new white cassocks and a black scapular and tried to look very dignified and a little aloof - and made sure by retreating to the First Class decks from where I watched the plebs having their vulgar fun! Yes, I know, Chicken!

One day I was invited on to the bridge by the Captain who asked if I would like to take a trick at the wheel! As you may imagine I did not hesitate for a moment. It was a tremendous experience. Here was this relatively small spoked wheel in the middle of the bridge; there outside the window was the whole forward part of the ship stretching into the distance and looking immense and solid. Turn round and look astern and there was the even larger after section. Wonder of wonders, this little pygmy standing here could make that enormous throbbing monster go in any direction he wished simply by turning this little wheel! The Captain indicated the binnacle in front of the wheel, the compass needle steady, as the sailor at the wheel kept the ship on course. He was told to stand aside for me to 'take the ship.' Remembering what I had learnt from Tom I took the wheel with both hands, grinned at the Captain and said, "I have the ship, sir." "Carry on Father," he said. As, with tiny adjustments, I kept the ship on course I could sense how sensitive it was to the least touch of the wheel; it was vibrant with life. The Captain then said I could steer just a little off course and then bring it back, to get a better feel of what I was doing. That was the culminating thrill, as the needle of the compass went first to starboard then to port, and then back on the original reading. Only a very slight deviation, but I had actually steered that monster; it had actually obeyed my commands! Was I chuffed!

After the heat on the equator the temperature gradually moderated as we approached the southern tip of Africa where it was mid-winter. So it was back to a black cassock and grey scapular again.

Everyone seemed to be on deck to see Table Mountain coming gradually into view, disappointingly without its famous white tablecloth. Disembarkation procedures were in full swing by the time we docked in Cape Town harbour. I was held up at Customs because Geoff had given me some flower seeds to plant in the garden at Sophiatown, and this created a bit of a stir because seeds could bring in crop diseases and their import into the country was very strictly controlled. However, after a lot of humming and hawing they decided that it was such a small quantity that they would let me keep them.

I said goodbye to my friends, all of us saying that we must meet again, but like most shipboard friendships they proved ephemeral, and with one exception we never did meet again. The exception was a businessman who very kindly put me up for a night when I was stranded in Port Elizabeth a couple of years later.

Tom Savage, at that time Dean of Cape Town Cathedral, and his wife Monica met me at the quayside and carried me off to the Deanery where I was to be their guest for a few days over the weekend before going up country to Johannesburg. As we walked to their car I was astonished to see, moored behind the Stirling Castle, the Royal Yacht, Britannia. That brought a lump to my throat and a wave of homesickness swept over me. However one could not be depressed for very long in Tom Savage's company. He had been trained at Mirfield, so we were soon swapping stories about the Community and College and felt we had known one another for years. Tom and Monica and their two teenage children were kindness itself and gave me a good tour of the Cape during the time I was with them, including a visit to Cecil Rhodes' house which had been left exactly as it was when he died.

Soon after we arrived at the Deanery, Tom said, "O Father, I've put you down to preach at Evensong in the Cathedral on Sunday, is that OK?" "O yes, I said, that's OK. Thank you very much." Then he added, "O yes, and it will be broadcast throughout

South Africa, we are 'on the air' that night. The Cathedral will be comfortably full, but you will have a much bigger audience than that." Phew! I'd never broadcast before and I was quite scared of the thought of it. He said I just had to be sure that I did not preach for more than twelve minutes. I did my best, but I don't think anyone was greatly inspired by what I had to say.

So - I had arrived in the Dark Continent at last. I wondered what it had in store for me ....

Next stop Johannesburg - and Sophiatown.

My heart quailed at the thought.

8

South Africa

Tom and Monica Savage put me on the Johannesburg train at Cape Town station for the nine hundred mile journey, which would take over twenty-six hours to complete and involved a night on the train.

After I had boarded the train, the Guard, seeing that I was what he would have called a *domine*, Afrikaans for 'minister', set about finding me a 'coupe' - a small compartment with only two bunks and a table and stainless steel washbasin. There was one free about the middle of the train and I was assured that I would have this to myself all the way to Johannesburg, so I really was travelling comfortably. It was wonderful what a cassock could do!

There was a 'coloured' attendant, that is a man of mixed race, for each coach, who came in to make up your bunk at night and stow it all away tidily each morning while you were having breakfast in the dining car. He would call you at whatever time you wished in the morning with a cup of splendid South African coffee. I soon found myself thoroughly enjoying this comfortable way of travelling, and it never lost its appeal for me all the time I was in that fascinating country.

At dusk we reached the brown parched scrub of the Karoo desert stretching in all directions as far as the eye could see.

Some time after I went to bed I heard lashing rain beating on the roof of the compartment and the roll of thunder. The next morning as I looked out of my window I had a wonderful surprise, for instead of unbroken brown sand and scrub there were flowers to be seen everywhere you looked. I realized how lucky I was to see this enchanting phenomenon of the desert on my very first trip across it - the rain had brought the flowers opening in the dawn and, as Holy Scripture says, 'the desert had blossomed like a rose.'

The next day we began to climb from the 'low veldt' to the 'high veldt', out of the Karoo desert to higher ground on which Johannesburg stands at 6,000 feet above sea level, so it became colder, and when I got down from the train at the occasional stops I began to feel the icy wind that blows on the high veldt for much of the winter months. From the window I saw the small flat-topped hills and mountains, known as *kopjes* (pronounced 'copies') and the piles of rocks that are typical of the South African landscape. Soon after breakfast we were running through the outskirts of Johannesburg and I began to see my first African areas, thousands of identical brick boxes with corrugated asbestos roofs, marching in serried ranks across the landscape, diminishing to the distant horizon. The 'roads' were red earth, and for every few houses there was a standpipe by the roadside, the only source of water, and an outside toilet shared by two or three houses. There was smoke rising on the cold morning air from the cooking fires as the women crouched over their pots preparing food.

We drew slowly into Johannesburg station, the front half of the train into the 'white' part of the station, the rear stopping at the non-white section where the African and other non-white passengers went their separated way.

There on the platform to meet me was my old friend and fellow novice, Jack Guinness with his wide welcoming grin, He had preceded me to Sophiatown about a year before. Jack had brought one of the community cars, and having stowed my luggage in the boot he took me to the community's headquarters, St Peter's Priory, Rosettenville. Here was Trevor Huddleston's real successor, Fr George Sidebotham, the new Provincial. I was given a warm greeting by all the brethren, including the three Africans whom I had not met before, Frs Leo Rakale, Ambrose Duba, and Simeon Nkuane. They were all very friendly but I seemed to 'click' specially with Leo Rakale, partly, I think, because he was completely unconscious of colour. He had a wonderful sense of humour and was great company. One could surely never be dull for very long in his company.

After lunch, once more with butterflies looping-the-loop in my tummy, Jack took me by a circuitous route through Johannesburg and out the other side to Sophiatown. Johannesburg was, and still is in my opinion, an ugly city, the semi-skyscrapers are brash and monolithic. The 'city of gold' they call it and it is completely dedicated to the acquisition of wealth, a temple to materialism, like most money markets and centres of business. Soon we ran out of the city through very pleasant residential areas, with good houses and beautiful gardens. Then the outer suburbs where the standard of living became progressively lower until we were running through the 'poor white' areas whose inhabitants did not see much of the gold of the Golden City. Then we crossed the tram tracks, and Jack said, "Welcome to Sophiatown!" We were driving up hill through a crowded street, with Africans, and a few Indians and Chinese milling around. As soon as they noticed the car the adults smiled and waved, and the children ran alongside waving and shouting, "Hello Fudder," "Hello Fudder," and grinning from ear to ear, the bolder ones jumping on the running board for a ride, Jack's face lit up as he returned the greetings that bombarded us at every turn of the wheels; it was clear that he was devoted to these people. What a vibrant and exciting place! Even driving slowly in the car I could feel the sheer *life force* of the place. The butterflies had begun to settle a little. Up the street we went, and there at the top was the famous church of Christ the King, its tall clock tower dominating the scene. Opposite the church we turned into the school playground, deserted now because the school is closed, and out the other side, across the rough and rocky road to the Priory of Christ the King, which was to be my home for the next few years.

The Priory was built of brick with a corrugated iron roof, on four sides of a square with a lawn and a large jacaranda tree in the middle. There was an open verandah, or *stoep*, all the way round from which opened the chapel, three brethren's rooms, a store, the wash-house, the kitchen and refectory. On the front of the Priory were the office and the 'parlour', which were outside the 'enclosure', and where lady visitors could be received. The 'front *stoep*' ran all along the front of the Priory, and it was here that callers waited until they could be seen in either parlour or office. In the 'enclosed' part of the house were four more rooms for brethren or guests and the community room or common room. Blue-gum (eucalyptus) and jacaranda trees and an avocado pear tree grew in the front garden, giving a lot of welcome shade to the house. The house was built for hot weather, not cold, and the bitter winds that blew across the Reef penetrated the house and cut one to the bone. I have never been so cold anywhere else on earth as I was during the Johannesburg winters. Each of us had an electric fire in his room, and there were fires in the public rooms as well, but they did little more than make the place just bearable. So in winter we would put on all our 'winter woollies', even to scarves and mittens indoors in order to keep passably warm. It reminded me of Tatterford in the late '30s. Of course in the daytime when the sun was shining from a cloudless sky one only had to go out and find a spot sheltered from the wind and one was immediately warmed right through.

I soon got into the way of things in Sophiatown and a very exciting place it was. Opposite the Priory on the other side of the road was Ekutuleni (House of Peace-Making) where various numbers of Wantage Sisters worked on the Mission. Ekutuleni had been begun by Dorothy Maude daughter of a one-time Bishop of Kensington, in the late 1920s. She had a consuming passion for social justice and worked untiringly for the welfare of the people of Sophiatown.

The township had been founded by a Pole who had bought the area some five or six miles from the centre of Johannesburg and had sold building plots to Africans, Indians and Chinese - and he had named it after his wife Sophia. Sophiatown, with neighbouring

Martindale and Newclare were the only places near Johannesburg where non-whites could be freeholders. Over the years the white suburbs of the city had gradually spread and by the 1940s had surrounded the township on three sides.

As the need for more and more cheap labour had increased over the years no new areas had been put aside to accommodate the burgeoning work-force, so workers coming in from the country districts had to crowd into the existing 'black' areas. In Sophiatown standholders built shacks on their plots, which they rented to those crowding into the township. As a result Sophiatown was a conglomeration of decent houses, each with its back yard full of shacks built of rusty corrugated iron and often lined with corrugated cardboard. The overcrowding was terrible, and I marvelled at the way people managed to keep clean and nicely dressed, as most did, when living in these conditions. From these shacks - as from similar ones in all the townships of Johannesburg, there came children in spotless clothes answering the church bell Sunday by Sunday.

The City Council had completely neglected Sophiatown, and it was only in the middle 1930s, when Raymond Raynes had been appointed Priest-in-Charge of the parish that things began to change. Raymond also had fire in his belly for social justice, and he and Dorothy Maude made a formidable pair. Through their efforts main drainage and street lighting had been installed, and the main roads metalled. It was said that when the gaunt figure of Raymond Raynes, with cassock and scapular flowing, stalked into any of the Council offices, the staff ran for cover. I suppose it could be said that notwithstanding his great work later as Superior of the Community and behind the scenes in the councils of the Church, the greatest work of his life was done in Sophiatown. He certainly enjoyed it more than he did anything else. When he was eventually recalled to become Superior of the Community he had wondered whether there could ever be anyone else in CR to whom he could confidently entrust his beloved Sophiatown. It is said that as soon as he met his then very junior brother Trevor Huddleston he knew that he had found a worthy successor. And so it proved, indeed Trevor went on to build on the firm foundations laid by Raymond, and it was he who put Sophiatown on the world map and trumpeted the evils of the Nationalist Government's policy of apartheid to every corner of the globe.

When I arrived in Sophiatown in 1956 Dominic Whitnall was Priest in Charge, with Jack Guinness as his second in command. On arrival at the Priory I was introduced to Auntie, who was our African cook, short and fat and on the whole jolly, but who had black moods that would come upon her suddenly and for no

179

apparent reason. Then there were the various young men, most notably Maurice Mabika, big and strong and dependable. I also met another Maurice, Maurice Manana who drove the jeep and the van for the Sisters at Ekutuleni across the road and was sometimes lent to us when our own car was not suitable for the job in hand. I was shown my room, which looked out onto the garden, beyond the fence of which was a brick house with its satellites of shacks.

Dominic then took me out of the front door across the deserted school playground to the great church of Christ the King.

Fr Raymond Raynes had built the church - he had said to the architect, "I haven't much money, so I want you to build me a huge garage." The result was a church that could seat a thousand people. It had a wide nave, side aisles with ample seating, Norman style arches, all of brick and precast concrete, and a very large sanctuary with a great High Altar against the East wall. There was room enough for all the ceremonial that anyone could desire. The whole place was full of light and colour. The smooth concrete steps leading up to the High Altar were always shining brightly with red Cardinal polish; the low walls surrounding the Sanctuary likewise gleaming with contrasting black polish. The ceiling of the Sanctuary was a pale blue, and the East wall and the walls of all the aisles and side chapels were filled with beautiful frescoes painted by one of the Wantage Sisters. The face of Christ the King was easily recognisable as the face of Raymond Raynes, and others of the Fathers featured in the various saints depicted on the walls. The roof was of corrugated iron painted dull red, and the simple but splendid tower held the clock with a face on all four sides, and the bell which was tolled several times every day. The clock faces could be seen from considerable distances in the township, for the church was built upon the highest outcrop of rock at the top of the hill upon which Sophiatown stood - from the church it was downhill in all directions. The inhabitants of Sophiatown relied upon the church clock and the ringing of the bell for their timekeeping. The bell was always rung at five-thirty every morning for the first mass at 6 o'clock. The Angelus was rung at 6am, 12 noon, and 6pm daily. One morning it was my duty to ring the first bell and I overslept, and did not ring it until just before I began the mass. That evening one of the men rebuked me gently saying, "Father did not ring the bell this morning - I was late for work."

I tried to capture the atmosphere of Sophiatown in one of the newsletters I regularly wrote for friends in England. Here was a typical day at the mission:

Haul in the rope, boom, boom, boom, goes the old bell....
Tap-tap-tap. here comes old blind Margaret Tlotleng to her

daily Mass (never misses a service in fact), led by her small niece, Yvonne, aged eight and a charmer. Paddle, paddle, paddle - the bare feet of my server.... Twenty people there by the end of the Preparation, and thirty-five to forty by the end of the Epistle..... We are just sitting down to breakfast when an African houseboy comes in and says, "John has been arrested, Father," so its saucers on top of cups and out we go to see the very usual sight of upwards of two dozen African men handcuffed together in a dismal crocodile - all are Pass offenders....... 8.20 am Prime and Terce sung in chapel. Greater Silence ends, There's no such thing as Lesser Silence in Sophiatown, for by 8.30 the place is buzzing with life and problems. Already there is a queue of folk on our front *stoep* .... Meanwhile the phone rings,"Please Father, I am a reporter from a German newspaper...." Better look in on old Ben on the way home (had his leg amputated just below the knee pushed under a bus by *tsotsies* (gangsters) - his message when he knew his leg had to come off was, "God is good, I've got to have my leg off Father." Lives in a corrugated iron (tenth-hand) shack with his dear old wife. The inside walls are corrugated cardboard from old Surf cartons.

So the day went on: confessions to be heard; couples to be prepared for marriage... people in distress, "My daughter has been raped Father;" "I have nowhere to sleep, Father." Evensong sung by a congregation of thirty, then clubs and organisations to visit; just before Compline a man turns up, "Wounded , Father"- first aid in the bathroom; the wound was not bad - he was very ticklish and everyone got the giggles - such a relief to laugh. Sometimes there are as many as fifteen or twenty wounds to be dressed. After Compline, bed - and the night noises of Sophiatown - maybe the man who smoked dagga (marujana) and had DTs, or the dogs howling, or the doorbell and a request to ring the Maternity Hospital (the Priory had one of the few phones in the area).

Sunday in Sophiatown was a weekly wonder of delight. There were two early masses, one at six and another at eight, but the great service of the day was the High Mass at ten. When I first arrived there would be six or seven hundred people in church - the small children massed in the central aisle looking like a huge flower bed. On Sundays, from the well-built and prosperous, and also from the poorest houses and shacks, came hordes of spic and span children, ebony skin shining in the sun, the girls in pretty coloured frocks, the boys in snow-white shirts and navy shorts or trousers. I was always amazed by the lengths to which the people would go to

181

be thoroughly clean - water often having to be brought to the shack from a distant standpipe. Even the poorest people seemed to have precious 'Sunday best' clothes stored away and freshly pressed on Sunday morning ready for church.

The service itself was in either English or one of the two main African languages, Xhosa and Sotho, but the hymns were sung in five languages simultaneously, the numbers displayed on an immense hymn-board. We had a first class choir under Michael Rantho, our very able choirmaster who could have been a professional had his skin not been black. The choir was massed at the West end of the church, in my opinion the best place for a choir in order to give the greatest 'lift' to the congregational singing. The sermon was preached from the huge pulpit that could accommodate the preacher and two interpreters with ease - and with plenty of room for all three to make expansive gestures. At first, preaching with two interpreters was a strange experience, for one thing a five minute address took fifteen minutes to deliver. I thought it would give more time to think about what one was going to say next, but on the contrary I found I had to hang on tight to what I was saying or I would forget and get into a muddle.

The worship at this service was so wonderful and inspiring that it beggars description. A number of white visitors from Johannesburg, including Deane Yates, the Headmaster of St John's College, and Dorothy his wife, came regularly Sunday by Sunday to worship with us at the High Mass and said they found the services in other churches insipid by comparison. There were also frequent visitors from all over the world who came to experience the worship in the famous Christ the King, Sophiatown - and without exception said they had never known anything like it anywhere else. Of course the liturgy was the old unreformed Anglo-Catholic High Mass, with Celebrant, Deacon and Subdeacon, holy water, incense, masses of candles, the servers in red cassocks and lace cottas - the lot! It was good 'theatre' by any standard, and a very natural way, it seemed to me, for Africans to express their worship of their Risen Lord, Christ the King. But perhaps it was the choir which made this service unique of its kind, at least for me and for many who came to worship with us. Africans have a natural flair for harmony, and the men and boys of the choir produced the most unimaginable harmonies that sent tingles of wonder and delight down the spine, and I listened specially for the deep organ-note sounds of the vibrant African bass voices. It was the singing that drew most comment from our visitors.

One of the most moving Sophiatown occasions was the Maundy Thursday Watch. The last Mass before Easter is sung on

Christ the King, Sophiatown 1957

Removals from Sophiatown, Father Hoey and I (right) watch impotently

With Sophiatown kids outside
the Priory 1958

Visiting among the shacks

Despair among the ruins of Sophiatown 1960

185

the evening of Maundy Thursday. We commemorate the Last Supper when Jesus took the bread and said, 'This is my body,' and the cup and said, 'This is my blood of the new covenant.' At the end of this Mass the consecrated Host is not consumed, but taken in solemn procession and placed upon the Altar of Repose. This altar has been carefully prepared beforehand and is decked in the best hangings and frontal, with many candles on the altar and surrounding it, as many flowers as are available. The consecrated Host upon the altar reminds us of the real presence of our Lord, the Light of the World, who tomorrow, Good Friday, is to be crucified. We are invited to keep watch with him all through the night.

Most churches I knew had a rota of people who promised to keep watch for an hour at a time to make sure that the Altar of Repose was not left unattended. No rota was necessary in Sophiatown. No sooner had the Host been placed upon the altar and all the candles lit than people crowded in to keep the vigil. People of all ages, from boys and girls to men and women in their prime, grannies and the halt and the blind. Old Miriam with Yvonne in attendance, was one of the first to settle down. All would kneel on the hard floor, many of them upright and unmoving for a long time. I noticed two or three mothers in the crowd with their babies in shawls on their backs in the African fashion. They would pray for half an hour or so, then taking the baby off their backs, they would curl up on the floor, settle the baby in their arms - and go to sleep. What wonderful prayer, I thought! For I was sure that in their subconscious minds their prayer was continuing while they slept. I made several visits to the Altar of Repose that night and always there were many coming and going, slipping quietly into the church and out again after their devotions - but many stayed the whole night.

Two things in Sophiatown symbolised most strongly for me the Community of the Resurrection's resistance to the oppressive racial laws of the South African government. The empty school buildings, and the gradual destruction of the homes of the people and their removal to Meadowlands, part of what later became Soweto.

The Bantu Education Act of the early 1950s limited by law the degree of education that the non-white races were permitted to receive. This was to make sure that the non-white majority would never be able to compete with the white man. Dr Verwoed, the evil genius of apartheid, had openly stated that the Bantu races were only to be educated in Afrikaans, and only to a certain very elementary level, just sufficient for them to be of use to the superior white race. The Community decided that it could have no part in such a travesty of education and accordingly closed all its schools and colleges in South Africa. This was a tremendous loss to the non-white population, but we could have done nothing less. The Community of the Resurrection had founded and run many schools for Africans, the best known being St Peter's Rosettenville, known as the Black Eton, where many well known Africans had been educated to the highest standards. And of course the schools at Sophiatown. So our schools stood empty, a perpetual silent reproach to the South African Government.

The steady destruction of the homes of Sophiatown had already begun when I arrived there. White Johannesburg having spread until it surrounded Sophiatown on three sides, Sophiatown had become a black spot in a white area, and this was an intolerable situation for the Afrikaans government. Hence the passing of the Group Areas Act, specifically designed to get rid of all such black spots and move the populations further out from the city to the distant areas that eventually came to be known as Soweto. The Act dealt not only with the removal of the population, but also with the unique problem of the non-europeans in Sophiatown who owned their own freehold. The Act stated that they were to be given 'comparable alternative accommodation' in Meadowlands, the designated area in which the people of Sophiatown were to be resettled. They were also to be given 'adequate compensation' for the loss of their freehold. It had become abundantly clear to the Community that neither of these provisions in the Act was being honoured. Indeed the clearance of Sophiatown was being carried out with no regard for the people at all. It was almost a daily occurrence for a truck to turn up outside a house without notice, and with a gang of men who would immediately proceed to load the contents of the house in the roughest possible way, barking orders at the occupiers. Last of all they themselves would be loaded on to the truck amongst their belongings, and driven off to Meadowlands where they would be dumped outside a small brick box - the 'comparable' alternative accommodation! There was no mention of compensation.

Dominic Whitnall, collaborating with Trevor Huddleston, had instructed a very fine firm of lawyers, the Epstein brothers, to prepare a case against the Government on behalf of the 'standholders' of Sophiatown to halt the piecemeal clearance of the township until the conditions of the Act had been fulfilled. Not long after my arrival Dominic, sadly, was not well and had to retire from Sophiatown and I took over the work of liaising between the lawyers in Johannesburg and the standholders in the township. This was a very exciting business and not a little scary. I would go regularly into the city to meet Jacob Epstein and his younger brother, Brian, and they would brief me on the progress of the case. Back in Sophiatown I would then call a meeting of the standholders in the disused school hall. On the appointed evening the hall would be packed with people, several hundred of them, and I would stand on the stage with two interpreters, and tell them what the lawyers had said. As I spoke I would see dotted about the hall as many as half a dozen men busily writing in their notebooks - the Special Branch Police, like the nuns in peaceful England, taking down every word I said. Cold shivers would run down my spine in spite of the heat of the hall on a balmy African night.

At that time, because we were trying to stand up for the basic human rights of our people against a callous and fanatical regime, we went to bed every night wondering whether before morning we would be in gaol. I had had my first brush with the Special Branch on my first day in Sophiatown. After breakfast on my first morning I had taken a camera and gone for a walk around the township to begin to get to know it. As I came down one of the main streets I saw coming towards me a line of African men handcuffed at intervals onto a long chain. I immediately focused on this sorry sight and took several photographs in quick succession. I looked up to see two white policemen with swagger-sticks bearing down upon me, and suddenly realizing that I should not have taken those pictures, I quickly opened the back of the camera and exposed the film to the light. They were very angry indeed and I thought I was going to be arrested on the spot, but after I had said I had only just arrived at the Priory and was just looking for 'local atmosphere', they gave me a good ticking off and left, to arrest more poor wretched men just because they had forgotten to bring their passes with them when they set off for work. (Every African man had to carry a passbook wherever he went to prove that he had a job and therefore had a right to be there). That afternoon two grim-faced men called at the Priory and demanded to see me - Special Branch officers who interrogated me for a long time on my reasons for wanting to take those pictures. They were clearly furious that I had managed to destroy them before the police had got to me. They would have loved to arrest me, but I had destroyed the evidence.

However, despite this episode, I took a camera with me wherever I went, and soon I was repeatedly being asked to 'take a snap' of the homes that were soon to be demolished. I often wanted to weep when a man or a woman, with big sad eyes would say to me, "Father must please take a snap of my place, before they pull it down, Father." I was soon a busy photographer, and was allowed to turn one of the school rooms into a really professional darkroom where I did all my own processing and enlarging. I sold enough of my photographs to make it possible to equip the darkroom and give many of my pictures away, especially to those whose houses I photographed. One day I thought I would go and take some pictures of the 'comparable alternative accommodation' at Meadowlands, so I got into the car and went over. There, stretching as far as the eye could see were hundreds of rows of little brick boxes with corrugated asbestos roofs, all absolutely identical, all equally spaced from one another, on both sides of identical red-dirt roads with the occasional high-slung street light. There were three small rooms inside, none had doors fitted - the only door was the front door. Where the corrugated asbestos roof rested upon the walls there was a line of holes because the corrugations had not been filled in. The internal walls were of plain brick like the exterior. The floors were rough concrete. The contrast between the often beautiful Sophiatown houses and these dreadful places was stark and cynical. It was outside one of these that our people from all the decent houses in Sophiatown were being unceremoniously dumped with all their goods and chattels in pathetic disarray while their lovely homes in the township were being bulldozed to the ground. I was filled with anger as I drove back to the Priory. There I immediately went to the darkroom and developed and printed the photographs I had taken. I was meeting the Epsteins in town the next day for one of our regular sessions, and I took a selection of the pictures with me, including a number of those of the nice houses in Sophiatown. I put the pack of pictures on Jacob's desk and said, "I thought you might like to see these - Group Areas Act, Before and After!" He picked them up and began to turn them over slowly, first the nice houses as I had carefully arranged them; then, without warning, suddenly the 'comparable alternative accommodation'. I saw his jaw harden; he looked up at me with flashing eye, and said, "This is *obscene!*" - and crashed his fist on the desk. "My sentiments exactly," I said. He thought for a moment and then said, "You know what I'm going to do, Father? *I'm going to bind up these photographs with our petition to the Court!*" "Gosh," I said, "Can you do that?" "You watch me!" he said.

The day when we all went to the court house in Johannesburg for the hearing was unforgettable. Jacob Epstein had retained a well-known QC to present the case of the Standholders of Sophiatown against the Government. The public gallery was crammed; it seemed as though half Sophiatown was there, all buzzing with barely suppressed excitement. I sat just behind Jacob Epstein and the QC. The judge in black gown first called upon our man to present his case, and while he was speaking I noticed that the judge seemed not to be listening. He was turning the pages of our petition - and I saw when he got to the photographs. He looked at each of them in turn, then went back to the beginning and looked at them all again. As he came to the last one for the second time, he tapped with his gavel and stopped our QC in his tracks. Said he, "Are these photographs a true representation of the facts?" "Yes, your honour, they are," said our QC. The judge said, "The Court will have to satisfy itself on that point. The case is adjourned until two o'clock tomorrow afternoon. At nine o'clock tomorrow morning the Court will visit all these premises to verify these photographs."

The next morning I was outside the first house in Sophiatown that was to be visited. I had been there well before nine, and eventually I saw a line of black limousines snaking its way toward us across the waste ground on the border of the township - looking like a funeral without a hearse. The Court was on its way! From the front car descended the judge - looking rather ordinary without his gown, and then the Clerk to the Court, and all the other officials. I conducted them through the house and they looked into every neat and clean room, at the kitchen with its sparkling pots and pans, its gleaming cooker and spotless fridge. I think we visited two more houses, then they all got back into their cars and, driving the Priory car, I led them out to Meadowlands where they solemnly observed the brick boxes in their serried ranks, and went inside one of them to see the doorless rooms and the daylight coming in around the eaves.

The case lasted two more days; the QC representing the Government spoke at length, but he hadn't got a hope really, for it was quite clear that the provisions in the Act for compensation and for the provision of comparable alternative accommodation were not being implemented. And so the Judge said, very forcefully, when he gave judgment in our favour. There was a tremendous outburst of applause from the public gallery, waving of arms, cries of delight and, of course it being Africa, the singing of victory songs and dancing. I was watching the two men who were in charge of the clearance and demolition of Sophiatown as the judgment was given; their large faces went brighter red than usual, they muttered to one another, glanced spitefully at me and fled the court.

But the fight was not over yet. The Government immediately announced that it would appeal against the verdict. That meant several more months to wait before we really knew, and in the meantime the clearance of Sophiatown went on at an accelerated pace, sometimes almost with frenzy. One night I was called after midnight by our stalwart Maurice Mabika who said, "Father they are knocking down a house while the children are in bed inside." So it was cassock over pyjamas, bare feet into shoes, and Maurice and I running to the garage for the car while I slung my belt round my middle, feeling the reassuring shape of my crucifix. They were indeed pulling the house down; we heard the bulldozer before we saw it. I waved and shouted at the men and thank goodness they stopped - they were all Africans, and of whatever faith or none, Africans always respected 'the cloth'. So we had an *indaba* (a conference) there outside the partly ruined house in the small hours. The thing had gone too far to stop altogether of course, but at least they waited while the distraught mother got the baby from its cot, covered in plaster dust from the collapsing ceiling, but unhurt. This was one of the poorer houses in the district, and there was not much in the way of 'goods and chattels' to be loaded onto the waiting truck. Fortunately as I had grabbed my belt and biretta from the chair in my room I had also swept up a camera, so in the light of the headlights of the car I was able to take a photograph of the sorry scene: the neighbours out in full force wrapped in their blankets - even summer nights in Johannesburg were decidedly nippy - the heartbroken family, the mother with the baby in her arms, the broken house and the partially loaded truck.

Another memorable day was when we all went to the High Court in Pretoria to hear the Government's appeal before three judges. The same arguments were rehearsed on both sides; again I was seated a few rows behind the government representatives. The appeal failed, the three judges confirming the original judgment in our favour. Again there was the irruption of victory shouts and signs - and again the government officials fled the court in anger and hatred. Again the people of Sophiatown swept out of the court in triumph. This time down the famous steps of the Pretoria High Court.

Back in Sophiatown there were parties and singing and dancing. The pace of the clearance of the township slowed down, people were given proper compensation for loss of freehold and their nice homes, and no more houses were destroyed while people were in them.

I did a lot of photography at this time, showing the death and destruction of Sophiatown. In one a gaunt dead tree was in the foreground, its tortured branches like the fingers of a dead hand. Behind it were half demolished houses, but, standing out in the distance and dominating everything, was the serene tower of the church of Christ the King. I called it Death of Sophiatown, but with the Christian hope of the Resurrection being the distant but dominant thought. Indeed so many of our displaced friends, with what they called their 'sore hearts', were nevertheless buoyed up with Christian hope as they went into what must have felt like exile. To do our best to encourage this hope and in some measure ease their pain, we began to build a new Church of the Resurrection at Meadowlands, so that although our people were being dragged away from their beloved Christ the King, they would at least before long have another beautiful church in which to worship in the place of their exile.

Soon after the court case I was made Housekeeper at the Priory. It had been the practice in the Community for all the brethren to gather in St Peter's Priory in Rosettenville for dinner in the evening of Christmas Day, and I suggested that we should invite the Rosettenville brethren to dinner with us for a change. This was voted a very good idea, and I looked forward to giving them a traditional English Christmas dinner with all the 'trimmings' Our cook, Auntie, was also very enthusiastic and relished the thought of cooking for all the fathers. As usual, people had been very generous in their Christmas presents, and my store cupboard shelves groaned under the weight of all the bottles we had been given - whiskey, brandy, gin, bottles of wine; enough to keep us going on saints days for many months when, on a feast day, the Prior should decree that, "Tonight we will have a sundowner." So I could see that we could be generous on Christmas night as well.

I spared no expense on that dinner, and got a mild rap over the knuckles later, but it was pretty half-hearted. We were all living under considerable strain and I decided that we deserved a bit of a treat. The huge turkey would hardly go into our electric oven, but it did, just, so I was satisfied that that would be all right when the time came. On Christmas afternoon I made a slap-up traditional English sherry trifle, with vast quantities of real custard, sponge fingers soaked in sherry, ratafias, glacé cherries, almonds and masses of whipped cream. We had been given two large Christmas puddings. About the time I thought the cooking ought to begin I went into the kitchen to see Auntie. It was empty. I stuck my head out of the kitchen door and shouted. No response. I banged on the door of the room shared by the houseboys and asked them if they had seen Auntie. They looked embarrassed and said, "Yes Father." "Well," I said, "Where is she?" "Auntie is seek, Father," one of them said. "Sick?" I said, with my heart in my mouth, "In her room?" "Yes Father." Then, shyly, "Auntie has been drinking skokiaan, Father." Skokiaan is gin illegally produced in a home made still - and laced with carbide as used in acetylene lamps, to give it kick, and it is pretty lethal. O no, I thought. I prayed almost in panic, *O Lord, please don't let her be incapable of cooking the dinner.*

192

But she was, almost. At that moment she came reeling into the garden from her room. It was quite quite clear that she was monumentally drunk. She was rolling, and so were her eyes. I tore a strip off her hoping to sober her up a bit.. But it was no good. I sat her at the kitchen table and made her drink strong black coffee - then I sent her back to her room and told her I would send one of the boys for her in an hour and a half, and by then she had better be capable of looking after the last part of the cooking.

So I switched on the oven and put the turkey in - I had never cooked one before and had no idea what heat to set. However, Auntie came back eventually and it seemed that my treatment had been partially successful. With great effort she was able to finish off the dinner. It turned out to be one of the most enjoyable evenings during all my years in Sophiatown. Everyone was in very good spirits, no doubt helped by the splendid bar I had been able to assemble!

After dinner we sat in the garden, for Christmas comes in the middle of the summer in South Africa, smoking the splendid cigars we had been given, drinking our coffee and sipping our brandy to the sound of the cicadas chirruping in the trees, with the magnificent velvet African sky above ablaze with stars, like the sequined gown of some dusky princess.

Not long after I arrived in South Africa I had been invited to a dinner party by Leon Levson and Freda his wife. She occasionally worshipped at Christ the King; he was the famous South African photographer. This dinner party had two enduring consequences for me. First, when Leon knew I was interested in photography he showed me his darkroom, and very generously offered to teach me how to process my own films and use the enlarger. It was through him that I was able to set up my little 'cottage industry' in photography in Sophiatown which became self-financing. Secondly, on that evening I encountered for the first time two remarkable doctors, Anthony and Maggie Barker. They had met each other when they were students at Birmingham Medical School. When he asked her to marry him she had said, "Yes, darling I'd love to, but if you marry me you will have to marry the Zulus too because I am committed to them for at least the first ten years of my professional life." He said, "O blow, I'd quite set my heart on putting up my plate in Harley Street - but as you seem adamant I suppose I shall have to give in and come to Zululand with you." So they married and gave thirty years of their professional life to the Zulus, taking over the tiny Charles Johnson Memorial Hospital at a village called Nqutu, consisting of three leaky tin huts. Thirty years later they left on the site a great modern hospital including a Nurses Home and School. I went home that evening with the exciting prospect of a holiday in Zululand as their guest.

The next time I was due for a couple of weeks holiday I set off by train from Johannesburg to Dundee in Natal, and there I boarded a country bus which tore along the corrugated red dirt roads towards the mountains of Zululand. I was eventually put down outside the hospital - a number of single-storey buildings gleaming white in the hot sunshine, all clustered about the beautiful church which was the centre of the life and work at Nqutu.

The medical staff were all very friendly and welcoming and lived very much as a close-knit community. Anthony and Maggie were the only married members but apart from breakfast had their meals in the common diningroom. I was delighted to find that Anthony also was a keen photographer and we used to take our cameras with us wherever we went. When he could spare the time we would develop and enlarge the day's 'bag' - then we would line them up against the wall of the sittingroom and the three of us would assess their merits. Anthony taught me a lot, and with Leon Levson I consider myself very lucky indeed to have had two such wonderful teachers.

Being of a somewhat ghoulish nature, I have always been interested in surgery, and Anthony would let me put on boots and gown and spend most of Thursdays with him in the theatre while he operated - always explaining everything as the operation proceeded. He was a born teacher, and after a few visits I felt I could have performed some of the operations myself - not that he ever let me loose on anyone, of course! But he did let me extract a tooth one day when we were up in the mountains at one of his outstation clinics - I managed to get it out in one go and one piece, and the old lady, whose permission had been asked first, of course, grinned delightedly because her tooth had been extracted by an *umfundis*, a priest.

I loved Zululand at first sight and it was there that Africa sank its talons into me, as happens to most people who live there for any length of time. I loved the *smell* of Africa, the combination of hot dried grass, baked red soil, acacia and blue-gum trees - and a unique fragrance that comes from I know not where. Even though there was a lot of anti-white feeling among the Zulus at that time I was able to go walking by myself in the countryside around the hospital on my 'photographic safaris' and feel completely safe. Once, at a time of heightened tension, I arrived at a *kraal* and was met by scowling looks from all the women and the only man who seemed to be around. So I just said, "Nqutu... Dr Barker" - and immediately the scowls turned into broad smiles and the man and several of the women came forward to give me the traditional African double-handshake that means, "I greet you from my heart." The sole man in the *kraal* that afternoon had worked on the mines in Johannesburg and therefore could speak some English. He told me that tomorrow there would be a wedding in the *kraal* and that the bride and her attendant were in a hut already dressed in the full tribal regalia. I asked if they would consent to come out of the hut so that I could photograph them. He looked very doubtful and said it was not the custom for a bride to emerge before the ceremony, but as I looked very disappointed he said he would go and ask.

About a quarter of an hour later he returned and said that both bride and attendant had agreed to be photographed, and sure enough after a few moments out they came, looking very solemn, for as in Sophiatown, it was considered very unlucky for a bride to smile. They really were an exotic sight and must have been wearing all the traditional beadwork of the tribe. Their pierced ear-lobes held circles of wood of at least two and a half inches in diameter, decorated with tiny beads. Their heads were bare apart from modest beadwork circlets, for until after they are married Zulu girls do not wear the traditional huge head-dress like a truncated and inverted cone, originally made of clay, over which their hair is trained and which is then completely covered by a kerchief. Around their necks they were hung with literally dozens of multicoloured necklaces made of the tiny traditional beads. These beads used to be made from ostrich egg shells, each bead no more than three sixteenths of an inch in diameter and the hole made by piercing with a thorn. Later they were factory made, possibly in Birmingham, and sold in the local country stores. Around their waists the two girls wore ropes of beadwork from which hung 'mini-skirts' made of masses and masses of multicoloured beads, the bride's skirt being more elaborate than her attendant's. Their legs were bare to the knee but from knee to ankle were covered thickly with literally dozens of bead bangles - perhaps over a hundred on each leg. Their feet were clad in what we would call 'trainers'; the bride's white, her attendants black and white. They wore knee length flimsy black cloaks caught at the neck but open below to display all this fine bead regalia. In their right hands they held loosely furled umbrellas looking rather Chaplinesque. Umbrellas and shoes struck a false note, but in spite of this they made a splendid picture as they solemnly posed for me, standing to the left of the low doorway of their beehive hut.

Anthony was very impressed by this photograph and chalked it up to me as a 'scoop' - he himself had never had such an opportunity, though no doubt he could have found one had he wished. I was very chuffed - but of course I would not have got my picture at all if I had not spoken the password to Zulu hearts on my arrival. 'Dr Barker' was the Open Sesame to hearts and homes all over Zululand, for Anthony and Maggie were beloved of the Zulus and their fame had long since spread to every corner of that enchanting land.

When they first arrived at the poor little original 'Charley J', Anthony went off to visit the *kraals* and introduce himself to the chiefs and headmen, and he always made a special point of greeting the witch doctor, whose hand he would shake as he gravely said, "We are members of the same profession." (Many years later Anthony was actually invited to attend a Witch Doctors' Conference away in a remote area attended by witch doctors from all over the country. Not even influential Zulus could hope to penetrate this very secret gathering, and would almost certainly be killed if caught trying. It was unprecedented for a white man to do so - yet Anthony went as an invited and honoured guest.)

I spent many holidays with the Barkers at Nqutu, and always enjoyed myself enormously. On one occasion Anthony and Maggie and I went to a village some miles away and stayed for a couple of nights in an hotel so that they could have a short break, for they were often under considerable strain. That was a memorable weekend. On arriving at the hotel we found that Tom Savage, my friend who had been Dean of Capetown when I arrived, was also there for the weekend. He was an old friend of Anthony and Maggie and had recently been consecrated Bishop of Zululand. He was on one of his official episcopal visitations. So we joined him and Monica his wife and had a wonderful time together. On the Sunday morning Anthony and I went to visit in the neighbouring *kraal*, which Anthony knew very well. "We shall probably be in time for a beer," Anthony said - and so we were, but not in the manner I had expected. We were given a warm welcome, and invited into a beehive hut, which we had to enter almost on hands and knees, on account of the low 'door' - little more than a hole in the wall of the hut. As our eyes became accustomed to the gloom we could see a single line of men sitting with their backs against the circular wall of the hut. Invited to take our place among them, I found it was surprisingly comfortable. The floor, made of earth stamped smooth, was curved up to join the wall, and when one sat with one's back against this it was like sitting in a well shaped chair. The floor, as was customary, was 'painted' over with wet cow-dung in which graceful patterns had been drawn; when dried out this floor looked most attractive, lightly green in colour and of a velvety texture - and

196

smelt only of new-mown hay. There was nothing remotely unpleasant about it.

For a short time after we were seated we were given polite greetings, our health and that of our families was enquired after, and Anthony on our behalf reciprocated in fluent Zulu with similar greetings and enquiries. When politeness and the social niceties had been satisfied, the important business of the gathering began - a large gourd was passed round from one man to the next, each taking a small swig and passing it on to his neighbour. This was my first taste of native, or *kaffir* beer. There was no lacing of this with carbide or anything else; it was a one hundred percent wholesome fermentation. I found it very refreshing: brewed from maize, or 'mealies' to use the South African term, it had the consistency of thin porridge and something of the taste of natural yogurt. I suppose when it began its rounds the gourd contained upwards of a gallon of beer, and it went round the circle several times. After four or five rounds both Anthony and I only pretended to sip and after an hour or so made our excuses and wandered back to the truck in time to join the others for lunch.

On another occasion I went one day with Anthony in the truck to a *kraal* not far from the hospital and wandered around while he held his clinic. I stopped by a group of children and smiled at them - the only form of greeting I could give of course, and a little girl of about six came running to me with a broad grin, grabbed my hand and hauled me around the village pointing to the various things that she wanted me to see - the *boma*, a great circle of piled up thorn bushes and tree trunks, surrounded in turn by the long green and spiky leaves of aloes, into which the cattle were driven at night to keep them safe from leopard and hyena and other marauding predators; the different beehive huts; the washing laid out on bushes in the sun to dry; and on the periphery the oxen pulling the wooden plough. It was a scene surely unchanged for hundreds of years. My little guide was dressed in the usual everyday 'mini skirt' of twisted woollen fronds, and nothing else except a plaited necklace of white beads, and a more elaborate bead charm round her throat as protection from the Evil Eye.

On our way back to the truck one of the African nurses came up with us and talked to this delightful child for a while. Then turned to me and said, Phethelephe says Father must come to see her again - and from then on one of the nurses would go with me in the truck on each of my visits to Nqutu, specially to visit my little girl-friend. The road was in the valley and the village above the road, so the familiar hospital truck could be seen from a distance - which was why whenever I went calling, Phethelephe was always sitting on top of the same rough stone wall at the entrance of the *kraal* waiting for me, with a broad grin on her face, and as soon as the nurse and I stopped the truck and got out she would come leaping over the stony ground with her bare feet, to grab my hand and take charge while we went round the *kraal* greeting everyone in sight.

Before Anthony and Maggie had been in Zululand for very long both could speak fluent Zulu, with all the 'clicks', and I used to love just sitting there in a corner of a 'consulting room' and watching while they dealt with the patients; dear Maggie always looking just a little anxious as though she really was sharing her patient's anxiety. With a broad relieved smile she might assure this one that all was well and there was nothing to worry about; or speak sympathetically and encouragingly if her diagnosis told a different story. The Zulus are a strong and self-reliant people, and as everyone knows, can be very fierce; the finest warriors in Africa; but as so often with the strong, they are a people who love laughter, and Anthony was specially good at making his patients laugh.

The hospital was home from home for me because I was able to use the church for mass every morning, and there were always a dozen or more nurses, patients and doctors on the weekdays, and a full church every Sunday. Anthony had been architect and builder of the whole hospital, and had actually cast on site the concrete blocks of which it was built.

I loved the 'Charlie J', with its white buildings surrounded by spacious lawns kept beautifully green by careful watering day and night. There were always many people sitting on the grass, outpatients waiting to see the doctors, relatives of in-patients sitting around until visiting time, all making a colourful display on the green grass and under the shade trees. There were not very many young men around, for most were in the Transvaal working in the gold mines, but their wives and sisters and children were in abundance. I was always fascinated as I wanderedamong them all. Off-duty nurses in their light western dresses would sit in the sun and do one another's hair, weaving it close to the scalp in intricate and beautiful patterns, all held in place with black thread. By contrast, sitting next to them would be women in traditional dress, with their oiled leather skirts, bare breasted, and with a few ropes of beadwork and a lucky charm or two, the married women wearing their dramatic head-dresses, and I was often amused to see one or two of them clutching a modern plastic handbag.

Anthony said one day that while he did not want to wish a Caesarean Section operation on any woman, he did hope that I would be there when one would be necessary. The next time I went

Zulu bride and
attendant 1959

'Photo-Safari' 1959

Phethelephe, Zululand 1959

'Roadside beauty' 1959

'Basutho Contours'
Basutholand (now Lesotho)

200

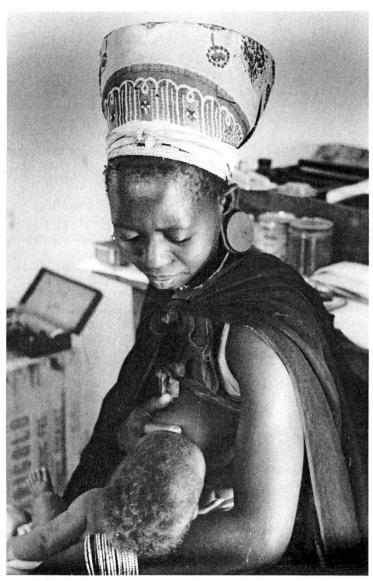

Zulu Mother

to stay he greeted me with, "We shall almost certainly have to do a Caesar today. Do you want to come and watch?" "Gosh," I said, "What do *you* think?" He gave me his bearded grin and said, "Suppose it has to be done in the middle of the night, do you want us to call you?" "Sure thing," I said, "I shall be mighty offended if you don't!" So he said he wanted me to have my camera and flash bulbs ready because he would like me to photograph each step of the procedure. The call came at two o'clock in the morning and I felt like a Battle of Britain pilot as I 'scrambled', flinging on clothes, pushing feet urgently into shoes, grabbing a handful of films and a camera and flash equipment, and flying down the concrete paths to the theatre where I donned gumboots, gown, cap and mask and entered the theatre as they wheeled the woman in on the trolley.

Having first asked the patient's permission for me to watch the operation, Anthony told me to stand at at the foot of the operating table and take all my pictures from that position. Maggie was the anaesthetist, and worked at the head of the table, Anthony, as surgeon, was on my left and his assistant surgeon on my right.

I watched that operation from first incision to the very end when the wound had been neatly sewn up and clipped, and it was one of the great experiences of my life. I was sometimes so engrossed that I forgot to take the pictures I should have taken.

But how could I help that when such drama was unfolding before my astonished eyes? From a relatively small transverse cut, there gradually appeared under Anthony's gentling touch, the head of the baby! Then a shoulder and an arm, with a tiny hand with fingers moving - the first little clutch at life in the world! Then the other shoulder and arm - and now in a rush the torso with its snaking umbilicus - and then Anthony was holding the baby up by his feet and it cried its first exciting cries and everyone smiled and then laughed aloud with joy! In no time the umbilical cord had been cut and the baby - who actually looked grey and wrinkly - had been carried off by a nurse to be washed and wrapped in a warm blanket, and everyone's attention was re-focused on the mother. She was soon attended to, neatly sewn and clipped, and wheeled to the recovery room where she would be watched over until she regained consciousness and was introduced to her new baby. Anthony had always said that whenever he had performed a Caesarean Section he wanted to kneel down and pray, and I knew exactly what he meant. Baby or mother or both would certainly have died if he had not performed that operation. Now, as I saw next morning when I went to the maternity ward, instead of death here was exultant life. The mother was beaming as she showed me proudly, not the little grey wrinkly thing of the operating theatre, but a chubby little black baby shining like polished ebony.

Unfortunately, I had not taken a full set of photographs, but when I apologised to Anthony he said that was OK, there was another mother who might need a Caesar today or tomorrow, so if that one came up I could photograph that as well and make up my deficiencies. And that is what I did, the very next day. So off to the darkroom, to emerge a few hours later with a quite respectable series of step-by-step photographs of the Caesarean Section Procedure. Anthony said he was pleased with the results and that he would use them when lecturing to the nurses on the subject. I kept my set stored in a large envelope, and marked in red 'NOT FOR THE SQUEAMISH!'

On another of my visits I found Anthony and Maggie tremendously excited, for Anthony's book had been accepted for publication! *The Man Next to Me* described their arrival at the Charles Johnson Memorial Hospital towards the end of the war, and their subsequent work in 'selling' western medicine to the Zulus and building the new hospital. It is a fascinating book and shows the deep commitment that both he and Maggie brought to their patients as people.

I was extremely lucky to have wonderful friends in South Africa, my most intimate being Deane and Dorothy Yates. He was headmaster of St John's College, run and largely staffed by the Community until 1935. From small beginnings under Father Nash in 1898 St John's had grown to become one of the leading boy's schools in South Africa. Its magnificent buildings, designed by Sir Herbert Baker (Lutyen's pupil, colleague and successor) stood on the mountain ridge of Houghton, a suburb of Johannesburg.

Deane and Dot made me feel a member of the family, and I could always go there for my occasional days off from Sophiatown. I found it a great relief and refreshment to have a night and a day with them in their lovely house in Houghton, away from the pressures of Sophiatown. I was also a frequent visitor at the College and often preached in the chapel. It was a wonderful school, and reminded me of Benenden. There was the same atmosphere of friendly cheerfulness among the boys and the staff, and a very high standard of education - some say the best in South Africa. Indeed it was my fairly frequent excursions to St John's College and other schools and to various white parishes that made Sophiatown bearable for me - just.

Deane and Dot even took me on holiday with them to the Kruger National Park Game Reserve and to White River, on the low veldt where the climate was sub-tropical - and I saw bananas growing for the first time! During the Second World war, Deane, an officer in the Royal Artillery, had often preferred to ride a motor-bike rather than a jeep. He earned the nickname 'Skid Yates' and he drove his car in the same manner! He was one of the most skilful drivers I had ever met, and with his swashbuckling driving he filled our journeys with excitement. Although his car was a modest Ford Popular he drove it as if it were far more powerful, hunched over the wheel and tearing along the wonderful South African National roads, slaughtering the occasional snake who had forgotten his 'kerb drill' and came to a bumpy end under the wheels of our modern Jehu. We three had hilarious times together, and I owe them a tremendous debt of gratitude, for from start to finish of my five years in South Africa they did more than anyone else to make my tour of duty bearable.

After the excitement of the court case, I found the gradual destruction of the township, the increasing piles of rubble, the dwindling population and the increasing squalor of the place, more and more unsettling. Unlike Trevor and some of the other brethren, I was not a political animal; I have to admit that there was no real fire in my belly for social justice - in the court case my emotions had certainly been engaged, but I had only carried on where someone else had left off; I cannot imagine myself ever initiating the proceedings. There was also the ever present possibility that we could be arrested any day - or night, which was more likely. Hannah Stanton, sister of Fr Timothy Stanton CR, who was working in Pretoria at this time, was imprisoned for six months without trial, before being deported. Knowing her so well, and hearing how magnificently she had coped with imprisonment, I knew I could not emulate her, and the possibility of following her into gaol filled me with craven fear, for I am no hero and certainly not martyr material.

I found all this increasingly unnerving, so my trips away from Sophiatown either for recreation or for other sorts of work were lifelines for me. I am sad to have to admit that I never became a true 'Africa man' like other members of the Community so often were.

Jonathan Graham who had recently succeeded Raymond Raynes as Superior of the Community, came out for his first visitation in early 1960 after I had been in Sophiatown for about four years, and we were all waiting to greet him outside the Priory as he arrived. Shaking hands with the brethren nearest to the car he turned and spotted me, "Ah," he said, "Ah, here's Paul, hating every moment of it I expect!" I shook his hand, giving him a sheepish grin. Not *every* moment of it, but quite a lot of it for a lot of the time, I thought. I suppose I had a love-hate attitude to South Africa; I loved the country districts, Zululand and Basutoland and Rhodesia, which I visited several times. I loved all the generous friends, both black and white, that I had made. I also loved the climate, apart from the worst of the winter weather. But I could not really cope with the political situation, with the unending fight against apartheid and defiance of the government. I had helped to take the evidence of the Sharpville shooting and it had torn my heart. It tore my heart also to see these lovely people being hounded out of Sophiatown. Every time I went out of the door I saw those who had been left behind in the ruins because they did not have the right papers that entitled them to resettlement in Meadowlands. They had simply been left to rot among the ruins; I felt impotent to help: there was nothing I could do. It was completely overwhelming, and I wanted out. So I have to admit that I longed for home more and more. - I had turned one of the old classrooms into a small cinema for the children and used to show British Council films which often included such London scenes as Piccadilly Circus, and when I saw the red buses going round the statue of Eros a large lump would form in my throat!

When Jonathan Graham had me in for a talk I told him just how I was feeling, and he said he quite understood and did not hold it against me. "I hope you can be patient for a while longer," he said, "I can't bring you home just yet, but I promise you it will not be long." I was greatly relieved after our talk, but even so became increasingly depressed.

It was at this time that I first had doubts about my vocation; I had been reading a book about the Religious Life and when I read the chapter on signs of a true vocation I began to feel that many of these 'signs' were not present in me and never had been. Once again I seemed to be drifting back to another 'square one'. This made me long even more for home and I often cried silently in my heart with the psalmist, *How long O Lord, how long?*

1959 South Africa

205

9

Return to England

The Superior recalled me to the Home Province towards the end of 1960. Wilful as usual, I asked permission to fly home as I could not face the long voyage by sea. George Sidebotham, the Provincial, suggested that I go by the 'slow' air route provided by a small airline on which one slept in a comfortable bed in an hotel each night and took four days to reach England from Johannesburg. This sounded splendid to me and I accepted the idea with alacrity. It did not quite work out that way, but I had a very pleasant trip indeed. We took off from Jan Smuts Airport at some ghastly hour like three o'clock in the morning, and my Prior, Francis Blake, with typical self-sacrifice, hauled himself out of bed in the middle of the night in order to drive me to the airport. I was absolutely astonished to find on arrival that about a dozen of my friends had done the same and were there to see me off and bid me *Bon Voyage*. What wonderful kindness. I had a large size lump in my throat as I bade them all goodbye, for it was unlikely that I would see any of them again unless I should be sent back to South Africa in years to come - which God forbid, I thought.

The flight was great fun. The aircraft was a four-engined turbo-prop machine, all one class and very comfortable, and had a German crew. I suppose there were about fifty passengers in my section, among whom by reason of my white cassock and black scapular I stood out like a panda. I also appeared to be something of a novelty to the young stewards and air hostesses who took me under their wing and proceeded to spoil me rotten. From time to time I was invited to little drinks parties in their compartment at the rear of the plane; they all spoke fluent English and there was much laughter and fun. The Captain and the other members of the crew were also very kind to me and invited me sit with them on the flight deck whenever I felt inclined to do so - an invitation of which I made frequent use during those four days. The officer in charge at the time would patiently answer my many and probably naive questions.

Unfortunately the flight plan was seriously disrupted - by the wind. Our first stop was at Windhoek in what used to be German West Africa. The intention was to land, pick up passengers, and take off again in just a matter of minutes. But, as its name implies, Windhoek is a place where the wind rules such matters. No sooner had we landed than it changed direction and we were told that we would not be able to take off until it had changed again to a favourable direction. The reason was that Windhoek was a small airport, and had only one runway for large aircraft. The airport was surrounded by mountains, and planes like ours could only take off when the wind was right. We waited in the aircraft for some considerable time hoping that this capricious element would change again soon and we would be able to continue our flight. But no, after a couple of hours or so, during which lunch was served, it was clear that the wind was unlikely to oblige, so we were bussed into town and put up in hotels. We were warned not to stray far from the hotel because we could be called at a moment's notice to be rushed back to the airport. It was extremely hot and humid and I determined not even to put my nose outside the hotel doors and favoured instead a good long rest on the bed in my comfortable air-conditioned room. I was in a deep sleep when the call came in the middle of the night and we returned to the airport.

The take-off was very alarming. The plane taxied to the beginning of the runway, chocks were put under the wheels and the brakes were put firmly on. The engines were then revved up - and up - and up - and up, until the whole plane was shaking and rattling and swaying, so much so that my brief-case on the rack above fell down upon my head. When the thing was in a state of juddering and rattling frenzy the chocks were whipped away and the brakes released - and we went tearing down the runway like a mighty unbroken stallion suddenly released from his bonds. We were heading straight for those formidable mountains that towered above and which were now coming towards us with sickening speed. Yawing from side to side like a very small boat in a very big storm, at long last, but I was sure too late, we felt the plane lumber into the air, with engines shrieking like four super-banshees. Too late, clearly too late: the mountains, black and menacing in the moonlight looming over us, I tried to reconcile myself to the fact that this was how it all ended, not with a whimper but with a bang, and began to cross myself and mutter commendatory prayers from the Last Rites - and then, O then, we were in fact looking *down* upon the mountain tops! In spite of all appearances we had made it - but I swear I could have reached out and touched those mountains as we passed.

Soon after dawn the Captain came over the tannoy and said that in a few moments we would be passing over Albert Schweitzer's mission hospital at Lambarene and sure enough there it was, a huddle of buildings and trees. I recalled the story of that great scholar and organist - who used to go on long lecture and concert tours all over the world from time to time to finance his mission - how when one day he was struggling to drag a large log to the mission to replenish the firewood, he saw a young African leaning languidly against a tree and picking his teeth with a thorn and said, in effect, "Be a good chap and give me a hand with this, will you?" To which the young man replied, "O no, I can't do that; you see, I am an intellectual."

Our Captain was a jovial man and at one point said, "We are just about to cross the equator - and if you look out off the starboard windows you will in fact just be able to see a faint line - NOW!" - and we all looked!

After Windhoek the only night we slept in a hotel bed was on Malta, where Father Hoey's sister Patricia and her husband were living. He was Chaplain to the RAF station there. They called for me the next morning and took me on a tour of the island, making a special point of visiting St Paul's Bay where my patron saint had been shipwrecked on his way to trial and martyrdom in Rome. After giving me a splendid lunch they took me to the airport and saw me off.

The weather was now considerably cooler and a light rain was falling as we took off from Malta. I had exchanged my tropical whites for black cassock and warmer clothes and spent several hours now on the flightdeck, watching as ice formed on the 'windscreen' in front of the pilots, to be dispersed by a screenwash of pure alcohol and wipers similar to those on a car. Pyrotechnics of lightning appeared dead ahead amid huge banks of swirling black cloud. "Heavy thunderstorm," said the Captain. "Lets see if we can get above it." Which we did, it seemed effortlessly, the big plane gently rising at an angle I am sure unnoticed by the passengers, until we could see the turbulence far below us and affecting us not at all.

All that day we had been getting reports that Heathrow was threatened with closure by freezing fog, and in consequence this plane would land at Dusseldorf. There I said goodbye to my good but short-time friends, the aircrew and cabin crew of this friendly aircraft, and sat for an hour or two awaiting a possible flight for the last leg home. After a time I was told that a seat had been found for me on a B.O.A.C. Comet that would land either at Heathrow or Prestwick according to the prevailing weather conditions. So eventually I was seated comfortably in a window seat on the Comet, still almost a legendary plane, and the first jet aircraft in which I had flown. I found it enormously exciting as we took off at what seemed to me an acute angle and after a few moments we were through the murk and drizzle of Dusseldorf, first into an eerie grey world, a flat surface of grey cloud below us, and a few thousand feet above us an identical flat grey ceiling, towards which we climbed steadily. On entering the 'ceiling', grey fog swirled about the windows for a few seconds before we burst through into glorious sunshine, the grey 'ceiling' now a white blanketed floor below us. Eventually the Captain came on the air to say that Heathrow was still open and we would be landing there in about three quarters of an hour.

So, from the equator to freezing fog in London in a few hours, and I breathed in the cold mist almost with delight as I stepped on to the Airport bus that took me to Victoria Station for the train to Worthing.

While I had been away in South Africa, Mother and Geoff had built their dream retirement bungalow in Findon Valley on the edge of the Downs behind Worthing, and I was to stay there for the weekend before going on to Mirfield. Mother and Aunt, bundled up in fur coats met me at the station and we took a cab to the bungalow. They had all three aged in the five years since I had last seen them, and of course there was no Gran to greet me as there always had been on all previous homecomings since I first began to go away from home. She had died after a fall a couple of years earlier at the age of ninety-five.

It took some time for us all to begin to feel at ease with one another - and poor old Geoff had never really been at ease with me in the house in my long black cassock and grey scapular.

I liked the new bungalow, and as was to be expected, Geoff had produced a magnificent garden from what had been a bare strip of meadow only a few years before. Even though it was December there was colour and beauty in Geoff's garden, the result of both his knowledge and the daily hours of hard work he put into it, in all weathers.

There followed a trip with the old folk to Coulsdon to see my brother Phil and his wife and their now very grown-up girls - and the latest surprise addition to their family of a year ago, David my nephew. Then on to Chessington to see our step-sister Joan and her husband with their little son Geoffrey and another baby on the way.

Next it was Kings Cross and the train to Wakefield and then the bus to Mirfield - much nicer than going to Mirfield station now even more depressing than before. It was wonderful to be recognised by a local man getting on the bus who seeing me sitting there greeted me with, "Eee, Faaarther are thee back from South Africa, are thee well, then?"

The bus set me down at the back door of the retreat house and I went in lugging my cases and meeting the old familiar smell of floor polish and soup. My shoes squeaked across the gleaming lino - and how good it was to be here! Evensong was in progress and everywhere was deserted, but I found the room allocated to me for the night, and by the time I had washed and brushed up and made it downstairs again the brethren were streaming into the hall ready to follow the Superior into the refectory for supper. A replay of many previous arrivals at this time of day, but the last time had been almost five years ago. I gave and received many grins and winks of greeting as we waited, and after the grace there was the usual warm welcome given to a brother when he returned from abroad. This is my true home, I reflected this is my real family, and no doubts raised their heads to trouble me.

The following day I went to the Hostel in Leeds, where the Superior had appointed me the new Sub-Warden, for the last two weeks of the term. In a couple of weeks I could learn the ropes and start fully briefed next term. The Hostel was an official Hall of Residence for Leeds University, built by the Community in 1910 to house our students while they studied for their degrees,

It stands, a massive pile of Edwardian gothic architecture in dark red brick and stone, near the top of Springfield Mount next door to the Mount hotel. In 1960 there was no Clean Air Act operating in the West Riding and all the buildings were blackened with soot and grime. This gave the Hostel a grim appearance, not much lightened either on entry, for the corridors were never fully lit and I found the whole place rather gloomy. The gloom was dispelled, however, by the students, and lunch and dinner in the refectory were hearty and cheerful meals. I had a warm welcome from Fr Hilary Beasley, the Warden. whom I had known since he was a student at the College at Mirfield. He showed me to my office and with some trepidation I sat in the chair of the Sub-Warden of the Hostel, a position that I never thought to hold and for which I felt singularly ill equipped. What had made me fearful was the Superior's airy mention that, as well as looking after the housekeeping, I would be 'doing a bit of tutoring.' Hilary asked me to take on a student who had to resit the English paper of his Matric while studying for the first year of his degree course. I thought, O heck, I have not done anything like this since I did my own cram course, and I knew I had forgotten most of that. Anyway, there were text books - and, I was delighted to discover, the set Shakespeare play was Macbeth - the very play I had myself studied for Matric all those years ago at Tatterford. So my spirits revived a little.

We started on the first day of the term. and by dint of keeping one chapter of each text book ahead of my student, I managed to help him to do his revision. I am sure no tutor waited for a student's examination results with more trepidation than I did for this young chap's, and my relief knew no bounds when he eventually came into my office with a broad grin on his face to say that he had passed! Like my own matriculation, this result also opened for him the door to ordination. He thanked me warmly for my help and I am sure he had no idea of how infinitesimally ahead of him his tutor had kept all that term!

My primary responsibility at the Hostel was the housekeeping, which involved doing the shopping, working out the menus, supervising the kitchen and the domestic staff, seeing that the place was kept clean and tidy and trying to ensure that it ran smoothly and that everyone had a balanced and adequate diet. In Hilary's absence I was in charge and presided at High Table - fortunately the Latin grace was the same as we used in all houses of the Community at that time, so I was spared blushes the first time I had to preside at dinner. The place was humming with life and although the routine was based on monastic principles, it was not by any means an oppressive regime, and there were a lot of high jinks and laughter among the students. All five members of the community on the staff joined in the merriment unreservedly, and it was a happy place. Our 'community room', the commonroom reserved for the brethren and their guests, was a comfortable room with an open fire in the winter, where coffee was served after lunch and dinner and where most days saw guests for afternoon tea.

The shopping, of course, was mostly for large quantities and involved sitting in my office and doing the ordering by telephone. I was once very dissatisfied with the quality of the Cheddar cheese, and asked the wholesaler to call to see me about it. The gentleman duly sat in my office while I made my complaint. He could not understand what I could find wrong with the cheese they supplied. I said I thought it was soapy, more suitable for the bathroom than the table, and it lacked the character of genuine Cheddar. He listened with a puzzled frown, and then suddenly his face cleared and he said, "O Father, are you talking about the sort of cheddar that you had before the war?" To which I replied, "Well yes, I suppose I am." Upon which he said, rather pityingly, "O but Father, you will not find that sort of cheese today, its made quite differently, and nowadays people would not like that old sort of cheese." I had to admit defeat and we went on eating soapy 'cheddar' cheese.

I delighted in the English spring weather when it eventually arrived. The crocuses and daffodils that pushed through the grime of the quadrangle garden were the first I had seen for five years and

I had forgotten how glorious it could all be when the reluctant English sun shone, as it did that year after the hard and bitter winter. In due course Spring gave on to a glorious hot summer, and having tried to quieten, calm and encourage the nervous students through their examinations during the previous term we waited with them anxiously in the summer heat for the results to come through. Thankfully there were no failures that year, and the worst that had to be faced were the degrees that were not as good as had been hoped and expected.

During that term the Superior, on one of his visits to us, came into my office and said he would like me to take over as Prior of our Cardiff house in August, in place of Fr Claude Lunniss who was going elsewhere. Even monks can be ambitious, and for a long time I had hoped that one day I would be put in charge of a house. I had never been to St Teilo's Priory and my immediate reaction was that it would not have been my first choice. All that changed however on my first visit.

St Teilo's Priory consisted of two Victorian semi-detached houses that had been knocked into one with a more modern building added at the back which the Community had made into a small retreat house and conference centre. Before we took it over it had been a hostel for university students. The chapel was a small Victorian Gothic building of no architectural merit but, I thought, crying out for a good face-lift. All three buildings were connected by a main corridor. The Priory was quite dilapidated and needed constant repair. Every board creaked ominously wherever one walked. Brother Paulinus, by trade a sculptor and painter, had been given *carte blanche* a few months before my arrival to brighten the place up, and he had certainly done so. The ceiling of every room was painted with a solid colour - royal blue, bright yellow, tomato red, or green. All the walls of rooms and corridors were in what the manufacturers called 'brilliant white'. So in spite of its narrow and decrepit Victorianism, the Priory presented a bright face to the world - and I loved it on sight.

I was shown what would be my room - obviously the 'master bedroom' of the original semi, and I was delighted with this also. It was spacious enough for a large desk and chair, a bed in the corner, a curtained 'cupboard' and a large chest of drawers. The floor was covered wall-to-wall with brown lino, highly polished. The desk was large and scruffy and had seen better days, but the drawers in the two pedestals ran smoothly. It stood in the bay window which looked out onto the well-kept flower beds of the eastern end of Roath Park; a very pleasant outlook indeed which gave me the

Cardiff Priory Chapel 1962 – myself in 1st stall on right

impression of living on a large and immaculately kept estate - just up my street!

There were seven or eight of us resident in the priory most of the time I was in Cardiff, and it was a very happy house. We were all very different characters with diverse backgrounds, but we lived and worked together in almost unbroken and affectionate harmony. I had always loved life at the Mother House, but I think that in Cardiff I experienced more fully than anywhere else the comradeship and fellowship of community life at its best. Of course, human nature being what it is - and monks are nothing if not 'human'! - there were the occasional spats of discord and misunderstanding, but they were soon over. As always it was the unbroken daily round of 'the immediate service and worship of God' that was the ground of this harmony, together with the grace of God, unfailingly given when people admit their faults to one another, thus seeking and finding mutual forgiveness.

I was glad that nothing had been done so far about the chapel and after I had settled in we made that our next priority. The proportions of this small Victorian gothic chapel were not at all bad, but it was a mess inside. The brethren's stalls were immediately inside the door and were of an insipid oak colour. The chairs for retreatants and guests were between the altar and the stalls. So they had the brethren breathing down their necks during services. We changed the lay out by putting the stalls in front and the chairs behind. We then painted chairs and stalls black and laid wall-to-wall plain grey carpeting, covering the horrible bright red plastic tiles. Walls and ceiling were painted white, and this completed the transformation. Over the altar we had a large cast-iron cross with a *Christus Regnans* figure, not clad in triumphal robes but in the traditional simple loin-cloth. Our Lord's head was up and his eyes open, looking straight out, with a wonderful serenity. This crucifix was the work of a friend of the Community, Frank Roper the renowned sculptor, who was head of Sculpture at Cardiff College of Art. The wrought iron cross had irregular spikes on both upright and cross-beam - he had said, "I have put the suffering in the cross." The figure was cast in aluminium, rough in texture and toned down to a dull mid-grey sheen. Beside the altar hung a white oil lamp with floating wick indicating the presence of the Blessed Sacrament, and inducing a sense of the numinous. The flickering light, the sheer white walls and ceiling, produced a quiet and serene atmosphere. We hoped this would be one of the healing elements for those who would use our retreats in order to 'come apart and rest awhile' away from the rush and tear and noise of their ordinary daily lives. And so it proved. A great number of people over the years came to value that little sanctuary of peace and inspiration, and returned again and again to refresh their spirits.

We were greatly blessed by the couple we employed to run the house and kitchen: Stanley and Gemima were both devoted Christians and lived in a tiny flat in the Retreat House. Stanley in particular was a man of great devotion and was often at his prayers in the chapel early in the morning, long before any of the brethren appeared on the scene.

Much of the work at St Teilo's centred upon the Retreat House where we held retreats for both laity and clergy, who came from all over the country as well as the principality of Wales. We also arranged various conferences and lectures for the clergy of the Church of Wales. The well known Dr Frank Lake, a professional psychiatrist and a devout Evangelical Christian, came regularly for the best part of two years to conduct his course on Clinical Theology. He had written a pioneering and monumental work on the interrelation between psychology and pastoral theology. In the 1960s it was all the rage, and Frank toured the country constantly lecturing on the subject. We felt very fortunate and privileged to receive the course from the great ,man himself, and all who sat under him were much helped in self-knowledge, and especially in their understanding of other people's psychological problems. I had first come in contact with Frank Lake when he wrote to me criticising an article I had written in the community quarterly magazine about the relation between the sin of *accidie*, or spiritual sloth, and depression. I had written to him from Cardiff thanking him for his criticism, the force of which I clearly saw, and asked him if he would consider conducting his course of lectures at St Teilo's for the benefit of the Welsh clergy and any laity who cared to attend. I was touched by his friendly reply - and he offered to start the course in a year's time, which he did. Ultimately Clinical Theology lost its appeal - I suspect that Frank's declining health and so the loss of his own charisma, had a lot to do with this - but there is no doubt that it gave a great deal of lasting value to all those who attended the courses up and down the country, and many priests and laity became better helpers of their fellow men and women as a result. I, for one, thank God for this devoted man and the new ways of helping people to which he introduced a whole generation of clergy and lay people.

At St Teilo's I revived my Whitsun Weekend instruction parties, and each year some of the same people would come to the Priory, but a significant number of new faces were to be seen each time, believers and agnostics usually in satisfactory proportions. In the 1960s, with the gradual loosening of some of the 'religious' inflexibilities or rigidities it became possible for women as well as men to live alongside a religious community and join in both worship and recreational activities and eat together in the refectory. The many letters we received after these events bore testimony to the help that this gave to the development of a 'rounded' Christian life in those who came to St Teilo's for these parties.

They were far from solemn occasions. The day would begin of course before the altar and after breakfast there would be a devotional address in chapel and time for prayer and meditation. Then at 'elevenses' the talking and laughter would begin, and for the rest of the day solemnity and gaiety in due proportions would go hand in hand. There was much serious discussion and much thought both corporate and private - in fact all experienced something of that 'fellowship' on every level inspired by the Holy Spirit that Christians from the time of the Acts of the Apostles have called *koinonia*. Nor was this a one sided affair - people did not come to be 'done good to,' or 'inspired' by 'The Fathers,' for all of us, brethren and visitors alike found our lives enriched, and we members of the Community acknowledged that we learnt as much as we taught, and received as much as we tried to give.

Apart from having a retreat house on the spot and all the work that that entailed, the brethren went away to conduct missions and retreats in other places, and to preach up and down the country, not only in Wales, but all over the British Isles, just as was done from other houses of the Community. And of course it was my job to see that the proper balance was kept between external work and time spent quietly at home in the immediate worship and service of God. I am not sure that I kept the proper balance myself, for as time went by I seemed to become increasingly busy and away from home a great deal.

I was lucky to have a very good Sub-Prior in Fr Gerard Beaumont, well known for his jolly hymn tunes. The children in a parish he visited called him 'The Honkytonk Father.' Gerard and I tried to make sure that one of us was at home when the other was away. In this way we kept a continuity of authority which ensured the smooth running of the house and the life. He was a wonderful chap; nothing rattled him and he could almost invariably inspire a laugh, without being frivolous, even in the most tense situations. One Christmas, all the brethren had gone off on assignments to help in parishes leaving him and me alone with a big problem. One of the brethren was a manic depressive and just at this time he was going through a particularly severe manic phase. In consultation with the doctors we had, with great sadness, come to the conclusion that he would have to be committed to a psychiatric hospital for a time, and on Christmas Eve he was taken from the priory, but not before a fight in which he attacked me and had to be subdued by the experts. When the ambulance had gone Gerard and I felt dreadful but we knew that however hard, we had acted in the brother's best interests. We both said Mass on Christmas day, and in the evening I had been invited to dinner at the house of Rollo and Joy Charles, great friends, who lived ten minutes walk away at the other end of Roath Park. They told me to bring Gerard along too if he would like to come - they knew the situation we had had to cope with. But Gerard said, "No thanks, if you and they don't mind, I think I would rather go and sit in a pub for the evening if I may." I knew Gerard and his visits to the pubs, and I readily agreed and told him he was free until he felt like coming home. So off I went to my quiet and civilised Christmas dinner, and Gerard just faded into the night.

Boxing Day being a feast day we had a talking breakfast together. He asked if I had enjoyed myself, and having told him I had, very much, I said, "And what did you get up to?" His eyes lit up as he said, "O I had a marvellous time. I went to that pub down by the docks and went into the Public Bar - no one was at the piano so having ordered my pint I said 'Happy Christmas All', downed half of it and then began to play - you know, all the old sentimental stuff and a few carols. They all gathered round and began to sing. After a while a chap came and said to me, 'You staying Father?' And when I said I was, he said, 'OK I'll go and get me drums.' Sure enough in a short time he was back with a complete set of drums and we played for the rest of the evening until closing time - a bit over to be honest, but who cares on Christmas night? O yes, I had a wonderful time." And he did a whole lot of good for the Church and the Faith, I am quite sure. Wherever he saw a piano he had to play it - with a cigarette dangling from the corner of his mouth, screwing up his eyes against the smoke, and the ash dribbling down the front of his cassock - a mess, but what a wonderful man and what a great lover of God and of people.

(He died of lung cancer in a South African hospital, bearing witness to the Faith and exercising his priestly ministry to those around him who were also dying of the same disease, cheerful and confident to the end and an inspiration to doctors, nurses and fellow patients alike).

I was so lucky to have men of great and diverse character in my priory. There was Peter Hewitt, well up in his seventies, a great wit and source of amusement to us. He had been a ballet dancer and could still tap the light fantastic toe for a few steps. He had been 'Uncle Peter' on the original 'London 2LO' programme in the early days of radio. Artistic and temperamental.

Then there was Andrew Blair, the Scotsman who still retained a faint suggestion of his original accent. He had been particularly kind to me and I was very fond of him. When he retired as Prior of the Mother House I asked if he could come to me. The Superior told me that Andrew had been delighted to be asked for, and he was a great asset to the house, portly, invariably cheerful and kindly, with a pungent wit and a keen mind he was a source of fun and wisdom, a splendid 'community' man. I loved and valued him greatly.

Brother Jeremy, our lay brother, another great character, a South African from a well to do family. He had been a fighter pilot during the war, ran out of fuel and made a false landing behind enemy lines in North Africa, only remembering as the Nazis came to take him prisoner that he had an emergency tank full of petrol that would have got him safely back to base, had he remembered to switch it on! So he spent the final years of the war in a POW camp. After the war he was the rich young play-boy in Johannesburg until his conversion, when he gave away all this money and possessions and joined CR wanting to dedicate himself to our Lord and to his poor.

In Cardiff he was assistant Prison Chaplain at Cardiff gaol. To Jeremy every released prisoner was a reformed character, an angel whose wings only needed a little extra polish, and "please could we put him up for a few nights, days, weeks?" Jeremy's 'angels' gave me many a headache, for they did all sorts of strange things - the last one, whose cause Jeremy had pleaded literally on his knees, was really off his rocker, and the crunch came when we were woken up in the middle of the night by this chap roaring through the Priory and Retreat House scattering communion wafers like confetti that he had filched from the sacristy. It was then that I had to put my foot down. I tried to explain to Jeremy, as I had done a dozen times before, that our community was not geared to deal with people like this, who were much more the sort of responsibility that other communities could take on. We were a teaching order more like the Dominicans than the Franciscans. Even Jeremy saw the point this time, and the man left the next day to be helped by an organisation that catered for released prisoners. I was very fond of Jeremy, this tall gangling man with the radiant smile and blue eyes. People of both sexes fell for him hook line and sinker. Fr Martin Jarrett-Kerr took him on his team when he conducted a mission at one of the redbrick universities, and he told me that any time of the day Jeremy could be seen crossing the campus, always with a trail of young people following him wherever he went Like the Pied Piper of Hamlyn.

Martin Jarrett-Kerr, short and lively, intense and intellectual, was the learned member of our little band. He could be noisy and boisterous and deeply concentrated in turn, always reading and able to do several things at once. We got a lot of amusement during silent breakfasts watching him reading one of his tomes, often a copy with uncut pages, his eyes never leaving the page as he methodically cut the forthcoming pages with his knife, or reached out for butter, marmalade or toast. He was another great asset to the house and we bathed in reflected glory when his name appeared, as it frequently did, above articles in learned journals, or he was quoted in *The Church Times*, or had letters published in *The Times*.

Then there was Fr Matthew Trelawney-Ross, getting old now. He had done sterling work in Sophiatown in the past and was greatly loved by Africans and whites alike. He was very musical and had done a lot to train the choir at Christ the King, Sophiatown. We had a grand piano in the common room of the retreat house, and Matthew would often be found playing classical music there in the afternoons. Where the rest of us would take a book with us to read on a long train journey, Matthew would take a piece of music, the score of an opera, or a symphony, and as the train rumbled on its way, Matthew would hear every note of the score he was reading. He also had a splendid if slightly eccentric sense of humour and was a very popular member of our priory family.

The three junior brethren at St Teilo's were Fr Hadrian White, a South African, Fr Robert Mercer, a Rhodesian (later to become Bishop of Mashonaland), and Fr Bernard Chamberlain. Hadrian was excellent with children's missions. Robert was a good retreat conductor. Bernard also conducted retreats and missions. All three were very caring people and made considerable contributions to a happy house. Robert's favourite reading was Crockford's Clerical Directory, which comprises the potted biography of all Anglican clergy in the United Kingdom and Ireland, and you could rarely mention the name of a priest anywhere the details of whose ordination and appointments Robert could not quote from memory. He was on a par with another brother, Fr Justin Pearce, who knew Baedeker's railway timetables by heart, and would spend a lot of time on a train journey looking out of the window, and, seeing a puff of smoke in the distance would say, "Oh yes, that's the 4:33 from X due at Y at 5:15 - Hm, running a bit late."

While in Cardiff I was elected to the Governing Body of the

Church in Wales, the equivalent to the Church of England General Synod, and this enabled me to get to know a great number of the Welsh clergy. Each year I attended the Annual Synod of the the Church in Wales. This was always held in Llandrindod Wells, where the Cardiff contingent, both clerical and lay, stayed at the Imperial Hotel.

The Bishop of Bangor asked me to be one of his Examining Chaplains with responsibility for helping the newly ordained clergy with their spiritual life, preaching, pastoral work and hearing confessions. I usually combined this work with my visits to the Church Teacher Training College in Bangor, where I was the external Chaplain and did a lot of work.

While I was at St Teilo's my old friend Guy Sanderson, who had been my spiritual director in Hendon, was consecrated Bishop of Plymouth. He did me the honour of inviting me to give the address at his consecration by the Archbishop of Canterbury in Southwark Cathedral. I found this a daunting prospect but of course could not refuse - in fact part of me was thrilled at the thought.

I had been trying to give up my beloved pipe - I was a very heavy smoker and had been smoking an ounce a day for many years. I had made several attempts to kick the filthy habit. I was in the midst of the latest of these attempts when Guy's invitation came and I was managing to keep going, with a struggle. Guy told me that the address must not be longer than nine minutes, and that having been conducted to the pulpit by the Cathedral Verger with his wand, I must wait to begin my address until the Archbishop and the five or six other bishops who were to be co-consecrators, had taken their seats immediately beneath the pulpit. Ye gods!, a terrifying prospect!

As I have said earlier, right from my early days in Portsmouth I have rarely been able to preach from notes, and never wrote out an address in full. This time I knew I must write it *and time it!* Nine minutes flat! Phew!

A few weeks before the event I wound some paper into my typewriter. I knew what I wanted to preach about and I had chosen my text, which I typed in red at the top of the paper, and underlined. Then I sat back and waited for the words to form in my mind so that I could type them neatly in black on the page. I waited - and waited - and waited. Precisely nothing came. I sat for a quarter of an hour, then got up and did a few other things, like going on a tour of the Priory for a while seeing that everything was in order. I had a few cheerful words with Gemima in the kitchen; she was happily cooking the lunch. Back then to my room to sit at my desk and gaze at my nice text, all neatly typed in red. I waited for the opening words of my address to appear on the blank screen of my mind. Not a flicker; the screen remained blank. *O Lord, please let it start to flow, show me what You want me to say.* But the Lord was not listening, or so it seemed to me.

O well, perhaps I was not meant to do it yet - plenty of time, over three weeks in fact. I decided to let it gestate a little longer. So out came the page with the neat red text at the top, and on I got with something that was interesting and absorbing - the red-headed sheet on a corner of the desk, in view but not being actively thought about. I had another go the next day, with precisely the same result - or lack of it. So out it came and went back on the corner of the desk. A fortnight went by. Still the same old red-headed sheet consigned again to the corner of the desk where it would soon take root I shouldn't wonder - it was getting a bit dog-eared now. Each time I sat down and looked at that sheet of paper my hands automatically went to the pockets of my cassock - one used to hold my pipe and the other my pouch. But of course, I'd forgotten, I'd given it up. O dear, it got to five days before the consecration. Panic stations! I was desperate; not a word written! I wound the paper into the typewriter for the millionth time. *Lord, please, You've got to help me. Dammit, (sorry Lord), but with all due respect, You've got me into this mess. I* can't *be expected to preach extempore for exactly nine minutes flat - do be reasonable! (Sorry Lord, but really!).* But like Don Camillo, I'm talking to a silent Lord, who is pretending He can't hear. Nothing; just absolutely and comprehensively nothing, absolutely *nothing* came.

I leaped up from my desk vowing that I would not take that piece of paper out of the typewriter until it was covered in black type. I strode down the corridor to Gerard's room and said, "Please take all my calls. If anyone wants to see me, tell them I am heavily engaged and do not know when I shall be free. Give me permission to miss chapel today if necessary, I'm going to get some tobacco and I'm not budging from my room until I have licked that blessed consecration sermon!"

Gerard coughed and laughed in his usual way and said, "OK, you get your baccy and start writing - and I'm sure it will be all right for you to miss chapel for this if necessary; its important. I'll bring you a cuppa when we have ours." So I nipped across the top end of Roath Park to the little Post Office and bought a couple of ounces of tobacco. Back at my desk I took out four pipes from the bottom drawer, nice and dry now having not been smoked for months. I filled them all, carefully tamping down the tobacco, and even that familiar action began to relax me. I lit my lighter and drew in the lovely fragrant smoke of Gold Block, that king of tobaccos, and through a dense cloud I looked at the red-headed sheet waiting innocently there in my typewriter. A reflective calm came over me; the tail end of an idea wafted into my mind and I began to type what I had 'seen' gently developing, the ideas running smoothly, like pulling on the free-floating end of a ball of nicely wound string, and down on the page it went in nice black type. I puffed on my pipe, and lo and behold the ideas continued to come, unrolling smoothly, idea after idea, each snicking smoothly into the last, like a series of nicely cut dovetails. A couple of hours later it was done. Beginning, middle and end - Introduction, Development, Conclusion. A little adjustment here and there and I reckoned it would not be far off the nine minute maximum allowed for the address.

I told myself that obviously the Lord did not want me to give up my pipe just yet! I did not try again until many years later when I got angina, and then it proved easy.

So life at St Teilo's was varied and fascinating and very, very busy - and for five years or more the doubts that had begun to nibble at my sense of vocation were subdued and for most of the time forgotten beneath the sense of fulfilment that I found as Prior of Cardiff.

Gradually, however, the sense of wellbeing began to fade: at first imperceptibly, but then with increasing momentum. I began to get periods of acute 'spiritual dryness'. At first I thought these to be the normal experience of all who try to live the life of prayer. But they persisted and after a couple of years or so I was feeling completely dead spiritually. I was still preaching and teaching and conducting retreats and hearing confessions - but I felt as though I was on auto-pilot and doing all these things simply routinely and without heart. Periods like this are not uncommon in the religious life, and if one is reasonably sure that there is not something in one's life that our Lord wishes one to change and one is refusing to do so, then the only thing to do is to wait patiently until the dryness lifts, the clouds roll away and the sun of confidence and peace shines again. But this did not happen, and July Chapter 1966 arrived when we closed the Priory for a month as usual and all went to Mirfield for General Chapter and the Community Retreat.

I told no one how I was feeling - and to this day I cannot fathom why I had not told my confessor. However, I decided that I simply could not keep the retreat properly. As Prior of a house I could not absent myself from the addresses, so I decided that I would attend these but the rest of the time I would spend on my bed reading novels. I felt not only spiritually but also physically exhausted. And that is what I did: I attended the two addresses a day and the daily office - and the rest of the time reading novels and sleeping. I was filled with despair and in the depths of depression.

It was on the last day of the retreat, the Friday, before we came out of retreat on the Saturday morning, that something occurred which was to alter radically the whole course of my life, something small but of enormous significance to me. A tiny slip of paper fell to the floor as I opened a letter from my mother - 'I thought you would be interested in the enclosed,' she had written, and when I bent to pick it up I found that it was *the obituary notice of Bar's husband, Bertie Page*, cut from the local paper. I was rooted to the spot as I read. I felt as though I had been hit hard over the heart, I had all the sensations that follow a physical blow, and I was winded and gasping for breath. Although I did not formulate it consciously at that time, I think I knew that this was a turning point. The realization grew, from that moment on, that I had never been able to forget, or completely leave aside, the The Girl in the Middle, *and now she was free!* I did not feel excited - but I had a sense of foreboding. I wrote to her at once and sent her my condolences and said that at the time of the funeral I would be in the Resurrection Chapel trying to 'hold her up'.

Even more astonishing, on the following morning when we had come out of retreat the Prior of the Mother House called me into his office and said, "Paul, you were in Hampton, weren't you?" "Yes, born and bred," I said. "All Saints, Hampton?" he asked. "My local church where I was confirmed." "Well, they have asked for someone to conduct a mission there, will you do it?" "Yes, OK," I said. "So, get in touch with the vicar, will you?" and he gave me the letter. Barbara was a member of that congregation and lived less than a quarter of a mile from the church!

It was several weeks later that I went to All Saints Hampton to make the preliminary arrangements for the mission in a year's time. I had had hardly any contact with All Saints since before I was ordained over twenty years previously. Bar had written to me acknowledging my letter of condolence. Later she wrote again when she had read about my going there to prepare the mission. She said, "If you do not come to see me when you are there I shall never speak to you again!" So I told her I would give her a ring when I had finished in the Vicarage on the Saturday afternoon after meeting the church wardens and members of the PCC. I felt sure I would be free in time to go for dinner. I was free about six and duly made the 'phone call; she said Tim would come to fetch me in his car. He arrived, a tall goodlooking young man in his twenties, driving a Mini-Cooper with great verve and panache. I had not seen him since he was a little boy but I recognised him at once. Barbara let me in while Tim put the car away - and it was between us just as it had always been; it was as though the intervening years had fallen away - and I knew instantly that I still loved her as much as I had always done since inching my way down that ladder all those years ago. We were suitably restrained however, and did not fall into one another's arms. Just a quick hug, and then we were getting to know what had happened in our lives since we had last met.

Tim had discreetly gone to his room and left us to talk, but we met at dinner and I heard all his news too. After leaving Cranleigh his education had not quite gone according to plan. However, he was now studying at Bromsgrove and before long would be looking for a job, preferably in the motor industry, cars being a great passion in his life, and trucks a specially absorbing interest. There was not much he did not know about either.

Bar told me that Bertie and his brother Phil Page had worked the two sides of the one business. Bertie was the nurseryman in charge of all the growing on their vast nursery next to the house. Phil managed the wholesale business in Covent Garden where the produce of the nursery was sold. It was a very good business indeed, so in the early years of their marriage, Bertie and Bar had been quite prosperous and Tim had been given a public school education. Unfortunately, there was discord in the family and Phil was persuaded to separate his half of the business from Bertie's. After that, while the Covent Garden business continued to flourish, the nursery went into a decline from which it never recovered.

For many years Bertie and other nurserymen in the area had been trying to get their land off the Green Belt, but to no avail. Now, Bertie having died, Bar was trying to sell both house and nursery because she could no longer afford to carry either on. The house was in need of urgent repair, was far too large for her in any case, and the nursery business was on the verge of bankruptcy. So when I turned up out of the past, things were in a pretty parlous state.

From then on I made it my business to call to see Bar whenever I came through London. I would stay a night before going on to my destination, and probably also on the way back to Cardiff.

All this time the tensions were mounting in me, and each visit made it worse, but I could not stay away and leave her and Tim to face the future alone. Bar was often distraught and tearful on my visits, and one day through her tears she gave me that rueful little grin I remembered so well of old, and said, "You always turn up at the times of crisis in my life, don't you?" It certainly seemed as if this had been so from the time we had first met.

I felt the old familiar surge of love for her, and I blurted out, *"Darling, I want to leave the Community and marry you!"* She looked at me in shocked disbelief and said, "O but you could not *possibly* do that!"

I was almost as shocked at what I had said as she was, but then heard myself saying, "Well, I don't know, there is a lot of thinking going on just now about the religious life, and some people believe that a man or woman can be called into a community for a number of years - and then called out. A lot of people believe that life vows should not be taken, because people and circumstances change." She was still not convinced, and was very troubled at what I had said. My own tensions had also increased; this was the first time I had expressed the thought that came into my mind very often now.

On my next visit to Bar I was on my way to St Mary's Convent, Wantage to conduct a retreat for the sisters. It was the day on which the *Yom Kippur* war began in Israel, and I read about it in the paper with a sinking heart on the train from Paddington to Didcot, where I was to be met. I was in turmoil also on my own account and dreading the thought of having to conduct this retreat. However, as I have said, I was 'flying on auto-pilot' at that time.

Half way through the week I felt I must talk to someone, so I borrowed the community car one afternoon and went into Oxford to see my old friend Mother Mary Clare, who was Superior of the Sisters of the Love of God, the wonderful Anglican contemplative community at Fairacres. She was a tall woman with one of the most loving and generous hearts I had ever met. She padded into the room with large bare feet in large sandals, hitching at her wimple which she never seemed able to keep straight, beaming her usual welcome as she gave me a big hug. "Mother Mary Clare, I'm in an awful mess," I said, and in an agonised voice it all came tumbling out. When I had finished, she got to her feet, came across to me and gave me another big hug and said, "My dear, I've known for a long time that you no longer have a vocation to this life - *I'm quite certain God is calling you out of CR to marry Bar!"* I was completely astonished, awed would not be too strong a word. Like so many contemplatives, she seemed to have X-ray eyes and could see clearly into a problem that remained an impenetrable fog to anyone else. She then went on to tell me how she had been concerned about me for some time and felt that this was to be the solution. Her parting shot as I left was, "My dear, you will probably learn more about poverty, chastity and obedience in married life than you ever did in the Community!" I returned to Wantage and the sisters' retreat feeling that the pressure had been released to some extent, but almost overwhelmed by the daunting prospect of the future. Not surprisingly, I was very limp and exhausted.

I rang Bar that evening and asked whether she would be free to come to fetch me from Wantage when the retreat finished, and she said she would. By the time she called for me at the convent I felt like a zombie. She had brought a picnic supper which we ate on the banks of the river at Henley (smoked salmon sandwiches, which somehow I managed to get down, but I have disliked smoked salmon ever since!) Bar told me later that she had been very worried about me, for I hardly spoke all the way home, and spent the whole evening looking straight in front of me and not saying a word. The following morning she brought me my breakfast in bed and said she had called her doctor, a family friend, to come in to see me. Rusty Hogbin gave me a certificate to say that I was suffering from an 'acute anxiety syndrome' and should not 'return to work' for at least ten days. I stayed in bed all day and in the evening Bar rang my brother Phil, who lived only a few miles away at Walton-on-Thames, and told him she was worried about me, and also for my reputation as people would soon know that I was staying alone with her in her house. Phil, my beloved and wonderful brother, was with us in a quarter of an hour flat saying he would take me home with him and I could stay as long as I wanted. It was from his house that, the following day, I spent most of the time writing to the Superior, Fr Hugh Bishop, telling him all.

When I got back to Cardiff there was a letter awaiting me from him. As was to be expected, he was very wise and kind about my problem and said that he did not think it impossible that I was being called out of the community to marry Barbara, but that of course, like any other vocation, it would have to be tested. He would talk to me about it at General Chapter which was only a week or two away - in the meantime I was to continue seeing Bar as I was already doing. During Chapter he reiterated his advice - and permission - that I should see Bar as often as I could for the next six months, "You will both have changed over the years," he said, "and you must get to know one another again - this may be a passing thing and it must be tested to see whether it is genuine."

Just at this time I had arranged for Canon John Townroe, then Principal of St Boniface Theological College, Warminster, to come to Cardiff for three days to give a series of lectures to the clergy of the Diocese of Llandaff on the subject of Spiritual Direction - the art of guiding people in their life of prayer and the use of the sacraments, particularly the sacrament of penance. I had not met

226

him before, but he was highly thought of in the church, especially for his teaching of this subject. After dinner on the first evening we served coffee to all those gathered for the course, and I managed to have a few words privately with him. I asked whether he was too tired after his long drive to spare me a few minutes of his time after Compline? "I shall be glad to see you Father," he said - and to my astonishment added, "Have you ever had a nervous breakdown?" I grinned sheepishly and said, no I hadn't but I felt as though one was fairly imminent. So after Compline I took him to my room and told him my story.

10

Called out

Like the good counsellor he is, John listened without interruption for over an hour until I had 'talked myself empty', and then helped me to get some sort of order into my tormented thoughts. He assured me that if I still wanted to do God's will I would in time be shown what that was to entail, and be given the strength to follow. He agreed that the Superior's advice was wise and that he was suggesting the correct course of action. On my way to or from London from then on, I frequently called at Warminster to see John, and he kept me afloat.

I think I managed to keep the Priory ticking over during that terribly difficult six months. I took my Sub-Prior, Gerard Beaumont, into my confidence and he was quite wonderful - full of strong sympathy and endless patience, as most days I spent a lot of his time talking incessantly. I was feeling so disorientated that I could not pray, at any rate not in my normal way, and I had a growing distaste for the recitation of the daily office. I would drag myself out of bed in the morning and recite the office mechanically; I would say Mass only rarely, and would sit in my stall wrapped in my cloak in a cocoon of pain, almost unaware of what was going on around me. I found some relief when I was with Bar, but even with her there was still the background of torment, in which she also shared, for she was still very uneasy about what was happening. She knew she wanted to be with me - but of course was still mourning Bertie whom she had sincerely and deeply loved, and could not think ahead. So Bar was muddled and disorientated also.

At least we could cry together, which we frequently did. I remember one day in particular. Having at last sold the big house and nursery in Hampton, I had helped Bar to move into the lovely riverside flat in Twickenham, I was spending my summer holiday with her. We felt cooped up indoors and needed to get out of the flat, find the silence and serenity of a church and 'be painful before God'. We were careful at that time not to be seen together too much in public, as we were both known in the area, so we tried to find a church a short distance away. We went first to Hanworth, then to Hounslow, but the only ones we could find were locked. Finally, Bar said she thought there was a church near Esher, off the beaten track. We went in search - and found All Saints, Weston Green. With the open space of the green before it, there stood this lovely Italianate church, modern and brilliant white. The West doors were wide open, the high altar in the sanctuary floodlit, clean and serene, cheerful and welcoming. Hand in hand we entered treading softly. On the North side we saw a small Lady Chapel with the white light flickering, indicating that the Blessed Sacrament was reserved there. It drew us like a magnet, and as we entered the chapel the deep silence and the pervading atmosphere of prayer enfolded us like the wings of love. We knelt side by side - and our tears flowed for a very long time. We left that church deeply comforted, and it was not long before we were laughing together again, for I must not give the impression that our six months 'together' was spent in unrelieved gloom. We shared a lot of laughter and spent a lot of time in relative peace. We were discovering that suffering and joy can co-exist, and often do.

Having helped with the move from the big house to the flat, on subsequent visits I came with my tools and did a lot of odd jobs, fitting shelves in cupboards, hanging pictures, fitting light fittings and all the other multifarious jobs that always present themselves when moving house. One job I was quite proud of was the fitting of a long working surface in the kitchen. Together we chose a formica topped kitchen table, and having taken meticulous measurements I proceeded to make in my workshop in Cardiff a working surface that would stretch the whole width of the kitchen covering the fridge, washing machine and rubbish bin. I covered it with formica to match the new kitchen table.

The job was completed a few days before I was due for my next visit. It was over two metres long and the problem now was how to get it from Cardiff to Twickenham. Tim came to the rescue. He had recently built a Lotus Elan sports car - a wonderful piece of work considering that the parts and all the nuts and bolts had arrived all jumbled together in a number of tea chests and packing cases. At the time he was studying in Bromsgrove and one Friday evening he came from there to Cardiff to pick up the working surface and my bag of tools. The poor chap had never set foot in a monastery before and I think was a bit apprehensive. That evening before Evensong and dinner I decreed that, as this was a special occasion, we would have drinks at 6 o'clock. I duly got out the bottle of gin we had been given some time before and we all drank gin and tonic. Tim said he had never been served such strong gin and tonics before! After supper we managed to get one end of the work surface into the passenger seat of the little car, and the tools into the boot, and just before we went into Compline Tim drove off with a formica work surface pointing skywards from the passenger seat of his fast little car. With the wind resistance it caused, I think it must have made the handling of the car a bit tricky to say the least, but I forgot to ask him about it when we next met. I had no real fears for him, however, for he had always been a superb driver. Driving was one of the great passions of his life. At that time, and later, he had many tensions in his life, and not least those caused by my reappearance on the scene, and often his only release was to drive miles and miles in his car at all times of the day and night.

So the first six months, our 'togetherness' months, wended their slow and painful way through our lives, and the time inevitably came when Father Hugh Bishop, the Superior, would come to interview us. One Sunday he was due to preach at the Parish Mass in Feltham, a few miles from Twickenham, so it was arranged that I would pick him up after the service and bring him to the flat for lunch, where he would meet both Bar and Tim.

Bar and I had lengthy sessions with him after lunch, and he said that as we had had six months together he would now have to ask us to have six months apart - for the sake of the Community. This we entirely understood and accepted, though with heavy hearts. After tea Bar and I took Hugh to Kings Cross for the evening train back to Mirfield. On the way home Bar told me that she had been greatly comforted by her talk with the Superior - "He told me," she said, "that he wanted me to know that he was quite satisfied that I am not trying to tempt you out of the Community; and that is a very great relief, I was afraid he would think I was." Christmas was just coming up and Hugh had said that I might have Christmas with Bar and then he would like me to attend the General Chapter at Mirfield, beginning the day after Boxing Day, when we would talk more about my six months apart from her.

On Boxing Day I went to call on the vicar of all Saints Weston Green, our welcoming church. I thought about ten o'clock in the morning would be all right and not too unsocial an hour even on Boxing Day. I rang the bell and waited ... and waited. I was about to go away when the door was opened by a pretty lady in a dressing-gown, with tousled hair and sleepy eyes, who simply said "Yes?" and yawned prodigiously. "I'm awfully sorry to disturb you so early on Boxing Day," I said, "but I'm a Mirfield Father and I have to go North tomorrow. I do rather urgently need to see your husband." "Did you say a Mirfield Father?" she interjected, with a little more liveliness, "That's right," I said. She grinned, opened the door wide, and said, "Oh well, that's different, come on in Father," with eyes that sparkled now with friendliness. As I stepped across the threshold her husband appeared, also in a dressing gown and so I met Michael and Jo Saunders for the first time.

I told Michael and Jo Bar's and my story and asked if he

would keep an eye on her for me while I was away for six months, and keep it confidential for the time being. They were both caught up by the romance of it all and he promised to keep an eye on Bar. He visited her at the flat the very next day after I had caught my train from Kings Cross, and he and Jo immediately became our very good friends.

During Chapter the Superior asked me into his office and said that it was obvious that for the next six months I could not live in a community house - was there anyone among my friends who might have me to stay for that time? I said I thought perhaps Robin and Liz Johnston might have me to stay at Plaxtol, a small village in Kent not far from Sevenoaks where they had recently bought 'The Grange,' a large rambling house on the edge of the village. A wonderful place in which to 'go to ground' while I made my agonising decision! Robin was the businessman whom I had met while I was at the London Priory in the early 50s. We had remained close friends ever since those days. His wife Dorothy had died of a heart attack while I was in Sophiatown, and I had kept in close touch by writing to him quite often. His letters of desolation had turned at long last to ones of joy. Robin had gone to a New Years Eve party, feeling pretty miserable, and there had met Liz whose husband had recently died; leaving her with two small daughters. He asked her if she would have dinner with him one evening, and from there they did not look back. Robin had written to me in South Africa and told me all about it.

I quite often stayed with Rob and Liz while I was at the Cardiff Priory. So I had no hesitation in telling the Superior that I thought Rob and Liz might take me in for six months. Hugh immediately reached for the 'phone and rang them. Rob said, "Of course he can come to stay; tell him to bring his tools - he can be Estate Carpenter while he is here - there's plenty to do." So I left Mirfield, stayed a few days with Bar, and then one day in January we drove down to Plaxtol with my suitcase and tools in the boot.

Bar took to Rob and Liz at once, and they were full of kindness and consideration for her. Liz had even gone to the trouble of buying her a printed canvas and all the necessary wools to make a tapestry cushion-cover - "You will need something to occupy you while he is away", she said. Bar was warmed by her thoughtfulness and kindness and went home that night feeling miserable yet at the same time comforted.

In one of the outbuildings at 'The Grange' there was an old carpenter's bench, and I proceeded to make this my workshop. I did many jobs around the house, the most ambitious being the building of a large storage cupboard in the basement, with two doors and slatted shelves. This particular section of the basement had been used as the coal-hole by the previous owners and still contained a daunting amount of coal and a small mountain of coal dust. The only way to clear it was by shovelling it into buckets and carrying them up the basement stairs, through the kitchen, down a corridor, and eventually dumping them near the compost heap in the garden. It was a filthy, backbreaking and strenuous job, which in retrospect I can see was just the sort of thing I needed to do at that time. For it was now, at Plaxtol, away from both sides of my awful dilemma, that the constant strain of the last year and more took its toll and I proceeded to have what I can only describe as a nervous and spiritual breakdown. I wept copiously while I shovelled coal dust until I was black in the face, and as I sawed and hammered.

Liz was wisdom personified and left me alone all the time I was working. When at teatime I was bathed and changed she would talk or listen and could often bring me back to a lighter-hearted mood.

By this time their joint family had grown from the original five, and three more boys had been added, two of whom were at prep school in Tonbridge. One of my regular jobs was to take the boys to school in one of the two minis and collect them again in the afternoon - always a hilarious and rowdy business, for we picked up a couple of their friends on the way and there was a lot of larking about as we sped down the country lanes to or from school. I occasionally had to stop the car and refuse to go any further until they piped down. They were wonderful children and gave me many lighter moments in my sombre moods.

With their unstinting generosity Rob and Liz lent me a car for my own use, and from time to time I would go down to Warminster to see John Townroe, and to visit other friends - which got me out of the family's hair for a while. Later I realized how difficult it must have been for Rob and Liz, having me there for all those months, but they never once allowed me to see any of the impatience, I am sure, they must often have felt..

Eventually the jobs were finished; the basement room newly whitewashed, the large cupboard gleaming down one wall - to be known from thenceforth, as 'Fr. Paul's cupboard'. Eventually also the 'six months apart' came to an end, and a few weeks before it did so I wrote a long 'Apologia pro Vita Mea' asking formally for my release from the Community and stating my reasons. and sent it to the Superior. Mother Mary Clare, with whom I had of course kept in touch, suggested that I consult a psychiatrist she knew in Oxford, to see whether he could help me to sort myself out. Hugh Bishop, the Superior thought this was a good idea. It happened that the psychiatrist was in the process of packing up preparatory to emigrating to Canada, but he generously agreed to see me in spite of having closed his consulting room door for the last time.

He read my *'apologia'*, and said that while he was sorry he would not be able to see me again, he felt quite confident from reading what I had written that I ought not to have joined the community, that I ought to be released - but he was not at all sure that I should marry Barbara! I am bound to say that this shook me rigid. I felt sure I had been called to the religious life in the community, but that I ought now to be released. I also believed that although we had not come to any firm decision, and would not for many months to come, I would in the end marry Bar.

By the same post by which I wrote to the Superior, I wrote to Paul Bird who had been Brother Paulinus CR for a number of years. There had been doubts about his vocation and he had never gone forward to Final Profession. No one was surprised that he eventually asked for his release. He had had a rough time getting back to life in the world, and I used to see as much of him as possible. Eventually he found just the right job - as Vice Principal of the Central School of Art and Design. A few years before, on one of my visits to him, he had told me that he wanted the School to appoint a Student Counsellor whose concern would be the welfare of students and staff, and later that a young Baptist minister had been appointed and was doing an excellent job. He was playing a big part in keeping the student body reasonably peaceful during that turbulent period in student politics of the later 1960s. When I asked for my release I knew I could not return to parish life - indeed at the time I was questioning whether my vocation to the priesthood, as well as to the religious life, was being withdrawn.

Accordingly I wrote to Paul Bird telling him of my decision and saying that I knew I could not return to parish life and would be in need of a job. 'If', I wrote, 'you should hear of a job as Student Counsellor being available in a London college, I would be grateful if you would let me know.' I had always worked with young people and felt I could still do so in a non-priestly fashion. He replied by return of post saying, "Our man at the Central School has just given in his resignation, so you had better apply for the job!"

He added that if I wished, I could live with him and his wife, whom I knew well, in their house in Chiswick when my release came through and I left Rob and Liz. Another generous friend, and another door opening as the most recent one closed. I was quite sure I ought not stay longer with Rob and Liz than the six months we had originally arranged. No friends could have been more generous, and I owe them an enormous debt of gratitude.

I went to the General Chapter after Easter when the votes on my release were to be counted - including those from the community houses in South Africa, Rhodesia and the West Indies. There was a final debate in the Chapter room at Mirfield before the brethren of the home province voted. While all this was going on in the Chapter Room I was sitting nervously in the Superior's office, and remembering that other occasion twenty years before, when I had waited for Chapter to vote me into the Community. But then I was with others; now I was alone. After an agonising hour or so I heard brisk and unmistakable footsteps approaching, the door flew open, and the Superior strode in. "The Community have voted in favour of your release, with just one vote against," he said. Then, overcome with emotion we gave one another a hug, for we were very fond of each other. I knelt and asked for his blessing and later that morning I was ready to leave for the last time. Fr Hilary Beasley, my old friend and previous boss at the Hostel, was now severely crippled and had been provided with an adapted Mini to make him mobile. He said he would drive me to Wakefield station for the midday train to Kings Cross. As I lifted my case into the back of the car the front door of the Mother House opened and all the brethren streamed out to shake my hand and say goodbye and wish me well. Among them was Brother Roger Castle. He came and gave me a hug, and looking at me through the lower lenses of his spectacles, as he habitually did, said, "Of course you are not *really* leaving us, you are just going off to do another job, that's all." We were great friends and he could not bear the thought of my leaving.

Paul Bird was waiting with his car at Kings Cross. He swept me back to Chiswick where I did a quick change into a pair of slacks and an old jacket (the only lay clothes I possessed), and then to Paddington Station. Here, by the skin of my teeth, I caught the train to Sidmouth where Bar was staying with her cousin by marriage, Michael Page, and a few black children from a foster home whom he befriended.

I took Bar out to dinner that night with the money the Bursar had given me. It was the first time I had been able to take someone out for a meal for twenty years. It gave me no end of a thrill and I felt very sophisticated!. We had a nice meal and were gradually able to relax with one another. I did not say anything about marriage for I had learnt that she was not yet ready to consider such a suggestion. She was still mourning Bertie and had once or twice felt that I was rushing her too much. I also had in my mind what the Oxford psychiatrist had said, and although it was Bertie's death that had precipitated all this, I now felt that I could not and should not make any firm commitments about the future for the time being. First I had to give myself time to assimilate all that had happened in the last two years, and to adjust to its implications. I also had to get a job, for apart from the money the Bursar had given me, which would not last long, I did not have two pennies to rub together, so a job was a pretty basic need.. After that would be time enough to plan for the future.

In the meantime we had a very happy weekend in Sidmouth with Michael, and Tim joined us on the Saturday morning. We went for a walk in the public gardens, and it felt very strange to know that I was no longer a religious, and that there was no earthly reason (or even a 'heavenly' one) why I should not be walking in public hand in hand with Bar. I reflected that I now had an entirely new life to build for myself, and I hoped that eventually and at long last my Girl in the Middle would take the central place in that life. But I knew I must keep an open mind on that subject for some time yet and wait until she was ready to think ahead a little more than she could at present. 'At present' is the clue, I thought. Live for today, leave the future in other hands until planning ahead clearly becomes part of the business of 'today'. So, with something like peace we sauntered hand in hand along the clean tarmac paths among the bright flowers shining in their formal beds. Like everyone else, we went into the tourist shop where Michael bought me a woollen tie to celebrate my release - my first item of new lay clothing!

Michael had proved a good friend: already Bar's trusted confidante, he had known about the whole business from the beginning, and had been most kind and supportive to both of us. A week or two later he invited us to the Post Office Tower restaurant in London for a celebratory dinner. But how could I go out to dinner, I had nothing to wear! I only had my slacks and a grotty old sports jacket. I would have to wear a suit at least if not a DJ for that prestigious restaurant. So Bar got on the phone to her sister Joan, who immediately said, "O I'm sure Chris will lend Paul a suit, they are much the same build." It turned out that we were not 'much the same' build but almost identical, and the suit Chris gave - not lent - me fitted as though made for me. From then on he gave me several suits from time to time that he no longer liked or needed, and they were always in very good condition and tided me over until I could afford to buy my own. As a result of this generosity I went quite smartly dressed with Bar and Michael to dinner in the revolving restaurant on the top of the Post Office Tower, and we watched fascinated as London slowly passed us by. The restaurant was closed not long afterwards when Arab terrorists tried to blow up the

Barbara 1967

Our Wedding Day 1968 – at last

236

tower, and it never re-opened.

Soon after moving into the flat in Twickenham, Bar had been asked by Dr 'Rusty' Hogbin, her doctor and friend of the family, to step in while his secretary was away on the sick list. The secretary died and the job became permanent. Bar loved this work and was very good at it; she worked every morning and some afternoons, so although living only a bus ride away in Chiswick I saw her only a few times a week. We decided that now I was no longer wearing my religious habit we must be discreet for the sake of her reputation. Mine no longer mattered very much!

A lot of my time while living with the Birds in Chiswick was spent in writing and rewriting my application for the job of Student Counsellor at the Central School. Paul was helping me to write my Curriculum Vitae. He was meticulous, even pernickety, in the phrasing of each paragraph and statement, and the placing of every comma. So it took a long long time and many, many re-writes before he thought it was good enough.

I had first known Diana, Paul's wife, as a devout young girl at the CR Summer School one year, when she had impressed me, among other things, by her utter stillness while at prayer in the chapel. I had not been surprised when I heard later that she had joined a contemplative community. I had occasionally talked to her through the grill when visiting the convent. When Diana had joined the community the 'enclosure' was very strictly enforced, but later in the sixties one of the ways that the new thought about the religious life had affected the enclosed communities was in modifying somewhat these strict rules. People from 'the world' began to be allowed to speak to the sisters, albeit still through the grille, about various topics of interest. Paul Bird, when still Brother Paulinus CR, had been asked to talk to the sisters about art. He told me afterwards of this visit and how, as he talked, he had noticed one of the younger sisters in particular who had fixed her eyes upon him with a great intensity. After his release from CR, he had returned to give a second lecture and the same thing had happened again; but this time their eyes had locked upon one another. He said he had had much the same sensation as I had had on opening that fateful letter from my mother enclosing the obituary notice of Bertie Page. He came away very troubled from that encounter, and told me that he felt absolutely certain that this young nun was miserable and did not have a vocation to that life. And so it proved, for about a year later she was released from the community and later still they were married.

Diana and Paul had been married for about two years when I went to live with them, and she and I talked a lot while Paul was at work at the school and I was preparing my application for the job. I think we were able to help one another a little over the very difficult business of coming out of a community and adjusting to life in 'the world'.

Paul came home each day to tell me about the growing total of requests for application forms that had been received. First it was, "We have so far had 50 requests for applications forms;" then it was seventy-five, then eighty-two. Before the requests finally ceased, over two hundred forms had been sent out. With each new total my spirits found a new low. Paul kept saying, "Oh yes, but a lot of these people will not actually apply." I cannot remember how many applications were received, but it seemed to me an overwhelming number. Eventually, however, a short list of eleven was drawn up: and I could hardly believe it when Paul told me that my name was on it!

Armed with this information I went off to see Bar that evening and told her I was on the short list and that I would soon hear from the Central School about the date of the Selection Board.

Shortly before this, on one of my visits to the flat, we had been looking out of the kitchen window at the people passing along the embankment and I kissed the back of her neck and told her I loved her. She turned into my arms, smiling at me, and I found myself going down on one knee, and taking her hand I said, "Darling, will you marry me?"

This time there was no hesitation as she cuddled my head to her and said, "Yes darling, I will - in fact I don't think I can live without you!"

Now, having told her about the short list and that the interviews would be in a month's time, I said, "What about taking a chance and getting married before the interviews, and just hoping against hope that I get the job?"

She said, "Oh yes, why not? - I can't believe that having given all those years to God in the community he has not got something for you to do now."

So I went to see the vicar of St Mary's Twickenham and put up the banns, which of course had to be read on three consecutive Sundays. We asked our dear friend Michael Saunders of All Saints, Weston Green, if he would marry us, and he said he gladly would.

We were both still under considerable strain and feeling a lot of nervous stress. Neither of us could bear the thought of a big wedding with masses of relations and friends, so we determined to make it as quiet as possible with just the bare minimum of people present. I had told Mother and Geoff that we were going to marry, and Mother had at once begun saying who she would like to be there. I had told her firmly that there were to be no wedding guests and we would not even tell anyone the date of the wedding. She did not like it a bit, but my brother Phil and Dorothy said they quite understood, and so did Bar's sister Joan and her mother.

We were married at St Mary's at 11am on Friday, 24th June 1968. I was still wearing the suit given me by Chris. I got a bus from Chiswick, and by the time I got to Twickenham it had begun to rain. I had not brought a raincoat and ducked into the florists near the bus stop and bought a dozen red roses and some maidenhair fern. I dodged along from shop awning to shop awning clutching my roses to my bosom, and arrived at the church rather damp. I found a vase and arranged the roses, which I put on the altar. As I awaited the arrival of my bride, I reflected that here was another momentous occasion in my life, another ambition at last on the verge of achievement. Now there was none of the bated-breath expectancy I had felt as I awaited my ordination to the priesthood in Portsmouth Cathedral twenty-six years ago. Now I was wondering whether that ought to have happened at all. Nor was there any sense of euphoria as I awaited my marriage at long last to my beloved Girl in the Middle. I had been so emotionally drained by the events of the past two years that all I could feel at that moment in St Mary's Twickenham, was a quiet satisfaction that at last Bar and I were going to be together. I was going to be united for the rest of my life to my 'other half,' for the affinity that I had felt with her since we first met had persisted down the years; for long periods unregarded and hidden beneath the surface of my mind, but now once again dominating my feelings. I simply felt a quiet satisfaction that after all the vicissitudes of life I was at last about to 'come home,' to be where I belonged, and everything else, even priesthood, paled into insignificance by comparison..

Tim gave Bar away, and Paul and Diana Bird were our witnesses, and that is all there were except for John Kendall the parish clerk.

As we got into our car to drive to the flat I kissed Bar and then said, "O damn, I've left my false teeth in Chiswick!" There was a moment of stunned silence, then we both fell about laughing and nearly had hysterics. Bar said those were the most romantic first words a newly wed bridegroom had ever said to his bride!

Michael Saunders, Tim and Paul and Diana Bird came back to the flat with us, where Bar's sister and Edie, her one-time housekeeper in the big house and still her great friend, were waiting to welcome us with a small champagne 'wedding breakfast.' Bar told them of my romantic first words to her as we got into the car, and there was more hilarious laughter. After a while we suddenly realized that Paul Bird was missing - he had gone back home to retrieve my denture, and thoughtfully returned with my raincoat also.

We had arranged to have a weekend mini-honeymoon at the Dudley Hotel in Hove, which Bar knew well. She said it was quiet and secluded and comfortable, and above all it was not far away - we did not want to spend hours driving. We had a late lunch just outside Dorking on the way down and Bar suddenly said, "Oh bother, I've left my beauty case in the bedroom" - so back we went to Twickenham to fetch it, and again set off on our honeymoon - dentures and beauty boxes; I think an indication of the state we were in.

We eventually reached the hotel feeling flaked out. We could hardly believe that after all the vicissitudes of life through which we had both passed since we had first fallen in love as teenagers, here we were, married at last! At dinner that night I did some mental arithmetic to see whether I could afford a bottle of champagne, and decided I could. So we toasted one another, recalling what an effort it had taken to come together at last, pledged to each other now for the rest of our lives. But we were not solemn about it; we chuckled and laughed a lot, if a little wearily. We had what we both most needed, a quiet and restful weekend.

Bar was always a water girl and loved the sea; nothing eased the tensions for her so much as a stroll along the shore by the edge of the sea, and at Hove of course there is always the lovely sound of the waves breaking and ebbing on the shingle. So hand in hand we would walk by the sea, and occasionally on the pier we would lean over and watch the water rising and falling against the limpet-encrusted piles, with the different seaweeds fanning and folding with the movement of the water.

There was one embarrassing moment at the very end of our mini-honeymoon. At lunch on the Sunday, after which we were to set off for home, we were chatting over our meal when, to my utter horror I saw at the very next table a party of four middle aged people which included one of the most avid of the Community 'camp followers,' a well-to-do good hearted but rather strident Yorkshire woman. I knew that if she spotted me she would be bound to leap up and come over and declaim for all to hear some such observation as " O Father, I'd heard you'd left Community, is this the wife then?" Absolutely not to be borne! I half covered my face with my hand, and muttered urgently across the table to Bar, "Eat up, quickly, we must get out of here!" Bar looked nonplussed and concerned, "Whatever's the matter, darling," she said, "you look awful." "Eat up - *quickly*" I said. We finished off, my hand still covering my face, gulped the last of the wine, and I fled the dining room, with Bar trailing behind. I went straight out into the street and then turned to wait for her. I was shaking and white as a sheet, Bar said. We walked along the pier while I told her what it was all about, and after a while I calmed down.

I could not bear to face anyone I had known in my previous life in the Community. It was not just that this was a person with whom I felt little affinity. I was still raw and hurting from the traumas entailed in the decision about whether or not to ask for my release. Probably it had a lot to do with my pride - I had been a fairly prominent member of CR and I knew that a lot of people up and down the country had relied upon me and valued what I had tried to do for them. Sure as I was that 'before God, I could have done no other' than leave the Community, I felt that I had let them all down, and was convinced that they would think this too. When I had recovered we returned to the hotel, almost looking round corners to see if the dreaded dumpy figure was lurking there, but thankfully we managed to check out and make it to the car without further ado.

We had decided to call on Mother and Geoff in Worthing on our way home and announce that we were now man and wife - gripping the nettle of Mother's disapproval and hurt as soon as possible. Mother was really very good about it and did not make our visit an unhappy one. She was always a realist and although clearly disappointed not to have been at the wedding, accepted the fact after a few moments and gave us a loving welcome. It helped that she had always been very fond of Bar and was delighted that at last we were together. In fact the affection was mutual and Bar's admiration for Mother increased as the years went by. But she would not allow her to bully or try to dominate her. Aunt, who had lived in Worthing until recently, had gone to a home for retired teachers in Paignton, so it was some time before we were able to go to see her. We were sorry not to be able to see her too.

We arrived home on the Sunday evening, and the interviews for the job were fixed for the following morning.

Monday was a blazing hot June day, and dressed in my suit and a collar and tie, I set off for the Central School with squadrons of butterflies looping the loop in my tummy. I was shown into the Senior Common Room where the other ten candidates had already assembled. They were all young men in jeans and sweaters or open necked shirts, and my heart went straight to my boots - Gosh, I thought, I stick out like a sore thumb in this lot; they all *look* like students and I clearly haven't a chance against opposition like this.

This is the sort of person they will appoint, not a stuffy looking old bloke like me! I was very depressed.

My turn to face the selection board came at long last, and I got through it somehow. I returned home to the flat as fast as I could and went straight to the bedroom where I took off my jacket. As I removed my tie I was telling Bar about the interview and about the other candidates and how I did not think I stood a chance - when the 'phone by the bedside rang. I lifted the receiver to hear a breathless voiced Paul Bird say, "I have just rushed out of the school to a public 'phone box to tell you *you've got the job!*" - and he burst into tears! I looked up at Bar and said, *"I've got the job!"* - and *I* burst into tears!. Her face lit up and she said, *"You've got the job!"* - and *she* burst into tears!!

When we had all calmed down a bit Paul added, "and what's more, the Principal said, 'We can't put a man of this experience on the minimum starting salary scale, we'll put him on the top scale from the start!' What jubilation! *O, thank you, thank you.....*

We asked Paul and Diana over for dinner to celebrate my appointment and to thank them for all the wonderful help they had given me. Before my appointment could be finally confirmed I had to be given a medical examination by an Inner London Education Authority (ILEA) doctor to make sure they were not accepting a health risk, and this included convincing them that I was not too deaf to deal with students. Butterflies were looping the loop again as a few mornings later I went to County Hall on the other side of Westminster Bridge for the medical check-up. I was really scared that I would be turned down on account of my deafness. I was seen by a friendly Indian doctor who pronounced me fit. He did not mention my hearing loss, so I thought I had better bring it up myself to save any possible future embarrassment. "I'm rather deaf," I said nervously. He immediately smiled and said, "But you seem to do pretty well with the hearing aid you are wearing." And that was that. My appointment was confirmed a few days later by the Chief Education Officer.

After the medical check-up I went on to the Central School to see the young man whom I would be succeeding and asked him many questions about the job. It was getting towards the end of the summer term and I could see that he was quite busy. He had built up a splendid filing system with confidential details of interviews with many students. We arranged that he would leave the student's names on file so that I would know they had been seen, but the details that had been told him in confidence he would destroy. He suggested that as his contract did not expire until the end of August I should ask if I could start work before the beginning of the term and overlap with him for the last month, with which the ILEA readily agreed. This was great from my point of view, for not only would it give me a whole month in which to learn the ropes from him, but also it would mean that I would be earning some money a month before I had expected to - an important consideration, for the small amount of money the Community had given me was fast running out.

All this having been satisfactorily arranged, life took on a rosier hue, and Bar and I decided to have a fortnight's proper honeymoon before I started work. We thought of Salcombe and were recommended to the Castle Point Hotel by some friends of Bar's. I spoke to the manager who also owned the hotel and asked if they had a room by any chance - I said this was our delayed honeymoon. Peter Brooks was so nice on the 'phone. He said the only room they had was at the top of the house, it was a bit cramped but had a comfortable bed. When I said we would take it, he said "O that's splendid; we've only been running the place for a few weeks, its our first season, so we'll have a double celebration when you are here on your honeymoon!" Peter Brooks was a naval Commander who had taken early retirement and he and his wife had decided to buy this hotel in order to run it together.

The room at the top of the house was just that, in fact it was tucked into the roof, the ceilings sloping on both sides. It was next door to the main water tank, and from the gurglings and rushings and dribblings that we heard must have been the spaghetti junction of all the plumbing in the house. On our first morning we had just been brought our early morning tea when there was a terrific gurgling noise and suddenly a great gout of water shot into the air from the waste of our washbasin. We shot up in bed and nearly crowned ourselves on the sloping ceiling, and ended up laughing hysterically. But we loved that holiday and had tremendous fun. We were able really to relax for the first time that we could remember since I had first contemplated asking to be released from the community. That trauma was behind us now; we were married at long last; I had a job to start in a couple of weeks time; Bar was already in a job she loved; we had a lovely home by the Thames, with wonderful river views from every window. I could sit on our balcony and throw crusts to the ducks! We felt we were greatly blessed.

One reason why we had chosen Salcombe for our honeymoon was that it was not far from Paignton and we wanted to see Aunt as soon as possible. She had written sweetly and kindly about our marriage, and we knew she was longing to see us as much as we were to see her. So a couple of days after our arrival we set off immediately after breakfast to visit her. We found a beautifully dressed elderly lady who gave us the warmest possible welcome and insisted on taking us out to lunch.

Like mother, Aunt had always been very fond of Bar and although they had not seen one another for many years they got on famously from the first. Aunt still had her dry and wry sense of humour and we had many laughs together. We arranged that we would come over on another day before we went home and this time we would take her out to lunch and for a little run in the car if she would like that.

On that occasion we had lunch in Paignton and afterwards took her on the ferry to Dartmouth. Aunt was sitting in the back of the car, and as we boarded the ferry we heard her murmur, "I hope I shall not suffer from *Mal de Mer*," in her gentle yet slightly schoolmistressy voice. How we laughed at, and with, her that afternoon! We gave her a Devonshire Cream Tea, with scones and what as children we used to call 'stand-up cream,' and strawberry jam. Tucking into this feast at about 4 o'clock she glanced at her watch and said reflectively, "I mustn't be late for my supper at 5:30!" Like so many elderly people who have to live an institutional life, the important events of the day were the meals. She was not hungry, nor was she greedy; it was simply that her days to a great extent revolved around the mealtimes.

Soon after our return from Salcombe I started work at the Central School. I had a small office in the main corridor on the ground floor opposite the Senior Common Room, strategically placed for both students and staff.

It took me a long time to settle into the job; some of my duties I found very daunting. I was responsible for doing what I could to find lodgings for the students, the majority of whom lived too far away to commute from home. There were so many colleges in London, apart from London University, that it was enormously difficult to find lodgings for new students starting their courses in September. My predecessor had done some work towards a lodgings list, and fortunately for me, being a methodical man, he had left a file full of addresses of possible digs and lodging houses. I did the best I could with this and produced a lodging list of sorts by the time the first fresher students began knocking on my door asking for help in finding somewhere to live.

There was much to learn, not least I had to know a great deal about student grants from local authorities in order to be able to advise possible future students about their rights to a grant, the qualifications needed in order to apply, and how to set about obtaining one.

I slowly mastered the technicalities of the job, but as the first year gradually developed into the second, I was conscious that the students were not bringing their problems to me as they had done to my predecessor and I felt that I was falling down on the most important part of the job. For instance, my predecessor had told me that one day a girl had come to see him in tears saying that she was in great trouble. From experience he asked what to him was the obvious question, "What's the trouble dear, are you pregnant?" - and was astonished when she wailed, "Oh no, its *much* worse than that: my boyfriend's parents think I am not socially acceptable!" No one had confided anything remotely like that to me, or indeed come to me in any sort of personal difficulty.

I wondered what to do, and after a lot of thought I decided to try two things. First, I would write a letter of welcome to every individual fresher student which they would receive on their first day in college, stating what my role was intended to be. I would emphasise that I was not a member of staff and had no disciplinary role whatever. Everything said to me in my office would be treated in absolute confidence and would be divulged to no member of staff or to anyone else at all. I would say I was there to prevent small problems from becoming big ones; that I could be talked to about any subject under the sun; that being rather 'long in the tooth' there was not very much about life that I did not know about, and so was completely unshockable.

Secondly, I decided, that during the first week of the new academic year I would address all the fresher students in the Jeanetta Cochran Theatre, which was part of the College, and tell them the story of my life, so that they would know something about this old guy who was responsible for being their 'counsellor'.

This double strategy proved to be just what was needed; they read the letter with interest, but the first meeting in the theatre was the real success. Luckily I managed to have them laughing their heads off - especially about the bit where Bar, my beautiful golden Girl in the Middle with the husky voice, lay in my arms looking up into my eyes and saying, "Ten little nigger boys digging in dead earnest, poor Ernest", as I explained why when I stopped being a monk I retained my community name of Paul. By the time I had finished my *spiel*, standing on the edge of the stage, I felt a warmth of friendship coming to me from the auditorium.

I had hardly made it back to my office before youngsters were coming in to see me, and before long I had to get an 'Engaged' notice to hang on my door to deter other callers when someone was with me. From spending a lot of my time almost twiddling my thumbs in my office I now became very busy. I took to working through my lunch hour as this seemed a time when students found it convenient to come to see me, and they soon got used to opening their hearts while I munched my bread and cheese and drank my glass of beer - in fact I think in some cases it helped them to relax and feel at home. After a difficult year I felt that at last I was earning my salary, at any rate to some extent. Paul Bird told me later that about this time the Principal had said to him that he did not think I was doing very well because students did not seem to be coming to see me - his office was a few yards down the corridor from mine. My new approach had almost simultaneously begun to bear fruit and Paul was able to say, in surprise, "But you can't get near him for students, they are round him like bees round a honeypot!" A considerable exaggeration of course, but from then on there was indeed a steady flow of people to see me, and it continued for the rest of the twelve years until I retired.

Another contributory factor in my getting closer to the students was the fact that a new Bursar asked if at the beginning of each term I would take over the responsibility for handing out grant cheques to students from their Local Education Authorities. Although it meant a considerable increase in my administrative work I gladly took on this job, for it allowed me to know more about the financial situation of individual students and therefore able to help with difficulties that might, and often did, arise. It also meant that I saw almost every student for a few moments at the beginning of every term and some of these brief encounters resulted in a return visit and a talk.

In time students felt free to come to me about difficulties they were having with their courses, and also personal ones with particular members of staff, and I was often able to act as mediator in difficult situations. Before long staff and students alike were coming to talk over their problems, and I was glad that I had emphasised from the start that I was an entirely independent entity, so all could come and speak freely to me in confidence.

During my first year the Association of Inner London Student Counsellors of which I was automatically a member, organised a two year in-training course in psychology, which I attended and found most helpful in my work, since it was specially geared to student problems.

The Central School of Art and Crafts, as it was originally called, was founded in 1896 by the London County Council. At the time, inspired by the Arts and Crafts Movement under the influence of William Morris, there was growing disillusionment with the quality of design owing to the mechanisation of production, and the movement was demanding a return to hand-production. According to this school of thought the machine was a social evil.

The first principal of the School, W R Lethaby, had a different conviction. He believed that science and modern industry had given the artist many new opportunities. Another thinker along these lines was C R Ashbee, who declared that modern civilization rests on machinery and no system that exists for the encouragement or endowment of the arts can be sound that does not recognise this. (paraphrased from the 1983-85 Prospectus). So the Central School became one of the most important influences in the return of good design and art to the world of modern production and its influence came to be felt in all fields. Perhaps this was most clearly seen in the work of Walter Gropius who in his early years had been greatly influenced by the Central School's concept of bringing aesthetics into industrial design and architecture, and at Dessau in Germany had built the Bauhaus. John David Morley writes, 'Visitors who arrived at Dessau station in the late Twenties were confronted by a building standing in the fields unlike anything they had ever seen before: a jumble of white squares and rectangles, the walls for the most part consisting of glass, and apparently without any roof at all ... it was the Bauhaus and it had just been built by Walter Gropius. There was nothing like it in the world. It was a declaration of war on all architecture that had gone before. It was the manifestation of architecture as the complete work of art in which architects, sculptors, painters and designers subscribed.' The influence of the Bauhaus was to be seen throughout industry and architecture in the Thirties, from 'modernistic' buildings to streamlined kitchen utensils and gadgets. It had particular vogue in the United States.

In 1976 an exhibition was mounted at the Central School to celebrate its 80th anniversary and one day during the exhibition Paul Bird, the Vice Principal, came into my office with a broad grin on his face. He said, "I was sitting at my desk this morning when there was a tap on the door, and in came a little man in a long raincoat, holding his hat against his chest with one hand and extending the other as he came across to shake my hand - and he said timidly, "I am Walter Gropius!" Paul was ecstatic, "What an honour! the great man himself! the author of the Bauhaus. I have just shown him round the exhibition, but he would not let me do the honours and take him out to lunch - he has just gone quietly on his way."

Once a year during the Easter term, two weeks were set aside when Foundation Students from all the other art colleges in the country were invited to visit the Central School to be shown round the departments so that they could make up their minds whether they wanted to apply to us for their degree courses. Hundreds of students wanted to avail themselves of this opportunity and over the years the numbers had grown to such an extent that it caused a serious disruption of the work in the departments for the whole of that fortnight. I was asked if I would take on the job of organising these visits and seeing that the students were shown round in an orderly fashion that would give them a good idea of what our courses had to offer and yet save the departments from major disruption. It was the sort of logistical and administrative job that I enjoyed, so I took it on. I am still not sure that I should have done this, but I could not resist the challenge.

Before Christmas I sent out a circular to every art college in the country with a list of the days and times on which each of our departments would be open to visitors, a booking form was enclosed. As these forms were returned the information was collated on large posters for each department and the name of the college and the number of students expected were entered. The day before the visit the department was informed of the numbers to be expected the following day and from which college the visitors would be coming.

Visitors were asked to arrive at least a quarter of an hour before the visit was due, and on arrival were assembled in the senior common room for an introductory talk by a member of staff before going up to the department to be shown round in an orderly way. The scheme worked very well. Prospective students saw the departments that interested them, and our staff and students were caused only minimal disruption. Although it gave me a lot of extra work I think it was of real service to the college and to the visitors. It also meant that those who eventually applied to us for a place and were accepted would already have had a brief contact with me.

When I finally retired in 1980, after twelve years at the Central School I felt that I had become part of the very fabric of the place and in some ways I was sorry to go. But I was really getting a bit old for the job and after twelve years the School needed a change. I looked forward to the prospect of having more time to be with Bar and to spend in my workshop. Paul Bird made the farewell speech at my retirement party to which a large number of students and most of the staff came. He said that I had been a 'one man band' in the school, available to both students and staff - and concluded, "So what more appropriate leaving present can we give him than a *band* saw" - at which he whisked off a tablecloth covering an object standing on the grand piano, to reveal a gleaming new band saw, which I am still using fourteen years later, one of the most useful presents I have ever had.

For the twelve years while at the Central School I had done a lot of carpentry in my garage which I could convert very quickly into a splendid workshop. The Community had generously given me the tools I had collected at the Cardiff Priory and to these I had added many more. Apart from making things for the flat I began taking on commissions for other people. The owner of the freehold of our small block of flats and of the larger block next door let me do a lot of the maintenance work for both blocks. Before long I had a flourishing - and lucrative - sideline, which was very acceptable in the years after our marriage when money was rather scarce. I found my carpentry was first-class occupational therapy, and for years I revelled in it. Most evenings and weekends would see me engrossed for hours at my bench. The only piece of equipment I had not been able to buy was a band saw, and now as I retired from the School in 1980, that lack was generously supplied.

11

The Wilderness Years

I had not anticipated the difficulties that would face me when I came back to the ordinary world after twenty years of the religious life. Because I had been a very active religious, travelling widely, spending a lot of time 'in the world,' staying for various lengths of time in other people's houses and having the privilege in many of being accepted as a 'member of the family,' I had expected that I would take to ordinary life as a duck takes to water. I could not have been more mistaken.

For twenty years there had been a definite framework to my life; everything had for the most part been 'regular' and predictable. Now I was married at long last to my love, and I found myself in an entirely different world; nothing was predictable, everything was new and strange. I now had to think of money and try to ensure that I was managing it responsibly. In our early years we had to be very careful of this, for us, rare commodity. So I worried about money in a way I had not needed to do while in CR, where all necessities of life had been provided from the common purse. Now every penny had to be looked at carefully before being parted with. Commuting to town every day was also a strange experience and learning this new job in the entirely new environment I found difficult and exhausting.

But these difficulties paled almost into insignificance compared with the adjustments that marriage itself made necessary. Twenty years of living the celibate life, with its trials and difficulties, is not the ideal preparation for marriage, to say the least. Nor were our ages. I was fifty-three and Bar fifty-two when we were married. Bar had been married twice before, and I was entirely inexperienced - and ignorant of many of the basic facts of the conjugal relationship to a degree that astonished and dismayed me.

As I have already recalled, sex was a forbidden subject when I was young and there had been only two occasions when it was referred to by my father. The first, when I was about eleven, my old Nanny was having tea with us one afternoon. I had asked innocently, "Where *do* babies come from?" My father had grabbed me in instant fury, flung me into the next room and closed the door on us while he angrily admonished me never to let him hear me mention the subject again, and had added,"You will learn about all that when you are older." The only other occasion was when I was about seventeen when he had come into the room and said in an agonised voice, "O Ernie, be very careful of women, they make you do terrible things!" I had been so astonished by this outburst of unsolicited advice that I had not said a word before he had turned hurriedly on his heel and left the room, no doubt highly embarrassed. All I knew at that time about sex therefore I had picked up for myself, in the smutty way that most of my contemporaries did in those days, relying on what we heard older boys saying; what we could glean from the crude drawings they sometimes left on classroom blackboards, and later of course, from erotic reading and the mild pornography that was all that was available in those days. Of course we combed the Bible for the 'dirty bits', and were grateful to friends who had sisters at home for the little they could tell us.

Reading some psychology and dealing with people enlarged one's knowledge, and during our courtship years when we were young, Bar and I had learned a lot from one another so far as Christian conventions and our uneasy consciences allowed. But there were areas of importance in the relationships between men and women of which I had remained in complete ignorance. Bar was infinitely kind and patient but as the difficult and traumatic months went by it became abundantly clear that I was not only ignorant but also psychologically impaired in my sexuality.

It is an abiding regret that in spite of all Bar's wonderful kindness and sympathy I was never able completely to overcome these difficulties and the physical side of our marriage never became fully normal. This was a great deprivation because for us there never was the experience of tenderness and fulfilment that can so often ease the frustrations and sufferings that are inevitable, on occasions, in any marriage. There was a lot of tenderness, but it was expressed in other ways, but I know there were times when she doubted whether I really loved her.

In consequence I did everything for her that I could think of to convince her that I was as devoted to her as I had always been. I suppose, as she said on more than one occasion, I 'spoiled her rotten.' Nor was Bar the only one who thought this. On one occasion quite early on in our marriage she was not well and we had promised to go down to Worthing to see Mother and Geoff. She insisted that I go alone, saying that she would be perfectly all right.

Mother took the opportunity of Bar's not being there to start telling me that I was spoiling her. I was furious at this intrusion and refused to listen, telling her angrily that I was not prepared to discuss my wife. I over-reacted of course, my hackles rising because I thought that here she was again, still trying to dominate and run

251

my life for me. I suppose I was over-compensating for my inadequacies.

We tried to get help about our problems in those early days of our marriage: we saw two different doctors at different times, but to no purpose.

Another early difficulty was poor old Tim. I had always been fond of him as a little boy, but I had been a rotten godfather to him; I wrote to him from South Africa when he was to be confirmed at Cranleigh, but that was all, and it was a great dereliction not only of duty but of affection. When we told him that we were going to get married I said I would try to be a better step-father to him than I had been godfather.

Tim was now nearly twenty-six, and was working with a firm in Crannock and coming home in his Lotus Elan at the weekends. He would not have been less than human if he had not much liked the arrival of a second stepfather. He was an unhappy chap at that time, and not long after we were married he left his job, and came home to live. He was in a very depressed state and was in fact having a mild nervous breakdown.

That made three very depressed people living in the small flat in Twickenham. Tim had the room at one end of the flat near the bathroom, and our bedroom and the sitting room and diningroom were at the other end. Many evenings saw Tim lying on his bed at one end of the flat, me in an armchair at the other end, and Bar working furiously in the kitchen in the middle. All of us in the depths of depression. Poor Bar, poor Tim, poor Paul! Bar used to say tearfully, "I feel like the jam in the sandwich."

The doctor said that Tim should not think of trying to get another job yet; that he should stay at home where he felt secure, and should occupy himself in some light occupation that interested him. He was always very clever with his hands, and to keep him occupied we bought him a large model speedboat kit to make up and he would pore over this for hours at a time and often late into the night. The day came when we went off to buy the little petrol engine and remote control unit for it, and having fitted those he took it to the Diana Pond in Bushey Park and set it off on its maiden voyage, controlling its speed and movements from the bank. Very exciting, and a real sense of achievement for him.

Eventually Tim was feeling sufficiently better to apply for a temporary job at Bentalls department store in Kingston during the Christmas shopping period. This did him a power of good, and one of the best things was that he met a girl who also did him a power of good. She was his supervisor who taught new members of staff the arts of selling, including the mysteries of the till. He left a note on the windscreen of her car one day, and soon afterwards brought her home to Sunday afternoon tea. She was such a lively character and had us all in fits of laughter. There was never anything serious on either side, but they were jolly good friends for a time, and exactly what Tim needed just then.

Meanwhile I was learning the ropes at the Central School, and among the files in my office I found some literature about the Vocational Guidance Association, which existed to help young people to make up their minds about what they wanted to do in life and helped them to discover where their aptitudes lay. I had heard of this association before and of the sometimes impressive help that they could give. Tim was in a quandary about what to do. His main interests were in cars and trucks, and he was very knowledgeable about the motor industry in general, but he did not know what sort of job he wanted. So I took all the literature home and showed it to him and Bar. After a good deal of thought Tim felt he would like to go to the VGA and see if they could help him. He had a preliminary interview, then did the tests, and when the results of those had come through he went for a final interview by a professional evaluator.

All three of us were quite astonished by the results. The tests suggested that he would be good at social work. Tim - *social* work? - Gosh, we thought! Very high on *journalism* and writing! More astonishment! Bar could not believe her eyes and ears, "But I have never been able to get you to write a thing - not even a Thank You letter!" she said.

The evaluator strongly urged Tim to do some social work and see how he liked it - and also, perhaps later, some writing. He was so much better as a result of this assessment that he felt confident enough to give it a try. But how to start? It happened that when I had been thinking of what to do myself after my release, in case the Central School job did not come my way, I had thought of helping with the welfare work that was organised at St Martin in the Fields. Austen Williams the Vicar had said he was sure he could find me a job. So it occurred to me to give him a ring about Tim.

That good man, with his immediate willingness to help, invited Tim to go and see him - with the result that for a long time Tim went to help man the 24 hour telephone helpline, and also to serve the homeless and the hungry in the soup kitchen in the crypt of the church on Sundays. He thus came in contact with a stratum of society that he had not known before.

To our delight and relief we saw a new Tim blossoming, and

253

it was through St Martin in the Fields that he got a full time job with the Voluntary Hostels Association. This involved sitting, with others, at a telephone all day finding hostel places for men and women about whom probation officers and welfare workers would telephone from all parts of the country. It was a very worthwhile job and it reintroduced him to full time working.

Tim had been doing this for quite some time when on the spur of the moment he rang the editor of the weekly magazine, *Commercial Motor*. Having told him of his experience and training he concluded by saying, "So I think I could be of use to you." The editor was a little taken aback and said, "Oh, er, yes, well you had better come and see me sometime," to which Tim replied, "What is wrong with now?" Of course, so brazen an approach could not be gainsaid and within half an hour Tim was in the editor's office.

He came away with the promise of being considered for a job as a journalist, and in his pocket a report numbering several pages of which he had been asked to make a precis of not more than 300 words. Tim had recently moved into a house shared by several young people in Putney, but this evening he came home to us for dinner and told us about the interview. We were tremendously impressed and very happy for him. We implored him to take his time over the precis, it was very important that he make a good job of it - in fact the job itself might depend upon it, and so on and on, just as fussy parents the world over would do. He said, "O yes, I shall."

The next day he rang us from work and told us that he had done the precis that night, that he had got his car out around midnight and driven to Trafalgar Square where he knew there was a late night post! His precis was on the editor's desk at 9 o'clock the next morning when he arrived for work! Needless to say Tim got the job and started his career in journalism about a week later - and had an article below his own by-line in the first issue after joining the paper. Thank you, Vocational Guidance Association! I have only heard of one person who found that the VGA did not help. After Tim had had a few years with *Commercial Motor* he applied for and got a job with the Ford Motor Company at their headquarters office at Warley, and stayed there for many years. In fact until just before he married at the age of forty-three.

After those difficult early years our relationship improved immensely; our mutual resentment and guardedness did not last for very long, and I believe was quite natural, given all the circumstances.

There was never really any doubt about Bar's and my

relationship. When difficulties arose we found our way through them and then, at the end, one or other would smile and say, "But we are all right really, aren't we?" And we would have a long hug and agree that we were. As the years went by we grew more and more into the unity of understanding, acceptance of one another 'warts and all', and the affection that is the basis of a sound marriage. We learned to live with our inabilities and frustrations, and only from time to time did the sense of deprivation and regret assail our unity and our peace. Except for the times when we were working we were rarely apart and wherever we walked together we would be holding hands. Fun and laughter were never very far away.

Bar had only been abroad once, because in the early years when they could afford good holidays, she and Bertie and Tim had gone to Scotland every year for the shooting and fishing, short breaks had been spent fishing the Test for trout, and the 'seaside' holidays had always been in Torquay. Bertie did not like 'the abroad' and thought holidays in Britain were the only ones worth having.

A year or so after he died some friends invited Bar to join them on their holiday at Miramar in the south of France. She had thoroughly enjoyed that holiday and often spoke about it. I was eager to go abroad again, for I had always loved travel, but we did not yet feel we could afford to go on to the Continent and indeed Bar was very nervous about the idea - she was not yet convinced that I was the intrepid and resourceful traveller I made myself out to be! In Miramar she had been with people who were accustomed to travelling all over Europe and knew France especially well, so she had felt quite safe with them. But if we went to foreign parts there would be only the two of us, and she was not ready for that sort of adventure yet.

So the year after our maxi-honeymoon in Salcombe, we went to Ireland, to stay just outside Dingle, near the very end of the Dingle peninsular. It was, after all, across the water, and they *did* speak English. We would not seem so far from home.

We had been recommended 'Molly's Guest House' as basic but comfortable, with good plain food - and not expensive. We took the car on the train to Fishguard and the ferry to Rosslare and then drove to Waterford where we put up at a medium priced hotel. Foolishly we had specified a double bed. That is what we got, but it was more a three-quarter sized bed than a double, and most of the springs were broken so that it sagged down in the middle even before you got into it! What a terrible night! We hardly slept a wink and were thankful to leave in the morning.

We set off across Ireland and were soon so enchanted that we forgot the Waterford bed and began really to enjoy our holiday. About mid-afternoon we ran through Dingle and out onto the road to the end of the peninsular - and 'Molly's'. A sea mist had crept in and, following directions, we came to a grim looking grey pebbled house, shrouded in swirls of mist, standing in a scruffy looking garden - we had arrived! Rather fearfully we carried our bags to the front door, which at our ring was opened to us by a twelve year old girl who recognised our name when we mentioned it. She told us Molly was out, but she would take us up to our room.

We followed her up a narrow staircase and she showed us into a room - with three single beds, on the middle one of which was a pair of man's braces: and in the washbasin a razor and shaving brush! Gosh, we thought, are we sharing a room with another man? By the time we had got over our astonishment we discovered that the girl had vanished. Turning to go and find out what was what I went out of the door to go downstairs when the door of the next room opened and out came a nun in full habit! I was deeply shocked, horrified and upset I rushed back into 'our' room and said to Bar, *"There's a nun next door!!"* Such an incident in Eire should not have occasioned such surprise, for there are priests and nuns everywhere. But so complete was my withdrawal from my previous life that I could not bear the sight of them, and I found the prospect of having a nun in the very next room completely unnerving.

However this inauspicious beginning gave on to a most enjoyable holiday. Molly was a real character and made us very welcome. The braces and razor disappeared from our room during 'high tea', the nun next door did not appear among us at all, and we found a fascinating variety of people as our fellow guests; a Canadian professor, a Norwegian academic of some sort, a Danish lady and two or three people from Belfast. Conversation in the evenings in the comfortable lounge was animated and as varied as the people involved.

This was 1969 and the 'Troubles' had just begun again in the North. Our friends from Belfast watched the News every night with growing anxiety, as indeed did we all. Between nine and half past in the evening Molly would put her head round the door and say, "Tea Up," at which we all trooped into the kitchen. There a large tin of biscuits waited in the middle of a huge scrubbed wooden table and on the black kitchen range stood a large brown enamelled pot of tea. Beside the range sat an old man in sailor's jersey and peaked cap - Molly's father. He was the reason for the presence of the young nun in the next room to ours. Nuns and priests were sent to him to be taught 'The Irish.' He did not speak much English, but was fluent in the ancient language and a renowned teacher of it. At that time the Roman church was making sure that as many priests and religious as possible could speak the native tongue, and this old man was a king pin in the teaching programme.

This pre-bedtime kitchen 'round table' was a regular feature of life at Molly's, and was greatly appreciated by the guests. She would regale us with Irish tales, and tell us of her travels in the United States where she had many relatives and spent several months of the year visiting. They all seemed larger than life, and we often wondered whether Molly had kissed the Blarney Stone more than once! We explored the Dingle peninsular and the Ring of Kerry; we basked in sunshine and shivered in torrential rain. We spent a day on one of the uninhabited Blasket islands where we were taken in a currough. The making of these boats had changed very little for hundreds of years - originally they were made of a wooden frame of withies over which skins were stretched. Now tarred canvas had replaced the skins, but the wood frame was much as it had always been. An outboard motor was now fitted to the stern. Our boat looked a flimsy affair, and there was quite a swell running when we embarked one sunny morning to cross the quarter of a mile of green sea to the Islands. Bar looked rather fearful as the five of us sat gingerly in the rising and falling boat, with the water only a few inches from the gunwale. But the boatmen were immensely skillful and we wove neatly among the rocks on the shore of the island and were soon deposited on a beach of pure white sand. Here we spent the day lazing on the beach, swimming in the icy cold waters of the Atlantic, chatting, and eating the excellent packed lunch that Molly had prepared for us. The currough called for us in time to get us home for the traditional 'high tea' at 5.30 - we were tingling with health, our faces aglow from the wind and the sun, and were ravenously hungry.

That holiday did us a lot of good, although the second week further North where we stayed at a four star hotel was a terrible come-down. Everyone seemed anti-English and we were the only ones there, all the rest being Irish or foreigners. The first landing on the moon occurred during our stay, and no one could get the television to work - all that could be seen was the 'snowstorm' of the wrongly adjusted set. My stock rose just a little when I managed to get the thing sufficiently tuned to see the landing. But hatred of the English was so endemic among the staff that even this did not improve the service we received. We were glad to leave and set off for home.

Our holiday ended on a very happy note, for we went home via Swansea to stay a couple of nights with my old friends Rollo and

Joy Charles who were now living outside Cardiff. They were eager to meet 'Father Paul's wife' and no one could have been more welcoming - they had even turned out of their own room for us, Joy into the single spare room, and Rollo with friends down the road! As we walked up their drive they came out to meet us, and Joy exclaimed, "Well, good gracious, so you *have* got legs after all!" - not having seen me before without my cassock. I was not wearing clerical gear, for I was by now drifting inexorably away from the Church.

After we were married we continued to go to church, first at Weston Green, and later at All Saints Hampton where we had been brought up. I rarely said Mass, but I preached a couple of times. But I was more and more uneasy. My problems had begun long before I left CR, and right from that time it seemed that I became increasingly 'spiritually cold' until after a couple of years I really felt frozen and lifeless. Nothing in church seemed to have any reality any more. We had begun soon after marriage to try to pray together, silently, on either side of the bed, but it seemed unreal. I think Bar would probably have carried on if I had wanted to, for with her usual generosity, she would have done anything to make me happy. But the whole thing seemed farcical to me and we soon gave it up.

In those early days we were both showing the classic symptoms of clinical depression, and we felt desperately in need of help. Unfortunately Michael Saunders had left Weston Green and there was no one we really knew to whom we could turn with any confidence, so we simply muddled along trying to cope with each day as it came.

What brought matters to a head was the death of Bar's mother. This was a terrible blow to her; she had idolised the old lady, and when she died she rather went to pieces. While we had been going to church at Weston Green we had met a fine young doctor who was a member of the congregation and a friend of Michael Saunders. He was very keen on co-operation between the clergy and doctors. It was clear that Bar was in greater need of help than I was, and in desperation I rang him up one day and asked if he would see her. I took her over the following afternoon and after he had seen her privately he said to me, "Your wife needs a priest not a doctor - *do something about it!*"

I was in a quandary; I knew few of the local clergy and did not feel any of them would be suitable. I then remembered being told that the Archdeacon of Middlesex, who lived in Kensington, did a lot of counselling, so I made an appointment to see him one morning. He told me that while he would be glad to help, he simply could not take on any more people at the moment, and that anyway it would be a long traipse from Twickenham for Bar to go up to see him. "However," he said, "I think you will find that help is much nearer at hand," and he told me about Maurice Kidd, the Rector of Hanworth, only a stone's throw from Twickenham. He said he was very impressed with the counselling work that Maurice was doing. "As soon as you go into his room you feel quietness and peace descending upon you," he said. This sounded marvellous to me, and I went home full of hope and told Bar about it. Her face fell. *"Hanworth? O No, not Hanworth!"* she cried. I was crestfallen as she explained that Hanworth, where she had lived until she married Peter and for periods after he was killed, had some of her saddest childhood memories and she would rather have had to go anywhere but there. Nevertheless, seeing how depressed I was, she said she was prepared to give it a go and see how she got on, if Maurice Kidd would see her. I said I would go first to spy out the land, and went that very evening. Maurice and I got on from the first, and I felt sure he would be able to help Bar. He was willing to take her on and we made a provisional date. He said, "Tell her it might be the very best thing for her, to start here in Hanworth that has such unhappy associations for her." It was that remark more than anything else that persuaded Bar to start her therapy in Hanworth where a lot of her unhappiness had its roots.

Maurice helped Bar for several years, and was quite literally a godsend to us.   After a while I began going to him as well, and he helped me as much as he helped Bar. I think for a long time he kept us both afloat and I am sure he was the pilot who saved our marriage from foundering on the rocks of our difficulties.

Not only did Maurice counsel us, but he and his lively young wife Pennie became our great friends. They really were wonderful to us, for we were very short of friends and they generously made us feel members of their family. Pennie was pregnant with their first child when we met, and all three of their lovely boys arrived while they were in Hanworth. We became 'honorary grandparents', sharing the status with a large number of others too of course, for they were very popular in the parish. They became our best local friends, unique and specially important to us in that they were the first new friends we made together. Bar had a few friends of her own age, whom we saw from time to time, but having married Bertie, who had lived in the same house most of his life, it was natural that his friends became hers, and most of them were his contemporaries - some twenty years older than Bar. A few of these older friends kept in touch with us for a time after we were married. It was however inevitable that they did not feel they had much in common with me, and contact with them gradually petered out. The sole exceptions were Douglas and Betty Roberts, old friends of Bertie and later of Bar, Jill and 'Mac' McMinn, and Naomi Hogbin, the widow of Bar's doctor, who were very generous to us and who became my great friends also,

Having been away from the area for so many years I hardly knew anyone locally; all my own friends were in other parts of the country, and in any case I now felt that, with very few exceptions, I could not face them any more, mainly because I had met most of them through the Community. Those I had known before joining CR were another matter, and in most cases I could still feel comfortable with them. Chief among these was Alastair Haggart, my old friend from Hendon days when we were fellow curates, now Principal of Edinburgh Theological College, and later Bishop of Edinburgh and Primus of Scotland.

One year, at Alastair and Peggy's suggestion, we decided to holiday in Scotland. We took the car on the train to Edinburgh. After having breakfast with Alastair and his wife Peggy we set off for Dornoch. It seemed an interminable road but the scenery was splendid. We passed through Inverness, and far out in the country we noticed that all the AA boxes we passed had 'Out of Order' signs on them. We hoped we would not break down and need them. Half an hour later the engine faltered and steam was rising from the bonnet of the car. I thought the radiator had run dry, and took an empty plastic container and stood by the roadside waving it at the passing cars. No one took the slightest notice, and after twenty minutes or so I was in despair. I stood glumly looking at the holiday traffic whizzing by, and then thought I would give it one more try. I forlornly lifted my bottle and waved apologetically at a car approaching - and lo and behold, he pulled in a few yards further on. I ran up to him and said, "Thank you so much for stopping, I am sorry to trouble you but my radiator seems to have run dry and I wonder whether you are carrying any water you can spare?" He smiled seraphically and said, "Would you mind if I had a look at your car, sir, you see I'm a motor mechanic!" I was astonished! I said a big thank you to St Christopher and to this earthly saviour, and took him back to our car. He took one look under the bonnet and said, "Your fan-belt has broken, that's your trouble sir, have you got a spare?" Thank goodness only the previous day, on the way to put the car on the train, I had stopped to get a spare fan-belt, so that was fine. My new friend was such a nice man, and obviously pleased to be able to help. I walked back to his car with him to fetch his tool kit - and invited his wife to come and sit and chat to Bar while the work was being done. She was, like him, a short and comfortable person full of the milk of human kindness, and was delighted by the invitation. Bar and she got on like a house on fire. Our 'friends in need' often came that way and knew a lot about the area. She was soon telling Bar about the best beaches and beauty spots around Dornoch.

We enjoyed our time in and around Dornoch and ranged far and wide, out into the magnificent forests of the extreme North West, to John O'Groats, and Thurso, and we paid a visit to the Castle of May, the Queen Mother's House. Bar was a great royalist so this pleased her very much.

Before returning to Twickenham we had a few nights with Alastair and Peggy in Edinburgh, and said many times how we wished we all lived nearer to one another.

So the first years of our marriage, a mixture of joy and suffering, tended to be rather lonely as far as local friendships were concerned. I could not face churchgoing at all for a number of years and this inevitably cut us off from people. Bar was the faithful one; she rarely missed the 8am Holy Communion Service at St Mary's parish church but as so often happens with this service she rarely talked to anyone and came straight home.. I used to stay in bed on a Sunday morning until it was time to get up in my dressing gown and prepare breakfast by the time Bar returned from church. She used to say from time to time, "I take you with me in my heart."

I have said that all this time I felt 'frozen', another way of putting it is to say that whenever I did go to a church I felt as though I was seeing the whole thing through thick plate glass; it all seemed to be happening in a sort of dream-state, as though soon I would wake up to reality. Nor could I pray in any normally accepted sense. Occasional ejaculatory or 'arrow prayer' was all that I could manage, and that not very often. While I sincerely believed when I sat down to think about it, that I had truly been called out of the Community to marry Bar, there was simultaneously in the back of my mind the question, "Are you not feeling guilty about abandoning your vows? Is it not possible that you have failed a great test of your vocation; that you should have suffered your way through that sense of spiritual deadness and that there, in the Community, you would have had a 'resurrection' after a time and have become a better religious as a result?" As I look back down the years, I think I must have been going through a crisis of conscience, and one that I did not deal with very well.

There were times, not of course uncommon in a marriage, when Bar and I both wondered whether it had been a mistake for us to marry after all those years of separation and separate development - but we did not mention these doubts to one another until they had passed, as they always did, and we were again feeling happy with ourselves.

The time came for Maurice Kidd to leave Hanworth for another job in the Diocese of Canterbury. This was a shock to both of us, for we had thought him a permanent fixture and assumed that he would go on being our counsellor indefinitely. Our reaction to the news that he was leaving was, *"O but we can't possibly do without you!"* Maurice, however, quickly assured us that before he left he would find us another counsellor in whose hands he felt confident in leaving us. This he certainly did when he recommended us to Heather Jones who lived and practised in Brentford, only a quarter of an hour away by car, hardly further than Maurice at Hanworth. So for several years we poured out our difficulties and depressions to dear Heather. She took us competently and lovingly forward from where Maurice had left off and we never ceased to be grateful to her. It was with Heather that both of us eventually uncovered events buried in our unconscious minds that were clues to the abiding difficulties that had dogged our steps all through our lives, and continued to do so.

Mine was the sudden uncovering of the fact that when I was a tiny boy two of our young maids used to take the opportunity when mother was out, of taking off their clothes and making me explore their bodies and play with them sexually. This was so deeply buried in my unconscious that I had no recollection of it until that very moment in the midst of talking to Heather. I knew enough psychology not to need Heather to tell me that this was almost certainly the root of my sexual problems, which had been further exacerbated by the frustrations and prohibitions of my adolescence.

One afternoon Bar came home from seeing Heather and said to me, "What do you think I found myself saying to Heather this afternoon?" "Tell me," I said. She said, "I found myself saying, 'I remember when I was a little girl of three my father coming into the room and looking down at me and saying, "Oh Barbie, when I knew you were another little girl I wanted to throw you out of the window!"

Bar was the youngest of three sisters, and her father had longed for a 'son and heir.' Few fathers today would say such a thing to a three year old, but in those days there was no 'popular psychology' to tell parents how careful they must be with the minds of children and how easy it is to do irreparable harm.

So, after years of counselling, we at last knew things about ourselves that must have contributed to our problems and unease all down the years. I am sure it was why Bar so easily felt rejected, and had always believed herself, in the last resort, to be unlovable.

262

She always responded with great generosity of spirit to people, and easily loved those who were prepared to love her - but if ever that love cooled or she imagined that she had had a 'brush-off', she was immediately ready to say to herself, "You see, I am not really lovable at all."

With Heather's help and guidance the time came when we could at last talk more freely to one another about these matters, facing unpalatable truths about ourselves. These were often very painful sessions, but in the end we would always look at one another, grin ruefully, and admit that we were both, like many other people, to some extent 'psychological cripples.' We were able to accept each other as such, and this resulted in a deepening of mutual understanding and a further development of our love for one another.

Meanwhile, my estrangement from the church seemed not to abate but to deepen. I still had in my cupboards my beautiful priest's cloak, two cassocks, some stoles, Bibles, notes of retreats, that I had conducted, and copies of lectures I had given, as well as a number of theological books. As time went by I could feel these things were anchoring me to a past from which I felt I wanted to be free. This feeling became so intense that one day I could bear it no longer, and I threw all the books and Bibles away, God forgive me. The clerical gear I put in a large suitcase and took to the Vicar of St Mary's, John Gann, and asked him to give it all away to anyone who might appreciate it. In spite of a feeling of guilt, that was a load off my mind. Bar was sad at what I had done, but she did not reproach me, for she saw that it was something I just had to do.

After that I had, on the whole, an easier mind and where ultimate things were concerned I went into a sort of neutral gear and coasted along through life for a time quite contentedly.

It was some fifteen years before I began to feel easier about the Church, and the time came when, at my suggestion, Bar and I began to go once a month to the Parish Communion at St Mary's parish church. We also plucked up courage and went over to the parish room for coffee after the service, and so started to meet a few people. One of our new acquaintances persuaded Bar to join the Twickenham Women Citizens Association which met once a month. So she began to make a few friends in that way.

My monthly church going gradually became fortnightly and then before long we were going to the Parish Communion every Sunday, and beginning to know more people of that very friendly and welcoming congregation. We found that we were accepted and as a result we felt our life expanding very happily.

Bar had always been a person who can find release of

tension in tears and from time to time I would notice her weeping during the service. Sometimes she would tell me why she had wept, and at other times not, but I never pressed her about it. One Sunday after we had been going to church every Sunday for some time, I noticed that she was weeping. When we got home I said, "Do you want to tell me why you were weeping in church this morning, or not? - you know you don't have to." She said, "Yes, I will tell you - I was weeping because I realized during the service *that for the first time you were really praying this morning!*" I was shaken - but realized at once that she was quite right; for the first time since I had been going to church again, I had really taken part in the service and found myself truly praying. Up until then I had been going to church through a reawakened but vague sense of duty. The 'plate glass' between me and what was going on had still been in place though the occasional shaft of light had begun to penetrate it. Today had been different, I had really found myself responding to the love of God in prayer. Today there had been no plate glass; it had not shattered in a dramatic moment; it had merely disappeared, so quietly and unobtrusively that until Bar had spoken I had not noticed its absence.

Barbara 1973

12

Return From The Wilderness

My emergence from the Wilderness Years was very gradual at first. I was still not feeling spiritually strong enough, for instance, to tell those that did not already know, that I was a priest.

In 1987, at the end of John Gann's time as Vicar of Twickenham, it fell to the young curate, Malcolm Tyler, to carry on during the year-long interregnum until the new vicar was appointed and installed. During Holy Week that year, Malcolm rang me up and said, "Paul, you can say 'No' if you want to, but would you read the Gospel on Easter Day at the Parish Communion?" Bar had come to the door of the room expecting the 'phone call to be for her, which it almost always was, and was looking at me anxiously, not knowing who was on the line. I hesitated, gulped, and then said in a rush, "OK yes, thank you Malcolm," and put the 'phone down quickly. Bar said, "Whatever is the matter? you have gone as white as a sheet!" I said, "I've agreed to read the Gospel on Easter Day!" Bar said, "Oh love, will you be all right?" The shock had begun to wear off and I said, "Oh yes, I expect so - I'm already beginning to look forward to it!"

The church was packed, as it usually is, especially on the great feast days. and I was very nervous as I left our pew at the end of the gradual hymn and went to the lectern. Of course, being me, I began and ended with a mistake - having announced the gospel I began reading at once and was drowned by the organ leading the people in singing 'Glory to Christ our Saviour.' However, I started off again and soon got back my confidence.

As I read, the most wonderful experience of deep peace possessed me - and I knew I was back!

When I told Bar about how I had felt she was delighted with this evidence of my return.

From that moment onwards things happened at an accelerating rate. One Saturday morning a few weeks later I said to Bar, "I've a good mind to start wearing my dog-collar again!" Her dear eyes lit up, and she said excitedly, "Oh darling, will you?" and added, "Oh, let me give you your new shirt and dog-collar. I'd love to do that."

So there and then we jumped into the car and went off to Vanheems in Brentford where she bought me one of the modern shirts with a little channel into which is inserted the while plastic strip collar, showing only about three inches in the front, instead of the all-round affair I had always worn before. This was another innovation since my day and a great improvement on the old fashioned collar.

Next morning, feeling very conspicuous in my new gear - like a deacon on his first Sunday - Bar and I went to church. A few people knew that I was ordained, but most did not, and there were several 'double-takes' as we went up the path and into the church. Several people who were in the know were very kind and came and shook my hand and said how pleased they were to see me 'in uniform'. I went into the clergy vestry for some reason I cannot remember. The only occupant was one of the servers, whose eyes opened wide and he said in some confusion, "Oh, er, hello, I er, didn't know you were a... well, *you* know!" Everybody seemed pleased - the Vicar even said something about my being very brave, but it had not occurred to me that this was a brave thing to do at all. During coffee after the service one of the choir girls gave me a grin and said, "I like your new bib and tucker!"

Alun Glyn-Jones, John Gann's successor as Vicar of Twickenham, had been inducted to the parish a year or so before this decisive moment of my return to the priestly ministry. I had gone to see him soon after his arrival and had told him the whole story. He had been wonderfully sympathetic and understanding. When I got to the point of recalling how a few months ago I had got rid of everything that had been part of my previous life, he immediately said, "And did you then feel *free?*" I had not formulated the thought for myself, but when he said this I realised to the full extent how free I had felt from that moment onwards. Later reflection has convinced me that that was the very moment, when I had shed all that was left of my previous professional life, that my return began. Finally, I said to Alun that now I was back and could pray again in the old familiar ways, I could not help thinking that however far I had felt from our Lord, I had never really been all that far away, and that in a sense I had been 'praying all the time'. As I spoke of this Alun reached over to one of his bookshelves and picked up a small card which he handed to me saying, "Do you know this?" It was called 'Footsteps in the Sand.' I had never seen it, but as I read I knew it put my situation in a nutshell. I have since learned that many people are familiar with this little piece of devotional writing by an unknown author, but for the sake of those who do not, I summarise it here:

> One night a man had a dream. He dreamed that he was walking across a desert, holding the hand of the Lord. and their footprints stretched away behind

them. As he looked back he saw that in several places there was only one set of footprints, and he noticed that these coincided with the very worst periods in his life. He said to the Lord, "Lord those were the times when I most needed You, why did You forsake me?" The Lord looked down on him and said, "My child, I would never forsake you; *those were the times when I was carrying you.."*

When I showed this to Bar later that day, she burst into tears and said, "Oh darling, that was *you*, wasn't it?" I told her I felt that this fitted my experience exactly.

Of course, I should not have been surprised at this 'mini-revelation', for Christian theology teaches that we are so indwelt by Christ, the Second Person of the Holy Trinity, that the life of the Holy Trinity is eternally being lived within us at the very core of our being, whether we are conscious of it or not.

To put this great mystery into ultimately inadequate but nevertheless not wildly untrue terms, it means that the Father the Creator and Sustainer of the Universe is, within us, eternally pouring out his eternal love to the Son, who is the creative word of God, and the Holy Spirit is the eternal Person who flows in an eternal outpouring of selfless love between the Persons of this mysterious Trinity in Unity. Christians believe that the whole purpose of human life is to become more and more aware through prayer and sacrament, of what they already are, living members of Christ and called to show forth that divine love in the world in spite of their unworthiness and sinfulness.

So theologically it was no surprise to me to realize that this mysterious activity had been going on at the core of my being, overlaid and hidden from me by preoccupation with my sufferings during the wilderness years. Now, as has happened in Christian experience all down the centuries at times of renewal, these great truths had begun to enter once more into my conscious mind, not by my own initiative, but by His.

The wearing of my dog-collar was but a logical progression of the renewal that had begun, so appropriately, on Easter Day as I read the Gospel - the Good News that Christ is Risen and lives for evermore. Surely no other day could have been more appropriate for a 'son of the Resurrection,' as I felt myself still to be, to 'come home' to the Risen Lord!

Those were the times when I was carrying you. I was now able to see clearly that I had always been in His hands; that even when I was blind and 'frozen' I had not been forsaken, for in retrospect I could now see how He had been at work all the time - during my years as Student Counsellor, in and through the trials and tribulations of secularisation and marriage, the times when I had almost, but not quite, despaired. Even without my usual sort of prayer; away from the sacraments and all the other 'means of grace', I now saw that He had been at work in me regardless of my feelings of alienation. Regardless also of my frequent stubborn refusals to do what I knew I should, as well as the many times when I did what I knew I should not. Times when, however dimly, I knew I was refusing the guidance of the Holy Spirit and following my own will instead. Times indeed when I could almost certainly have begun my return had I accepted the help that was offered by wise and faithful friends and would-be mentors.

When I had I left the Community, Bishop Guy Sanderson was one of my friends, together with Bishop Alastair Haggart and a few others, who gave me their unstinted understanding and acceptance during the wilderness years. Guy had been very upset by what appeared to all of us as my loss of faith, and every now and again would tentatively suggest a book that might help. I had pretended that I did not want to be helped. I must have hurt him by declaring that I was quite happy being a 'layman' again. I realized how saddened he was by my withdrawal from the Church. He had had great faith in me and while I was at St Teilo's had suggested me as the missioner when one of the parishes in his area had wanted a conductor for their parish mission. I had taken a good team of sisters, students and lay men and women, and the thing had gone with a bang. After the last service there had been a parish party and Bishop Guy had enthralled everyone by sitting at the piano and playing pop tunes and all the old songs - some of which his father, the composer Wilfred Sanderson, had written. To see me later, acting as a non-churchgoing layman troubled him deeply. Sadly, Guy had died before, what Alun Glyn-Jones called, 'Paul's resurrection' occurred. On the Sunday I donned my new dog collar, Bar had said, "O wouldn't Guy have been happy to see you now!"

This 'resurrection' was really profound; I found myself increasingly called to the type of contemplative prayer that I had known before the 'dying' had crept upon me in the Community, and with this grew a desire for the necessary periods of solitude and silence. This was easily attained without disturbing our normal life-style, for Bar by now needed to rest a lot in the course of the day; her spine was becoming increasingly arthritic and she rested on her bed after lunch for a good part of the afternoon. Meanwhile I would sit in my armchair and have plenty of time for silence and solitude, either before or after my postprandial snooze, until I took her a cup of tea later.

Unfortunately, but perhaps inevitably, Bar felt I was 'leaving her behind' and she desperately wanted to 'be with me' in all of this reawakening. For a time she was quite upset that she could not manage to 'keep up' as she put it. But Bar was always a realist and it was not long before she told me that she now realized that she could not possibly keep pace with me. I tried to explain that it was not a matter of one being 'ahead' of the other; each in his or her own way has a unique personal relationship with God and given the desire to try to love and serve Him and the desire to pray, then whatever that relationship is at any specific time is the one that is right and that He wills.

Two things helped Bar to stop worrying about 'keeping up'. One was Alun, telling her that in the Christian faith it is not *knowing* a lot that matters, but *loving* much. She found those wise words of great encouragement.

The second thing that helped her came about by my asking a Roman Catholic friend whether the Roman church still had the service of Benediction. This service centres upon the adoration of our Lord present to us in a unique and mysterious way signified by the consecrated Host in the Eucharist. The Host is placed in a monstrance, a circular glass case surrounded by a nimbus of rays made sometimes of gold. These represent the 'glory' that shone about Christ on the Mount of Transfiguration. At the end of this service the monstrance containing the Host is lifted and the sign of the cross is made with it over the congregation. It is important to remember that it is not the bread that is worshipped, but the living Christ whose actual presence, unseen but real, is signified by the bread that has been consecrated in the Eucharist. This service of Benediction used to be celebrated quite regularly in Anglo Catholic parishes; it still is in a few, but in todays climate of faith it is not as popular as it once was. My friend did not seem to have heard of Benediction and said, "I don't know, but once a month on a Friday evening we have Exposition of the Blessed Sacrament and a three hour Watch before it from eight 'til eleven. You ought to come to it sometime, there is a lot of silent prayer, and it is lovely." I pricked up my ears at this, for it sounded just the sort of thing I felt attracted by. Right from my teenage years under Jock Murray at Hampton, I had felt moved to pray in the presence of the

Blessed Sacrament whenever possible. The church where the Watch was held was not far from our flat, and when I told Bar about it she immediately said, "Oh I would like to go to that sometime for a little while, but not for three hours." I explained that very few people would stay for the whole time, most would go in for half an hour or an hour.

As we entered the church we were immediately welcomed by the lady whom we later learned organized the Watch who gave us the necessary hymn and prayer books. We sat near the back, settled down and proceeded to take it all in. The altar was brightly lit and ablaze with candles surrounding the monstrance. The rest of the church was in darkness apart from the large crucifix hanging from the chancel arch, which was spot-lit. Before us, silhouetted against the lights of the sanctuary and altar, we could see many figures kneeling upright and still. A wonderfully warm atmosphere of peace and prayer pervaded the still and silent church. I felt myself relaxing and absorbing it, and I could sense Bar doing the same. When I took a little glance at her I saw that her attention was fixed upon the rood crucifix, the figure stark white upon the black cross. After half an hour of complete silence the lady who had welcomed us began the recitation of the Rosary. I knew this would be totally foreign to Bar - and indeed I did not find it congenial myself at that moment - so slowly rising from our seats we nodded to our welcoming friend and quietly left the church.

I could see that Bar had been profoundly affected. We got into the car and drove home silently. When we were taking our coats off at home, Bar said, "Wasn't that *wonderful?* - and that crucifix; it's the most beautiful crucifix I have *ever* seen." I was so delighted for her, for I realized that she had had a genuine spiritual experience. From then on there was no more talk of 'trying to keep pace' or desperately seeking knowledge to redress her ignorance. My love now *knew* just as I had *known* while I read the Easter Gospel. I realized that my darling had taken a great leap forward because our Lord had revealed himself to her while she was relaxed, silent and receptive. *Blessed be His Holy Name.*

We were flooded with peace that night, and from then on we went whenever we could to take part in the Watch before the Blessed Sacrament on the second Friday of the month.

Alun was kindness and gentleness personified as I gradually groped my way back to exercising my ministry. When I said I would like to celebrate the Eucharist again, he took me firmly in hand saying, "Right, I shall treat you like a young deacon preparing to celebrate for the first time, and I think it best if you do so at a Wednesday morning service at 10 o'clock." So - shades of Portsmouth in 1942! - we met in church one evening and he got out a chalice and paten and the service book, and saw me through the old Prayer Book rite of 1662 - which I used to know by heart, but over which I stumbled woefully that evening. I would never have dreamed that I could have forgotten 'the ropes' as thoroughly as I had.

A good many of the general congregation came to the service when I celebrated for the first time. Alun served me and prompted me when I needed it, which was often! My mind would go completely blank and I would have no idea what should come next. I felt very emotional - having reached the age when I had begun to cry easily - but managed to get to the end, not without mistakes, but without breaking down. When we got back to the vestry Alun gave me a big hug and said something like, "Well done; welcome back!" We then went to the back of the church where I felt exactly like a newly ordained priest receiving the congratulations and good wishes of the congregation after his first Mass. Bar, bless her, was so proud, and had had several quiet little weeps of happiness during the service.

It was only some six months after this that Bar began having more indigestion than usual, and one morning she sat on the edge of the bed saying she had a bad pain, and rubbing her chest. Soon the pain passed and she was moving about as usual. The following day she had the pain again at the same time, and we decided to make an appointment to see the doctor that evening. We had arranged to go into Richmond that morning to see our financial adviser in Parkshot. Bar said the pain had gone again so we went by bus because it would set us down nearer than we could park the car, but even this involved a walk. Afterwards Bar wanted to go to Marks and Spencers to do some shopping, and this meant a longer walk. Half way there she seemed puffed but did not complain of her pain again, so we sat on a low wall for a few minutes, then she smiled and said, "OK let's go on." We got to the store, and fortunately there was a chair by the exit so she sat down gratefully and said she would stay there while I did the shopping. When I came back I suggested that I get a taxi to take us home, but she said, "Oh no, I'm all right now, let's get the bus." Which we did, and got home all right. I cannot think why the danger signs did not register with me. I guess that she was covering up because she did not want me to worry, but I must have been blind as a bat not to realise

271

that she was really ill.

Bar rested on the bed for a while and then got the lunch as usual and had her rest in the afternoon until it was time to go to the doctor. He said, "This is a very difficult diagnosis for a doctor to make; I *think* it is a sort of indigestion that you have not had before. However, it would be a good idea if you went to the West Middlesex Hospital tomorrow morning and had an ECG."

Next morning Bar was washing up the breakfast things and said to me, "Shall we go to the West Mid first?" - we had decided to do a few other things that morning. I said, "Oh yes, of course, the ECG takes priority today." So we got into the car and fortunately I was able to park not far from the entrance to the ECG department.

There were several people waiting and Bar seemed all right and talked a little, though not very much, and quietly, as one does in hospital queues. We did not have to wait long before her turn came and she went into the cubicle to undress. After a while a nurse came out and asked us all to draw our chairs closer together in the confined space, as "There is a stretcher coming through." I thought, I suppose they are bringing an in-patient down for an ECG, but when the trolley arrived a few moments later it was empty, and I was surprised. Then the nurse came back and said to me, "We do not like what we are seeing on your wife's ECG, so we are taking her straight across to Casualty." I leaped up and followed her into the ECG department. Bar was already on the stretcher and they were bundling her clothes on to the rack beneath it. I smiled weakly at her and said something fatuous like, "Don't worry love, it will be all right," and then walked alongside the trolley holding her hand as she was pushed quickly out of doors, across the road and into the Casualty Department.

This was full of people on trollies waiting to be seen, but as soon as we appeared we were shown straight into an empty cubicle by a doctor and a nurse. The doctor started talking non-stop, with a strong Irish accent, and in a jocular manner, while he frantically rushed about setting up a drip, putting a needle into the back of Bar's hand and connecting it to the drip - "Well love," he said, "sure and you're actually having a heart attack at this very moment now; but not to worry, this is the latest thing in this drip, and it will prevent your heart from getting damaged, so it will be all right, see?" The nurse was also very busy; I forget what she was doing, but I got the impression that she was furious with the doctor for his ham-handed approach and frantic chatter. I was hovering around not knowing what to do or say and feeling desperately worried though trying not to show it. Apparently this drip was doing its work for after a little while the situation seemed to calm down. Bar was wheeled out to join the long queue of patients waiting on trollies. The nurse told me that they were trying to get a bed for her in the Coronary Care Unit, in other words in Intensive Care. Bar was able to talk a little and she was worried about my having no food, for by now it was long past lunch time, so I went off and found a refreshment trolley and bought a soft drink and some chocolate. I munched away and drank whatever it was I had bought and Bar stopped worrying.

After what seemed an interminable wait we were at last told that there was a bed ready in Coronary Care. Here she was received by a most delightful and obviously efficient Sister who let me see Bar for a few minutes after they had put her to bed. They had wired her up to all sorts of modern wizardry including the usual television monitor. I was only able to stay a few minutes, but as I left she looked better - she felt secure, I think, under the care of the Sister in charge of the unit, and the pain had gone. Sister told me I could return at 8pm for half an hour. I went home knowing that my girl was very ill, but hoping that the new treatment she had been given would limit the damage to the heart and that in time she would recover.

I found her able to talk a little that evening and she was quite cheerful, telling me that the tests had shown that it had been only a mild heart attack and that there was no great damage to her heart. She had a card which showed a date three months hence when she was to return to the hospital to have another dose of the wonder treatment that the Irish doctor had given her. For the time being she had had as much of the drug as could be given and must wait three months for a further injection. Bar was cheerful and pleased with what she had been told. I left the hospital feeling thankful and relieved.

I rang the Unit in the morning to hear that she had had a good night and had been transferred to the main ward on the floor above. What they did not tell me was that I could visit her on that ward at any time, so I waited until the 2:30 visiting time that had obtained in the Coronary Care Unit.

I found her by herself in a cubicle of the ward. She was slumped down in the bed and as I went in she looked at me with a little smile as I said "Hello Darling, how are you today?" She said in a small voice, "All the better for seeing you!" I said, "Not very good?" "No," she said, and began to tell me all about it. As she spoke she became more and more breathless, and began obviously to be in great pain. I rushed to her and held her in my arms telling her not to talk, and stroking her forehead. She went grey and her lips were blue and she came out in a fearful cold sweat. She whispered to me, "I had a little chat with our Lord a little while ago and I told Him I knew how much He had suffered for me, and I was quite prepared to suffer for Him" - she always spoke of her prayers as 'having a little chat ...' I felt as though my heart was breaking, and said "Stay as still as you can darling, and I will go for the nurse."

I rushed out of the cubicle looking frantically for a nurse. The nursing station was deserted; I tore down the corridor looking into every room and cubicle, but there was not a uniform to be seen. At the end of the ward I saw someone sitting in an office typing; I burst into the room and said, "My wife is having another coronary and I can't find a nurse or a doctor anywhere!" Bless her, she leaped to her feet and said, "I'll find someone," and sped off. I rushed back to Bar who was in a terrible way; quiet but grey-faced and racked with frightful pain. I held her in my arms again, and she whispered, "I have never known pain like this."

A few moments later a nurse and young lady doctor came briskly in and took over. They carried another of the gadgets that had been used in Casualty to inject the special drug, and quickly fitted it - but it was faulty and did not work. Another was found, and that did not work either. Eventually, probably only a few minutes, but an eternity to Bar and me in our different agonies, one was found that worked properly.

While they were at work I left the cubicle as I was really getting in the way, and as soon as I got outside Alun appeared from the entrance to the ward. I'm afraid I burst into tears when I saw him, and he led me to a seat and hung on to me while through my tears I said, "I'm afraid Bar is very ill; she is having another heart attack." After a while the doctor and nurse came out and said they were going to take Bar back to the Coronary Care Unit, and left to arrange for her transfer. Alun and I went to her and she now had more colour and was without pain though obviously exhausted. She greeted Alun with a smile, and after a while he prayed with her and left, saying he would be in again. I stayed with her until they had transferred her to the CC unit and she was once more wired up to the monitors and put on a drip. Sister said that I need not stick to the rigid visiting times, but could stay as long as I liked, or that if I wanted to go home I could come back whenever I wished.

It was now getting on for six o'clock in the evening, so, Bar seeming stabilised for the time being anyway, I decided to go home and have a meal and then come back later. Sister said I could stay as long as I liked that night - the whole night if I wished. Bar whispered that she was anxious that I should not drive after dark, and although I was quite capable of doing so I knew she would worry if I did. I said I would ask David Pearce, our good friend and neighbour to bring me back to the hospital. Which is what I did, and returned armed with some biscuits and a thermos of coffee.

I stayed all night, and my poor love was in a lot of discomfort and very restless. She kept twisting and turning on the bed and messing up the tangle of wires from the pressure pads to the monitor so that the screen went crazy - it looked as though if it had had a voice it would be screaming. I kept untangling them and after a while the screen would return to normal with the straight line and that awful little blip appearing at regular, and sometimes irregular, intervals as she either calmed down or became agitated again.

I did so want her to get some sleep, and I stroked her forehead for a long, long time. I had brought her communion earlier and had given her the Laying on of Hands. This was something she had always valued greatly. I thought of the first time I had given it to her when she was in the early stages of mourning for Peter while staying with Minka, her mother-in-law. She had said she could not sleep, and I had told her that if she called me when she was ready to settle down I would give her the Laying on of Hands which would help her to relax and sleep. This I had done and she had had a good night's sleep. This time it was more difficult and it was a long time before she managed to have some sleep of a sort. At about two in the morning she was awake again and smiled wanly at me but then looked very anxious as she said, "Oh darling, do see if there is a bed you could lie down on and get some sleep, you've been here for hours, and you must look after yourself." I am bound to say I was feeling pretty jaded, and Sister said there was a room on the next floor where I could use the bed and try to get some sleep. It was good to stretch out but of course I could not sleep, and after a couple of hours or so I had some more coffee and went back to resume my vigil. Bar was looking a little better, but she was still anxious about me - (it was her constant fear that I would have a heart attack and die before she did and I knew she was thinking this now) - but I said I felt quite rested after the time I had had on the bed. Just before five she said she was feeling better now

275

and would I not please go home and go to bed - "and darling, please ask them if you can ring for a car to fetch you; don't try to go home by bus." I promised I would do this, for it was clear that it would distress her if I stayed, and that was to be avoided at all costs.   I felt I could not ask to use the 'phone in the unit; they were all so busy monitoring the patients on their television screens, so I decided to wait until I got to the gatehouse and ask the porter if I could use his 'phone. It was quite a long walk to the gate - right the other side of the hospital. When I got to the gatehouse it was all locked up and dark and there was no one on duty. I could see the bus stop from where I was standing, and a bus was approaching - I ran as best I could, but it had stopped and moved away long before I reached the stop. There was no traffic; everywhere was deserted. I doubled back into the hospital drive and saw lights and people moving about in a building a little way along. I trotted to this building, up the steps - a nurse crossed the end of the lit corridor as I arrived, so I thought, Thank goodness, they will let me use the 'phone here. I pulled, then pushed the door handle - locked! Oh no! I waited for a while hoping to attract someone's attention, but not another soul appeared.   Feeling very tired I slowly retraced my footsteps to the lonely bus stop, dimly lit by a not very efficient street lamp, all amongst the darkened windows of the row of houses on the other side of the road - and as I went I prayed, *Please Lord, let another bus come along.* I got to the stop, turned to look up the road - and lo and behold, in the distance a brightly lit bus making its way towards me! I stepped into the road, waving my arms, making sure my dog-collar was clearly visible. The bus stopped; the doors swung open and I jumped aboard. It was completely empty and being driven by a young woman, who smiled at me as she closed the doors and started up, and said, "Where do you want to go to sir?" I said, "I'm making for Twickenham - how much is the fare?" She said, "Oh this bus is not in service, I'm just taking it to where it has to be at eight o'clock this morning. I don't want any money, but I think I can catch up the bus ahead which will take you into Twickenham, but don't worry, if I can't catch him I'll take you there myself." So I sat down wondering at the wonderful kindness and sympathy of this young woman - I suppose I was showing some of my tiredness and distress. Did she make that bus move! Phew, I hung on with both hands as we roared through the night. After some time, sure enough, ahead of us we saw the lights of another bus which was decorously stopping at every bus stop. With her foot firmly pressing the accelerator to the floor we charged down the deserted road in hot pursuit. Soon we were almost on his tail as he drew into another bus stop, and with a masterly double swerve my female Jehu drew out and around our quarry and, braking hard, stopped in front of him. She said, a little breathlessly but with triumph in her eyes, "There you are sir, he'll take you home." I tried to give her a tip but she would have none of it and said, "Cheerio sir, good luck." The other bus, knowing itself beaten in the race, opened friendly doors to me and I stumbled aboard. Another empty bus, and this time the driver was a man, who said, "Where do you want to go to sir?" I told him I'd love to be dropped in King Street, Twickenham by the traffic lights. "Righteo sir," he said, "no problem - no, I don't want any money, its too early in the morning." A few minutes later he dropped me at the corner of Wharf Lane that gives on to the back gate of our flats. A few more minutes and I was home at last. I got myself some hot milk with a good slug of whiskey, and dropped into bed.

I awoke to a cheerless dawn and lay for some time depressed and anxious. I knew that yesterday's coronary had been massive and that great damage had been done to Bar's heart. Strangely I did not think at that time about what the future might hold - perhaps I dared not. Had I done so I would have wondered whether Bar would be able to continue living in the flat, with its seventeen stairs to our front door - and she so loved the flat and especially living so close to the river, for as I have said, she was essentially a water girl. Given the damage to her heart, would she even be able to walk again; would she be almost or completely bedridden? No, no, I dared not think these thoughts.

I rang the hospital as early as I thought reasonable and heard that Bar was again back in the ward upstairs, but this time with others and not alone in a cubicle.

As I had been doing regularly, of course, I rang Tim and told him the news. He had come over the previous evening to visit Bar. I rang other relations and friends as well to keep them up to date. Bar had said that at present she did not want to see anyone but Tim and me, and people understood this. Tim said he would go to the hospital just before lunch and I said I would be there at the same time. This was Saturday 2nd November 1991, the day of the World Cup Rugby Final at Twickenham, and the town was full of fans from all over the world. Tim and I had decided that just before lunch would be a good time to go to the hospital as later the roads would be choked with traffic on account of the match. We coincided in the ward at midday and found Bar looking much better; she had some colour in her cheeks and was quite cheerful. We were vastly relieved to see this and considerably heartened. She was still very anxious about me and pleaded with me to go home and go to bed as I must be exhausted after being there all night. Tim said the same, "Yes, you must look after yourself Paul, it's very important that you keep well." So I stayed only a few minutes and then went home and after a meal undressed fully and went thankfully to bed with a slightly easier mind. - I had kept my hearing aids in so that I would hear any calls. It was about 5 o'clock in the afternoon when the bedside telephone rang. The Sister in charge of the Coronary Care unit said, "Mr Singleton, I'm afraid your wife is having another heart attack, sir, and I feel sure you would want to be here." I said I would come at once and then heard myself asking, "What is the prognosis Sister?" to which she replied, "Not very good I am afraid, sir." I immediately rang Tim and told him I was going straight to the hospital and he said he would set off at once too. My good friends David and Carol in the flat below had said that they would take me to the hospital at any time of day or night, so instead of trusting myself to drive, I gave them a ring and David said he would take me at once - I dragged on some clothes and within a few minutes we were off - expecting to have to find our way through massive crowds. But most of the traffic had already dispersed after the match, and we made our swift way to the hospital unimpeded. He dropped me outside the Medical block and I took the lift to the CC unit.

As I walked along the corridor I could see the curtains were drawn around Bar's bed, and the Sister met me at the door with a grave face and asked me to sit down. "I am afraid I have terrible news for you sir, Mrs Singleton passed away a few minutes ago." My heart shrieked, *O NO!!* Then, incredibly, I immediately felt completely calm, and rising slowly to my feet I said, "I would like to see her please." She said, "Not just at the moment sir, the doctors are still with her, and it would be better if you waited for a short while." I said, "It's all right Sister, I am used to these things, I would like to see her at once please - I shall be quite all right." Without formulating the thought, I knew that I must try to say the Commendatory prayers for her immediately. So seeing my determination, she went and put her head round the bed curtains and asked the three young doctors to leave. They came straight out, and I went in. Sister softly drew the curtains behind me, as I gazed at my beautiful, now grey, but for me always golden Bar, my Girl in the Middle.

My darling was stretched across the bed in a position that

clearly showed her final agony. My heart constricted at the thought of her pain. I managed to say, *"Go forth from this world, O Christian soul...."* before I broke. I wept the first of many many tears there at the bedside.

When I had recovered sufficiently I went out and rejoined the anxious Sister. She made me sit down and sent for a cup of tea for me with plenty of sugar. She asked if there was anything else she could give me. I had not brought my angina pills with me so, as a precaution I asked if she could possibly give me a TNT tablet to put under my tongue - I said, "I'm all right at the moment, but the shock might catch up with me...." She said, "Yes, of course", and immediately produced the tablet.

After a while I could not bear to sit still any longer and went out of the ward and walked up and down, up and down, by the lifts, waiting for poor old Tim to arrive for whom I knew this would be a terrible shock. He had a long way to come - from Bourne End near Maidenhead, and I found myself praying that he would drive carefully and not have an accident on the motorway. But he is one of the best drivers I know, so I was not really worried. At long last the doors of the lift opened and he came straight to me. Before I could say anything he knew, and bless him, he gave me a big hug. As we clung together he said, "Oh Paul, Oh Paul." I cannot remember whether the doctors in the meantime had composed Bar, but I encouraged Tim to go in to see her. This was perhaps a mistake, for he suffered dreadfully from shock in the following week.

I have always felt that if possible people should see the bodies of their dear departed ones, otherwise there is a greater danger that a part of the mind that may not come to terms with their absence and be unable 'believe they have gone.'

Tim took me home and we called on David and Carol who were most distressed to hear the news, for they both loved Bar dearly. They came up with us to the flat and we all had a drink together while I rang Alun, who came round immediately and he and I went into another room where he talked to me and we prayed together.

Alun was a great support all through that terrible weekend and for a long time afterwards. I went to church as usual on Sunday morning. I did not sit in my stall in choir, but in the congregation in the pew that Bar and I had shared for several years. Now it was Alun's wife Christine, who took over the care of me and sat with me in the pew and held my arm tight when I broke down - especially in the hymns which were Bar's favourite times for weeping during the course of church services! All through

279

the weeks and months of mourning, Alun and Christine gave me wonderfully loving care and support, and I reckon them two of my greatest friends.

On the Monday morning Tim came over and took me to the hospital for the heartrending business of collecting Bar's belongings - her rings and the few clothes that I had not already brought home, and the medical 'certification of death'. We then went to the undertaker and arranged the funeral. I put the announcement of Bar's death in *The Times* and *The Telegraph*, and the letters seemed to pour in from all over the country. Everyone who knew Bar was shocked at her short illness and completely unexpected death. I had always known that she was popular wherever she went of course, but the letters expressed a deep affection and appreciation that warmed my heart. Many people mentioned her lovely sense of humour. And I was reminded that only a few days before she died, Bar and I had been laughing over our early morning tea about something one or other of us had said. As she wiped the tears from her eyes she had said, "Aren't we lucky? There can't be many couples of our age who rarely get out of bed in the morning without laughing their heads off about something or other!"

I had arranged for the lesson at the funeral service to be those immortal words of St Paul in 1 Corinthians 13 about love, and I had said that I would like to read the lesson myself if I felt up to it - but I asked Alun to be ready to take over if I found in the end that I could not manage it. Tim and Charlotte sat with me in the front pew, as Bar's coffin was carried in. I was rather cross and put out because although the young funeral director with whom we had made the arrangements had said that he himself would be conducting the funeral, it had turned out that a young woman had been given the job instead. I said in my heart, *Sorry darling, I did not know about this - I know how you hate to see a woman conducting a funeral, but there's nothing I can do about it.* I managed to read the lesson all right, but broke down when I got back to my seat, which of course did not matter at all. Charlotte was so kind to me and hung on to my arm until I recovered myself. Alun preached a very good address to a packed church.

In spite of being November the weather was sunny and mild and so it was no hardship for anyone as Tim and Charlotte and I stood outside to greet the congregation as they came out of the church. Several were in tears and could only give me a little wave and rush away. Everyone said what a splendid and moving funeral service it had been; the emphasis, as I had wanted it to be, had been on love and praise and joyful submission to the will of God. We sang 'Praise to the Holiest in the Height', and, 'Just as I am without one plea', both favourite hymns of Bar's. Several said that it was the most moving funeral service they had ever been to.

Afterwards our good friend, Mary Oughtred, in the flat above, provided a buffet lunch for the family and those who had come from a distance. This turned out to be a quietly happy occasion and everyone was very grateful for Mary's hospitality.

When at last it was all over, I closed the door of the flat with a mixture of relief and sadness - and recognised that my life had changed radically once more - more radically than ever before in fact, for My Girl in the Middle, who had been in the centre of my life and always 'there' wherever I had been and whatever I had been doing, was, irrevocably, there no longer. For a long time I could not think at all. I was just conscious of being very, very tired - and completely hollow and empty inside.

One of the letters of condolence I had received was from a wise lady in our congregation who said, among other things, "I do hope you are not going to try to be 'brave' - do not try not to cry - when my mother died my father used to switch on the Hoover and *howl!*" I awoke on the morning after the funeral, as I had on every morning since my love had died, and found myself howling before I could get to the Hoover.

When I had quietened down I became increasingly conscious of all Bar's possessions - cupboards and drawers crammed with her things, and this produced another paroxysm of grief. "O darling, whatever am I to do? - all your sweet things, all those dresses - the ones we both liked so much, that came alive when you wore them?" and, with a little weepy grin, "...and sweetie, those I couldn't stand but never told you so, for *you* liked them!" Whatever was I going to do about them? - every piece so personal, almost a part of her, and for a time I was paralysed by the thought of it all. Thank God I could pray again now - though prayer comes naturally to people in times of crisis and distress. I kept on asking myself: Whatever could I do?

As I gradually composed myself I recalled how some people cannot touch the clothes and possessions of their dear ones who have died and have to leave everything just as it was when they last touched it. I had always thought it a very morbid practice, and I knew I could never do that. I remembered those who said that it had been many months before they could bring themselves to deal with their husband's or wife's possessions. I gradually began to realize that I could not do that either. By the time I dragged myself out of bed I knew that for me there was only one course to take; however heartless it might seem to other people, I had to do this terrible job without delay; I must begin today. Which is what I did. I had to give myself a psychological anaesthetic so that I could do the job almost clinically, without a thought beyond whether this or that would be acceptable to this or that relation or friend, and whether this or that should go to charity. Armed with a number of large black sacks labelled appropriately, I spent most of the day sorting clothes and possessions. Carol's son Chris helped me such a lot with his sympathetic understanding and practical help, coming with me to the Normansfield Psychiatric Hospital in Teddington who had said they would be glad of any clothes. Many precious possessions and family 'heirlooms' went to Tim of course.

Naturally it took me some time to get over this clearance when the 'psychological anaesthetic' wore off, as it soon did. Even so, I was satisfied that I had done the right thing.

There is a finality about death that cannot be gainsaid and in my view it is unhealthy to pretend that it is not so and try to hang on to a departed loved one by clinging to possessions. I kept photographs, of course, but they are different it seems to me; they simply help to reawaken the sense of the abiding presence of the beloved in one's heart. Indeed I found the very first photograph I ever took of my Girl in the Middle, just those few months after I had had my 'vision', soon after we had properly met and were seeing one another regularly. I had taken it on my mother's little old Box Brownie camera, a favourite family camera in the 1920s - I suppose it must have been in the early 20s when Mother had bought the camera with the twelve shillings and sixpence she had won in a sweepstake on the Derby. Bar was standing in the orchard at her home, with a background of fruit trees. It was a tiny print about two inches by two and a half. A friend who has a photographic business went to a great deal of trouble to have it photographed, enlarged and 'intensified' for me by the wonders of modern technology. The result is that I have a splendid enlargement of the very first picture I took of Bar. I also have the last one - a group of herself with David and Carol Pearce taken on the shore in the Isle of Wight only three weeks or so before she died. We had stayed three nights in Portsmouth, partly as a nostalgic visit for me to the Cathedral where I had been priested, and we had spent a day on the Island. We all had a very jolly time, and I am so grateful to David and Carol for making Bar's last little holiday such a happy one. We had laughed such a lot as we always did when the four of us were together.

As the slow days and short nights after Bar's death gradually lost their shock and immediate pain, I found myself realizing that sad and sudden as it had been, Bar had got her wish - and in fact so had I. She had died before me as she had always hoped she would. I had survived her, as I had always hoped, because I feared she would never be able to manage by herself, either physically or psychologically. I had hoped she would go first, but found myself saying quite illogically, "Yes, but not as soon as this." Yet the recollection of this was a great help to me in coming to terms with her now irrevocable absence from my life.

A month or so after the funeral I told Alun, "This week I have been going around with one phrase echoing in my head all the time: *Consummatum est*, 'It is finished', 'It is completed', and at the same time I have been remembering Brother Roger Castle saying to me as I said goodbye to the brethren at Mirfield in 1968, 'Of course, you are not really leaving us, you are just going off to do another job, that's all!'" Naturally I had not looked upon marrying Bar as 'just another job', except in the sense that I strongly felt and still feel that it was something I was called to do, and was very very happy to do. That, I think, does not preclude the sense that I now had, that something had indeed been 'completed'. What I had been called to do had now been done. My thought continued that while not exactly the 'shepherd', I had in fact been called, in a sense, to leave the 'ninety and nine' in the wilderness and go to love and help the one that was 'lost'. And there is no doubt in my own mind that Bar was indeed 'lost' - in sadness, in anxiety and in depression, and needed a lot of loving care and undivided attention. This also was a comforting thought, and helped me in the early stages of bereavement.

Some of the best help at this time came through the loving concern of Tim and his wife Charlotte. Had he been 'bone of my bone and flesh of my flesh' Tim could not have been more sympathetic, kind and helpful, and he and Charlotte kept in close touch for many weeks and gave me wonderful support.

On another level was the affection and prayers of the local Christian Family at the parish church. I had always taught how powerful intercessory prayer is in helping people in particular difficulties or distress, and many had told me in the course of my ministry how in illness and bereavement and other sorts of trouble, they had felt borne up on a wave of prayer. It was now my own turn to experience this for myself, more fully than ever before. Even in the darkest moments of grief and despair I was always aware of being 'held', or 'upheld' by a powerful wave of strength-giving comfort, and I knew exactly what it was - it was the love of God mediated, as it so often is, through the caring prayers of many many people far and near, but especially of the wonderfully caring and supportive congregation at my parish church. I shall never be able adequately to express my gratitude for this. Nor was the help and support only spiritual. It was practical too. For weeks I had Sunday lunch at home only once, and that was when Tim came over on business and I made lunch for us both. On all the other Sundays, a particularly sensitive day, I was invited to Sunday lunch - an English institution - in the homes of members of the congregation.

Several months after Bar died I went to the ten o'clock Eucharist one Wednesday morning. I was depressed that day and feeling out of sorts. As I knelt in my pew I accepted my depression as we all have to do, for all of us have our depressions from time to time. I was not specifically thinking of Bar that morning but I had as usual 'offered her up' during the intercessions and of course she is never far from my thoughts. I think the root of that particular depression was just simple loneliness. I went to the altar to make my communion, still in my depression. On my return to my pew I knelt to make my thanksgiving - and I felt a gentle warmth suffuse me, sweeping through my body from head to toe. My spirits lifted, like the sun gently coming from behind cloud. I felt comforted and cheered - quietly, not ecstatically. I felt as I used to feel when Bar gave me a hug when I was feeling down. It was the same warmth, and I felt that this had come from her and that she was very close; I thought, *Good heavens, she has hugged me!* I cannot justify this feeling theologically. Psychologically it can be explained as purely subjective, a 'bereavement hallucination'. Be that as it may, the experience had a profound effect upon me, and I think it is true to say that from that moment I ceased actively mourning my Girl in the Middle. She still lives in my heart, of course, and always will. But I have said Goodbye to her until the General Resurrection on the Last Day, whatever that is going to be like, and none of us know or can imagine. However, I was now, and have remained, at peace about Bar.

The 'Oldie Goldies' 1988

With Carol and David Pearce –
three weeks before she died

13

The Big Bang

From then on it was as though a 'Big Bang' occurred in my life, for it seemed to explode in all directions. Primarily I felt 'filled with the Spirit' and a new joy had entered my life, the joy of wholehearted belief in our Lord and the 'glory of his Resurrection' - and the consequent certainty that He was directing my life completely. I felt I wanted to preach about this, and I had my first opportunity on Easter Day when I was asked to conduct the 8 o'clock Eucharist at the parish church that morning. I had not known that I had been put down for this when I had said at the Staff Meeting, "Don't you think that on Easter Day, of all days in the year, there ought to be a short address at the 8 o'clock service?" Alun Glyn-Jones, the Vicar, said at once, "Yes I agree," as everyone else murmured agreement. He continued, "OK, you will preach it because I've put you down to celebrate at that service!" Hoist by my own petard!

I was in fact delighted to have the opportunity of doing this. On Easter Sunday evening there was to be a television programme in which three or four clergy and ministers were going to say why they did not believe in the resurrection of our Lord, and I wanted to say something about this and 'bear witness to the Resurrection.' At the end of the Creed the congregation were surprised when I asked them to sit while I left the altar and came down to stand on the chancel step, in the exact spot where I had stood to read the Gospel on Easter Day four years before. I warned the congregation against being upset by this programme. I said that whatever people thought or said about the historical event, the real proof of the resurrection is to be seen in the fact that the Risen Lord still changes people's lives. He does so just as radically today as He did in his earthly ministry and in the early Church and has done in the Church down the ages. I said I knew this from personal experience, because the Risen Lord had changed my life not once, but twice. First when I was a young man, then again on this very spot where I am standing now, four years ago on Easter Day, after nearly twenty years estranged from the Church, the Risen Lord 'revealed' Himself to me as I stood reading the Easter Gospel at the Parish Communion. He changed my life in that moment, and I 'knew' again that He had risen from the dead, the Resurrection was true.

As I stood bidding people a Happy Easter after the

service, one man came up to me and said, "Thank you for the reassurance - I needed it!"

Suddenly doors that had been kept locked were now standing open; where there had been darkness in my life there was now a glorious light.

One of the first doors to open was the door to the Community of the Resurrection. Not long before Bar died I had said, "Darling I would love to take you to see Mirfield!" She had replied quite excitedly, "Oh would you really? - I've always wanted to go there and see what it is like - are you sure you would like to do that? Because if you are I would absolutely love to go!" I had written to the Superior, Fr Silvanus Berry, who had been a newly professed brother when I left, and had been very kind to me in those dark days when I was wondering whether I should ask for my release or not. He had replied with a very friendly letter saying that we would be very welcome. Sadly that was a trip we were never able to make. When Bar died a few months later I had a very kind and sympathetic letter from the Superior, who had seen the announcement in the paper.

The now unlocked door of Mirfield was beckoning me and not long after my 'warming' experience in the church I arranged a visit.

I had mixed feelings as I drove in at the main gates and drew up before the front door - from which I had last emerged twenty-four years ago and had not seen since. The first thing I noticed was the tight security that now pertained. In my day on arrival I could have opened the front door and walked in. Not now. Now the door was locked and I had to await an answer to my ring. In spite of the warmth of the Superior's letters and a notable one from my old friend Fr Aelred Stubbs, I half expected a polite but slightly distant welcome and was quite prepared for this - indeed I would have considered it perfectly natural.

The door was opened by the Guestmaster, Fr Clifford Green - and immediately we were in a bearhug as he gave me a wonderful welcome, the first of many. It seemed that I was generally accepted - a very different attitude from that shown to ex-brethren in my time in the Community. I remembered being very frosty myself to a priest who had left CR and returned later to visit, just as I was doing now. I said as much to one of my contemporaries and he said, "Oh well, we have learnt a lot about acceptance and about personal relationships since those days." It was quite wonderful to be in the dear old place once more. One of the first places I visited was the Chapel of the Resurrection, the large apsidal chapel behind the High Altar where the Blessed Sacrament is reserved. It was still as I had always found it, full of serenity and prayer, still my Mecca, and spiritually at any rate I felt that I had come home. Fr Silvanus Berry, my erstwhile junior brother, now Superior of the Community, very kindly found time to take me round to see the changes that had occurred in the church since I had left. The altars in the upper church were as they had always been, but in the lower church, still used as the College chapel, the six side altars had gone, leaving only the main altar. He showed me the lower church sacristy, where in my day there had been seven vesting tables, one for each altar, each with full sets of vestments in all liturgical colours in a chest below. These had all been cleared out and the long room turned into a chapel specially set aside for retreatants. It had a cosy feel to it, softly carpeted, and with an amazing lighting console from which many styles of lighting could be arranged for the chapel, - a brilliant sanctuary and shaded nave, with a spotlight on the retreat conductor's chair, or on the free-standing crucifix that stood at the south end of the altar, or on the altar itself - or the whole chapel lit just sufficiently to make your way to your seat. The Bishop of Wakefield had given special permission for the Blessed Sacrament to be reserved here as well as in the Resurrection chapel. Certainly there was a very distinct stillness and serenity about this chapel - the sort of stillness that says to the believer, 'Be still, and *know*' and where if we compose ourselves to stillness, we are often given a real blessing of peace.

Some may dismiss the special lighting effects as mere gimmickry. Not I. I have always believed that whatever we can do to encourage a devotional atmosphere in a church or chapel is quite justified. After all, we are not simply 'spiritual' beings, we are 'body-souls' and each side of our nature affects the other, so if we can induce spiritual relaxation and stillness by physical means, that is perfectly justified and good, and means that the whole person is relaxed. For lights slowly to be dimmed at the end of a retreat address and a crucifix slowly illuminated, will help retreatants to relax into the spiritual and physical posture for the deepening of prayer and renewal that is one of the important purposes of a retreat. Nothing but good can result. I was delighted to see that all this had been provided for the physical and spiritual refreshment of retreatants.

My room in the retreat house was one in which I had stayed from time to time while I was a member of CR all those years ago, and the place brought back many memories. I am thankful that it was not the same room in which I had opened the fateful letter from my mother enclosing the obituary notice of Bar's husband. I think that would have recalled my spiritual struggle too abruptly. As it was, I believe I was in a room on the same corridor as the one in which I had stayed on my very first visit to Mirfield, sometime in the early 1940s, when Dick Herrick and I had come there from Portsmouth for our annual priests' retreat.

I decided that for the time being I would not think very much - I would walk around the house, the church, and the grounds and just soak it all in like a sponge. It was a lovely spring day and the West Riding was looking its most gracious in the sunshine. The spring flowers were in full bloom in the garden as I made my way along old familiar paths to the little copses on the edge of the cricket field where I had taken the photograph in the 1960s of one of the brethren walking away from me in the dappled shade, just as it was now - the picture I called, with brilliant imagination, 'In a Monastery Garden'! Then through the cemetery with its lines of oak crosses on the graves bearing the dates of a brother's birth, profession and death. In my day we had had a splendid gardener named Stanley Harford who had an unfortunate stutter. He told me one day that Fr Bell the Custos in charge of the grounds, had decided to widen the cemetery on one side by felling some trees - as brethren died we were needing more space. Stanley was incensed at this lopsided plan and told me with great indignation, "Father- Father - Father Bell-Bell, he didn't-didn't ought to do-do-do that-that, Father-Father, it-it will-will-will des-des-destroy the sym-sym-sym- symmetry of the cem-cem-cem-cemetery, Father-Father No Father he didn't ought, *No* Father!" There were many more of the beautiful oak crosses now and the part that had destroyed the sym-symmetry of the cem-cemetery was full.

Through the lych gate I went at the other end of the cemetery into the Calvary Garden, always one of my favourite spots, with the life-size figure on the huge cross, looking out over the Calder Valley with its railway lines, the River Calder, no longer polluted as it had been in my day, the canal with the occasional barge still plying along its still waters, and then to the moors rising beyond, with the drystone walling criss-crossing the green turf. I sat for a few moments gazing, as I had done hundreds of times before, at the silent figure, the Dying One who by His Resurrection brought the whole Christian, and yes, the whole of the Western civilised world into being. The carpenter from Nazareth who still changed lives after two thousand years. The most incredible story in the world. A story, I felt, that was so incredible that it just had to be true. Full of nostalgia, I made my way along the little narrow path bordered by the drystone wall on the edge of the sheer drop down towards the main Dewsbury to Huddersfield Road. Just around the corner the quarry from which most of the stone for the church and many of the additions to the original house had been obtained. In the very early days of the community immediately after the removal of the necessary stone, this quarry had been turned into a great amphitheatre on the model of a Greek theatre and would seat upwards of two thousand people. The acoustics were very good and in those days many Christian Socialist meetings had been held there and had drawn crowds of men from all over the West Riding to hear some of the famous Socialist politicians, including Keir Hardie.

Up another slope from the far side of the quarry and there was the College of the Resurrection, the training place for generations of priests, many with backgrounds of relative poverty and original lack of schooling like mine. And so back to the great church, like an old lion crouching there upon the sloping hillside. Into the lower church, up the southern spiral staircase into the cool peace of the upper church, silent and still with the afternoon sun softly gleaming through the circular clerestory windows. Down the south aisle, past the chantry chapel of Walter Frere, the first Superior, into the Chapel of the Ascension where there is now a Greek Orthodox icon standing in front of the altar before which I lit some candles to symbolise my prayer and affection for all my friends and loved ones. Finally through the arch - to my 'Mecca' once more, the Chapel of the Resurrection, in a real sense still 'home' to me.

Now I felt I had absorbed the whole wonderful and dear place once again - its life had begun to enter my bloodstream once more and was coursing through my veins.

Next, tea in the refectory, quite informal; two large stainless steel double-handled teapots on a hot-plate near the door; a collection of mugs and a couple of jugs of milk. On the tables, plates of bread and butter. You took your mug of tea and sat where you wished. The brethren were all very friendly and still welcoming. I sat with some of my aging contemporaries, each of us in turn saying, "Do you remember...?" Each reminiscence and story being capped by another; much laughter; such fun. When silence fell between us and we lapsed into quiet reflection, I saw the refectory as it had been in my day - not the decent oak tables at which we were now sitting, but rather scruffy ones covered in plain grey linoleum, and I saw the shades of departed brethren of my own era - Father Doctor Lionel Thornton, alone at the head of an empty table practising the 'Common Life in the Body of Christ' in solitude! - about which he was writing his *magnum opus*; and Raymond Raynes, my first Superior, wrapped in his shoulder-cape, with shaven head and beaklike nose, declaiming on the latest sins of British Rail. I could hear him saying, "*I* could solve all British Rail's problems overnight - *cut the fares in half!* Simple! That's the way to do it, everyone would travel by train then, and there would be plenty of money to improve things!" There was Brother Roger, keeping the little knot of brethren that always collected around him in fits of laughter - and many others, now at rest in the cemetery where I had just visited them and read their dates of birth, profession and death on their lovely oak crosses.

Many of the younger brethren whom I had not met came and introduced themselves and were very friendly, which was most heartening.

I think what impressed me most on this first visit was the way in which, under the influence of the Liturgical Movement which was only just beginning to have its influence when I left, the worship of the community had developed and changed. Now there was only a very small minority of brethren who liked to say their own Mass on most days. The great majority were happy to celebrate only occasionally as their turn came round, and for the rest of the time to remain in the 'congregation of the Faithful' for the daily 'Conventual Mass'. This was celebrated at either the High Altar on major feast days, or more often in the Chapel of the Resurrection. The ceremonial had been drastically simplified and was far less fussy than the old 'Western Rite' that I remembered. The reforms I had seen begun, I now saw in all their radical simplicity, and I warmed to them immediately. Gone were all the jerky 'manual acts' preceding and during the consecration of the bread and wine. All was conducted smoothly, quietly and in an unhurried manner which I found very devotional and an inducement to prayer.

The psalms of course form about a third of Matins and Evensong, and the greater part of the Midday Office, and it seemed to me that these too were now said or sung more recollectedly than I remembered; certainly there was a much longer pause observed at the colon in the middle of each verse, and this was another great improvement. The reason for the colon is that in the psalms the second half of the verse frequently repeats in different words the thought expressed in the first half. To pause here at the colon gives time for the thought to be assimilated by mind and heart before it is affirmed by its repetition in the second half of the verse. In the psalms we have an enormously rich mine of spirituality - there we can find every aspiration and appreciation that down the ages has expressed every side of man's relationship with God. The psalter is a universal treasury of spirituality, and the more it can be used creatively, so much the more is it capable of feeding the soul of modern man just as it has fed the souls of men and women in every age since these incomparable verses were first composed - in many cases centuries before they were first written down. But if they are to 'release' their meaning for us in our day, we have to learn to recite them recollectedly, and that means without hurry. The psalter can become a great treasury of prayer for us today as it was in the past for our forebears, if we will take the trouble to learn again how to use it with unhurried devotion.

At Mirfield, as in all religious communities, the psalter is recited antiphonally - that is, each side of the choir reciting or singing the verses alternately. The psalms are said quietly, only a little above a murmur but each word having its due weight, with quite a long pause at the colon - the time taken by a leisurely breath, in, and out. For visitors this takes a little getting used to, and at first I found myself starting the second half of the verse while the brethren were still silent - quite embarrassing! However once one has learned to keep the proper pace it soon becomes clear that saying the psalms in this way produces what can best be described as a reflective rhythm - and this in turn allows the psalter to begin 'speaking to the soul'. Recited this way it is astonishing how much the sentiments and cries-from-the-heart, written so many centuries ago, chime in with and express the aspirations and fears of our own hearts, separated though we are not only by many centuries but also by vastly differing cultures. How sad to see the psalter so often abused by being rushed through with no chance of recollection or reflective application. But how good to know that in some parish churches today the quieter method is being used and the laity introduced to the treasure house of the psalter.

Again, opportunity for reflective prayer is given by the practice of keeping a period of silence after the reading of the passages of Holy Scripture that are used in the Daily Office.

Evensong is sung to Gregorian chants at Mirfield, and in term time the students at the College join the community for this office. When I was in the community there were always musical students with good voices, and it seems that the same is true today. This brings a great enrichment to the community worship, and there is plenty of back-up for the Precentor who forms a group of cantors, composed of brethren and students, to lead the choir.

My first Evensong after an absence of nearly a quarter of a century was another great experience. I was delighted to hear those limpid plainsong chants soaring into the barrel vault of the church with a melodious resonance that sent shivers down my spine! I experienced again how singing the psalter to plainsong chants also 'releases' the spirituality and inspiration of those immortal words and phrases. I always think of plainsong as the authentic 'music of the spheres', the cadences born to carry man's soul into the heavenly places, instinct with the thirst for God. I could only sit and listen to all this wonder; I did not dare to open my mouth and try to sing - I remembered that soon after I had become a novice the Precentor had told me only to sing very softly because, "You cannot sing in tune!" So I remained silent, but in my mind and heart the notes of worship were soaring in *crescendo* and *diminuendo* with the rest, and all that evening the chants were filling my mind, and they sang me to sleep that night.

Before I left Mirfield I determined to come back in July for the Centenary 'Commemoration Day' celebrations. On Commemoration Day each year friends of the Community, old students and well-wishers, converge on Mirfield in large numbers. In my day we would expect anything between four and five thousand people from all over the country, and indeed from all over the world. The day would begin with High Mass either in the community church, or, more commonly in later years, in a huge marquee erected on the front lawn. After this there would be a picnic lunch on the cricket field, and tea would be served from huge coppers on the edge of the field that were heated by open fires. I remember the Assistant Custos, Brother Barnabas, one year reporting to General Chapter that on Commemoration Day 400 gallons of tea had been served - and there had been a twenty-minute queue at the loos! Commemoration Day was always a wonderfully friendly and exhilarating occasion, and I knew I could not miss the one which would mark the centenary of the Community, so I collected my tickets before I left for home.

One of the letters of condolence I received after Bar died was from my old friends in Johannesburg, Deane and Dorothy Yates. When I wrote to thank them I told them that I was going to Commemoration Day and had booked a room in the small local motel. A week or two later the 'phone rang at 8am and I was asked to write down a cable from Johannesburg. *Can you get us room motel two nights over Commem? phone Johannesburg number Collect. Dot.* Gosh, they were coming to England and I would meet them again at Commem.! I found the number of the owner of the motel, grabbed the phone again, kept my fingers crossed hoping she would be in and awake at 8am. A friendly Yorkshire voice said, "Hello, can I help you?" and when I had explained, "Yes, sir, there is a room in your cottage which they can have." I was to have the ground floor room, they the one upstairs. She said she would book Mr and Mrs Yates for those dates, and yes she would accept a deposit from me. I promised to get the cheque in the post that morning, so all was fixed.

I immediately dialled the Johannesburg number, perfectly happy for the call to go on to my bill. Immediately the bell was ringing six thousand miles away and, as if it had been in Twickenham, I heard the cool collected and infinitely polite voice saying, with a lilt, "This is Dorothy Yates speaking, Good morning." - "Good morning Dotty," I said, "How are you?" "Who is this?" she asked. "This is Paul Singleton ringing from Twickenham!" A shocked pause, then, *"Daaaarling"* - three tones higher and with a boost of decibels. Then dead silence for a space. She was always generous with her 'Darlings's - all and sundry, black and white came into the orbit of her love and affection. "So soon!" she said at last, "I can't believe this, I only sent the cable less than an hour ago, and here you are already, and you say you have booked us a room! *Wonderful!*" "I always was a fast worker" I claimed smugly. She told me their expected time of arrival of their train to Leeds on the day before Commem. They would take a taxi to Mirfield. I told her I would be waiting for them. As I put the 'phone down I felt the years since the three of us last met already melting away, and a rising excitement at the prospect of our meeting again before many weeks were past.

I went to Mirfield a few days before Commem. and moved into my room at the motel - which was the conversion of a row of workmen's cottages near the dreary station at Mirfield. Each consisted of two rooms, one up and one down with a tiny bathroom next to the upstairs room; there were five of these sets of rooms, four to let, while the middle one of the row had been turned into a small dining room and kitchen where a good full Yorkshire cooked breakfast was served every morning by a lady who came in for the purpose and to clean the rooms and make the beds. It was quite comfortable, if small and basic.

Deane and Dot were due to arrive on the afternoon of the day before Commem. I decided to sit in the car outside the front door as I awaited their arrival in case the driver of the Leeds cab did not know the motel - I thought if I kept an eye open I might prevent them from flashing by. While I waited I played Andrew Lloyd Webber's 'Phantom of the Opera' tape in the car. As each cab approached I scanned it closely and made myself as visible as possible in the hope that they would see me, hoping also that I would recognise them. After several had gone by, I half noticed one that had someone wearing a red coat, but as it swept on I decided it could not be them. So I sat back in the car with the door wide open listening to Michael Crawford's lovely voice and still keeping an eye open for a cab. None came, and it was now past the time I had expected them. I was just coming to the conclusion that they must have missed the train when suddenly a brawny arm came round the door of the car and clasped me round the shoulders. I was out of the car in a trice and Deane and I were pummelling one another's backs and saying stupid things like "You haven't changed a bit you old Devil" - then I turned and there was Dotty - red coat of *course* - and a great hug and kiss this time instead of backslapping! "Wonderful, how wonderful to see you - come on in, the kettle has boiled." " Where can I spend a penny?" - "Oh yes, up the stairs and straight ahead - your room is on the left ... Hi Deane, come on in, park yourself in that chair, I'll make the tea, how was your flight?" "Oh, OK, not bad, but we had a mess up over tickets for the train and only just caught it..." Dotty began to speak as she reached the last steps of the staircase and was in full blast as she came into the room. As we sipped our tea the sun of our mutual friendship burned away the mists of time and warmed us all from a clear sky.

The first of our reunion excitement over, it was clear they were both dead tired after their eleven hour flight the night before and the five hour train and taxi journey today, so off they went to sample the motel beds, and I put my feet up on mine also. They re-emerged much refreshed around six, with Deane bearing a large bottle of Duty Free Scotch, which was a sight for sore eyes. We decided to have dinner at the pub next door and then go up to the Community House to greet some of the brethren.

When we arrived at the Mother House they were just coming out into the front garden after supper and Deane and Dot got a great welcome from many of them whom they had known for years both in South Africa and in this country.

The Centenary Commemoration Day dawned grey and threatening and we were afraid that it was going to be spoilt by rain. I was glad I had armed myself with an extra large golfing umbrella so that if the worst came to the worst we could all three shelter under its ample spread. We parked the car in the meadow opposite the back gates of the community as it began to drizzle and the three of us walked arm in arm under the umbrella to the huge open-sided marquee on the front lawn. Hundreds of people were pouring through the gates from dozens of coaches and private cars that had come from all over the North of England and beyond. We managed to find ourselves three seats inside the marquee which we 'booked' with raincoats and the big brolly. Luckily the drizzle had stopped for the time being, so we were able to mingle with the crowds, from time to time meeting people we knew. Twice I was accosted with, "Excuse me Father, aren't you Father Singleton? - I remember you when you came to do a mission...." and again, "Ee, this is champion, if it isn't Father Singleton. 'ow are y'then Faaather!" Such warmth; such gratitude and tenderness in my heart. A little later one of the Whitby sisters, already talking to Deane and Dot whom she had known in South Africa, now wringing my hand and saying it was good to see me again. No recriminations, no turning away from a 'defector'.

The High mass that morning was something to remember for a lifetime. It was celebrated by the Superior, Fr Silvanus Berry, in the presence of George Carey, Archbishop of Canterbury, and Nigel McCulloch, the Bishop of Wakefield. There were eighteen concelebrating priest members of the Community in a great arc around the central High Altar. The front lawn has high grass banks surrounding it on three sides, and, the weather just managing to hold off from rain, the banks were crowded with the people unable to get into the marquee, and these were able to see the altar and take a full part in the service which, was also broadcast to a large area by the audio system. The Archbishop preached a magnificent sermon on the importance of the Religious Life in the life of the Church, and the great contribution made over the past hundred years by the Community of the Resurrection, both in this country and overseas. The service took me back to the High Mass celebrated in the White City Stadium in the 1930s during the Anglo Catholic Congress that had had such a formative influence upon my life as a Christian. But this was much more of a family affair. Eight thousand of us made our communion that day and we all felt that we knew one another, that we 'belonged', just like one big family that is normally scattered abroad, but has now gathered here in the ancestral home to celebrate one hundred years of family history. The eighteen concelebrants all wearing identical vestments and each with an assistant, went to eighteen chosen points around the garden, marked by specially painted heraldic signs, to give communion to the vast number of communicants. They did so, not from silver or gold chalices, but from simple ceramic chalices and patens, more like household utensils than conventional sacred vessels - another seemly simplification due to the Liturgical reforms of recent years.

After the High Mass Deane and Dot and I stayed for a while, mingling with the crowds and then, none of us being as young as we used to be and now feeling pretty tired, we repaired to our little motel rooms for a snack lunch and a good postprandial snooze. Catching up with news of mutual friends and our own activities over the years, we had another excellent dinner in our pub, and went early to bed.

Sunday morning saw us once more with the Community for the normal conventual High Mass of Sunday in the community church. Deane and Dot, like me, were very impressed by the simple dignity of the rite.

At lunch, again in our now familiar pub, came the wonderful invitation - "Paul, why don't you come out and stay with us next winter - your winter, our summer?" Phew! - the thought had never entered my head! To stay with them, as of old, after all these years! To see South Africa again! To feel that heavy sunshine beating down from the cloudless sky! To smell the unique smell of Africa again!

"The exchange rate is very much in your favour at the moment," Deane was saying. "About five Rands to the Pound sterling - it will hardly cost you any more than staying at home - in fact if you stayed for a few months you would probably save your fare!"

My goodness! What a wonderful invitation! "Come for two or three months," they said, "you can stay with us". "With your own bathroom and loo," said Dot, "for as long as you like." "We can go on a few trips, perhaps the Game Reserve - do you remember when we went in the 50s, and hardly saw an animal? This time we'll make sure we see some real game, not just the odd giraffe and zebra, which are two a penny anyway. You will be able to see some of your old friends too, both black and white. *Go on, do come!*"

Who could resist? Who would want to? Two of my oldest friends, resurrected here at "t' Resurrection" at Mirfield. I could not bear the thought that this afternoon when I took them to Leeds for their train back to London to begin their Scandinavian and European tour, I would not see them again for years - perhaps not again in this life. No - by hook or by crook, next January would see me setting off for African sunshine and another reunion with Deane and Dot, and through them with many others whom I had not seen for over thirty years. 'Resurrections' would be going on all over the place!

It needed neither hook nor crook to get me to Africa. When I told Tim and Charlotte about this magnificent invitation there was no pursing of dubious lips, no hesitation, "But of *course* you must go Paul." And so, six months later I boarded Flight BA 057 from Heathrow, due eleven hours later at Jan Smuts airport, Johannesburg.

14

Return To Africa

I arrived at Jan Smuts Airport, Johannesburg on the morning of 16 January 1993 and set foot on African soil for the first time for thirty-three years - I did not go down on hands and knees and emulate the Pope by kissing the tarmac, but I felt like doing so. I was still wearing the winter clothing that I had had to wear to Heathrow, but it was 8.30 in the morning and the African sun was not yet high in the sky. Therefore as Johannesburg is 6,000 feet above sea level it was still quite cool, and I did not feel too hot. At the barrier there was the now familiar red jacket as Dot and Deane waved to get my attention. Then, with 'Skid Yates' at the wheel we barged down the motorways to Kew, the district in which they had now been living for some three years in order to be as near as possible to the Alexandra Township. Both utterly committed to the pursuit of peace and welfare of the African and coloured inhabitants of that often violent and largely impoverished township.

Deane resigned the Headmastership of St John's College, Johannesburg in December 1970 in order, as he put it, "to do something for the underprivileged and to witness against apartheid." This consisted of founding the multi-racial school of Maru a Pula in Botswana. where he and Dot worked indefatigably for ten years. He retired from Maru a Pula in 1981, having been invited to return to the Union to found the New Era Schools Trust (NEST). The purpose of which was to build non-racial schools in South Africa - this was a very brave thing to do and three such schools had been founded long before apartheid had begun to be dismantled.

When Deane eventually retired in 1990 he and Dot decided that they would give the rest of their active lives to the service of the people of the Alexandra Township ('Alex'). Deane became Chairman of the Security Task Force of the Interim Crisis Committee which sought to resolve crises by negotiation instead of violence, and worked generally for peace in the township. Dot continued the welfare work, especially among the elderly in the Itlhokomeleng old people's home. Everyone knows 'Mama Yates' and she is greatly loved by all and sundry. Her welfare work in Alex began when she was in her twenties, the young wife of the young Headmaster of St Johns College. At that time she was involved with the African Children's Feeding Scheme. As soon as they began their retirement work in the township they became regular members of the Anglican Church of St Michael and All Angels there. For most of the time they were the only white members of this black congregation. In 1980 Deane was voted onto the Parish Council, becoming a churchwarden in 1981 and a Lay Minister in 1986.

As we drove on our way from the airport through the suburbs of Johannesburg I was already noticing many changes since I had last known this city. Where in my day front gardens had often sloped down to the public footpath without even a fence or hedge to claim privacy, now there were high walls topped by wicked razor-wire, and with large notices beside the steel and padlocked gates, warning of immediate 'armed response' and that intruders would be shot on sight. Bluff in many cases of course, but by no means all. There is such a notice on the gatepost of Deane and Dot's house, put there by the previous owner. They themselves have never possessed a gun and never would. But they have to take security very seriously. There are massive steel bars over every window, and the front door is of thick and solid wood with, on the outside, a double-locking steel security door. The double gates and the security doors over both front and back doors are kept locked at all times. It is like walking through a prison; the steel gate is unlocked to let you through and immediately relocked behind you, the front door security gate likewise. However, notwithstanding the obvious security measures and fortress-like exterior, they have a very comfortable house indeed, standing in well-kept grounds, with a fenced off swimming pool to one side. The house is named *Kagiso* - 'place of peace' which describes both the atmosphere of the house itself, and the mission of its owners.

Kagiso is three minutes from the Alexandra Township, which was much in the news in the 80s and early 90s for the internecine warfare between the Inkhatha Freedom Party (the Zulus engaged in 'the armed struggle' for freedom from white domination) based mostly in a huge men's hostel that towers over the shacks and houses of the township, and the ANC (African National Congress) who are spread over the rest of Alexandra and to which the majority of the inhabitants gave allegiance. When the violence was at its height in the late 80s and early 90s Inkhatha invaded a whole area of decent houses nearby and with great violence threw the people out of their homes, killing many of them, razing their houses to the ground, and leaving the rest gutted and derelict. The area became known as 'Beirut' for this very reason and it soon became a 'no man's land' under the guns of the hostel. Those who had to flee their homes either built shacks in the already overcrowded township, squeezed in with relations and friends or left the area altogether. Some two hundred people occupied the Mayor's parlour in the administrative buildings of Alexandra. Dot took me to visit these families and it was an astonishing sight to see small areas in each corner and down both sides and ends of the large hall, formed by a fridge, a deepfreeze, a couple of beds etc., all that had been salvaged from the homes ravaged in 'Beirut'.

Within a few hours of my arrival at their house in Kew, I was on a conducted tour and looking aghast at the ruins of well-built houses in 'Beirut' with Deane saying, "Now we are in the most dangerous area of this township." A small shiver of apprehension crawled down my spine. I felt as if I was in Sophiatown again. The years rolling away as I looked at splendid homes wantonly destroyed because one section of the community hated another - this time not whites destroying black homes, but even more sadly, blacks destroying black homes. As we toured the township that evening, Deane introduced me to numbers of men and women saying, "This is Fr Paul who used to work in Sophiatown." At the mention of Sophiatown faces lightened and handshakes became warmer, for it is still a name that inspires pride and respect and no little wonder. For men and women who were only toddlers or not even born in the days of Sophiatown the name of Fr Huddleston strikes an immediate chord of folklore that is almost mystical, sometimes saying,with a faraway look in their eyes, *Hau, Hau, Father Huddleston!!*

I went with Deane and Dot to the 9 o'clock Parish Mass the following Sunday and before the notices were given out the parish priest asked all visitors to stand. There were half a dozen or so of us, and when he got to me he asked who I was and where I came from: "I am Father Paul from Twickenham in England where they play rugby," I said. He shouted to the congregation, "He is Fr Paul from Twickenham in England *where he plays rugby!*" The entire congregation took one look at my figure and burst into laughter.

A few weeks later I was asked to preach, and as I took my place on the chancel step I was joined by an African interpreter. I began by telling the congregation the story of one of the Fathers in Sophiatown when I was there preaching at the High Mass with an interpreter. This particular Father knew a little Sotho, but not enough to preach in the language, so he had an interpreter. After the service he said to the interpreter, "I don't think you said what I said." The interpreter replied "No Father, I said what you *ought* to have said." When the laughter had subsided, I continued, "So I hope that if my interpreter friend here does not think I am preaching you a good enough sermon, he will preach you a better one himself!" I then preached on the theme of forgiveness. I said that both blacks and whites in South Africa must learn to forgive one another, for both had done bad things to the other. "We white people must ask our black brothers and sisters to forgive us for all the bad and terrible things we have done. But our black brothers and sisters have done bad things also for which they must ask forgiveness - without forgiveness from both sides there can be no true peace." I said that I, as a white priest, also had to ask for forgiveness of my black brothers and sisters because I had to admit that when I was in Sophiatown I had not done as much as I could have done for them. I had done a little, but not as much as I could and should have done. "Therefore today I tell you, my black brothers and sisters of another generation, that I am very sorry I did not do what I could have done in Sophiatown, and I ask you of your charity, to forgive me." And I meant that.

I was wondering increasingly as the days went by, why it was that I had been so eager to leave South Africa in 1960 and return to England. Why had I not been as fascinated by the work among African people as Deane and Dot always had been, ever since leaving St John's college, and even before that? I do not know the answer to that question. Or do I? I suspect it was partly cultural and partly cowardice - I could not adapt to dealing with people who had little or no educational background - and I was petrified of being put in prison. I had found the same cultural difficulties in England among the uneducated and impoverished people in Portsmouth during the war. I used to say I had a very limited range - I could cope with people who had had some education, so long as it was not too much! However, what I do know now is that I was thrilled to be back in Africa. Once that beloved country gets its claws into you it never lets go.

I had wonderful reunions with people, both black and white, that I had not met for over thirty years. Head and shoulders above everyone else, of course were Deane and Dot themselves. The intervening years had simply rolled away when we met in 1992 at the Centenary Commemoration Day at Mirfield, and having taken me again to their hearts they now took me to their home which became mine for nearly three months, and no more generous hosts could a man ever have. I was again accepted as a member of the family, with the two dogs, two cats, plus Bella the wonderful Xhosa cook-housekeeper and her various children and grandchildren who all lived together here at Kagiso, the Place of Peace.

For the whole of my stay Dot, the indefatigable hostess, was constantly on the telephone ringing up the people who might still remember me, arranging dates, providing transport in her battered little yellow VW Golf car.

The 'phone when not being used by the family, was always ringing with pleas for Dot's help in the township, for Deane to go hotfoot - or rather burning rubber - to try to sort out some trouble, defuse a potentially dangerous situation and prevent violence, or investigate it when it had occurred. On my third evening we were just about to start the sweet course at dinner one evening when the 'phone rang and Deane came back with a frown on his face to say that someone was firing with a revolver at passers-by in the Township and that one man had already been killed. He said, "I'm sorry, but I shall have to go." "Shall I come with you?" I asked, confident that he would say, "Oh no, Paul you stay here with Dot" - instead of which he said gratefully, "I wish you would." I was wearing an open necked shirt and went off to my room quickly to don my dog collar. Then off we went in Deane's car, down the 'white' road, round the corner, across the main road, and then an 'S' bend into the dark and brooding township. We did not fasten seat belts in case we had to make a hasty exit from the car, but locked the doors against any attempted hi-jack. I had forgotten that darkness could be so dark; it was thick - accentuated by the occasional single light-bulb on a pole that went for street lighting in Alex.

A huge shape loomed up in the headlights and we stopped by a police armoured vehicle, known as a Casspir. The faces of the black and white policemen were eerily lit as they dragged on their cigarettes. No, they had not patrolled the area; yes, they had heard about the alleged shooting, but no, they had not heard anything themselves or seen a body. So we left the car and walked along the dark street to the 'fence' of a house, consisting of sheets of corrugated iron topped by strands of razor wire. Deane tapped on the corrugated iron and said quietly but insistently, "Agnes, are you there?" One of the sheets of iron shifted aside and a little frightened black face peered out, "Yes, Mr Yates." "Do you know where the shooting was?" "Yes, Mr Yates, down that way; a man has been shot." "Do you know who it was?" "No, but the body has been taken off the street; there has been no more shooting for about an hour." We went looking with a torch but could see nothing. The whole place seemed deserted; but we knew that hundreds of people were locked and barricaded into their houses for safety and were lying low.

We went back and talked to the police, and asked them to patrol the area all night, especially this and the adjacent roads, and they said they would.

Deane was not satisfied with this assurance and said he wanted to make sure that something would be done about the situation if possible, so it was back to the car and a mile or so further into the township to the police headquarters.

As we got out of the car, two khaki-clad paramilitary policemen with AK47s at the ready, fingers on triggers, appeared out of the gloom, who on recognising Deane, let us into the command post compound. We crossed a yard where there were fourteen or fifteen Casspirs and other armoured vehicles parked ready to move off at a moment's notice. I was reminded of Portsmouth during the war. Deane with the confidence of familiarity led through a lit doorway into a concrete corridor and down a flight of concrete stairs to the entrance to the command post proper, where a couple of white officers and several black police were manning computers and television monitors. Deane talked to the officer in charge and after a while got an assurance that the necessary patrols would be mounted.

That was all that we could do; so it was back home and into the dining room about an hour after we left, to eat the sweet course with Dotty, who had waited for our return. Next day a body had been found, but no patrols had been mounted. Thankfully there had been no more shooting, but Deane said that the people had been reassured by our presence and grateful for our efforts.

A few days later I went to the new St Peter's Priory of the Community of the Resurrection, a much smaller one in Turffontein where they have recently moved from the old priory I knew in Rosettenville, now far too large for the reduced numbers of the community in South Africa. In Turffontein two bungalows had been linked by a corridor giving extra bathrooms, a medium sized chapel, commonroom, kitchen etc. A very satisfying set-up for five brethren plus numerous guests. I found a pervading atmosphere of peace and stillness. This was obviously a place of prayer and worship, with, as usual, the *opus Dei,* 'the work of God', being given priority in the life. From here the brethren went out to serve the Church and the people, of all races, in many different ways.

I made several trips into Soweto with Fr Kingston Erson and he took me to see old friends. One day we went to the parish of St Francis to see Abel and Pauline Molefe, whose wedding photographs I took in 1960. He was now rector of a lovely church with a large and thriving congregation and lives in a very pleasant rectory - I found them their first house in the African Native Township next to Sophiatown, and decorated it for them myself, causing some scandal in those days of strict apartheid. While I was with Abel and Pauline two other men turned up who, as boys, had known me in Sophiatown, one, Maurice Manana had been the driver and general handyman for the sisters at Ekutuleni - I told him I always remembered a piece of advice he had given me on one occasion when he was driving me through Johannesburg - "Always be sure you look often in your rear view mirror when you are driving, Father - very important." It pleased him that I had remembered. He had done quite well and had now retired from whatever business it was in which he had worked. I set up my camera on a tripod and we have a photograph of us all standing against the large palm tree in the garden of the rectory. Before going home I went in to see the church, which is beautiful, with the atmosphere that tells you it is a church that is prayed in.

It was splendid to see how Fr Kingston was known all over Soweto; wherever we went people greeted him like the old friend he was. He told me that on one occasion during the recent waves of unrest half a brick was thrown at his car and smashed the rear window; another hit the windscreen but did not shatter it, and then he was surrounded by a crowd of young African men who proceeded to lift the car intending to turn it over. Suddenly, he said, there was a shout, *"Stop, Stop! - its Father,"* and in the twinkling of an eye they dropped the car - and the whole crowd vanished like a puff of smoke. He was left a little shaken but none the worse. It was almost a carbon copy of my own experience thirty or so years before in Sophiatown during the first General Strike of African workers. It was good to see the same respect for 'the Fathers' here as there was in Sophiatown thirty years ago.

A few mornings later when I came to breakfast Dot told me that Isaac Meletse had rung up about an hour before, saying that he heard I was staying with them and he was coming in to see me at 8.30 this morning on his way to Pretoria! Isaac Meletse - Gosh! The last time I had seen him he was a bright eyed little boy with his shirt hanging out of a hole in his trousers, grinning up at me and saying he would be coming to England one day and would see me there! He had not come to England but, with no help from anyone and simply through his own prodigious efforts, had got himself educated and was now a king-pin in a large organisation that rehabilitates ex-prisoners.

Sure enough, he drove through the gates just as I was finishing my breakfast, and again it was huge hugs and the slapping of backs in affectionate reunion. He was accompanied by an albino African whom I also remembered as one of the children of Sophiatown, though I had never known him as well as I had Isaac. We had a wonderful half hour talking over old times before they had to be off for their day's work.

One of the happiest reunions however was with a lady who was the subject of one of the best portrait photographs I have ever taken. When I was in Sophiatown, Felicia Mabusa was twelve years old, a very pretty little girl. One day I sat her at a desk in one of the old disused classrooms that I had fitted up as a studio. She had an open book in front of her, and was resting her elbows on the desk, with her beautifully long-fingered hands on her temples. She was smiling at me as I took her photograph. It is a lovely picture. Showing the picture to Fr Francis Blake, who had been my Prior in Sophiatown, I asked him if he knew what had happened to Felicia Mabusa? He smiled and said indeed he knew - "After you left Sophiatown," he said, "Felicia went to the USA and got a good education. She married a Canadian psychiatrist and they have two daughters. They live in Atlanta, but at the present time Felicia is here in South Africa - and you can see her on the television any Sunday evening at 6 o'clock hosting her Top Level programme - the show that is advertised as the one that 'Gets South Africa Talking'. Here, this is her 'phone number, give her a ring, I'm sure she would be pleased to hear from you." So I rang the number of the South African Broadcasting Corporation and asked for Mrs Mabusa-Suttle. When the lady came on the line and I told her who I was, there was a moment of dead silence and then she squealed, "Father Singleton! Father Singleton! I never thought I would ever hear from you again!!"

Felicia came out to Deane and Dot's house for drinks one evening. She got lost on the way and rang us up; Deane knew just where she was and told her to wait there and we would come along to meet her very soon. She told us she was driving her uncle's green Mercedes, and sure enough I saw her from a distance, pulled to the side of the road and standing by the car. I got out and wove my way through the traffic - and in full view of passers by, there were hugs and kisses and squeals of delight - there on the sidewalk! An old white man and a young African lady! In 1960 we would both have been arrested on the spot.

Now, very aware of the passers-by I saw not so much as a raised eyebrow!

Back home over our celebratory drinks she told us about her home and her children - the two girls, 16 and 14 years of age, were both very keen and very good tennis players - the younger one was very good indeed and was determined to play in the Wimbledon Championships one day. Felicia thought she might well do that. Of course out came the camera and I took a picture of Felicia holding the portrait I had taken of her as a little girl.

A quite unpredictable encounter occurred while I was staying in Simons Town in the Cape with my old friends from college days, Walter and Freda Lovegrove. He was chaplain to the Retired Clergy Association in the Cape Province and invited me to a luncheon he had arranged for the Association. In his talk before the meal he introduced me, and afterwards a greyhaired priest came up to me and asked, "Paul Singleton, were you ever *George* Singleton?" I said, "Yes I was," and in great astonishment "and you were *Gussie Davis!*" "Quite right," he said. I went on, as I pumped his hand, "And you were my next senior at St Mark's Portsea during the war, and you left after I had been there a couple of years to become a Chaplain in the Navy - and what's more, we all envied you like mad because you married a smashing Wren officer!" "Quite right," he said again, "and here she is!" And he pulled a sweet, grey-haired lady towards us, and I recognised her immediately. It was fifty-one years since I had seen or heard anything of them.

Another astonishing reunion occurred when Deane and Dot took me to Botswana for the weekend to see Maru a Pula, the school they had founded just outside the capital, Gaborone. After leaving St John's College Johannesburg they had lived in a tent right out in the bush in Botswana while their house and the school were being built - Dot said the snakes were a real nuisance. Against tremendous odds with many setbacks, against entrenched prejudice and health-undermining conditions, and many financial crises, they left, ten years later, a first class non-racial school of the highest academic standard. Their successors have continued the good work, and I was very pleased to meet the present headmaster and his delightful family.

On the Sunday morning we went to Gaborone Cathedral for the High Mass. The huge building was packed when we arrived twenty minutes before the service was due to begin and we just managed to find three seats in one of the back rows in the Nave. It took my eyes several moments to adjust to the relative gloom after the brilliant sunshine outside, but when they

307

had done so I noticed that there were seven candles on the altar, not the usual six. I thought to myself, Oh, there must be a bishop who is going to preside, for a bishop rates an extra candle. Sure enough, after a while I could see sufficiently clearly to make out a bishop in cope and mitre seated in the presidential chair immediately behind the altar. When he began to speak he had a deeply resonant voice that reminded me of Paul Robeson, and his whole manner of celebrating thrilled me to the core. What reverence! What *gravitas*! What inspiring devotion and lack of hurry! I thought to myself, I have not heard Mass celebrated with this degree of recollection and devotion for many a long year. The devotion at the altar was matched by that of the vast congregation, and I reflected that this is worship at its best and as it always ought to be. It was a most inspiring act of worship.

Afterwards, as we wended our slow way out of the Cathedral back into the fierce sunshine and heat, I saw that there was a long queue of people waiting to greet the bishop, and I could see him far ahead, a black man in his purple cassock and skullcap shaking the hands of the faithful as they slowly passed. So I joined the queue. When I got to him I took his hand, was about to kiss his ring in the ancient traditional way, when I glanced at his face - and stopped in astonishment - "Good heavens, *You!*," I said. Then we were hugging and slapping one another on the back. I had known Walter Makulu when he used to come to Sophiatown as a student to worship with us on Sunday mornings and often stayed to lunch. I had always liked him and thought what a splendid chap he was. I did not know, or had forgotten, that he was going to be ordained, and of course once I had returned to England in 1960 I had completely lost touch with him. Leaving the community also meant that I had had no news of him since those days. Now here he was - a bishop, and not only that but no less a personage than Archbishop of Central Africa! I could not stay long shaking his hand for there was still a formidable queue of people behind. So I left him - and went to join the queue again at the back so that I could come to him a second time. This time I was among the last, so I could spend a little longer. I said, "O Walter, when I recognised you just now I nearly wept." "Paul," he said, "When they told me you were in the congregation, I *did* weep!" He told me that he had married an English girl and had two children - and they had a house in Fulham - only a few miles from my flat in Twickenham!

Further reunions followed. While I had been in Sophiatown I had been asked on one occasion to go to Masite in what was then Basutoland to act as Chaplain for a couple of weeks to the Society of the Precious Blood, a women's contemplative community whose Mother House is at Burnham near Maidenhead in England. The Bishop, who was their chaplain, was going away for a couple of weeks, and I was to look after the sisters in his absence. Fr Kingston Erson now visited this and other communities in Lesotho twice a year as External Confessor, and we had arranged that during my stay I would hire a car and we would go together on his 'Confessional safari' so that I could revisit the country and the communities.

Kingston knew a director of the Toyota car company in Vereenigig who had said he would arrange for me to hire a car from them at a generously low rental. On the appointed day we were taken to Vereenigig and the director being away, his secretary gave me the necessary papers to sign, then took us the garage. We had expected a jalopy or some small car and were astonished when she led us to a beautiful air-conditioned saloon, with power steering and automatic gear box! We were delighted of course and drove away in fine style. I made Kingston drive - I was not going to drive a car like that through the city traffic. I also decided that before we left town I was going to buy a locking-bar for the steering wheel, because car theft was rife all over Southern Africa and I was not about to take any risks with this splendid car. Kingston however said he was not going to stop that car in the city in case he could not start it again - it had one of these remote control gadgets that locks and unlocks the car from a distance and could also immobilise the engine. Neither of us had used one before. So he drove round and round the town while I went into the store to buy the locking bar - and when I got back onto the street I had to wait some time until he appeared once more. I was wondering what I would do if he had stalled the car some streets away and could not start it again! But he eventually turned up and I got aboard and we set off on our tour. After a while we both began to feel a little chilly; the air conditioning was going full blast. I looked in the glove compartment for the Owner's manual to see how to adjust it, but there wasn't one - they had forgotten to put it in the car. I fiddled with knobs but it did not seem to make any difference. So, with the brilliant sun beating down outside, we got colder and colder.

Shortly, a small roadside cafe hove in sight with a single petrol pump outside. Kingston gingerly drove in and parked and we opened the doors and stepped out gratefully into the heat of the sun. We were soon warm enough to appreciate the couple of cold fruit drinks we bought in the cafe. We were right out in the veldt on a long road stretching straight as an arrow into the distance, so I decided to try my hand with the car. I clicked the gadget and the car obediently unlocked itself, but when I tried to start the engine nothing at all happened. I tried several times; then Kingston had a few goes, but all to no avail. What to do? At that moment a large truck drew up at the one petrol pump and out stepped an enormous Afrikaner farmer wearing a tight pair of shorts over thick red legs, an open necked shirt, hairy arms and big round red face. Plucking up my courage I approached him and using my one Afrikaans word, I said, "Excuse me Meneer, I cannot get this hire-car to start, do you know how to work these things?" I hoped he understood, for this was a predominantly Afrikaans area - the people in the cafe could speak nothing else. He gave me a scornful glare, snatched the gadget from my hand, clicked it near the steering wheel, put in the ignition key, turned it, and the engine started at once! Giving me another scornful look he thrust the gadget into my hand and, without a word, stalked back to his truck. In the end we managed to figure out the air conditioning and the ignition, so all was well.

Our first visit was to the Community of the Holy Name at Leribe, not far inside the Lesotho border. I had known their Mother House in Malvern slightly when I was in Cardiff, so it was very good to see this flourishing branch house with so many African as well as white sisters. When we arrived I was introduced to the sisters while we were given tea on the *stoep*, and one of the white sisters said, "Oh I know of you, Fr Singleton - I took over St Teilo's Priory when your Community had to withdraw, and you had been the last Prior." So I met my successor six thousand miles away and twenty-five years later! Another white sister came saying, "Oh yes, Father, I was in one of your retreats at the community retreat house in Hemingford Grey many years ago!"

I was very impressed with the community at Leribe; apart from living the religious life of prayer and worship they were doing some very good work. One of the black sisters, who had a good degree after studying in America, was lecturing in the local polytechnic in Maseru, the capital. Two were working among students at the Anglican theological college which was part of the Roman Catholic University of Roma a few miles away from Maseru. White and black sisters were running the Craft Centre next to the convent for disabled African girls. At this centre they specialised in working with mohair and they taught every process, from taking the raw hair, carding it, spinning and dying it, to weaving it into lengths of material for making up into many types of garment. The finished products were on view and on sale in the front vestibule of the Craft Centre. Once a year one of the sisters and the chaplain set off in his car to go on a tour of many centres in Southern Africa selling their products to wholesalers and shops. The little industry was self-supporting.

Our next stop was at Masite where we arrived at 7.30am, having taken two Leribe sisters to Maseru Airport for an early plane. Kingston got out of the car as I stopped at the gate and said he would go and see whether the sisters had finished Mass. A few moments later down the rocky and stony drive, running with bare feet, came Sister Magdalene Mary, whom I had known as Rosemary Baron and whom I had introduced to Masite all those years ago. She had found that she had a contemplative vocation and had been professed in this community many years before.

Back in Johannesburg, Dot said one morning, "We are going over to St Benedict's House for morning tea with the sisters." CR had built St Benedict's House opposite their Priory at Rosettenville in the late 1940's. It was here that Trevor Huddleston had started the Shoe Parties that had become famous by the time he was recalled, and that we had copied at the London Priory. During my time in South Africa I had conducted many retreats there, and it was a place I was always particularly fond of. Originally St Benedict's had been run by a female Warden, but it had been taken over by the Whitby Sisters soon after I had arrived at Sophiatown. Dot told me it was still run by four Whitby Sisters. So I was delighted to go to 'Morning Tea', a great South African institution. As Deane was locking the car outside the house, I was first at the security gate and rang the bell. The nun who opened the door pointed at me straight away and said, "Here is the man who is responsible for my being here!" I was astonished and taken aback. "You don't remember me, do you?" she asked, and I had to confess that she had the advantage of me. "Well," she said, as we walked up the path towards the *stoep*. "When you were at your London Priory in Holland Park you were Chaplain of Bickersteth House. I came there to live while teaching in London. I was a wishy-washy Evangelical with no great convictions, and the first evening I met you, you pointed your finger at me and said, 'What you need my girl is the full Catholic Faith of the Anglican Church!' I was so upset by this, that I had to go round the corner to the little cafe there and have a cup of tea and a bun to get over it! And after that, you gave me an instruction every Friday evening, and each

311

time I had to go to the cafe for a cup of tea and a bun to get over what you had been telling me!"

As she spoke, distant and long lost memories did begin to stir in my mind, and looking closely at her face I began to see the eager, but at the same time rather frightened, face of the young teacher to whom I had been giving the 'Catholic Faith of the Anglican Church' straight from the shoulder. She told me that some years later she had written to me saying that she thought she probably ought to try her vocation to the Religious Life, and that I had told her to go to see the Reverend Mother of the Order of the Holy Paraclete at Whitby. She had entered the novitiate there and in due course was approaching her profession in the community. She then wrote to me saying that she was scared stiff at the thought of joining all those funny looking women for the rest of her life. "And you wrote back to me," she said, "and quoted Jeremiah, 'Be not afraid of their faces' - and then it was all right!" "Oh Lor," I said, "do you hold all this against me?" "No-o-o," she said, "This is where I have always been meant to be."

15

Back To The Future

One of my favourite contemporaries in CR was Father Cedma Mack, a delightful Irishman with, as one of the brethren remarked, 'leprechaun ears.' He was the sort of man who inspired 'Irish jokes' and had that endearing gift of being able to laugh at himself. A man of profound spirituality, he had to suffer a lot of physical pain in the latter part of his life but his humour and his serenity were never impaired. I arrived from Leeds unexpectedly one day to be greeted, in his soft Irish voice, with, "O, hello Paul, its lovely to see you - I've just written to you, have you had it yet? - oh no, of course not, I haven't posted it!" - and he dissolved into uncontrollable giggles.

A few years ago, long after I had left CR, Cedma was to preach in the Community church on Advent Sunday. He took his place at the lectern after the Gospel and said, "Advent is a time for looking back, and looking forward..." And he dropped down dead!

I feel I have come to a sort of Advent period in my life - knocking eighty as I write, and at the end of this story. It seems a good place to look back, and to look forward.

As I look back, the quotation that comes into my mind is from the Book of Ecclesiastes, *'Cast your bread upon the waters, and it shall return to you after many days'* for this seems to sum up so much of my experience. I seem to have done a great deal of 'casting my bread upon the waters' in the course of my life, and this same bread has so often 'returned to me after many days.' Most of it seems to have been at the call of Him who first placed his hand upon me when I was a teenager during that Lent course at All Saints, Hampton.

The most radical of my 'castings of bread' of course was when I had to cast my wonderful Girl in the Middle upon the waters of life without me - and lo and behold, after very many days, she returned to me. But in order for that to happen I had to cast my beloved community upon the waters - and lo and behold after almost as many days, they also returned to me. In neither case has the bread that has returned been in exactly the same form as when it was cast upon the waters; the form has changed, but the essence has been the same; an older Bar but the same love; not renewal of membership of CR, but something of the same 'love of the brethren' generously extended to me. And then all the friendships that, for good or ill, I felt I had to cast upon the waters. So many of those have also returned to me after many days - with such wonderful generosity and affection and, so far, with no recriminations. All of which prompts the reflection that our Lord always rewards sacrifices that are made in His name - and not infrequently by giving back that which in previous circumstances we have been asked to give up.

In the course of telling this story I have expressed the hope that when I have said I see the guidance of God in it all, I have not been rationalising a guilty conscience. However, the very writing, and the consequent need to try for accurate recall and honest facing of the facts, has now brought me to a greater conviction than before. I believe that ever since that teenage 'conversion' my life has not only been sustained but definitely and firmly guided by God for His mysterious purposes and in His unimaginable and undeserved love. That the whole tortuous course that I have travelled, has been according to His will in spite of my many deliberate sins and refusals. Even in the wilderness years when I felt I was wandering disconsolate through the desert sands, I was in fact being carried to where He wanted me to be.

I suppose it is possible to say that what impelled me to get rid of all my clerical gear and books and notes and everything else remaining of my previous life, was another very radical casting of bread upon the waters, for it was symbolic of finally cutting myself off from my priesthood, the very priesthood for which I had cast away so much of the bread of my youth, and for which I had struggled so long. In my blindness I had, as I thought, cut myself free once and for all from the exercise of the priestly ministry. How mysteriously God works! Even mistakes and failures and defections can be grist to His mill, for there is now no doubt in my mind that it was at that very moment, when at last I stood stripped of all that had gone before, that He began to bring me back. It now seems that I *had* to come to that point before He could begin to do so. Which of course is one of the classical truths of the spiritual life - that the soul has eventually to be stripped of all before it can proceed further.

It soon became clear that this 'bread' of the last remnants and reminders of my past life was also to return. The 'resurrection' experience during the reading of the Easter Gospel not only expressed itself in a return to prayer and an acknowledgement of my priesthood, but in a growing desire to exercise the priestly ministry once more. The first manifestation of this was the desire to pray, the second to celebrate the

Eucharist again, and the third to preach. In fact the more frequently I celebrated, the deeper became the desire for prayer and the more insistent the urge to preach.

Alun, my dear friend and vicar, was wonderfully understanding about all this, generously giving me opportunities both to celebrate and to preach.

As I have said, Bar died before I began to preach again, and my return to prayer had not progressed very far by the time she had her final illness. It was only after the 'warming' experience after my communion one weekday when it felt as though Bar had hugged me, that the life of prayer returned to me in full force. From then on prayer and preaching seemed to go together.

I had been set on course for the very simple 'prayer of silence', or 'contemplative prayer', when I was a teenager, and this had developed as I struggled to gain Matric at Tatterford, and while reading theology at St Augustine's College. I was blessed with good spiritual directors in both my parishes who saw to it that I did not fall by the wayside, seduced from prayer by the busy-ness of parish life, as so often happens. Naturally the life of prayer had deepened considerably during my years in the Community. Now on my return to active ministry I became increasingly convinced that a lot of people in this frantically busy and noisy - and *wordy* - world were being called to contemplative prayer.

One Sunday, when I had been asked to preach, I decided to do so on this subject. It was not until Saturday that I found that the theme set for that Sunday was 'Faith'. As soon as I realized this I remembered that someone had commented recently that there are people today who go regularly to church but do not believe in God, and I knew this to be true from what people had said to me; often adding, "But I wish I *could* have faith in God." Surely then, I ought not to preach about prayer, but about faith?

I had often sat under clergymen who exhorted us from the pulpit to 'have faith'. I could not however recall hearing any of them trying to answer the perfectly reasonable question, "Yes, but *how* can I 'have faith'?" So, I asked myself, how am I going to try to answer that question tomorrow? How *do* we find, or 'have' faith?

I was rather kicking myself at this point for not having looked up the Sunday theme earlier in the week; had I done so I would have had time to give the subject of faith more thought. As it was I had been thinking all the week about prayer, and consequently my mind kept going back to what I had intended to say about *prayer*. For a while I kept dragging it back to think about *faith*.

Then the penny dropped. Faith is a gift of God and I saw the essential connection between faith and prayer, for if you do not pray you are not very likely to be 'open' to God and therefore able to receive His gift of faith: clearly if people did not *pray* they could not hope to have much in the way of *faith*.

It is often claimed that many churchgoers do not in fact see much point in personal prayer. For many it is only the corporate prayer used in public worship on Sundays that has much meaning for them. This sort of prayer often consists almost entirely of expressing our thoughts in words, or using the words that express the thoughts of the Church in the set prayers of the liturgy and the prayerbook. And because of over-familiarity it is all too easy for these prayers to become little more than thoughtless repetition. The corporate prayers of the church in sacramental worship and in the Divine Offices (including Matins and Evensong) are important, but they lose a lot of their meaning and force if they are not backed up by the personal prayer of the individual Christian.

So my theme for Sunday was that we could come to faith through learning that prayer was not only saying things to God, but much more importantly it was learning to be still in heart and mind and allowing God to come to us, in stillness and silence. That if we learned to be still and 'listen', the time would certainly come, and before long, when we would be aware of another dimension in life; we would become aware of God in an unmistakable if 'obscure' way. We would find that we come to have an *intuitive* awareness that God is real, and that he is present with us - in other words we would be given the gift of *faith*. For God to be real to us we do not have to use our minds, our intellects - for God is ultimately beyond the reach of the intellect. We 'find' Him best by learning to be still and silent so that *He* can find *us*.

The last few moments of the address were spent in encouraging the congregation to relax, there and then, into stillness and silence and remember what our Lord says through his psalmist, *Be still and know that I am God.* - Be *still* and *know*. In fact a short exercise in Contemplation.

It became clear afterwards that this address had struck a cord in the minds of several people in the congregation, and a little later with the encouragement of the vicar we formed a

Contemplative Prayer Group that would meet once a fortnight. We let it be known that this group was not intended to be exclusively for Anglicans of our own congregation, but for those from other parishes and other denominations who would be interested to explore and learn this type of very simple but very profound prayer, for of course in this type of prayer denominational divisions are refreshingly irrelevant. The United Reformed Church, the Roman Catholic Church and another Anglican parish are represented in the Contemplative Prayer groups that now meet in our parish.

I think that those who have now been practising contemplative prayer for nearly two years would agree that they have become more aware of a hitherto unsuspected, or only vaguely suspected, side to their human nature. They have discovered that as they gradually learn to keep their *thoughts* on the periphery of their minds they are aware of another reality which does not depend at all upon thinking. They are becoming aware that this 'other reality' is feeding a depth in their nature that cannot be fed by any amount of thought. In Christian terms they are discovering the *mystical* side of their human nature - the side that responds only to what is beyond the reach of the intellect. It is the mystical side of our nature that responds to mystery, that can search for and find its rest in transcendence. One of the deepest hungers of mankind is for the experience of mystery and transcendence. Indeed it can be said that without some experience of this there can be no truly human life. It is the part of us that responds to great music and art, but neither of these can fully satisfy us.

There seems to be some realization of this truth growing among Christians today and many are re-discovering the treasures of the mystical tradition of the Church. Books on the spiritual life pour from the presses; there is a new interest in the 16th Century spiritual masters, St John of the Cross and St Theresa of Avila who are widely read. The teaching of the unknown 14th Century author of *The Cloud of Unknowing* forms the basis of most instruction in Contemplative Prayer. But most popular of all are the Revelations of Divine Love by the 14th Century anchorite, the Lady Julian of Norwich. Interest in her Revelations has exploded throughout the Western world and in this country has resulted in many groups of men and women up and down the country holding regular 'Julian Meetings' for contemplative prayer.

Some people today prefer to use 'contemplation' and

317

'meditation' as synonymous terms, but I have always distinguished between the two, and I believe the distinction is important, for they refer to two quite different sorts of prayer.

Meditation is the use of the mind, the intellect, in thinking about the relevance to our own lives of whatever part of Christian truth is under consideration, and resolving in what way we should modify our lives in order to conform to that truth. Meditation is therefore based upon *mental activity*. Indeed, one of the alternatives names for this type of prayer is 'Mental Prayer'.

In Contemplation, however, the reasoning mind is only used, if at all, as a spring-board to launch us into the prayer itself - a means of awakening in our hearts the desire for God and thus to start us off on our prayer, which consists of simply 'being' in the presence of God and learning to remain passive and open so that He may do His gracious work upon us. In all the other types of prayer we tend to be the 'workers' as it were; we are actively engaged. In Vocal Prayer we are *saying* our prayers; in Meditation we are *thinking*; in Affective prayer we *repeat* devotional phrases over and over. All these are excellent ways of praying and play an important role in a balanced spiritual life - but in all of them *we* are taking the initiative all the time. In Contemplative Prayer the initiative is God's, not ours. We simply prepare ourselves by learning to relax the body into stillness and silence, and to allow the teeming mind to slow down so that the multitudinous thoughts that crowd our mind are banished gently to the periphery of our consciousness. We then simply and silently and without thought, 'open ourselves' so that we are alert to the presence of God with us and within us. This prayer involves discovering that silence and stillness are not threatening as some people fear, but a wonderful refreshment of mind, body and spirit in our busy and noisy world. Contemplative Prayer is the simplest and deepest prayer of all and probably the most needed type of prayer for Christians today, for the emphasis is on learning how to be passive and 'available' so that God can take us and remake us in His own image. A modern writer, Jim Borst, has said, 'Stillness before God has little to do with achieving and a lot to do with receiving' and in contemplative prayer the emphasis is on 'being done to' rather than on 'doing'.

So there are two main sorts of Christian prayer. Fr Basil Pennington, in his book *Centring Prayer*, calls them 'the effortful and the effortless'. Contemplative Prayer is the latter and it is uniquely suited to the stressful lives that most of us live today. With physical noise in the environment battering our eardrums and the mental noise of ceaseless information and the stream of ideas assaulting our minds just as ruthlessly, St Augustine's cry, 'O God thou hast made us for thyself, and our hearts are restless until they find their rest in thee' has never had more relevance. Once we have admitted to ourselves and accepted the fact that God has made us for himself we realize that our souls are indeed restless until they find their *rest* in him. Rest - learning to be still and silent so that entering upon our prayer gradually becomes like slipping into a warm bath and letting all the tensions seep out of us as we realize that God wants us to let him enfold us in his love in order that he may do His gracious work upon us. We all need to learn that inactivity is not laziness - to take to heart our Lord's words to Martha who complained that her sister Mary was simply sitting at his feet and listening to him while she herself was left to do all the serving and chores, "Martha, Martha, you worry and fret about so many things, and yet few are needed, indeed only one. It is Mary who has chosen the better part, and it is not to be taken from her" (Luke 10.41). Simply to sit at the feet of our Lord and listen to him: that is contemplation. We do not hear him speak in words; but He communicates with us, or 'communes' with us, in the silence of our realization of his presence, however vague or intuitive that may be. One of my favourite stories about the utter simplicity and depth of this sort of prayer is the one told of the Curé d'Ars who noticed that one of the peasant men of his congregation used to go into the church every day on his way home from the fields and he would kneel for a long time in complete stillness before the crucifix hanging in the chancel arch. The Cure asked him one day what it was that he did in this time of prayer after his work, and the old man replied, "Well, Monsieur le Curé, I look up at him, and he looks down at me...." The wordless communion of love between persons.

We must of course use our minds and intellects in learning about our Faith and use them as vehicles to bring us to a deeper conviction - the minds that we have been given must be used to their fullest extent for His service. But intellectual application can do little more than lead us to a deeper knowledge *about* God. *Ultimate* reality is beyond the reach of the intellect. It is by prayer alone that we can come to *know* God. "Be *still*", he says, "and *know* that I am God." Be *still,* and *know.* We must allow him to help us to know that there is silence and stillness *behind* the noise and bustle of life, and as we tune-in to that silence and stillness, to *know* that he is there. We must learn to swim against the tide of our materialistic and secular culture. We must deny that the truth can only be found by the exercise of the intellect. It can be a great relief verging on excitement to realize that we are in fact able to enter into the truths that our minds cannot encompass.

Another of the effects of our culture is that it has robbed us of the experience of mystery, and one of the basic needs of men and women is to rediscover awe and wonder before the transcendent mystery of God himself. What in Christian terms we call the the Great Mysteries - of God's nature as Trinity in Unity, of the Incarnation and the Resurrection - are not mysteries in the sense that detective novels present us with mysteries that can be solved. Christian mysteries are the great truths that are beyond the reach of reason but are not contrary to it. Mysteries that, through the indwelling Christ, are made operative in our lives by his grace through sacrament and prayer.

As I look back I see an unbroken thread of the guidance of God stretching all the way from the present old man 'knocking eighty' to the youngster of seventeen in the pew at All Saints Hampton. Looking back I am filled with thanksgiving for the rich and multi-faceted life He has given me. Thanksgiving for the vocation to His priesthood, the greatest honour than can be done to man. Thanksgiving for a Religious vocation when for twenty years I tried to love Him direct and through the 'love of the brethren'. Thanksgiving for another twenty years of loving Bar my wonderful Girl in the Middle. Thanksgiving for all the other people, my many friends, through whom He continues to mediate His love and fills my heart with joy. Thanksgiving for showing me such of His truth as I have been able to comprehend. Thanksgiving for assuring me that even during the wilderness years when I felt far from him, and in spite of all my unfaithfulness and backsliding, His hand has been upon me the whole time. Thanksgiving that He has shown me that He uses all that happens to us in our lives in order to bring us to Himself and to our own full stature, our true humanity.

All this gives me immense confidence in facing the future. Twice He has put His hand upon me and brought radical change to my life, this last time bringing me out of darkness into the glorious light of his resurrection. Since that day, he has certainly poured upon me a cornucopia of blessings. Masses and masses of bread returning upon the waters! There seems to be no end to it - as a friend said to me the other day, "Paul, things *keep on* happening to you!" and so they do. What next, I wonder?

One day, of course, his hand will touch me again, and I myself will be cast upon the waters. I am confident that they will be the Waters that spring up unto Eternal Life, as he has promised - and *I* know that he never reneges on a promise. I *should* know that by now, shouldn't I? I look to the future with great curiosity and sometimes even with excitement. Just *how* will it all happen? *What* will all those truths be like that are far beyond the capacity of our minds and that even the greatest intellects and wisest saints have never been able to express - but which inspired human hearts can know? What *will* it be like in 'The Kingdom'? After 'seeing through a glass darkly', *what* will it be like to *'see*, face to face'? What will the full glory be like that we have from time to time sensed vaguely but so sweetly in our prayer? There will be no more loneliness, that's for sure; it will be an eternity of loving that will dwarf all our earthy experiences of bliss in an unimaginable glory. It will, I confidently hope, be a reunion of all whom we have loved and lost. 'Heaven' will not be a vast collection of individuals all *privately* loving God; it will be a *community* of lovers, loving one another in and with Supreme Love Himself, what we call 'the whole company of heaven' Thomas Merton in his *Seeds of Contemplation* has put the point better than I ever could:

> *I will have more joy in heaven and in the contemplation of God, if you are also there to share it with me; and the more of us there will be to share it the greater will be the joy of all. For contemplation is not ultimately perfect unless it is shared. We do not finally taste the full exultation of God's glory until we share His infinite gift of it by overflowing and transmitting glory all over heaven, and seeing God in all the others who are there, and knowing that He is the Life of all of us and that we are all One in Him.*

Until the day arrives for me to embark upon the next stage of my journey to that unimaginably glorious fulfilment, I try to say 'YES' to all that comes, confident now that nothing happens without Him and, that *all* things work together for good for those who try to love him.

To him be the Glory; to him be the praise. Amen.